South University Library
Richmond Campus
2151 Old Brick Road
Glen Allen, Va 23060

MAR 0 6 2018

Global Cases in
Best and Worst Practice
in Crisis and Emergency
Management

Global Cases in Best and Worst Practice in Crisis and Emergency Management

Edited by Ali Farazmand

CRC Press
Taylor & Francis Group
Boca Raton London New York

CRC Press is an imprint of the
Taylor & Francis Group, an **informa** business

Cover image courtesy of NOAA.

CRC Press
Taylor & Francis Group
6000 Broken Sound Parkway NW, Suite 300
Boca Raton, FL 33487-2742

© 2016 by Taylor & Francis Group, LLC
CRC Press is an imprint of Taylor & Francis Group, an Informa business

No claim to original U.S. Government works

Printed on acid-free paper
Version Date: 20160122

International Standard Book Number-13: 978-1-4665-7936-1 (Hardback)

This book contains information obtained from authentic and highly regarded sources. Reasonable efforts have been made to publish reliable data and information, but the author and publisher cannot assume responsibility for the validity of all materials or the consequences of their use. The authors and publishers have attempted to trace the copyright holders of all material reproduced in this publication and apologize to copyright holders if permission to publish in this form has not been obtained. If any copyright material has not been acknowledged please write and let us know so we may rectify in any future reprint.

Except as permitted under U.S. Copyright Law, no part of this book may be reprinted, reproduced, transmitted, or utilized in any form by any electronic, mechanical, or other means, now known or hereafter invented, including photocopying, microfilming, and recording, or in any information storage or retrieval system, without written permission from the publishers.

For permission to photocopy or use material electronically from this work, please access www.copyright.com (http://www.copyright.com/) or contact the Copyright Clearance Center, Inc. (CCC), 222 Rosewood Drive, Danvers, MA 01923, 978-750-8400. CCC is a not-for-profit organization that provides licenses and registration for a variety of users. For organizations that have been granted a photocopy license by the CCC, a separate system of payment has been arranged.

Trademark Notice: Product or corporate names may be trademarks or registered trademarks, and are used only for identification and explanation without intent to infringe.

Library of Congress Cataloging-in-Publication Data

Names: Farazmand, Ali, editor.
Title: Global cases in best and worst practice in crisis and emergency management / editor, Ali Farazmand.
Description: Boca Raton, FL : CRC Press, 2016. | "2015 | Includes bibliographical references and index.
Identifiers: LCCN 2015044149 | ISBN 9781466579361 (alk. paper)
Subjects: LCSH: Crisis management--Case studies. | Emergency management--Case studies.
Classification: LCC HD49 .G563 2016 | DDC 363.34--dc23
LC record available at http://lccn.loc.gov/2015044149

Visit the Taylor & Francis Web site at
http://www.taylorandfrancis.com

and the CRC Press Web site at
http://www.crcpress.com

Dedication

I dedicate this publication to my son Cyrus, who is in graduate school, and to my late parents, who were the victims of catastrophic disasters that took the life of one and totally altered another's. I am deeply indebted to my parents, who taught me the lessons of humbleness, humanity, work ethics, resiliency, and perseverance, as well as the public values of education, integrity, and responsibility—"education is an inexhaustible treasure," a statement my parents often reminded me of.

Contents

Preface ix
Acknowledgments xi
Editor xiii
Contributors xv

1 Studying Crisis and Emergency Management
  Using Global Cases of Best and Worst Practices 1
  ALI FARAZMAND

SECTION I GLOBAL CASES OF CRISIS AND EMERGENCY MANAGEMENT: A MACRO POLICY PERSPECTIVE

2 Hurricane Katrina as a Global Case of Grand Failure:
  Lessons for Future Crisis and Emergency Management... 17
  ALI FARAZMAND

3 Fukushima Nuclear Disaster and Ensuring Necessary
  Government Crisis and Risk Communication 33
  ITOKO SUZUKI AND YUKO KANEKO

4 Early Warning Success in Qinglong County, China, for the
  Magnitude 7.8 Tangshan Earthquake: Some Policy Lessons in Integrating
  Public Administration, Science, and Citizen Engagement...53
  JEANNE-MARIE COL

5 Emergency Management for Radiological Events: Lessons Learned
  from Three Mile Island, Chernobyl, and Fukushima Reactor Accidents 89
  FRANCES L. EDWARDS

SECTION II GLOBAL CASES OF BEST AND WORST PRACTICE IN CRISIS AND EMERGENCY MANAGEMENT

6 Hurricane Katrina and the Crisis of Emergency Management 109
  CAROLE L. JURKIEWICZ

7 Katrina: A Case of Manmade and Natural Disaster...123
  STEVEN G. KOVEN

vii

8 Managing at the Edge of Chaos: Lessons Learned
from the 2006 Bam Earthquake in Iran...135
ALI FARAZMAND

9 The United States: Emergency Management
and the September 11, 2001, Terrorist Attacks..149
WILLIAM L. WAUGH, JR. AND CHRISTINE ALLISON CANAVAN

10 Wilma and Sandy: Lessons Learned from Public Servants 161
JOHN J. CARROLL

11 Lessons Learned from Managing Governance Crises in the Arab States 179
JAMIL JREISAT

SECTION III MITIGATION CAPACITY BUILDING FOR CRISIS AND EMERGENCY MANAGEMENT: LESSONS FROM GLOBAL CASES

12 Resilience Capacity Building for Global Crisis and Emergency Management 197
CLIFFORD R. BRAGDON

13 Building Disaster Resilience: The Communities
Advancing Resilience Toolkit (CART) 223
ROSE L. PFEFFERBAUM

14 Learning from Transboundary Crises and
Disasters: The 2010 Haiti Earthquake 237
ALKA SAPAT AND ANN-MARGARET ESNARD

15 Planning for Response to Weapons of Mass Destruction
and CBRNE Events: A Local and Federal Partnership...259
FRANCES L. EDWARDS

Index 283

Preface

Over 15 years have passed since the publication of the first edition of *Crisis and Emergency Management* in 2001. At that time, it was the most comprehensive book on the twin fields of crisis and emergency management that was available in the world. Indeed, three months after its publication, the tragic events of September 11, 2001, took place and the volume immediately found itself on the desks of the U.S. President and many politicians, senior administrators, policymakers, and public managers, as well as specialists on crisis and emergency management around the world. I was told that the publisher could not keep up with the growing demands, and the book was a monumental success, with numerous applications for public, private, and nonprofit sector organizations across the globe.

A lot of changes have occurred since the publication of that first edition, prompting the publication of a second edition with many new chapters and revised original ones. Published in 2014, the new edition received a new title, *Crisis and Emergency Management: Theory and Practice*, and it again was the most comprehensive book on the global market. These past 15 years have witnessed incalculable changes, disasters, crises, and emergencies. The list is long, but the following highlights some of the events with relevance to and implications for crisis and emergency management: September 11, 2001, terrorist attacks and ensuing global war on terrorism; U.S. invasions of Iraq and Afghanistan that caused massive destruction, hundreds of thousands of human casualties, and refugee crises; bombings in London and Madrid; massive earthquakes in the southeast ancient city of Bam in Iran and in Sichuan in southwest China; Indian Ocean earthquake and tsunami in 2004; Hurricane Katrina in New Orleans; the earthquake, tsunami, and ensuing Fukushima nuclear power station meltdown in Japan; Hurricane Wilma in Florida and Hurricane Sandy in the Northeast; economic collapse of several European countries, such as Greece, Ireland, Portugal, and Spain; collapse of the Wall Street financial empire and ensuing American economic crisis; global crisis of capitalism and a crisis of governance in the Western world; rising unemployment as a result of economic recessions; Israeli invasions of Lebanon, Gaza, and the West Bank; ongoing crises of terrorism and violence in Syria, ISIL terrorism; Saudi Arabia's air bombardments of the impoverished country of Yemen that have produced a humanitarian crisis; and global immigration crises.

In each of these crisis events, the loss of human lives and the maiming of others have been enormous, running into the thousands, tens of thousands, and, in the case of Afghanistan and Iraq, many hundreds of thousands. To this cost must be added the destruction of property, looting, violation of human rights, abuse of children and women, internment and torture of many suspected terrorists around the world, as well as the systematic persecution of suspect groups and religions across the globe. We must also consider the many millions of working-class people all around the world who have experienced serious distress and even violence as a result of the economic crises brought about by the predatory globalization and capitalism that have forced them into a "race to the bottom" and inflicted major blows to the competitive free-market system and human freedom. We might also add the issue of global warming, a devastating phenomenon causing the destruction of species and their ecological environments, in addition to affecting entire ecosystems of our planet. The age of predatory globalization has had both expected and unexpected consequences affecting the world's environments, social systems, and governance and public administration systems.

How do the victims cope with such disasters and catastrophes? How do communities and countries cope with and manage them? How do the world's collective governance bodies deal with disaster? Are the voices of the poor, of women and children being heard? How are these disasters and emergencies managed, and what lessons have been learned from global crises and emergencies? This case book addresses these and other relevant questions by analyzing the causes and effects of several disasters and crises; by identifying policy and managerial lessons to be learned; and by proposing ideas, models, perspectives, theories, and suggestions for capacity building in crisis and emergency management. This is the first global textbook that focuses on select global cases of best and worst practice in crisis and emergency management around the world. It is intended to serve as either a primary textbook or a companion reading text for courses in crisis and disaster management, public administration, political science, global crisis studies, and emergency management at upper undergraduate and graduate levels. The chapters were carefully selected and include chapter learning objectives, analysis of presented materials, and lessons learned for future crisis leadership and emergency management. The chapters discuss situations that illustrate the good, the bad, and the ugly of crisis and emergency management. Instructors, students, researchers, policy experts, and practitioners will find the case studies illuminating, the theories eye opening, and the practices refreshing.

Global Cases in Best and Worst Practice in Crisis and Emergency Management is a case study follow-up of the earlier two editions of *Crisis and Emergency Management: Theory and Practice*. It is hoped that this book will inform scholars, instructors, students, practitioners, policymakers, crisis and emergency management experts, and public administrators. It will be followed shortly by a smaller, single-authored book, *Advancing Crisis and Emergency Management: Theory and Practice*.

Acknowledgments

It took several years to complete this publication and accomplish its intended form. Enormous time, energy, and cooperation were invested to this project, mostly by the contributing authors, who responded to my numerous calls for revisions and updates and who patiently and eagerly contributed to the body of knowledge contained in this textbook. All credit goes to them, and the responsibilities for any errors are mine. I am most grateful to them, for their patience, continuous cooperation, and contributions. I also appreciate the valuable assistance of my doctoral student, Arjola Balilaj, who helped me finish the last stage of this book and get it to production; her special assistance has been of the highest quality and effective. Additionally, I thank the CRC publisher Richard O'Hanley for his encouragement to publish this book, and his publication editor, Lara Zoble, at Taylor & Francis, for their patience, guidance, and assistance in getting the project off the ground.

Editor

Ali Farazmand, PhD, is a professor of public administration and policy at Florida Atlantic University, where he teaches courses in the intellectual development (philosophy and theory) of public administration, organization theory and behavior, organization change and public management, public personnel and labor relations, collective bargaining/negotiation, administrative ethics and accountability, globalization and sound governance, comparative/development public administration, modern systems of government, bureaucratic politics and administrative theory, and executive leadership. Farazmand earned his doctorate and master's of public administration from the Maxwell School of Syracuse University, in addition to earning a master's of science degree in educational administration from Syracuse University and a bachelor's degree in business administration from Tehran University.

He is the author and editor of 24 authored and edited books and over 150 refereed journal articles and book chapters. His articles have appeared in *Public Administration Review, Administration & Society, Public Organization Review, International Review of Administrative Sciences, Public Administration Quarterly, International Journal of Public Administration, Public Finance and Management, Asia Pacific Journal of Public Administration,* and *American Review of Public Administration.* He is the founding editor in chief of *Public Organization Review: A Global Journal* and editor in chief of the *International Journal of Public Administration.* Dr. Farazmand is a globally recognized international scholar and a global consultant on public administration and governance reforms, organizational change and public management, organization design and performance, crisis and emergency management, public sector quality and productivity management, leadership and performance management, and globalization and global studies. He has made groundbreaking contributions to various areas of social sciences, including organization theory/behavior, bureaucratic politics and administrative theory, chaos and transformation theories, institutional theory, crisis and emergency management, surprise management theory, organizational elite theory, administrative state, sound governance, and globalization. He has also served as a global consultant on governance and public administration reforms to the United Nations for over 17 years.

Farazmand's previous publications include *The State, Bureaucracy, and Revolution: Development or System Maintenance?*; *Modern Systems of Government: Exploring the Bureaucrats and Politicians' Relationships*; *Modern Organizations: Theory and Practice,* 1st and 2nd editions; *Administrative Reform in Developing Nations*; *Handbook of Comparative and Development Public Administration,* 1st and 2nd editions; *Public Enterprise Management*; *Privatization or Reform?*; *Crisis and Emergency Management*; *Sound Governance*; *Strategic Public Personnel Administration: Building* and *Managing Human Capital for the 21st Century*; *Handbook of Globalization, Governance, and Public Administration*; *Bureaucracy and Administration*; and *Crisis and Emergency Management: Theory and Practice*. His forthcoming books include *Public Administration in a Globalized World*, *Advances in Crisis and Emergency Management*, *Institutional Theory and Public Administration*, and *The Administrative State Revisited: Globalization and Transformation*.

Contributors

Clifford R. Bragdon
Florida Tech Research Park
Florida Institute of Technology
Melbourne, Florida

Christine Allison Canavan
Andrew Young School of Policy Studies
Georgia State University
Atlanta, Georgia

John J. Carroll
Huizenga School of Business and
    Entrepreneurship
Nova Southeastern University
Fort Lauderdale, Florida

Jeanne-Marie Col
John Jay College
New York, New York

Frances L. Edwards
Department of Political Sciences
San Jose State University
San Jose, California

Ann-Margaret Esnard
Andrew Young School of Policy Studies
Georgia State University
Atlanta, Georgia

Ali Farazmand
School of Public Administration
Florida Atlantic University
Boca Raton, Florida

Jamil Jreisat
School of Public Affairs
University of South Florida
Tampa, Florida

Carole L. Jurkiewicz
McCormack College of Management
University of Massachusetts
Boston, Massachusetts

Yuko Kaneko
Department of Social Sciences
Yamagata University
Yamagata, Japan

Steven G. Koven
School of Urban and Public Affairs
University of Louisville
Louisville, Kentucky

Rose L. Pfefferbaum
Terrorism and Disaster Center
University of Oklahoma Health Sciences
    Center
Oklahoma City, Oklahoma

Alka Sapat
School of Public Administration
Florida Atlantic University
Boca Raton, Florida

Itoko Suzuki
United Nations Department of Economic and
  Social Affairs (formerly)
Shizuoka, Japan

William L. Waugh, Jr.
Department of Public Management and Policy
Andrew Young School of Policy Studies
Georgia State University
Atlanta, Georgia

Chapter 1

Studying Crisis and Emergency Management Using Global Cases of Best and Worst Practices

Ali Farazmand

Contents

Chapter Goals 1
Introduction 2
Globalization 3
Theoretical Knowledge on Crisis Management and Emergency Governance 4
Nature of Crises 6
Managing Crises and Emergencies 7
Case Study Approach to Crisis and Emergency Management 9
Plan of the Book 10
Questions for Discussion 11
Additional Reading 11
References 12

Chapter Goals

By the end of this chapter, readers will have a full understanding of the following:

1. Crisis and emergency management meanings, forms, types, and kinds
2. Pros and cons of globalization and their implications for crisis and emergency management studies
3. Theories of crisis management and emergency governance

4. Nature and characteristics of crises and emergencies
5. Managing crises and emergencies and what is required for effective crisis and emergency management
6. Advantages of the case study approach to the study and practice of crisis and emergency management
7. Cases of best and worst practice in crisis and emergency management
8. Plan of the book and chapter descriptions

Introduction

Has the world always seen as many conflicts, wars, and challenges throughout its history as it has for the last several decades? Has the world ever faced so many challenges, chaotic changes, and crises threatening peace, stability, prosperity, systems' survival, and hopes as it has the last several decades? Answering these questions requires extensive empirical as well as theoretical studies, much beyond the scope of this rather small book. Conflicts create tensions, tensions cause conflicts, and forces benefiting from such developments tend to fuel them, making things worse. Conflicts leading to wars may benefit some but they disrupt life and destroy lives, property, and environments. Chaos arises when unexpected events develop, and the unanticipated consequences have surprising effects. The outcomes of chaos-driven crises are extremely difficult if not totally impossible to predict, and the inevitable consequences may have costly results from which few people would benefit. The end of the Cold War raised hopes for prosperity and opportunities among the poor and underprivileged worldwide that have not materialized.

Crises of various degrees of intensity impose an urgency and a call for emergency management requiring immediate attention and solutions. Unfortunately, not all such crisis situations receive adequate attention in a world full of faction politics and interest groups or nations with superior powers that seek to further their interests. At the end of the day, many conflicts have further worsened the *status quo* for millions enduring chronic crises, while the privileged few have benefited even more. Just a few examples are the perpetual crisis of Palestinians under occupation, the current Yemeni crisis under Saudi Arabia's constant military bombardment, the continuing global refugee crises, and the spiraling terrorism plaguing Middle East nations that can be attributed to al-Qaeda and ISIL, who are routinely committing crimes against humanity (supported by regional powers in some cases). A world filled with such massive contrasts between justice and injustice, wealth and poverty, and hegemony and powerlessness will only fuel further despair and desperate measures (including terrorism) to obtain perceived equality and justice.

The last several decades have witnessed many such developments, so many that global observers have lamented the possibility of reaching an apocalyptic conclusion. It seems that the world has entered an age of unreason in which all order has been turned upside down. Governmental reports declare nation-states to be at major risk of losing territorial sovereignty and control of their independence in the age of predatory globalization. The political and military threats posed by predatory globalization and global capitalism transcend national boundaries and defy the conventional notions of statehood and democratic ideals; they have broken the world peace, violated international laws, and put the world on the brink of a possible third world war, one that could be nuclear (Ohmae, 1990, 1995; Korten, 1995; Farazmand, 1999, 2012).

Globalization

The rise of the globalization of capital and its negative consequences for both developing and more developed nations of the industrialized West have raised many concerns embracing economics, environmental ecology, labor, culture, traditions, governance, administration, and politics. Energized by technological innovations, globalization has produced some positive effects, such as bringing more markets and products to consumers with money and facilitating communication and travel among people around the globe. But, it has also had many adverse consequences worldwide—increases in child and slave labor, wage slavery, environmental degradation, human rights violations, loss of control over national and local resources, loss of the democratic rights of citizens to make independent decisions, and powerlessness in the face of globalized finance capital backed by the most powerful (and potentially deadly) nations—the United States and its European allies. Today, predatory globalization has established an iron grip on nation-states' sovereignties, forced governments to impose austerity measures at the expense of the working and middle classes worldwide, and placed billions into virtual slavery. The new barons of the global village—as it has been characterized by proponents of predatory globalization—have tried to flatten the world with the ideology and practices of market supremacy and corporate structure as the ideal organization for governance and administration (for more on this topic, see Farazmand, 2012).

Until 1991, the world had been governed for 70 years by a dual world order, a two-world-systems model under the shared leadership of the Soviet Union representing socialism and the United States representing corporate capitalism; there existed a global order in which the rules of the game and engagements were fairly defined and understood. Conflicts that developed were resolved by both systems and through global governance institutions that reflected the two superpower preferences. With the fall of the Union of Soviet Socialist Republics in 1991, global capitalism and its hegemonic state, the United States, declared a triumph of corporate capitalism and market ideology over socialism. Initially, many overly optimistic proponents of corporate globalization rushed to paint rosy pictures of a world with no wars, conflict, or poverty—they were proven wrong rather quickly, as this author and many other critics warned and predicted (Korten, 1995; Farazmand, 1999). Multidimensional crises caused by predatory globalization and affecting various peoples, nation-states, governments, and cultures have arisen since then. Under the one-world ideological system of capitalism and market ideology, all voices of opposition and protest are silenced, and alternative forms of governance and socioeconomic order are crushed by military and other coercive forces, all in the name of a self-proclaimed ideology of market supremacy and a capitalist democracy in which the wealthy and corporate elites rule (Korten, 1995; Farazmand, 1999). Crises are now being transformed into opportunities for further accumulation of capital throughout the world, which is now considered a "global village" ruled by the feudal barons of the new world order. *Profit*, *social control*, and *capitalism* are the key operative words for the new era.

It is within this volatile environment of globalization that critics have found ample reason to express concerns. As examples, Rifkin (1996) announced the "end of work," Wilson (1997) highlighted the loss of urban jobs, Mele (1996) and Knox (1997) argued about the loss of a sense of community and urban infrastructure, Cox (1993) discussed the loss of territorial sovereignty of nation-states, and Korbin (1996) warned about a "return back to medievalism." Although proponents of globalization presented an optimistic view of a new world order under corporate globalization, opponents warned against its devastating effects. Fukuyama (1992) spoke of the "end of history and of man," and Huntington (1996) spoke of a "clash of civilizations." Brecher and Costello (1994) warned of a "global pillage," Parenti (1995) spoke of global "corpocracy and plutocracy," Farazmand (1999) predicted a "rise of wage slavery and mercenary systems of socioeconomic order," and Stever (1988) anticipated an end of public administration. Crises of institutions have reached a higher level of criticality. Of these, governability crises in the West and in the core of global capitalism, as well as in the community and family institutions that form the backbones of society, have deepened. Today, the world witnesses daily continuation of wars throughout the Middle East and widespread governability crises that extend to parts of Europe, such as Greece and Spain.

Popular books signal a shift in global paradigms away from stable patterns, thus both challenging and reinforcing the *status quo*. Information technology has broken down barriers among nations, organizations, and people around the globe. No longer can organizations and governments rely on continuity and stability. No longer can individuals predict and feel secure about their futures. No longer can anyone escape the devastating impacts of crises—crises that have reached a new level and have been eroding the fundamental underpinnings and basic assumptions of humanity. Unfortunately, these crises are routinely covered up by the military, communication, and financial arms of the globally dominant states. A growing sense of powerlessness and insecurity has led people worldwide to seek ways to escape degradation, dehumanization, resentment, and exploitation—it has become a matter of survival. They are forced into practicing self-censorship and role playing as the new culture of globalism and global order becomes more invasive. Alienation—work, social, and self—is increasingly seeping into people's personal and social lives, but many are resisting it and are struggling to maintain their identity.

Some are putting up the pretense of being part of the *status quo* to survive, but they may be walking time bombs ready to explode at any time. Some take their lives and those of others because they think they have nothing to lose. Potential crises hover at various levels of criticality until they explode, perhaps globally. The Occupy Wall Street protest movement was transformed into a global movement of counter-globalization, counter-repression, and counter-exploitation, reclaiming the people's power from the elites and bringing about fundamental institutional, political, and economic system changes (Farazmand, 2015). These global movements may have subsided for the time being but they are not gone and will likely resurface as the crises of governability continue, compounded by manmade and natural disasters that often lead to chaotic situations and emergencies.

Theoretical Knowledge on Crisis Management and Emergency Governance

A growing body of knowledge on crisis management and emergency governance is leading to the development of theories to explain what can be done in the case of emergencies and crises facing modern governments. Ancient powers, such as Rome and Persia, implemented highly flexible emergency management systems throughout their far-flung territories. These were a component of strategic public management that featured efficient bureaucracies and administrative systems to deal with floods, storms, earthquakes, and political or military emergencies (Farazmand, 2001). Modern theories of emergency governance and crisis management inform us with far fresher knowledge as to how "sound governance" (Farazmand, 2004) could be performed in such situations. Sound governance is key to modern governance and governability capacity building (Schumpeter, 1942; Schmitt, 1963; Allison and Zelikow, 1999; Dror, 2001).

The growing body of literature on the twin fields of crisis management and emergency governance spans nations, cultures, security administrations, terrorism, disasters, and catastrophes (Perrow, 1984; Comfort, 1988; Waugh, 2000; Farazmand, 2001; Wise, 2006). With regard to emergency and crisis governance, a crucial mandate appears to distinguish between the routine governance of public organizations across the board from those functions considered extraordinary and emerging situations such as political riots and upheavals, revolts and revolutions, foreign military threats, and even economic breakdowns with potential consequences threatening political system collapse. These destabilizing forces of chaos and crisis threaten modern systems of government, democratic or not, and cause breakdowns in social systems and their capacities to govern (Dror, 2001). Some of these breakdowns may be "birth pangs of a better future" and constitute what Schumpeter called "creative breakdowns" (Schumpeter, 1942). We still have very little knowledge of transformational breakdowns, but we can learn from the growing body of knowledge on "chaos theory" (Prigogine and Stengers, 1984; Kiel, 1989; Dror, 2001; Farazmand, 2004). What we do know, however, is that catastrophic and chaotic breakdowns can become very disruptive and brutal and cause much human suffering due to subsequent aggressive behavior. Thus, emergency and crisis-driven breakdowns require temporary extraordinary governance and politics and demand an emergency management regime to cope with and manage the situation (Schmitt, 1963). The authority of sovereign power to declare a state of emergency to cope with emergency situations (McCormick, 2000) is recognized in governance theory (Schmitt, 1963). This must, of course, be done with care and stop short of putting into place a dictatorial regime—including imperial presidencies or constitutional dictatorships—that threatens democracy and civil liberties. Emergency regimes are dangerous and no one likes them, especially when they adopt unnecessarily harsh policy measures (Leng, 1990; Gomien, 1993); such regimes tend to become aggressive and perpetuate themselves. Other devastating situations arise when "no government can be maintained, law and order breaks down and societies approach total collapse" (Dror, 2001, p. 206). Crisis and emergency governance arrangements must be developed and constantly upgraded to respond to the needs of the time, especially by such global institutions as the United Nations, in an age of rapid globalization and global threats of violence, terrorism, conflicts, war, poverty, and insecurity (Bartholemew, 2006; Hoffmann, 2006).

What exactly emergency governance regimes must do in crisis situations is a subject of much scholarly debate, but the key responsibility of emergency government is to first bring under control an evolving crisis or emergency situation that has the potential to transform into chaos. Projecting a sense of being in charge through a central command system can provide the control necessary in most emergency situations. Steps taken after this stage may include implementing response strategies that can help modify the extraordinary situation and make it possible to move on from emergency governance and to learn from the experience. Obviously, not all emergencies produce crises, and not all crises demand declaring a state of emergency, but all crises and emergency situations signal an *urgency* to take action before higher levels of criticality are reached. Despite the proven effectiveness of an emergency and crisis regime, there is no guarantee that such governance measures will always succeed, especially when the political legitimacy of the regime is questioned. Key to emergency governance is the application of a specialized expertise outside the bureaucratic structure of government, one that is flexible, robust, upgraded constantly, and well informed; yet, the bureaucratic structure provides the necessary power to the state in crisis situations.

Military emergencies require a military bureaucracy with special forces behind the flexible central command structure. For many social crises and emergencies, however, such a bureaucracy may be too slow to act as a leader and must be supplanted by a central command system that can mobilize government forces (the bureaucracy) and a host of other organizations such as various networked systems, voluntary forces, and foreign assistance agencies. An important aspect of crisis and emergency governance is sharp and timely recognition of a situation as being an emergency or crisis, as opposed to a routine disturbance. Such distinction is not often easy, as there may not be an immediate consensus among key actors or leaders as to what constitutes a crisis. Nevertheless, governance theories do inform us of a necessity for emergency regimes and crisis governance systems. The leaders and people of the United States and the Soviet Union experienced this unpleasant situation during the Cuban Missile Crisis of the 1960s, and both countries came to realize the possibility of mutual destruction in the face of a potential thermonuclear conflict and agreed to a collaborative working relationship against it by the 1970s (Allison and Zeliko, 1999).

Modern crises are characterized by complexity, interdependence, and politicization. "Tomorrow's crisis, in turn, will look different from today and yesterday's crises" (Rosenthal et al., 2001, p. 6). This reality is not widely understood, as assumptions and perceptions about emergency and crisis management are still based on traditional beliefs. For example, Schneider (1995, pp. 36–37) identified six major (false) assumptions that hinder current emergency and crisis management:

1. Only a local response is necessary when the location of a natural disaster is within a limited geographical area.
2. All levels of government will cooperate closely (May and Williams, 1986).
3. The administrative capacity and resources necessary to handle disasters or crises exist.
4. Public officials have an awareness and understanding of crises and are able to handle them.
5. The Federal Emergency Management Agency (FEMA) holds state and local governments responsible for their response systems.
6. People outside the response system understand how the system operates.

At first glance, these might be considered good assumptions; however, according to Schneider (1995), reality paints a different picture: First, different levels of government and their officials have different perspectives based on what works to their own advantage. Second, crisis and emergency officials often encounter difficulties when trying to manage the actions of other participants in the process. Third, emergency relief operations are generally underfunded and do not take top priority in government agendas (Waugh, 1990). Finally, the credibility of any emergency management operation is generally low, as such operations generally suffer from a lack of respect within the overall government system. There is a perception that people working in emergency management are untrained and unprepared for the job, that they are "old military personnel or political hacks who cannot find other employment" (Schneider, 1995, p. 39). Unfortunately, cases such as Hurricane Katrina reinforced most of these assumptions.

Nature of Crises

Crises occur at all levels and appear in all guises. Some are long-term processes of deterioration, while others are rapid ruptures. Some have their origins and roots in the past, while others are created by chance and the risks posed by a particular environment. Some are caused internally, others externally. Some crises simmer over time due to, for example, corrupt dictatorships, while others may occur suddenly, such as the Stock Market Crash of 1929, which led to the Great Depression. Crises come in a variety of forms and always have disruptive effects.

Crises scramble plans, interrupt continuities, and brutally paralyze normal operations and human lives. Most crises have trigger points so critical as to leave historical marks on nations, groups, and individual lives. Crises are historical points of reference, distinguishing between the past and present. Memories persist for anyone involved in disasters, hijackings, riots, revolts, and revolutions. Years, months, and days become historic points of demarcation (e.g., 1914, 1917, 1929, 1940, and 1978/79), and crisis events become memorable, including the Cuban Missile Crisis, the Vietnam War, the Middle East crisis, Arab Spring, Black Friday, the February Revolution in Iran, the October Revolution in Russia, the invasion of Iraq, and the 9/11 tragedy (Rosenthal and Kouzmin, 1993; Farazmand, 1996, 2001).

Crises come in a variety of forms—terrorism, natural disasters, nuclear power plant accidents, riots, business and organizational emergencies—often resulting in life-or-death situations. Some crises can be managed effectively, while others lead to failures and further disasters. Some bring about new and positive changes, while others result in further calamities. Crises consist of a short chain of events that can destroy or drastically weaken a condition of equilibrium and the effectiveness of a system or regime within a period of days, weeks, or hours rather than years. In this sense, a crisis is not the same as tensions or process-oriented crises; thus, two types of crises can be identified: (1) process-oriented crises developing over a period of time, and (2) sudden ruptures that develop within weeks, days, hours, or even minutes (Farazmand, 1996). The latter type of crisis is "fraught with far-reaching implications. It threatens to involve large segments of society in violent actions" (Dogan and Higley, 1996, p. 5).

Managing Crises and Emergencies

A central feature of all crises is a sense of urgency, and in many cases urgency becomes the most compelling issue. Situations change so dramatically and rapidly that no one seems to be able to predict the chain of events or the possible outcomes. An important aspect of such crisis situations is the dynamics that evolve over days, hours, and even minutes. In a revolutionary crisis, such unpredictability, uncertainty, and change characterize the dynamics of the unfolding events. Leaders and decision-makers are often caught by surprise by the many forces involved, including the people, strengths or weaknesses of the regime and ruling elite, external or internal actors, climatic conditions, and national characters. Surprises characterize crisis situations (Farazmand, 1996, 2001, 2007).

Some crises are processes of events leading to a level of criticality or degree of intensity generally out of control. Crises often originate in the past, and diagnosing their original sources can help to understand and manage a particular crisis or lead to an alternative outcome. But, as mentioned, some crises are sudden and abrupt events that can paralyze a regime, a community, or economic system. Understanding the dynamics of crises can help develop a better understanding of crisis evolution and its management. Intense crisis analysis needs to move beyond a focus on human error as being the origin of crises. Deficiencies in organization, leadership, and systems must be diagnosed to achieve effective crisis management outcomes. Many organizations develop over time a culture devoid of the ability to detect environmental threats challenging their survival, and many crises develop as a result of managerial incompetence (Perrow, 1984; Rosenthal and Kouzmin, 1993). Public organizations are not immune from this maladaptation of bureaucratic culture caused by bureau deficiencies and vulnerabilities. Crises are destructive, but they may also represent opportunities for a new order, changes that may produce positive results; therefore, crises create their own antitheses, which may dialectically reinforce and complement forces of a positive nature.

Timely and accurate evaluation of the criticality of problems and the dynamics of the events that ensue is key to crisis management. Doing so requires knowledge, skills, courageous leadership, risk-taking ability, and vigilance. Successful crisis management also requires motivation, a sense of urgency, commitment, and creative thinking with a long-term strategic vision while being mindful of daily operational imperatives. In the management of crises, established organizational norms, culture, rules, and procedures can become major obstacles. Administrators and bureaucrats tend to protect themselves by playing bureaucratic games and hiding behind organizational and legal shelters. A sense of urgency gives way to inertia, organizational sheltering, and self-protection by managers and staff alike. This is the most devastating institutional obstacle to the effective management of any crisis. Successful crisis management requires (1) sensing the urgency of the matter at hand; (2) thinking creatively and strategically to address the crisis to the degree and scope required; (3) taking bold actions and acting courageously and sincerely; (4) breaking away from the self-protective organizational culture by taking risks and actions that could produce optimum solutions with no significant losers; and (5) maintaining vigilance and a continuous presence during the rapidly changing situations as they unfold. Reason, creative thinking, and perseverance must be the guiding forces for those involved in crisis management and crisis resolution. Any error or misjudgment can lead to further disasters, causing irreparable damage to human lives.

The primary function of any government is to protect the lives and property of its citizens. Crises and emergencies generally test the competency of governments. Throughout the history of human civilizations, policymakers have sought to anticipate the unexpected "in order to reduce the risk to human life and safety posed by intermittently occurring natural and manmade hazardous events" (Petak, 1985, p. 3). This notion needs to be capitalized on as a noble policy and as the primary strategic choice of collective action. Unfortunately, not everyone thinks this way in a crisis situation; history is full of cases where opportunists have taken advantage of chaos and disorder to enrich themselves, to establish power bases, and to steal what does not belong to them.

Literature refers to the desirability of the emergence of "synthetic groups" in urban disasters (Wolensky and Wolensky, 1990) that operate as working coalitions of key actors and agents at different levels to provide command-and-control systems and to facilitate damage assessment and resource deployment (Dluhy, 1990). The absence of such command-and-control systems can create serious problems and add to the crisis situation, as occurred in Miami, Florida, during Hurricane Andrew in 1992: "Dade County emergency managers had no way to enforce cooperation. ... Organization chaos and weak command and control were the characteristic mode of the EOC [Emergency Operations Center] during the crisis period" (Averch and Dluhy, 1997, p. 84). Despite the federal, state, and local government assistance, empirical research shows that minorities, especially blacks and Hispanics, and immigrant workers suffered most from the consequences of Hurricane Andrew. Crisis and emergency management was least effective for these groups, who had to rely on their family and relatives for help and assistance. Long after the crisis, their suffering continued in the form of joblessness, loss of housing, hunger, disease, socially and economically driven problems of crime, and a host of other associated crises (see studies in Peacock et al., 1997).

The efforts of past decision makers, administrators, citizens, researchers, and all those involved in crisis and emergency management have provided the foundation for the current focus on these twin subfields of public administration in the United States and abroad. Not all emergency situations are caused by crises, and, in fact, many have nothing to do with any crisis at all. But, all crises cause emergency situations, which must be dealt with very carefully. As a central activity of public administration, emergency management is generally a process of developing and implementing policies and actions that involve the following (Petak, 1985; Farazmand, 2001):

1. *Mitigation*—A course of action to detect the risk to society or the health of people and to reduce the risk
2. *Preparedness*—A response plan of action to reduce loss of life and to increase the chance of successful response to the disaster or catastrophe
3. *Response*—Provision of emergency aid and assistance
4. *Recovery*—Provision of immediate support to return life back to normalcy

The emergence of chaos theory in the social sciences has contributed to the development of an understanding of crises that emanate from or are exacerbated by sudden chaotic events. Chaos theory has its roots in the physical sciences; its application to the social sciences is a rather new development that has proven useful to explain disequilibrium, disorder, and nonlinear changing conditions. The cycle of chaos/disorder/order is an evolutionary process that contributes to the transformation of social systems, including organizations with political and managerial implications. Stability and equilibria carry with them potential forces of change and disruption, which can trigger system instability and disorder and place the system on the verge of chaos and disorder. Patterns of change and instability characterize this chaos. The key to understanding and managing these changes is the application of nonlinear and multicausal or noncausal thinking within organizations and social systems. Long-term transformation results from short-term chaotic changes that cause system disequilibrium, a phenomenon that has major implications for crisis and emergency management (for details on chaos theory, see, for example, Jantsch, 1980; Prigogine and Stengers, 1984; Lazlo, 1987; Loye and Eisler, 1987; Kiel, 1989; Pascal, 1990; Farazmand, 2004 and Chapter 2 in this volume). An even more recent development in line with chaos and transformation theories is *surprise management theory* (Farazmand, 2007, 2009, 2015).

Case Study Approach to Crisis and Emergency Management

Case study approaches offer useful pedagogical and practical methods for the analysis and understanding of phenomena, issues, and problems, as well as solutions. Case studies provide the focused, in-depth, and detailed information necessary to analyze situations and apply concepts, theories, and models within the realities of a particular period of time. They are particularly useful in areas where knowledge is limited and exploration and examination are required to establish novel ideas based on empirical evidence. Thus, case studies can provide the important evidence necessary to support claims or solve problems of a similar nature (Farazmand, 2001). Case studies also provide a means for investigating what changes in a program have occurred and how they occurred over time, what results they produced, and whether those results were due to external interventions or internal dynamics (Farazmand, 2001; Leedy and Ormrod, 2010). As a reliable methodology, case studies offer a wealth of information often unexplored or overlooked by regular research. Using primary and secondary data, the case study approach offers one of the best empirical methods for social science research. In crisis and emergency management, case studies are actually ideal for gathering and analyzing the data necessary for policy and organizational decision making and comparative capacity building in knowledge management.

Application of the case study approach to the analysis of the global cases covered in this textbook is ideal for a variety of reasons. First, the cases selected for this book are among the most extensively discussed and analyzed worldwide, and they represent some of the most complex ones for consideration. Second, these cases are representatives of some of the best and worst practices in crisis and emergency management worldwide. Third, these cases have major implications for the future study and practice of crisis and emergency management and offer clear lessons on crisis leadership, organizational structures, command systems development, managerial coordination, communication, decision making, and so on. Fourth, these cases represent disaster management in different countries. Finally, the cases in this textbook are intended to serve as the basis for further focused analysis of issues, theories, and concepts offered in courses on crisis and emergency or disaster management. Like concrete cases studied in law schools, these cases offer students concrete, real-world situations to analyze and understand and the opportunity to apply lessons learned as needed.

Plan of the Book

This book is divided into three main parts after this introductory chapter. Each chapter includes references, and some provide a short list of additional reading. Part I presents five cases of best and worst practices in crisis and emergency management. Chapter 2 analyzes Hurricane Katrina and the crisis that ensued when New Orleans flooded as a result of levee breaches, causing chaos and crisis. This is a case that has received extensive global coverage by media, politicians, experts, and administrators and is one of the most extensively studied cases of all time. Chapter 3 focuses on the 2011 Fukushima nuclear power plant disaster caused by the tsunami that hit Japan and offers major policy lessons. Chapter 4 focuses on the early warnings of the imminent Tangshan earthquake that hit China with 7.8 magnitude in the 1970s. The in-depth discussion addresses how the early warning saved millions of lives and how that system has the potential to save more lives and property in the future. Chapter 5 offers a comparative analysis of three global cases of nuclear reactor meltdowns: Three Mile Island, Chernobyl, and Fukushima. The chapter provides a useful analysis of these cases and suggests policy and managerial suggestions for future crisis and emergency management.

The six chapters in Part II include comprehensive analyses of major global cases of best and worst practices in crisis and emergency management over the last two decades. Chapter 6 details the emergency management crisis that occurred in the case of Hurricane Katrina. Chapter 7 follows with an analysis of Hurricane Katrina as both a manmade and a natural disaster; there is much to be learned from the various aspects of the Hurricane Katrina disaster as a global case of crisis management worst practice. Chapter 8 presents an analysis of the devastating Iranian Bam earthquake, which claimed over 50,000 lives and destroyed the entire ancient city of Bam, including the world's largest adobe structure, the Citadel of Bam. It also offers several lessons from that disaster for future crisis and emergency management. Chapter 9 focuses on September 11, 2001, in the United States and offers a clear analysis of that disaster, the ensuing crisis and emergency management that followed, and the worldwide implications that led to devastating wars of destruction in the Middle East and the subjugation of millions of people worldwide to various antiterrorism and security measures. The focus is on the emergency management of that historical disaster, with lessons for future emergency management. Chapter 10 compares Hurricane Wilma and Hurricane Sandy with lessons learned from the perspective of a public servant. Finally, Chapter 11 delves into the crisis of governance in the revolutionary Arab world that began in 2011 and has continued for years. It also offers an interesting discussion of that region's development, which has been plagued by legitimacy and other problems.

Part III focuses on mitigation and capacity building for crisis and emergency management. The five chapters offer detailed analyses of various new cases with the purpose of mitigation and resilient capacity building for future crisis and emergency management in the 21st century. Here, Chapter 12 offers extensive analysis on building community resilience capacity and makes a strong case for such capacity building not only nationally but also globally, while offering lessons for future resilience capacity building. Chapter 13 provides a lengthy analysis of building disaster resilience and offers powerful lessons in resilience capacity building for future crisis and emergency management. Chapter 14 presents an interesting discussion on transboundary crises and the lessons to be learned from the aftermath of Haiti's massive earthquake in 2010. Finally, Chapter 15 offers a detailed and cogent discussion on how to plan responses to weapons of mass destruction. Focusing on federal and local partnerships, the chapter presents excellent points and offers clear lessons for future crisis and emergency management in a world full of crises, uncertainties, and trust issues.

This book of case studies is designed to serve as a textbook for upper undergraduate and graduate-level courses in public administration, public policy, crisis and emergency management, disaster management, chaos and transformation theories, political science, business management, security studies, and other related social science programs. It can be adopted as either (1) an undergraduate senior or graduate-level course textbook or (2) a companion/required reader in crisis and emergency management. Each chapter has a list of learning objectives at the beginning and a list of references at the end.

Questions for Discussion

1. What is meant by *globalization* and *predatory globalization*?
2. What is meant by *crisis management* and *emergency governance*, and what is their difference?
3. Do all emergencies turn into crises? Do all crises require emergency responses? Why?
4. What is meant by nonlinear, chaotic thinking about crisis and emergency management? What is linear crisis management thinking?
5. What is meant by *creative breakdown*?
6. Why is emergency governance dangerous and undesirable? Why is it sometimes necessary?
7. What is the difference between mitigation and a response system in crisis and emergency management?
8. What are the benefits of a case study text approach?

Additional Reading

Comfort, L.K., Ed. (1988). *Managing Disaster: Strategies and Policy Perspectives*. Durham, NC: Duke University Press.
Farazmand, A., Ed. (2001). *Handbook of Crisis and Emergency Management*. New York: Marcel Dekker.
Farazmand, A. (2014). *Crisis and Emergency Management: Theory and Practice*. Boca Raton, FL: CRC Press.
Freeman, A. and Kagarlitsky, B., Eds. (2004). *The Politics of Empire: Globalization in Crisis*. London: Pluto Press.
Haddow, G.D. and Bullock, J.A. (2006). *Introduction to Emergency Management*, 2nd ed. New York: Elsevier.
Hermann, C.E. (1969). *Crises in Foreign Policy: A Simulation Analysis*. Indianapolis, IN: Bobbs Merrill.
Hewitt, K., Ed. (1983). *Interpretations of Calamity: From the Viewpoint of Human Ecology*. Boston: Allen & Unwin.
Mitroff, I. (2004). *Crisis Leadership: Planning for the Unthinkable*. Hoboken, NJ: Wiley.
Pinsdorf, M.K. (2004). *All Crises Are Global: Managing to Escape Chaos*. New York: Fordham University Press.
Reich, R.B. (1991). *The Work of Nations: Preparing for the 21st Century Capitalism*. New York: Simon & Schuster.
Regester, M. and Larkin, J. (2005). *Risk Issues and Crisis Management*, 3rd ed. London: Kogan Page.
Stacey, R.D. (1992). *Managing the Unknowable: Strategic Boundaries between Order and Chaos in Organizations*. San Francisco: Jossey-Bass.

Steinberg, T. (2000). *Acts of God: The Unnatural History of Natural Disaster in America.* Oxford, UK: Oxford University Press.
Waldrop, M.M. (1992). *Complexity: The Emerging Science at the Edge of Order and Chaos.* New York: Simon & Schuster.
Weick, K.E. and Sutcliffe, K.M. (2001). *Managing the Unexpected: Assuring High Performance in an Age of Complexity.* San Francisco: Jossey-Bass.

References

Allison, G. and Zelikow, P. (1999). *Essence of Decision: Explaining the Cuban Missile Crisis*, 2nd ed. New York: Longman.
Averch, H. and Dluhy, M. (1997). Crisis decision making and management. In Peacock, W.G., Morrow, B.H., and Gladwin, H., Eds., *Hurricane Andrew: Ethnicity, Gender, and the Sociology of Disasters*, pp. 75–91. New York: Routledge.
Bartholomew, A., Ed. (2006). *Empire's Law: The American Imperial Project and the "War to Remake the World."* London: Pluto Press.
Brecher, J. and Costello, T. (1994). *Global Village or Global Pillage: Economic Reconstruction from the Bottom Up.* Boston, MA: South End Press.
Comfort, L.K. (1988). *Managing Disaster: Strategies and Policy Perspectives.* Durham, NC: Duke University Press.
Cox, R.W. (1993). Structural issues of global governance. In Gill, S., Ed., *Gramci, Historical Materialism, and International Relations*, pp. 259–289. Cambridge, UK: Cambridge University Press.
Dluhy, M.J. (1990). *Building Coalitions in the Human Services.* Newbury Park, CA: Sage.
Dogan, M. and Higley, J. (1996). Crises, Elite Change, and Regime Change, paper presented at the International Conference on Regime Change and Elite Change, El Paular, Spain, May 30–June 1.
Dror, Y. (2001). *The Capacity to Govern: A Report to the Club of Rome.* Abingdon: Routledge.
Farazmand, A. (1996). Regime Change and Elite Change: The Iranian Revolution of 1978–79, paper presented at the International Conference on Regime Change and Elite Change, El Paular, Spain, May 30–June 1.
Farazmand, A. (1999). Globalization and public administration. *Public Admin. Rev.*, 59(6): 509–522.
Farazmand, A. (2001). Crisis and emergency management: theory and practice. In Farazmand, A., Ed., *Crisis and Emergency Management: Theory and Practice*, Chap. 1. New York: Marcel Dekker.
Farazmand, A. (2004). Chaos and transformation theories: a theoretical analysis with implications for organization theory and public management. *Public Org. Rev.*, 3(4): 339–372.
Farazmand, A. (2007). Learning from Katrina crisis: a global and international perspective with implications for future crisis management. *Public Admin. Rev.*, 67(Suppl.): 149–159.
Farazmand, A. (2009). Building administrative capacity for the age of rapid globalization: a modest prescription for survival. *Public Admin. Rev.*, 69(6): 1007–1020.
Farazmand, A. (2012). The future of public administration: challenges and opportunities; a critical essay. *Admin. Soc.*, 44(4): 487–517.
Farazmand, A. (2015). *Advances in Crisis and Emergency Management.* Boca Raton, FL: CRC Press.
Fukuyama, F. (1992). *The End of History and of the Last Man.* New York: Free Press.
Gomien, D., Ed. (1993). *Broadening the Frontiers of Human Rights: Essays in Honor of Asbjorne Eide.* Oslo: Scandinavian University Press.
Hoffmann, S. (2006). *Chaos and Violence: What Globalization, Failed States, and Terrorism Mean for U.S. Foreign Policy.* Lanham, MD: Rowman & Littlefield.
Huntington, S. (1996). *The Clash of Civilizations and the Remaking of the World Order.* New York: Simon & Schuster.
Jantsch, E. (1980). *The Self-Organizing Universe.* New York: Pergamon.
Kiel, D.L. (1989). Nonequilibrium theory and its implications for public administration. *Public Admin. Rev.*, 49(6): 544–551.

Knox, P. (1997). Globalization and urban economic change. *Ann. Am. Acad. Polit. Soc. Sci.*, 551: 17–27.
Korbin, S. (1996). Back to the future: neo-medievalism and the postmodern digital world economy. *J. Int. Affairs*, 51(2): 367–409.
Korten, D. (1995). *When Corporations Rule the World*. Bloomfield, CT: Kumarian Press.
Lazlo, E. (1987). *Evolution: The Grand Synthesis*. Boston: Shambhala New Science Library.
Leedy, P.D. and Ormrod, J.E. (2010). *Practical Design: Planning and Design*, 9th ed. Hoboken, NJ: Pearson.
Leng, S.-C., Ed. (1990). *Coping with Crises: How Governments Deal with Crises*. Lanham, MD: University Press of America.
Loye, D. and Eisler, R. (1987). Chaos and transformation: implications of nonequilibrium theory for social science and society. *Behav. Sci.*, 32: 53–65.
May, P.J. and Williams, W. (1986). *Disaster Policy Implementation: Managing Programs under Shared Governance*. New York: Plenum Press.
McCormick, J.P. (2000). *Carl Schmitt's Critique of Liberalism: Against Politics as Technology*. Cambridge, UK: Cambridge University Press.
Mele, C. (1996). Globalization, culture, and neighborhood change: reinventing the Lower East Side of New York. *Urban Affairs Rev.*, 17(9): 1663–1677.
Ohmae, K. (1990). *The Borderless World: Power and Strategy in an Interlinked Economy*. New York: Harper Business.
Ohmae, K. (1995). *The End of Nation States: The Rise of Regional Economics*. London: Harper Collins.
Parenti, M. (1995). *Democracy for the Few*. New York: St. Martin's Press.
Pascal, R. (1990). *Managing on the Edge of Chaos*. London: Viking.
Peacock, G.W., Morrow, B.H., and Gladwin, H., Eds. (1997). *Hurricane Andrew: Ethnicity, Gender and the Sociology of Disasters*. New York: Routledge.
Perrow, C. (1984). *Normal Accidents: Living with High-Risk Technologies*. New York: Basic Books.
Petak, W.J. (1985). Emergency management: a challenge for public administration. *Public Admin. Rev.*, 45(1): 3–6.
Prigogine, I. and Stengers, I. (1984). *Order Out of Chaos*. New York: Bantam.
Rifkin, J. (1996). *The End of Work*. New York: G.P. Putnam's Sons.
Rosenthal, U. and Kouzmin, A. (1993). Globalizing an agenda for contingencies and crisis management: an editorial statement. *J. Conting. Crisis Manage.*, 1(1): 1–12.
Rosenthal, U., Boin, R.A., and Comfort, L. (2001). *Managing Crises: Threats, Dilemmas, and Opportunities*. Springfield, IL: Charles C Thomas.
Schmitt, C. (1963). *Der Begriffdes Politischen [The Concept of the Political]*. Berlin: Duncker & Humblot.
Schneider, S.K. (1995). *Flirting with Disaster: Public Management in Crisis Situations*. Armonk, NY: M.E. Sharpe.
Schumpeter, J. (1942). *Capitalism, Socialism, and Democracy*, 2nd ed. New York: Harper & Brothers.
Stever, J. (1988). *The End of Public Administration*. New York: International Publications.
Waugh, Jr., W.L. (1990). Regionalizing emergency and the state and local government capacity. In Sylves, R.T. and Waugh, Jr., W.L., Eds., *Cities and Disaster: North American Studies in Emergency Management*, pp. 221–238. Springfield, IL: Charles C Thomas.
Waugh, Jr., W.L. (2000). *Living with Hazards: Dealing with Disasters*. Armonk, NY. M.E. Sharpe.
Wilson, D. (1997). Preface. *Ann. Am. Acad. Polit. Soc. Sci.*, 551: 8–16.
Wise, C.R. (2006). Organizing for homeland security after Katrina: is adaptive management what's missing? *Public Admin. Rev.*, 66(3): 302–318.
Wolensky, R.P. and Wolensky, K.C. (1990). Local government's problem with disaster management: a literature review and structural analysis. *Policy Stud. Rev.*, 9: 703–725.

GLOBAL CASES OF CRISIS AND EMERGENCY MANAGEMENT: A MACRO POLICY PERSPECTIVE

Chapter 2

Hurricane Katrina as a Global Case of Grand Failure: Lessons for Future Crisis and Emergency Management

Ali Farazmand

Contents

Chapter Goals	17
Introduction	18
Theories of Emergency Governance and Crisis Management	20
Katrina: A Global Case of Grand Failure in Governance and Emergency Management	23
Lessons Learned and Their Implications for Future Crisis Management	26
Building Capacity with Anticipatory Surprise Management	27
Surprise Management Theory	28
Concept and Principles of Surprise Management Theory	28
Strategic Conditions for Surprise Management	28
Requirements for Surprise Management	29
Capacity Building in Surprise Management	29
Questions for Discussion	29
References	30

Chapter Goals

The goals of this chapter are to

1. Analyze a historical case of grand failure in crisis and emergency management.
2. Present a global perspective on Hurricane Katrina crisis and emergency management.

3. Present a candid analysis of Hurricane Katrina crisis-driven failures in leadership, organizational coordination, intergovernmental relations, chaos management, resource mobilization, emergency preparedness, response systems, and recovery dynamics.
4. Examine causes and consequences of policy, political, organizational, and managerial failures with regard to Hurricane Katrina crisis and emergency management.
5. Offer critical and concrete lessons to be learned from the Hurricane Katrina crisis and applied to future crisis and emergency management.
6. Offer a novel theory of surprise management.

Introduction

Throughout history, the competence of governments has been tested during crises and emergencies with regard to preventing or managing catastrophic disasters, saving lives and property, and providing security for their citizens. Incompetence has brought down governments and triggered regime-changing revolutions. This test of competence is even more critical today than ever before, as modern governments are better equipped technologically and usually must rely on legitimacy and the trust of their people to govern.

Failure to respond to and govern effectively during crisis situations and to manage disaster-driven emergencies may result in a loss of legitimacy and lead to a system breakdown, accompanied by chaos and crises with far-reaching consequences and uncontrollable outcomes. Political crises led to the collapse of the French government several times from the 19th century well into the mid-20th century. They also caused the fall of the Soviet Union at the height of its global position as a superpower, and a similar political crisis—of both legitimacy and performance—led to the Revolution of 1979 and the fall of the Shah's absolute monarchy in Iran. A vivid illustration of the test of governmental competence is initiation of the Iraqi war during the administrations of then-President George W. Bush and former Prime Minister Tony Blair, which caused a lingering legitimacy crisis that forced Blair out of office and sank the Bush presidency to the lowest level in recorded U.S. public opinion history. Similarly, the poor performance of the Israeli army—one of the largest in the world—in its 31-day war against a small Hezbollah group in Lebanon in 2006 caused a deep crisis of legitimacy for the Ehud Olmert government and left a broken image of a once-formidable army.

No government is immune to chaotic crises that can cause system breakdowns and transformation or regime change. Modern public management's ability to handle natural disasters and cope with the inconceivable and uncertain consequences is also a key test of sound governance. Floods, earthquakes, hurricanes, and tsunamis are disasters that, unless managed effectively, can have dire consequences. Similarly, terrorist attacks and violent revolutions can produce crises with potentially chaotic dynamics and far-reaching repercussions, unpredictable outcomes, and system breakdowns. Terrorist attacks and violent revolutions usually feature unmistakable warning signs that offer time for response planning and preparation; they may be the outcomes of earlier ill preparation, poor governance, and mismanagement. They are consequential crises, whereas natural disasters are chaotic, sudden, and nonlinear, with complex and potentially unknown outcomes. A central feature of all these crises is the sense of *urgency* demanded in managing them. Yet, if this is the story of yesterday's and today's emergency and crisis management systems, tomorrow's will be a much more complex one, as we will be facing a world of much more "inconceivable" (Dror, 2001), "unthinkable" (Handy, 1998), and "unknowable" challenges (Stacey, 1992).

Crises are usually borne out of a short chain of events; they are often unpredicted and unexpected, but they develop with dynamic and unfolding events over a span of months, days, hours, even minutes. They disrupt the routine events of life and governance, disturb established systems, and cause severe anxieties. They produce dynamics no one can predict or control. This has been the case for most popular revolutions and certainly was the case for Hurricane Katrina in 2005, a crisis resulting from a grand failure in emergency management and governance that reflected significant mismanagement and poor governance and resulted in a leadership crisis of great magnitude. Hurricane Katrina disaster management was instantly elevated to one of chaotic crisis management, which required a set of knowledge, skills, and sense of urgency unfortunately absent in the preparation and response stages of crisis management in New Orleans.

This chapter presents a global perspective on Hurricane Katrina crisis management—or, rather, its leadership and management crisis—with implications and lessons for future crisis governance and management. Hurricane Katrina was a catastrophic disaster that grabbed the attention of the entire world, giving rise to expressions of sympathy, concern, shock … and criticism. In the age of information technology and globalization, the global community was able to watch the unfolding events throughout the day. What shocked many was the lack of preparedness of the city, state, and federal governments and their inability to effectively manage the crisis that ultimately engulfed New Orleans. Real-time coverage revealed how an advanced nation like the United States could be caught by surprise and be unprepared to deal with a large-scale system crisis that seemed to paralyze the entire administrative and governance capacities. Many wondered whether the United States would be capable of responding to simultaneous crises throughout the world. Was it capable of helping its allies? What implications did this crisis have for future crisis and emergency management in developed and developing nations? What lessons learned from Hurricane Katrina could be applied to the research and practice of emergency and crisis management worldwide?

The inadequate response to Hurricane Katrina has raised many questions for scholars, experts, citizens, policymakers, and practitioners worldwide, not only in public management and administration but also governance and international relations. Knowing that New Orleans lies under sea level, why were the levees not built to withstand a Category 5 hurricane in the first place? Why was the entire emergency response system so unprepared? Why was a management system not in place to deal with such a situation? Why did the leadership at all levels of government fail to act in time? Why did it take 5 days for the federal government to act? Why were people not evacuated when warnings were issued in advance? How did this response affect the image of the United States as a superpower? These are big questions in need of book-length presentations. No doubt there are many implications beyond the administrative and policy ones that can affect our way of thinking about the management and governance of an increasingly unknowable world of uncertainty and about crisis management theory and practice.

This chapter takes a global approach, from outside in, to study Hurricane Katrina crisis and emergency management. It presents several key lessons learned, suggests some possible global implications, and makes recommendations for future crisis and emergency management. The chapter argues that crises and complex situations demand new ways of thinking, a new mindset. Handling them well requires a complexity-driven management system—what the author refers to as *surprise management*—that can accurately interpret the unfolding dynamics and surprises arising out of chaos and crisis. This is a prescription for survival in an age of rapid globalization, change, complexity, and an "unknowable world" (Stacey, 1992). This study benefits from over 50 informal interviews conducted since Hurricane Katrina with international scholars, ordinary people (e.g., taxi drivers, teachers, shopkeepers), government officials, and crisis and emergency experts representing 13 countries (France, Germany, Netherlands, Iran, India, England, South Korea, China, Japan, Chile, Venezuela, Trinidad and Tobago, and South Africa).

The next section presents a theoretical analysis of emergency governance and crisis management, followed by a detailed discussion of Hurricane Katrina as a global case of crisis governance and management failure, the international implications, and the key areas of failure as revealed in post-storm investigations, scholarly studies, and reports. Several important lessons learned from Katrina—good, bad, and ugly—are then presented in the hope that they may help us understand the mistakes and better prepare for the future. Finally, recommendations are offered for capacity building—through *anticipatory surprise management*—in emergency governance and crisis management, education, and training in an age of globalization and uncertainty.

Theories of Emergency Governance and Crisis Management

Theories of crisis governance and management have been developed based on the rich knowledge base of what must be done in emergencies and crises facing governments, societies, and individuals. The great powers of ancient Rome and the Achaemenid Persian empire had elaborate and highly flexible emergency management systems in place in their far-flung territories as part of their strategic public management to deal with floods, storms, earthquakes, and political or military emergencies (Olmstead, 1948; Cook, 1984; Farazmand, 2001, 2007, 2014), and they were effective in their time. However, modern theories of emergency and crisis governance reflect fresh knowledge on how sound governance (Farazmand, 2004) should perform in such situations (Schumpeter, 1942; Schmitt, 1963; Leng, 1990; Balke, 1996; Allison and Zelikow, 1999; McCormick, 2000; Dror, 2001). The world has changed dramatically, and the chances of accidents, disasters, and other types of emergencies have increased with advances being made in technology and more powerful governments being able to using them for political, economic, military, and geopolitical purposes (Perrow, 1984).

The growing body of literature on the twin fields of crisis management and emergency management spans nations, cultures, security administrations, terrorism, disasters, and catastrophes (Perrow, 1984; Comfort, 1988; Rosenthal et al., 1991; Sagan, 1993; Schneider, 1995, 2005; Steinberg, 2000; Waugh, 2000; Farazmand, 2001; Mitroff, 2004; Pinsdorf, 2004; Haddow and Bullock, 2006; Wise, 2006). With regard to emergency and crisis governance, a crucial mandate appears to distinguish between the routine governance of public organizations across the board from those functions considered extraordinary and emerging situations such as political riots and upheavals, revolts and revolutions, foreign military threats, and even economic breakdowns with potential consequences threatening political system collapse. These destabilizing forces of chaos and crisis threaten modern systems of government, democratic or not, and cause breakdowns in social systems and their capacities to govern (Dror, 2001). Global transformations may inevitably produce major breakdowns in social systems, engulf major countries and regions, and "constitute a major challenge to capacities to govern in the foreseeable future" (Dror, 2001, p. 204).

Some of these breakdowns may be "birth pangs of a better future" and constitute what Schumpeter called "creative breakdowns" (Schumpeter, 1942). We still have very little knowledge of transformational breakdowns, but we can learn from the growing body of knowledge on "chaos theory" (Prigogine and Stengers, 1984; Kiel, 1989; Dror, 2001; Farazmand, 2004, 2014). What we do know, however, is that catastrophic and chaotic breakdowns can become very disruptive and brutal and cause much human suffering due to subsequent aggressive behavior. Thus, emergency and crisis-driven breakdowns require temporary extraordinary governance and politics and demand an emergency management regime to cope with and manage the situation (Schmitt, 1963; Balke, 1996). The authority of sovereign power to declare a state of emergency to cope with emergency situations (McCormick, 2000) is recognized in governance theory (Schmitt, 1963). This must, of course, be done with care and stop short of putting into place a dictatorial regime—including imperial presidencies or constitutional dictatorships—that threatens democracy and civil liberties. Emergency regimes are dangerous and no one likes them, especially when they adopt unnecessarily harsh policy measures (Leng, 1990; Gomein, 1993); such regimes tend to become aggressive and perpetuate themselves. Other devastating situations arise when "no government can be maintained, law and order breaks down and societies approach total collapse" (Dror, 2001, p. 206). Crisis and emergency governance arrangements must be developed and constantly upgraded to respond to the needs of the time, especially by such global institutions as the United Nations, in an age of rapid globalization and global threats of violence, terrorism, conflicts, war, poverty, and insecurity (Bartholemew, 2006; Hoffmann, 2006).

What exactly emergency governance regimes must do in crisis situations is a subject of much scholarly debate, but the key responsibility of emergency government is to first bring under control the evolving crisis or emergency situation that has the potential to transform into chaos. Projecting a sense of being in charge through a central command system can provide the control necessary in most emergency situations. Steps taken after this stage may include implementing response strategies that can help modify the extraordinary situation and make it possible to move on from emergency governance and to learn from the experience. Obviously, not all emergencies produce crises, and not all crises demand declaring a state of emergency, but all crises and emergency situations signal an *urgency* to take action before higher levels of criticality are reached. Despite the proven effectiveness of an emergency and crisis regime, there is no guarantee that such governance measures will always succeed, especially when the political legitimacy of the regime is questioned. Examples include the revolutions in France, Russia, Iran, Nicaragua, and elsewhere around the world. In all these cases, the emergency regimes trying to stop the revolutionary movements failed due to a legitimacy crisis, but such measures did seem to work in situations such as the social upheaval in Los Angeles in the 1980s and France in 2006. Key to emergency governance is the application of a specialized expertise outside the bureaucratic structure of government, one that is flexible, robust, upgraded constantly, and well informed; yet, the bureaucratic structure provides the necessary power to the state in crisis situations.

Military emergencies require a military bureaucracy with special forces behind the flexible central command structure. For many social crises and emergencies, however, such a bureaucracy may be too slow to act as a leader and must be supplanted by a central command system that can mobilize government forces (the bureaucracy) and a host of other organizations such as various networked systems, voluntary forces, and foreign assistance agencies. An important aspect of crisis and emergency governance is sharp and timely recognition of a situation as being an emergency or crisis, as opposed to a routine disturbance. Such distinction is not often easy, as there may not be an immediate consensus among key actors or leaders as to what constitutes a crisis. Nevertheless, governance theories do inform us of a necessity for emergency regimes and crisis governance systems. The leaders and people of the United States and the Soviet Union experienced this unpleasant situation during the Cuban Missile Crisis of the 1960s, and both countries came to realize the possibility of mutual destruction in the face of a thermonuclear conflict and agreed to a collaborative working relationship against it by the 1970s (Allison and Zeliko, 1999).

The study of crisis and emergency management in public administration has been growing slowly but steadily. Recent national and global events (e.g., 9/11, Oklahoma bombing, London and Madrid train bombings) and the potential threats of nuclear and biological attacks, as well as hazardous material accidents, have established an urgent need for the development of a body of knowledge in crisis and emergency management. At the global level, this imperative has been addressed by the United Nations and its member-states who have established plans and programs to mitigate risks to societies, prepare for natural and manmade disasters, and respond better in crisis and emergency situations. The Asian tsunami disaster of 2005 affected several nations and claimed over 200,000 lives; the entire global community was involved in coping with the crisis and the devastation left behind. Other recent global crises include the Darfur and Palestinian–Israeli conflicts, the Iraq war, the refugee crisis, widespread poverty, and natural disasters that demand global solutions (Farazmand, 2007).

In public administration, the body of knowledge in crisis and emergency management is expanding beyond its traditional scope to address new concepts, approaches, and capacity building techniques through the study of chaos and complexity theories, as well as the development of adaptive and flexible system designs, as the world experiences rapid globalization. Traditionally, crises were considered to be a manifestation of "unness" (Hewitt, 1983). Natural disasters were viewed as acts of God that were "unwanted, unexpected, unprecedented, and almost unmanageable, causing widespread unbelief and uncertainty" (Rosenthal et al., 2001, p. 5). Today's concepts of crises and emergencies are no longer mainly externally oriented; they are everywhere with us, and they have become part of our lives.

Modern crises are characterized by complexity, interdependence, and politicization. "Tomorrow's crisis, in turn, will look different from today and yesterday's crises" (Rosenthal et al., 2001, p. 6). This reality is not widely understood, as assumptions and perceptions about emergency and crisis management are still based on traditional beliefs; for example, Schneider (1995) identified six major (false) assumptions that hinder current crisis and emergency management:

1. Only a local response is necessary when the location of a natural disaster is within a limited geographical area.
2. All levels of government will cooperate closely (May and Williams, 1986).
3. The administrative capacity and resources necessary to handle disasters or crises exist.
4. Public officials have an awareness and understanding of crises and are able to handle them.
5. The Federal Emergency Management Agency (FEMA) holds state and local governments responsible for their response systems.
6. People outside the response system understand how the system operates.

At first glance, these might be considered good assumptions; however, according to Schneider (1995), reality paints a different picture: First, different levels of government and their officials have different perspectives based on what works to their own advantage. Second, crisis and emergency officials often encounter difficulties when trying to manage the actions of other participants in the process. Third, emergency relief operations are generally underfunded and do not take top priority in government agendas (Waugh, 1990). Finally, the credibility of any emergency management operation is generally low, as such operations generally suffer from a lack of respect within the overall government system. There is a perception that people working in emergency management are untrained and unprepared for the job, that they are "old military personnel or political hacks who cannot find other employment" (Wamsley, 1993; Schneider, 1995, p. 39). Unfortunately, cases such as Hurricane Katrina reinforced most of these assumptions.

We must search for new ways of thinking about crisis and emergency management. Recent studies have shed some light on and highlighted the complexity and imperative of developing crisis and emergency management in both theory and practice, through education and training. Today, the field is growing, and a new body of knowledge is emerging that can guide theory and practice in crisis public management (e.g., Waugh, 2000; Farazmand, 2001, 2009; Haddow and Bullock, 2006; Wise, 2006). What is emerging is an understanding that effective management of crises and emergencies requires serious preventive planning and preparation, institutionalized response systems with a strong central command structure, a well-coordinated network of response and recovery systems, a specialized crisis management team along with decentralized field commands armed with flexibility, and the presence of a functioning expertise in distinct areas of crisis situations (Farazmand, 2001).

Increasingly important to this new way of thinking and capacity building is taking a *global* perspective to guide nation-state governments and administrative systems, learning lessons from each and every crisis and emergency incident occurring all over the world, and bringing this understanding to the forefront of theory and practice to help mitigate and manage future crises.

Katrina: A Global Case of Grand Failure in Governance and Emergency Management

If there is any single description that characterizes Hurricane Katrina crisis management it would be "grand failure." This grand failure was manifest in every dimension of governance and public administration at all levels; however, what was most disturbing about this catastrophic disaster was the international implications of this grand failure for worldwide governance and public administration. Scholarly and governmental studies have examined the Katrina crisis extensively, and there is a growing body of literature on what went wrong during that disaster and what can be done to prevent similar crises in the future. For the foreseeable future, Katrina studies will continue to cover areas of governance and public administration, emergency and crisis management, and the capacity to manage crises and emergencies. Sadly, few or no success stories have come out of the Katrina case. This short essay does not detail what went wrong in Katrina and how the ensuing crisis was mismanaged, as these topics have been documented by others (e.g., Schneider, 2005; Wise, 2006; Kiefer and Montjoy, 2006; Brennan and Koven, 2008; Farazmand, 2009).

What is missing in most of these studies, however, is a global perspective of this grand failure and the serious implications it has for global crises management, international peace and security, and future emergency management theory and practice worldwide. As part of this study, the author has conducted over 50 personal interviews since Katrina. This discussion uses a positive lens to focus on a short list of the critical failures, with the hope of identifying several major global lessons to be learned from the Katrina crisis that may serve as principles central to effective crisis and emergency management in the future. Finally, to advance knowledge and improve the practice of emergency governance and crisis management, a theory of anticipatory surprise management is offered. Global observations and perspectives of the Katrina crisis management may be grouped into three major areas: (1) governance capacity to manage Katrina-like emergencies and crises by an advanced country such as the United States, (2) ability of nation-states to cope with chaotic crises and extreme emergencies and the role of the United States in the global community, and (3) strategic global and international implications of this grand failure for the United States as a superpower.

Regarding the first, the entire world watched with disbelief when the world's most advanced nation was caught by complete surprise, unprepared and unable to cope with the Katrina crisis. The world watched a case of disaster mismanagement quickly turn into a crisis of management and leadership. It should be noted that the capacity to govern under an extreme crisis is paralyzing no matter how powerful and resourceful a country is. The situation in New Orleans resembled that which might occur in an extremely underdeveloped African nation; despite gaining the attention of the world, nothing seemed to be happening. It was not just bad governance, but ugly governance. Sadly, this ugly picture also had implications for democratic governance, human rights, and the role of race, color, and minority status in American society. In response to this author's inquiry of what they thought of the crisis situation, the vast majority of those interviewed (52 out of 57) wondered, if this was what can happen to the American poor and minorities on their own land, what could people around the world in developing countries expect of America under similar situations elsewhere? This is a devastating observation with far-reaching implications for modern governance and international relations. Undoubtedly, the image of the United States was tarnished in the global community, but perhaps a more disturbing impact of the Katrina crisis has to do with the country's ability to cope with and manage multiple crises and emergency situations. What would happen if two or three Katrina-like crises were to hit a country like the United States, a country that has extended its military forces to over 100 nations worldwide on over 737 bases (Bartholomew, 2006; Hoffmann, 2006)?

The Katrina crisis mismanagement and governance failure also affected the ability of nation-states to cope with crises and emergencies in both negative and positive ways. The negative impact was primarily a psychological one that reinforced the traditional perspective of viewing disasters and crises as acts of God such that little or nothing can be done about them (Hewitt, 1983; Rosenthal et al., 2001). The inability of the United States to cope with the Katrina crisis has produced a fatalistic and helpless attitude among many poor and developing countries toward disaster management. Paradoxically, at the same time, a positive impact of the Katrina crisis can also be observed—that is, a stronger sense of self-reliance, self-confidence, and self-capacity building for future crisis management. "Actually, we have not been doing bad at all; in fact, we have done even better in many cases," was a view that many interviewed shared with this author. This attitude has had a positive effect on building confidence among developing nations. Thus, the ability of nation-states to cope with serious crises can be positively or negatively affected by other nation-states' successes or failures in managing disasters and crisis situations. We may also expect the United Nations to play a greater role in promoting crisis prevention, preparation, and response systems across the globe.

Perhaps the most important long-term impact of the Katrina crisis mismanagement is its effects on the perception of the United States as a superpower within the global community. This is a barely considered and highly neglected subject of study but is the most important global perspective of the Katrina crisis. Great powers, mighty empires, and strong governments are often tested by unexpected or sudden crises and chaotic incidents. Most great powers have failed with far-reaching consequences. In chaos theory, this is known as the *butterfly effect*; a small chaotic change or challenge may produce large-scale changes by sending severe shock waves into the nerve systems of an empire, organization, or organism, pushing the system to the edge of chaos and breakdown with unpredictable outcomes.

The ability of the system to survive a potential breakdown and return to autopoiesis is highly dependent on its quality of self-reorganization and self-renewal (Prigogine and Stengers, 1984; Farazmand, 2004). The failure of the Katrina crisis management sent shock waves throughout the world, especially among the developing and less developed nations and revolutionary organizations, with regard to the ability of the United States to maintain its status as a global superpower (Freeman and Kagarlitsky, 2004; Hoffmann, 2006).

The motivation to challenge this global hegemony has certainly become stronger since Katrina, which revealed this superpower's weaknesses. What happens if the United States faces simultaneous crises of revolution across the globe, such as in Latin America, Africa, and Asia, further challenging its hegemonic dominance? How would the U.S. government cope with two or three Katrina crises and perhaps more 9/11 situations? These are serious questions with long-term implications for the United States among its allies and adversaries. International relations are shaped by power positions and the ability of nation-states to exercise diplomacy and politics in regional and global affairs, and this ability is tested by time, crises, and the capacity to govern under extreme emergencies (Dror, 2001).

As a global case of grand failure, the Katrina crisis revealed a number of lessons to be learned for future crisis and emergency management theory and practice. Evidence shows that there was prior knowledge that due to land erosion New Orleans and its levees could not withstand a large Category 4 or 5 hurricane, yet nothing was done about it (Carter, 2005). The 2002 U.S. Army Corps of Engineers' recommendation to upgrade the levees to withstand a Category 5 hurricane at a cost of $2.5 billion was ignored (Carter, 2005). The lack of preparation to mitigate potential disaster or its impacts was a major cause of the catastrophic result, as evidenced by the 2004–2005 simulations that exposed major problems with evacuation but which were never corrected (Glasser and Grunwald, 2005). Despite several days of warnings, local and state government leaders failed to evacuate the local population, most of whom were poor and ended up stranded when they attempted to evacuate just before the storm's landfall. It was too late, and their mobilization efforts were doomed to fail because most transportation facilities were useless under the flood water.

Leadership failure was also evident at the federal level. Governor Blanco requested that a state of emergency be declared under the special power provision contained within the National Response Plan (NRP) that gives the president the authority to bypass state and local governments in catastrophic situations, but the power was not used during Katrina (Wise, 2006). The federal government waited 5 days after landfall to undertake a coordinated action whereby the federal military and coast guards were put into action, which was far too late. The Federal Emergency Management Agency (FEMA) and its director at the time, Michael Brown, failed to coordinate a network of organizations and volunteers during the response process. Appointed on a patronage basis, the FEMA director had neither experience nor specialized expertise in crisis or emergency management and to some seemed more interested in his media image than responding to the crisis (Schneider, 2005). Volunteer forces across the country were ordered by Brown to undergo a 2-day pre-response training in Atlanta instead of actually being taken into the field. Because of the lack of a central command structure to provide leadership and coordinate state and local efforts, hundreds of network organizations and volunteers were unable to work together in a flexible and collaborative way. Conditions at the Superdome and the Convention Center deteriorated quickly. Local Homeland Security officials and Brown claimed not to know that people had taken refuge at the Convention Center and failed to provide immediate help there. There was a total communication failure among the police as well as other government agencies, resulting in chaos and a crisis situation that no one was trained or prepared to cope with (Baum, 2006).

The total intergovernmental management failure occurred at the local, state, and federal levels, resulting in a lack of coordination among the nongovernmental, nonprofit, and volunteer organizations present at the scene; in fact, the lack of coordination and leadership constituted the biggest failures in dealing with Katrina (Wise, 2006; Brennan and Koven, 2008). Karl Marx would have admonished the bourgeois ruling class at all levels of government for its failure to manage a crisis that did not touch the ruling privileged class and only affected the working class poor. Based on the ideas of Marx, it would seem that the image of conducting a global war on terrorism was more important for the national governing elite than caring for the working class citizens trapped in the disaster. The stakeholders were poor, black, and underclass, and they had no power to influence the governing elites.

Lessons Learned and Their Implications for Future Crisis Management

1. Never compromise the long-term strategic goals of a nation, system, or organization for short-term political or economic benefit. Building and upgrading the infrastructure necessary to withstand a Category 5 hurricane might have cost around $2.5 billion; however, doing so would have saved over $200 billion in damages plus human lives. This suggests that sound governance matters.
2. Build capacity. Preparation is key to mitigation and response systems. Never compromise in prevention and response preparation plans, and never leave specialized crisis and disaster management tasks to generalist politicians more interested in their image than saving lives and property. This is a lesson originally learned over 2500 years ago when Persians under Darius the Great King organized specialized emergency task forces to deal with trouble spots and disasters occurring across their far-flung empire (Olmstead, 1948; Cook, 1984). Capacity building requires education, training, practice, technological and financial support, and competent human resources with the expertise to meet the challenges of an increasingly unknowable world.
3. Coordination is also key to response systems. Both vertical and horizontal coordination are critical, as are process and cultural coordination systems. Establishing these requires serious cultural unlearning and relearning for tomorrow's crisis management. This was a big failure in Katrina.
4. Leadership and central command structures are the most important elements in crisis and emergency management. There is no substitute for sound leadership with a central command structure positioned well in advance that can provide flexible and well-coordinated command in the field capable of adapting to changing conditions as they unfold. Being able to take timely and decisive action during the unfolding dynamics of a crisis situation is a key characteristic of effective crisis leadership.
5. Traditional emergency management techniques are no longer useful. Prepare with updated, nonlinear chaos management systems that can be effective beyond tomorrow. Prepare for an unknowable world (Stacey, 1992), and manage crises effectively. Train and develop crisis expertise using what might seem to be inconceivable scenarios.
6. Learn from past experiences and build capacity for the future. Learn from other nations and global best practices. The approaches to flood control in the Netherlands and Great Britain can teach us quite a bit. In Iran, implementations of the earthquake preparation and response systems, as well as the country's effective crisis management system, can shed light on future crisis and emergency management systems around the world. Iran evacuated over

a million people in 2007 without a single loss of life when Hurricane Guno, a Category 3 storm, approached. It hit the southern coast of the country and claimed over 50 lives in the southern shore towns of Oman (*Hamshahri Daily*, June 9, 2007, p. 1).
7. Governments are tested for their competency in saving lives and property in disasters and crises. They are the institutions ultimately held responsible for poor crisis management outcomes. Democracy matters, but failing to act quickly during an extreme emergency can have far-reaching adverse consequences for a country's citizens, governance, and democratic ideals. Large bureaucracies may be too slow to act and unsuitable to handle crises, but they can lend a vast reservoir of expertise to crisis leaders and managers and should not be overlooked.
8. Engage people and be honest with them. Establishing a partnership with the people involved in a crisis situation is essential to reducing anxiety and minimizing opportunities for panic and chaos. These people know the locale better than any one else. Local institutions and community and neighborhood organizations are essential partners in crisis and emergency management. People who know the culture and speak the language, whom locals consider to be "one of us," should be a main part of the process.
9. Prepare for simultaneous and multiple crises or disasters, and institutionalize a new way of thinking about crises as sudden, unexpected, and inconceivable events that may happen any time and any place. This capacity must be institutionalized to avoid surprises. Upgrade capacity all the time.
10. As John F. Kennedy observed with regard to the failed Bay of Pigs invasion, "Success has a thousand fathers; defeat is an orphan" (Pinsdorf, 2004, p. 107). This may apply in many cases, but not to Katrina, where every official and even the Red Cross failed to do their job.

Building Capacity with Anticipatory Surprise Management

There is generally a big gap between the routine tasks of governance and administration and the emergency, non-routine tasks that demand urgency in attention and action (Schneider, 1995). Bureaucratic expertise may be suitable for routine tasks, but bureaucracies are no match for crisis- and emergency-driven events with chaotic and unfolding dynamics. The latter require a different way of thinking, a new mindset outside of the traditional box filled with rules, controls, and procedures. Such emergencies demand new knowledge, skills, and attitudes that can anticipate inconceivable and unthinkable impossibilities. Doing so is usually beyond the realm of ordinary management and governance capacity.

A key characteristic of all chaos and dynamic crisis situations—such as spontaneous revolutions or natural disasters—is the presence of a high degree of surprise. Officials and organizational actors are totally caught by surprise, and the entire response system becomes paralyzed, producing more chaos and surprise, triggering disaster after disaster. Such situations can be avoided by building in a capacity to deal with chaos through surprise management. We simply cannot manage chaos with routine administration and governance. Surprise management is necessary to manage the emergencies and crises that arise in an age of globalization when short-term profits take priority over long-term strategic issues of our planet (Regester and Larkin, 2005).

The most damaging forces of nature—tornadoes, earthquakes, and floods—strike unexpectedly; in this age of rapid globalization and nonlinear chaotic changes, surprise may be the "most commanding dimension of uncertainty" (Hermann, 1969, p. 29). To manage surprises one must acquire the knowledge, skills, and experience of surprise management. Unprepared policymakers and their planners can have an adverse effect on desired outcomes, but to an intelligent analyst everything is expected and "nothing will outdo the impact of the full-fledged surprise attack" (Kam, 1998; Rosenthal et al., 2001, p. 7). Anticipatory crisis management must integrate the element of surprise for effective governance and public administration. Lack of such capacity building—planning, preparation, response flexibilities—will surely lead to total paralysis in the face of surprises.

Crises and emergencies produce complexities, and complex situations require complex management systems that are adaptive, have extraordinary capabilities, and are responsive to the worst possible scenarios. Chaos and rapidly unfolding dynamics are inherent to complex situations, whose unpredictable outcomes often result in disorder, but an anticipatory capacity can mitigate the effects of such outcomes and reduce the level of criticality by arresting chaos in the earliest stages of crisis management.

In 2004, an earthquake totally destroyed the ancient southeast Iranian city of Bam (including its 2500-year-old standing citadel) before dawn, killing over 50,000 of the city's population of 80,000 and leading to the immediate collapse of the entire system of governance and administration within hundreds of miles. By 3:00 p.m. that same day, a centralized national command structure had already been set up and was in operation in Tehran to dispense information and coordinate multiple vertical and horizontal networks of organizational and voluntary response systems. In less than 24 hours, the situation was under control, and the response system was so effective that international response teams found little to do upon their arrival. Key to such effective emergency and crisis management was the combination of surprise management with a five-step, forward-reading strategy that anticipated all possibilities and impossibilities beyond five levels, including sudden desert sand storms, potential foreign invasion, and more (personal interviews).

Surprise Management Theory

Concept and Principles of Surprise Management Theory

Surprise management draws on chaos and complexity theories (Prigogine and Stengers, 1984; Pascale, 1990; Stacey, 1992; Waldrop, 1992; Kiel, 1994; Weick and Sutcliffe, 2001; Farazmand, 2007, 2014). As a social and political construction, the theory of surprise management is based on at least four principles. First, it rejects anything that is routine and expected. Second, by extension, it is fluid and constantly changing in nature, degree of flexibility, and adaptability. Third, situations must have certain preconditions to qualify as surprising and chaotic, nonlinear and unexplainable, as distinct from linear and predictable causal behaviors. Finally, surprise management requires cutting-edge knowledge, skills, and attitudes beyond the comprehension of most people in routine environments of governance and administration. Finally, it requires extraordinary and yet disciplined authority and power with unrestrained resources. Properly developed surprise management thrives on chaos and crisis situations.

Strategic Conditions for Surprise Management

Surprise managers and their teams find short-term thinking boring; thus, strategic thinking is the essence of the concept. Surprise management sharpens its teeth on small and short-term crisis conditions. Surprise management is expensive to develop and maintain, but it is a national asset with no substitute. Democracies require surprise management systems more than any other type of political system, and the idea must be nurtured to institutionalize its values. Strategic management has four key components: foci, loci, positions, and whos. *Foci* are the areas of focus or stress in crisis situations (e.g., political, social, international relations). *Loci* are the locations, organizational levels, and governance areas (local, state, federal, global) affected by the crisis. *Positions* are the strategic positioning and repositioning of key players, actors, and participants in the crisis or surprise management process. Finally, the *whos* are the individuals and institutional actors in strategic positions to make crucial decisions and act accordingly (Farazmand, 2007).

Requirements for Surprise Management

Surprise management requires ample resources to operate, with no constraints. It also requires critical opportunities to practice its operation. It demands full attention, talent, and effective communication, as well as the extraordinary skills necessary to evaluate extremely unthinkable conditions and circumstances, people, and dynamics. Surprise management requires specialized and rigorous training and development to address the foci, loci, and dynamic positioning requirements of crisis management. Surprise management requires autonomy and authority in its performance, but it is also accountable to democracy. Nothing comes as a surprise to its players (Farazmand, 2007).

Capacity Building in Surprise Management

Educational and training programs, formal and informal, periodic and continuous, are required to train and develop surprise management teams and leaders for crisis management. Weick (1995) reminded us that most managers make a mistake by trying to solve organizational problems through linear thinking; they must get out of this mindset and think both strategically and nonlinearly to manage the "unexpected" (Weick and Sutcliffe, 2001). Managing complexity on the "edge of chaos" (Pascale, 1990) requires a different type of organizational learning (Waldrop, 1992). Recent studies have suggested *adaptive management* imperatives to cope with crises and disasters (Wise, 2006). Others have argued for collaboration over adaptability (Jenkins, 2006), and still others have endorsed a network-based organizational system for crisis management.

The theory of surprise management integrates all features of the authoritative, collaborative, participative, and adaptive models, along with self-organizing fluidity and flexibility. It offers an unmatched capacity for crisis and emergency management (Farazmand, 2007, 2014). It is suggested here that universities and institutions of higher education across the globe develop and offer academic degrees and professional courses in chaos and surprise management as part of capacity building for future emergency governance and crisis management in an age of increasing global insecurity, risks, disasters, and inconceivable surprises.

Questions for Discussion

1. What is meant by "global case of grand failure"?
2. What are the central components of grand failure in the Hurricane Katrina crisis?
3. What is the difference between crisis and emergency management, crises, and emergencies?
4. Why did the Hurricane Katrina emergency situation turn into a high-level crisis situation?
5. Who were the key players or actors in the Hurricane Katrina crisis?
6. What factors contributed to Hurricane Katrina crisis mismanagement?

7. What can crisis management learn from chaos theory?
8. What lessons can be learned from Hurricane Katrina crisis management or mismanagement?
9. What is meant by surprise management theory?
10. What are the key properties of surprise management theory in practice?
11. What have you learned from the Hurricane Katrina crisis that can be applied to future crisis and emergency management?

References

Allison, G. and Zelikow, P. (1999). *Essence of Decision: Explaining the Cuban Missile Crisis*, 2nd ed. New York: Longman.
Balke, F. (1996). *Der Staat nacch sceinem Ende: Die Versuchung Carl Schmitt*. Munchen: Wilhelm Fink.
Bartholomew, A., Ed. (2006). *Empire's Law: The American Imperial Project and the "War to Remake the World."* London: Pluto Press.
Baum, D. (2006). Deluged. *The New Yorker*, January 9, pp. 50–63.
Brennan, M. and Koven, S. (2008). Hurricane Katrina: preparedness, response and the politics administration dichotomy. In Farazmand, A., Ed., *Handbook of Crisis and Emergency Management*, 2nd ed., revised and updated. Boca Raton, FL: Taylor & Francis.
Carter, N.T. (2005). *New Orleans Levees and the Floodwalls: Hurricane Damage Protection*, Congressional Research Service Report for Congress RS22238. Washington, DC: Library of Congress.
Comfort, L.K. (1988). *Managing Disaster: Strategies and Policy Perspectives*. Durham, NC: Duke University Press.
Cook, J. (1984). *The Persian Empire*. New York: Schoken.
Dror, Y. (2001). *The Capacity to Govern: A Report to the Club of Rome*. Abingdon: Routledge.
Farazmand, A. (2001). *Handbook of Crisis and Emergency Management*. New York: Taylor & Francis.
Farazmand, A. (2004). Chaos and transformation theories: a theoretical analysis with implications for organization theory and public management. *Public Org. Rev.*, 3(4): 339–372.
Farazmand, A. (2007). Learning from Katrina crisis: a global and international perspective with implications for future crisis management. *Public Admin. Rev.*, 67(Suppl.): 149–159.
Farazmand, A. (2009). Building administrative capacity for the age of rapid globalization: a modest prescription for survival. *Public Admin. Rev.*, 69(6): 1007–1020.
Farazmand, A., Ed. (2014). *Crisis and Emergency Management: Theory and Practice*, 2nd ed., revised and updated. Boca Raton, FL: Taylor & Francis.
Freeman, A. and Kagarlitsky, B., Eds. (2004). *The Politics of Empire*. London: Pluto Press.
Glasser, S. and Grunwald, M. (2005). The steady buildup to a city's chaos. *Washington Post*, September 11.
Gomien, D., Ed. (1993). *Broadening the Frontiers of Human Rights: Essays in Honor of Asbjorne Eide*. Oslo: Scandinavian University Press.
Haddow, G. and Bullock, J. (2006). *Emergency Management*, 2nd ed. New York: Elsevier.
Handy, C. (1998). *Beyond Certainty*. Cambridge, MA: Harvard University Press.
Hermann, C. (1969). *Crisis in Foreign Policy*. Indianapolis, IN: Bobbs–Merrill.
Hewitt, K., Ed. 1983. *Interpretations of Calamity: From the Viewpoint of Human Ecology*. Boston: Allen & Unwin.
Hoffmann, S. (2006). *Chaos and Violence: What Globalization, Failed States, and Terrorism Mean for U.S. Foreign Policy*. Lanham, MD: Rowman & Littlefield.
Jenkins, W. (2006). Collaboration over adaptation: the case for interoperable communications in homeland security. *Public Admin. Rev.*, 66 (3): 319–331.
Kam, P. (1998). *Surprise Attack*. Cambridge, MA: Harvard University Press.
Kiefer, J. and Montjoy, R. (2006). Incrementalism before the storm: network performance for evacuation of New Orleans. *Public Admin. Rev.*, 66(6): 123–130.
Kiel, D. (1994). *Managing Chaos and Complexity in Government*. San Francisco, CA: Jossey-Bass.

Leng, S.-C., Ed. (1990). *Coping with Crises: How Governments Deal with Crises*. Lanham, MD: University Press of America.
May, P.J. and Williams, W. (1986). *Disaster Policy Implementation: Managing Programs under Shared Governance*. New York: Plenum Press.
McCormick, J.P. (2000). *Carl Schmitt's Critique of Liberalism: Against Politics as Technology*. Cambridge, UK: Cambridge University Press.
Mitroff, I. (2004). *Crisis Leadership: Planning for the Unthinkable*. New York: John Wiley & Sons.
Olmstead, A. (1948). *History of the Persian Empire: Achaemenid Period*. Chicago, IL: University of Chicago Press.
Pascal, R. (1990). *Managing on the Edge of Chaos*. London: Viking.
Perrow, C. (1984). *Normal Accidents: Living with High-Risk Technologies*. New York: Basic Books.
Pinsdorf, M. (2004). *All Crises Are Global*. New York: Fordham University Press.
Prigogine, I. and Stengers, I. (1984). *Order Out of Chaos*. New York: Bantam.
Regester, M. and Larkin, J. (2005). *Risk Issues and Crisis Management: A Casebook of Best Practice*, 3rd ed. Philadelphia, PA: Kogan Page.
Rosenthal, U., Boin, R.A., and Comfort, L. (2001). *Managing Crises: Threats, Dilemmas, and Opportunities*. Springfield, IL: Charles C Thomas.
Sagan, S. (1993). *The Limits of Safety*. Princeton, NJ: Princeton University Press.
Schmitt, C. (1963). *Der Begriffdes Politischen [The Concept of the Political]*. Berlin: Duncker & Humblot.
Schneider, S.K. (1995). *Flirting with Disaster: Public Management in Crisis Situations*. Armonk, NY: M.E. Sharpe.
Schneider, S.K. (2005). Administrative breakdowns in the governmental response to Hurricane Katrina." *Public Admin. Rev.*, 65(5): 515–516.
Schumpeter, J. (1942). *Capitalism, Socialism, and Democracy*, 2nd ed. New York: Harper & Brothers.
Stacey, R. (1992). *Managing the Unknowable*. San Francisco, CA: Jossey-Bass.
Steinberg, T. (2000). *Acts of God: The Unnatural History of Natural Disasters in America*. Oxford, UK: Oxford University Press.
Waldrop, M. (1992). *Complexity: The Emerging Science at the Edge of Order and Chaos*. New York: Simon & Schuster.
Wamsley, G. (1993). *The Pathologies of Trying to Control Bureaucracy and Policy: The Case of FEMA and Emergency Management*. Blacksburg, VA: Polytechnic Institute and State University.
Waugh, Jr., W.L. (1990). Regionalizing emergency and the state and local government capacity. In Sylves, R.T. and Waugh, Jr., W.L., Eds., *Cities and Disaster: North American Studies in Emergency Managements*, pp. 221–238. Springfield, IL: Charles C Thomas.
Waugh, Jr., W.L. (2000). *Living with Hazards: Dealing with Disasters*. Armonk, NY: M.E. Sharpe.
Weick, K. (1995). *Sensemaking in Organizations*. Thousand Oaks, CA: Sage.
Weick, K. and Sutcliffe, K. (2001). *Managing the Unexpected: Assuring High Performance in Age of Uncertainty*. San Francisco, CA: Jossey-Bass.
Wise, C. (2006). Organizing for homeland security after Katrina: is adaptive management what's missing? *Public Admin. Rev.*, 66(3): 302–318.

Chapter 3

Fukushima Nuclear Disaster and Ensuring Necessary Government Crisis and Risk Communication

Itoko Suzuki and Yuko Kaneko

Contents

Chapter Goals 34
Introduction 34
    Great East Japan Earthquake: A Three Pronged Disaster—
    Two Natural and One Manmade 34
    Major Initial Damage 35
Description of the Case 36
    Research Theme and Basic Framework of Analyses 36
    Building Nuclear Power Stations in Disaster-Prone Countries Such as Japan 37
    Organizations Involved in the 3.11 Disaster 37
    Sequence of Initial Events 38
Analysis of Management of the Fukushima Nuclear Disaster 38
    Manmade Disaster Caused by Lack of Preparedness and Not Learning from the Past 38
    Manmade Disaster Caused by Ineffective Organizational and
    Management Procedures and Requiring Radical Reforms for Recovery 41
    Failure to Disclose Crisis Information to the Public 41
        Delays in Disclosing Crisis Information in Japan 41
        Delays in Disclosing Crisis Information to Local Residents 41
    Failure to Disclose Crisis Information to Emergency Relief Organizations 42

Failure to Disclose Crisis Information Due to Inadequate
Business Practices and a Lack of Government Transparency 42
Institutional Reforms to Aid Recovery from the Fukushima Disaster 43
Key Central Government Organizations Established
for Nuclear Safety Recovery and Regulations 44
    Nuclear Regulation Authority 44
    Nuclear Emergency Preparedness System 44
Ongoing Effects of the Fukushima NPS Accident 45
Government Takes Major Responsibility for
Decommissioning and Radioactive Water Issues 45
Evaluation and Analysis Based on Information
Disclosed by Government, Statistics, and Media 45
Lessons and Implications for NPS Crisis and Emergency Management 49
    Establish Effective, Transparent, and Accountable
    System of Government Crisis Communication 49
    Establish Accountable and Transparent Government Records Management to
    Facilitate an End to the Fukushima Nuclear Disaster and Mitigate Future Disasters 49
    Resilient Capacity Building, Citizens' Rights, and Government
    Responsibility: Learning from the 3.11 Nuclear Disaster 50
Conclusions 51
Questions for Discussion 51
Additional Reading 51
References 52

Chapter Goals

The goals of this chapter are to

1. Share some lessons learned from the Fukushima nuclear disaster.
2. Review and analyze government crisis and risk communication problems during the Fukushima nuclear disaster based on information and data disclosed to citizens.
3. Suggest how to strengthen accountable and transparent government risk and crisis communication management for nuclear emergency preparedness.
4. Explore resiliency capacity building for the safety of Japan's citizens and for nuclear disaster mitigation.

Introduction

Great East Japan Earthquake: A Three Pronged Disaster—Two Natural and One Manmade

The Great East Japan earthquake occurred off the Pacific coast area of Tohoku on March 11, 2011 (hereafter cited as the 3.11 disaster). The 3.11 disaster was three pronged:

1. *Earthquake*—Magnitude 9 on the Richter scale
2. *Tsunamis*—Over 20 meters high

3. *Accidents*—International Nuclear Events Scale (INES) Level 7 Fukushima Daiichi Nuclear Power Station (NPS) accidents, manmade disasters triggered by the tsunamis and possibly also by the earthquake (hereafter cited as the Fukushima nuclear disaster)

Major Initial Damage

Although this chapter deals only with the the Fukushima nuclear disaster and the immediate damage caused (the entire scope of damage has not yet been fully investigated or evaluated), the following information provides some understanding of the magnitude of the 3.11 disaster (Suzuki and Kaneko, 2013):

- Almost 16,000 deaths occurred and nearly 3000 people were missing.
- At least 130,436 housing units were demolished, 262,975 half destroyed, and 717,768 partially destroyed.
- The estimated damage was approximately 16.9 trillion yen (not including damage caused by the Fukushima NPS accident, which are still not known or disclosed); the initial 5-year (2011–2015) recovery cost has been estimated at around 25 trillion yen.
- Recovery work is being financed by a reconstruction income tax that citizens will pay for 25 years.
- About 470,000 evacuees lost their homes.

It is difficult to estimate the initial damage caused by the Fukushima nuclear disaster, as the situation is ongoing. The government and Tokyo Electric Power Company (TEPCO) from the beginning withheld necessary and critical information, even from evacuees. A valid scenario to end the crisis and estimates of the initial economic damage and recovery costs have yet to be determined. It is clear that the social and economic costs of the Fukushima nuclear disaster are substantially greater than the costs associated with the earthquake itself and subsequent tsunami disasters. Following is information that has been disclosed by the government that may help illustrate the huge scale of the damage caused by the Fukushima nuclear disaster (Reconstruction Agency, 2014a,b):[*]

- Over 150,000 evacuees have not returned to their homes; as of 2014, at least 100,000 were unable to return home due to radiation leaks or contaminated environment. The number of evacuees would grow even higher if it included citizens from the afflicted region who have chosen not to return to their homes.
- Although there were no immediate direct deaths, 1704 indirect deaths have been attributed to the disaster, as certified by the government.
- Operation of all of the remaining 48 nuclear reactors in Japan has been suspended for reassessment of their safety (there were 54 nuclear reactors before the 3.11 disaster).
- Afflicted residents and communities are to be compensated by TEPCO, which has been held liable, but also by government-aided payments of at least 9 trillion yen.
- Cleaning of radioactive contaminated soils began immediately, with the initial cost of approximately 5 trillion yen to be covered by the government from taxes.
- Costs associated with decommissioning the damaged nuclear power station are unknown but have been estimated at approximately 15 trillion yen by a government think tank.

---

[*] Cost estimate figures were obtained from various Japanese media outlets, including NHK Global Media Services and *Yomiuri Shimbun*.

Description of the Case

Research Theme and Basic Framework of Analyses

(See details reflected and cited in Suzuki and Kaneko, 2013.) Although TEPCO by law must assume major responsibility for recovery from the Fukushima nuclear disaster, the government has taken significant steps to provide relief, and since September 2013 has taken primary responsibility to facilitate recovery. In the years following the 3.11 disaster, the citizens of Japan gradually came to learn what happened from those directly involved in the 3.11 disaster or its emergency response. The government did not immediately disclose critical information at the time of the emergency, even to those ordered to evacuate. Reports issued in 2012 by the three major NPS accident investigation groups (Government Investigation Committee, Nuclear Accident Independent Investigation Commission, and Rebuild Japan Initiative Foundation) emphasized the failure to disclose nuclear risk and crisis information in a timely manner and pointed out that critical crisis information had not been shared by government emergency managers (central or local, particularly municipal governments, which are primarily responsible for local disaster management in Japan's disaster governance system).

In emergency management, two critical government communication issues arise with regard to not aggravating the situation further: (1) disclosing government information to the public so they can make informed decisions, as is the citizens' right; and (2) sharing information among the many government organizations involved in crisis management. Government crisis communication is not only for the public but also for the governmental organizations themselves to make them more effective and accountable during the emergency. Government crisis communication is a crucial part of the crisis management function. The key trait that government crisis management must have is transparency, as the government is in the end held accountable to the public, both nationally and globally.

Informed citizens can decide how best to proceed for their own safety. Emergency managers in various parts of the government, at the central or local level, need to have prompt and transparent crisis information shared among them so they can respond suitably to the emergency situation and facilitate safe evacuation of the affected citizens. Transparent information disclosure and timely government communication are becoming increasingly important in ensuring accountability and effectiveness of governance. This is particularly true at a time when a variety of communication resources are available to local citizens and the world community simultaneously.

In Japan, accountability is generally interpreted and used to mean the responsibility only to explain what happened, without taking on the responsibility of the results of the measures taken by the organization or individual managers. Individual accountability is rarely pursued, as it is considered difficult to do because of the traditional, consensus-oriented decision-making system and practices within Japanese organizations. Accountability is thus rather ambiguous in the collective decision-making system. To avoid assuming liability, bureaucratic organizations in government and in big business generally are resistant to disclosing information; hence, transparent information disclosure is not likely to be practiced.

This chapter concentrates on government crisis information disclosures that occurred at the time of the Fukushima nuclear disaster emergency and on the ensuing crisis responses taken by the government as of 2014. It is hoped that this focused undertaking will clarify the lessons to be learned from the nuclear disaster in Japan and provide some insight into establishing the safety resiliency necessary for disaster mitigation.

Building Nuclear Power Stations in Disaster-Prone Countries Such as Japan

The two major reasons why Japan has so many nuclear power stations are as follows:

1. Nuclear power station use has been promoted by political leaders, industries, and scientists as a significant source of electricity since 1956, after establishment of the United Nations' Atoms for Peace organization and the International Atomic Energy Agency (IAEA).
2. The use of nuclear power stations became particularly desirable after the 1973 and 1979 world oil crises and when environment pollution problems arose during the 1970s, as well as for environmental conservation reasons. The goal was to have nuclear power stations produce 50% of the electricity in Japan, which lacks natural energy resources.

When the 3.11 disaster occurred, the 54 nuclear reactors in Japan were producing 25% of the country's electricity.

Organizations Involved in the 3.11 Disaster

Below is a list of the organizations involved and the roles they played in the Fukushima nuclear disaster:

- The Nuclear Safety Commission (NSC), an advisory organization comprised of scientists and located within the Cabinet Office of the central government, from the beginning of the accident emergency provided direct technical advice to the prime minister.
- The Ministry of Education, Culture, Sports, Science, and Technology (MEXT) conducted SPEEDI radiation monitoring.
- According to the laws on disaster governance in Japan, local municipal governments are primarily responsible for local disaster preparedness, response, and mitigation; providing local emergency relief; and evacuating afflicted communities and citizens. They coordinate with and receive support from central and prefectural government emergency organizations, as well as non-governmental organizations.
- The Nuclear and Industrial Safety Agency (NISA) is the NPS safety regulator located within the NPS-promoting Ministry of Economy, Trade and Industry (METI), with local branch staff stationed at the Fukushima NPS.
- The Tokyo Electric Power Company (TEPCO), the leading private sector company, operated the Fukushima NPS under license of METI. The electricity company has assumed primary responsibility for the accidents, including the emergency response, recovery costs, and disaster liabilities.

In addition, for severe nuclear emergencies, the Nuclear Emergency Response Headquarters in Tokyo (headed by the Prime Minister), the Local Nuclear Emergency Response Headquarters located offsite in Fukushima, and the Joint Council for Nuclear Emergency Response were organized, as stipulated in the Special Law on Emergency Preparedness for Nuclear Disaster. These are set up as shown in Figure 3.1. The difficulties encountered during the 3.11 disaster under this institutional setup are analyzed in the following sections.

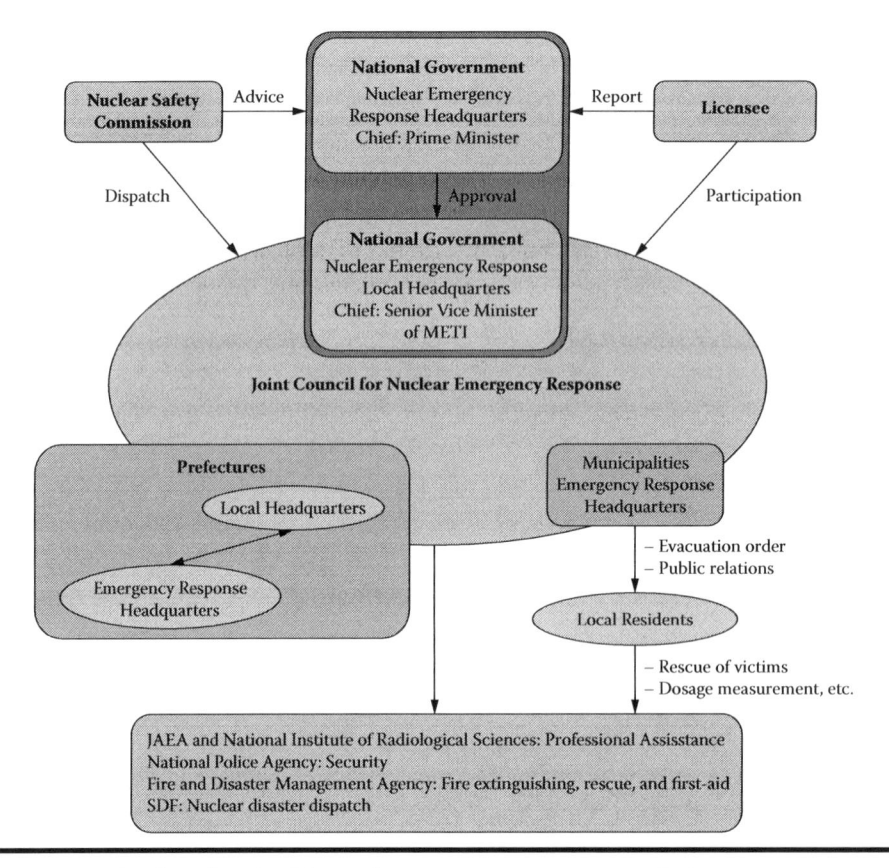

Figure 3.1 Organizations involved in nuclear emergency responses in Japan.

Sequence of Initial Events

The sequence of events at the Fukushima nuclear power stations are detailed in Table 3.1. It should be noted that the declaration of a state of nuclear emergency was issued immediately on the first day, together with an evacuation order for those living within a 3-km radius from the accident site. The accident was reported as being INES Level 3 by NISA on the second day of the accident, but that status was soon changed to Level 4 and within a month's time to Level 7, equivalent to the Chernobyl nuclear power station accidents. However, the meltdown, radiation levels, and direction in which the radiation was moving were not disclosed to the public at the time.

Analysis of Management of the Fukushima Nuclear Disaster

Manmade Disaster Caused by Lack of Preparedness and Not Learning from the Past

Despite being triggered by a natural disaster, the 3.11 Fukushima nuclear disaster was a manmade one caused by a lack of emergency preparedness to deal with multiple NPS accidents. Government safety regulators and advisors and NPS operators did not see the need to install the necessary safety mechanisms to protect against the occurrence of severe accidents, thus ignoring previous

Table 3.1 Sequence of Accident Events from March 11 to April 12, 2011

Date	Events
March 11	Earthquake hits Japan. Fukushima Daiichi NPS accident occurs. Prime Minister declares a state of nuclear emergency, establishing the Nuclear Emergency Response Headquarters, but tells the press that no impact from radioactive materials outside of the facilities had been confirmed. Radioactivity is not, in fact, leaking out of any of the nuclear facilities. A nuclear disaster dispatch order is issued to the self-defense forces. Fukushima governor instructs mayors of Okuma Town and Futaba Town to evacuate their residents within a 2-km radius from the Fukushima Daiichi NPS. Prime Minister instructs the heads of Fukushima prefecture and four towns to evacuate their residents within a 3-km radius from the NPS and orders those within a 10-km radius to stay inside their homes. Chief Cabinet Secretary announces that the reactors have lost their cooling capability. A radiation leak was possible, but there was no danger of radiation spreading beyond the NPS site. The evacuation order has been issued merely as a precaution.
March 12	NISA rates the accident as INES Level 3. Chief Cabinet Secretary informs the public that no health danger is posed by radiation spreading in the evacuation zones; no concrete data indicates as such. Chief Cabinet Secretary announces that TEPCO needs to vent pressure in the Unit 1 core containment vessel. Prime Minister instructs residents within a 10-km radius from the NPS to evacuate. Prime Minister flies by helicopter to the Fukushima Daiichi NPS. NISA is informed of the possibility that the Unit 2 core containment vessel might cause a meltdown. Unit 1 explodes; no indication of danger is issued by the government. NISA reports that no reactor containment vessel meltdown can be confirmed. Prime Minister instructs the heads of relevant municipalities to evacuate their residents within a 20-km radius from the NPS due to risks posed by the reactors. Chief Cabinet Secretary announces that the explosions have not occurred in the containment vessels but in the reactor building due to the accumulation of hydrogen, so there has been no leakage beyond the site.
March 13	Chief Cabinet Secretary acknowledges the possibility of a hydrogen explosion in Unit 3; no suggestion of danger outside the plant facility is given.

(Continued)

Table 3.1 (Continued) Sequence of Accident Events from March 11 to April 12, 2011

Date	Events
March 14	NISA reveals the first environmental radiation monitoring information gathered by the Local Nuclear Emergency Response Headquarters.
	Chief Cabinet Secretary verifies an explosion in Unit 3 but makes no suggestion of severe leakage of radioactivity; there is no indication of any danger.
	Chief Cabinet Secretary announces that the hydrogen explosion in Unit 3 has caused no damage to the containment vessel and no meltdown is presumed.
	Chief Cabinet Secretary announces that all units of the NPS are idle.
	Chief Cabinet Secretary reports that the cooling system resumed operation at 20:00 after Unit 2 fuel rods were exposed for some time.
March 15	TEPCO announces that the fuel rods in Unit 2 have again been exposed, at around 23:00 on March 14.
	Prime Minister meets with the TEPCO president and announces the establishment of Joint Nuclear Emergency Headquarters at the TEPCO Tokyo office to share information.
	Explosion occurs in Unit 2.
	Chief Cabinet Secretary announces that the suppression room connecting the reactor containment vessel of Unit 2 has been damaged.
	Fire breaks out in Unit 4.
	Prime Minister instructs the heads of relevant municipalities to order residents within a 20- to 30-km radius to seek refuge indoors.
	Chief Cabinet Secretary reports the fire that broke out in Unit 4; radiation levels around Unit 3 reach 400 µSv/hr, possibly affecting human health.
March 18	NISA raises the rating to INES Level 5.
March 25	Contaminated radioactive water is found in the basement of the NPS.
March 28	Contaminated radioactive water is found outside of the turbine buildings.
April 2	Contaminated radioactive water is found accumulated in a pit near the intake channel of Unit 2; the water is flowing out into the sea from a crack on the lateral surface of the pit.
April 4	TEPCO discharges low-level radioactive water to the sea.
April 12	NISA raises the rating to INES Level 7 and announces meltdown.

lessons learned from the Three Mile Island and Chernobyl accidents, as well as from many past NPS accidents in Japan (GIC, 2012; NAIIC, 2012; Rebuild Japan Initiative Foundation, 2012). If information from the government nuclear safety regulatory organizations had been made transparent and shared with the public, such consequences might have been avoided.

Manmade Disaster Caused by Ineffective Organizational and Management Procedures and Requiring Radical Reforms for Recovery

According to reports by the Fukushima disaster investigation commissions (GIC, 2012; NAIIC, 2012; Rebuild Japan Initiative Foundation, 2012), the NPS safety regulatory organizational system was guilty of gross negligence with regard to preparedness for potential nuclear accidents despite actively promoting the use of nuclear power stations. It was found that

- The NPS safety regulatory system was established by NPS-promoting METI.
- Components of the regulatory system were scattered among several ministries, each with a different sector-oriented bureaucratic system, making it difficult to share necessary information necessary for decision making.
- Collusion among safety regulators and government promoters of NPS, NPS operators such as TEPCO, scientists, and the media worked to produce a myth of NPS safety and deflected any safety concerns.
- Organizational management based on a life-time employment system, groupism, and collective responsibility-based decision making were typical in organizations and society throughout Japan.

Such a system can easily result in a failure to disclose crisis information to the public and to share such information among the emergency managers from different ministries, as a collective and consensus decision-making system was the practice to safeguard ministry positions that offered employment for life (NAIIC, 2012; Suzuki and Kaneko, 2013).

Failure to Disclose Crisis Information to the Public

The Fukushima nuclear crisis resulted in a serious loss of citizens' trust in government due to its inadequate crisis management, as exemplified by the government's failure to disclose critical information to the public, particularly the evacuees.

Delays in Disclosing Crisis Information in Japan

Substantial delays in the disclosure of crisis and risk information to the public were apparent in the gaps of information disclosed overseas and in Japan (see Table 3.2). Much of what was being reported by foreign media earlier on had not been released to the citizens of Japan, which deprived them of the opportunity to make informed decisions about their safety.

Delays in Disclosing Crisis Information to Local Residents

Communication delays caused much hardship among the evacuees from areas close to the Fukushima nuclear power station. They were not given information about the crisis or risk of radiation necessary to make sound decisions, which sabotaged their efforts to help themselves for a long period of time.

Table 3.2 Comparison of Information Disclosed Overseas and in Japan

Critical Information Disclosed	Overseas (Date Reported in Foreign Media)	Japan (Date Publicly Released by Japanese Government)
Radioactive water in basement would soon overflow and it would be necessary to release it to the sea.	March 14, 2011	April 4, 2011
Radioactive releases by the NPS could continue for months.	March 14, 2011	April 12, 2011
Conditions could quickly lead to melting and ultimately to full meltdown.	March 14, 2011	April 18, 2011
Evacuees may not be able to return to their homes for a considerable period of time.	March 14, 2011	August 21, 2011

Source: Adapted from Suzuki, I. and Kaneko, Y., *Japan's Disaster Governance*, Springer, New York, 2013.

MEXT, in charge of radioactive monitoring by SPEEDI, did not confirm until July 27, 2012, that the radioactive contamination information was available from SPEEDI data from the beginning, and the agency acknowledged with regret that it did not release that information to the public.

Failure to Disclose Crisis Information to Emergency Relief Organizations

Insufficient sharing of crisis and risk information resulted in serious mistakes being made; for example, the Nuclear Emergency Response Headquarters issued a wrong evacuation order and became involved in an excessively detailed technical intervention that further delayed critical emergency responses. Such mismanagement can be attributed to the following causes:

- Lack of sufficient clarification in the relevant laws as to the roles of those engaged in nuclear accident emergencies, although the roles and step-by-step procedures of private-sector NPS operators were detailed
- Failure of TEPCO to disclose critical information and share it with members of the Nuclear Emergency Response Headquarters
- Insufficient or total lack of information sharing due to the compartmentalized Japanese bureaucracy within the Nuclear Emergency Response Headquarters, as well as among the various emergency organizations involved

Failure to Disclose Crisis Information Due to Inadequate Business Practices and a Lack of Government Transparency

During the process of investigating the 3.11 nuclear disaster, the National Diet of the Fukushima Nuclear Accident Independent Investigation Commission (NAIIC) discovered that the government did not keep records of the meetings held at the Nuclear Emergency Response Headquarters or other conferences immediately after the disaster. Parliament released this finding to the public. Its disclosure testified to the lack of transparency and accountability among those involved in Japan's crisis management and revealed weaknesses in its information disclosure and records management.

More recently, Japanese media reported that the Government Investigation Committee had conducted hearings with key government and NPS emergency managers, including the director of the nuclear power station. The media also reported that government investigation records included transcripts of hearings with nuclear crisis managers involved in the early stage of the nuclear disaster that would clarify what happened there. Despite a newly promulgated public records management law, the government continues to resist releasing the transcripts, using the excuse that public disclosure may endanger the privacy of the individual managers involved.

Institutional Reforms to Aid Recovery from the Fukushima Disaster

The existing emergency institutions were found to be inadequate to handle the necessary recovery activities. To promote the nuclear safety regulatory functions of the government and to add impetus to the Fukushima disaster recovery, new institutions were established with the enactment of 14 new Acts (see the Table 3.3).

Table 3.3 Acts Promulgated to Aid Recovery from the Fukushima Disaster

Date	Act
August 5, 2011	Act on emergency measures for the 2011 nuclear accident damages
August 10, 2011	Act on the establishment of the Nuclear Damage Compensation Support Authority
August 12, 2011	Act on the exceptional treatment of paperwork concerning the evacuees from the nuclear power plant accidents
August 30, 2011	Act on the special measures for environmental contamination by the radioactive materials emitted by the nuclear power plant accidents by the Great East Japan Earthquake
October 7, 2011	Act on the establishment of the investigative committee for TEPCO's Fukushima Nuclear Power Plant accidents
November 28, 2011	Act on providing life support to the TEPCO nuclear accident victims
March 31, 2012	Act on the special measures for reconstruction and development of Fukushima prefecture
June 27, 2012	Nuclear Regulation Authority Establishment Act Act on the promotion of life support measures for residents of the radioactive contaminated areas by the Fukushima accidents Amendment to the Disaster Countermeasures Basic Act
May 10, 2013	Amendment to the Act on the special measures for reconstruction and development of Fukushima Prefecture
June 5, 2013	Act on the special treatment of the nullification of prescriptions in the nuclear damage compensation dispute mediation procedure.
November 22, 2013	Act on the dissolution of the Japan Nuclear Energy Safety Organization
December 11, 2013	Act on swift and secure compensation for the 2011 nuclear damages

Key Central Government Organizations Established for Nuclear Safety Recovery and Regulations

Nuclear Regulation Authority

The Nuclear Regulation Authority (NRA) was established in 2012 as an external organ of the Ministry of the Environment (MOE) to maintain a separation between safety regulatory functions and the ministries that promote nuclear power station use (e.g., METI) and to integrate various regulatory functions that were at one time fulfilled by several different ministries. The NRA is expected to enhance transparency and neutrality in decision making regarding nuclear safety through transparent information disclosures. The NRA does not have the authority to grant licenses to electric power companies or promote NPSs so it may have an impartial relationship with electricity companies. It has improved technical expertise by inviting occasional international experts from the United States, United Kingdom, and France. The merger of the Japan Nuclear Energy Safety Organization with the NRA in 2014 was expected to further strengthen the NRA's technical expertise.

Nuclear Emergency Preparedness System

In 2012, the nuclear emergency preparedness system shown in Figure 3.2 was organized, with the NRA being the central nuclear safety regulatory management organization.

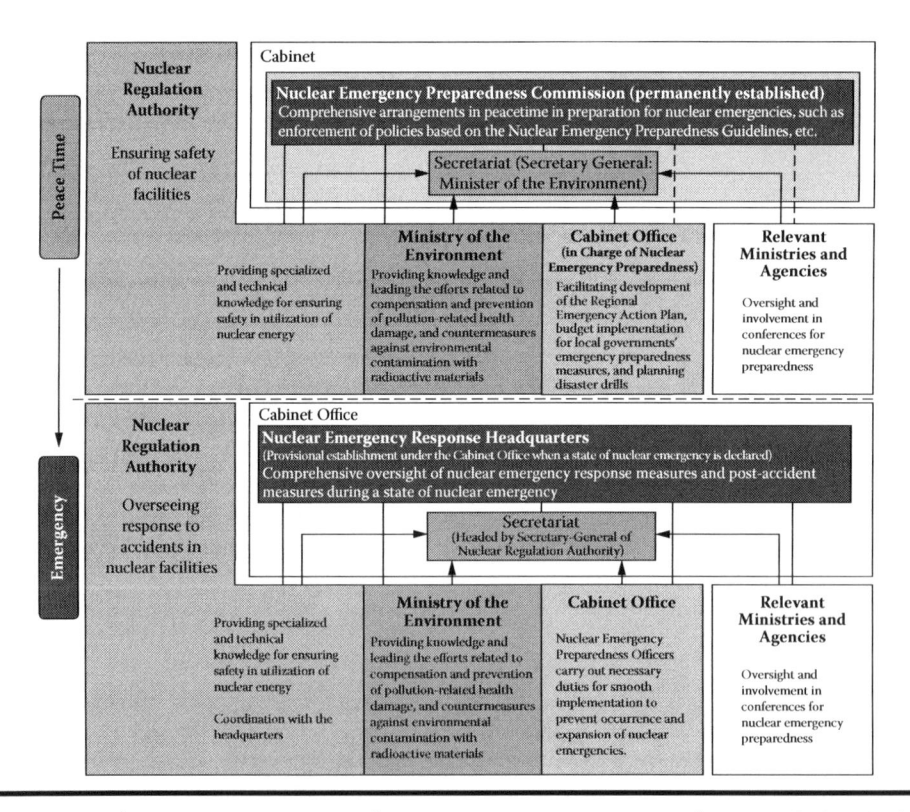

Figure 3.2 Nuclear emergency preparedness system (METI, 2013; Nuclear Regulation Authority, 2013).

Ongoing Effects of the Fukushima NPS Accident

As early as March 25, 2011, contaminated radioactive water was found at the Fukushima NPS site. After that, leakage of contaminated water continued, probably because of damage to the containment vessels. Another accident on March 18, 2013, resulted in a cooling system shutdown. On August 19, 2013, TEPCO discovered that contaminated water had leaked from the tanks. NRA first evaluated this accident as INES Level 1 but later revised their estimate to INES Level 3 after consultation with the International Atomic Energy Agency (IAEA) on August 28, 2013 (see Table 3.4 for details).

Government Takes Major Responsibility for Decommissioning and Radioactive Water Issues

As contaminated water leakage and decommissioning of the damaged NPS issues became serious issues, the Nuclear Emergency Response Headquarters, established on March 11, 2011, when the nuclear crisis occurred, assumed the major responsibility for dealing with them on September 3, 2013. The Inter-Ministerial Council for Contaminated Water and Decommissioning Issues was established on September 10, 2013. This council organized teams to address tasks associated with mitigating the contaminated water situation and with decommissioning.

As Figure 3.3 shows, the government appointed the Minister of Economy, Trade and Industry to be a team leader with METI bureaucrats, assuming secretarial functions in the implementation of concrete measures to cope with various contaminated water and decommissioning issues. The NRA's chairman is a member of the team, and the NRA is still responsible for nuclear safety checkups and technical examination and assessment of the validity of NPS-related safety issues. The Minister of Economy, Trade and Industry is now responsible for providing information on their policies and decisions with regard to the Fukushima nuclear disaster recovery to all responsible safety managers as well as the citizens. His accountability must now be monitored to ensure continuing crisis and risk information disclosure to the public and sharing among all the nuclear disaster recovery managers. It is particularly important as the current government is aiming at resumption of NPS operations as soon as the NRA completes the safety assessment.

Evaluation and Analysis Based on Information Disclosed by Government, Statistics, and Media

A scientific evaluation of the emergency management associated with the 3.11 disaster would require that some emergency management standards be established; however, this discussion does not offer such a scientific review. It does provide examples, both good and bad, as judged by the citizens immediately after the 3.11 disaster, and it highlights the nuclear crisis responses taken by the government. The evaluations provided here are more or less those shared by the majority of citizens in Japan, as determined by published polls and by the discourses of disaster investigation and research groups.

Relief and rescue operations immediately put into place by the responsible organizations after the earthquake were conducted in accordance with current laws, and the systems functioned as well as expected. These initial relief and rescue efforts were evaluated highly by the public. The relevant government organizations had actively reformed their systems to prepare for such emergency responses, and many collaborative arrangements had been made with nonprofit organizations

Table 3.4 Sequence of Accident Events from June 2011 to May 2014

Year	Date	Events
2011	June 9	METI instructed TEPCO to install treatment and storage facilities for highly radioactive contaminated water and to submit reports periodically.
2012	April 5	TEPCO announced leakage of radioactive water from the transfer pipe connecting to a desalination plant and a radioactive contaminated water storage tank.
	September 9	Nuclear Regulation Authority was inaugurated.
2013	March 18	TEPCO reported that the cooling system was shut down because of power failure.
	April 7	Media reported that contaminated radioactive water had leaked from the basement of the NPS site and contaminated water storage tanks.
	April 10	TEPCO announced a plan to transfer contaminated water to the groundwater storage tanks.
	April 26	Government organized a contaminated water treatment countermeasures committee to initiate discussion of how to reduce contaminated water leaks from NPS.
	June 19	TEPCO announced that underground water from seaside turbine buildings was highly radioactive contaminated.
	July 22	TEPCO announced that contaminated underground water was leaking into the power station port.
	July 31	NRA released their evaluation of the underground water contamination level.
	August 7	Government held a meeting at the Nuclear Emergency Response Headquarters to deliberate the contaminated water issues.
	August 8	METI convened the contaminated water treatment committee.
	August 19	TEPCO discovered leakage of about 300 cubic meters of contaminated water from the ground tanks. NRA rated this accident as INES Level 1 and later upgraded it to Level 3.
	August 26	METI minister visited the accident site and presented countermeasures to serve as the new principles behind plans to deal with the leak; government announced it would finance costs associated with solving the contaminated water issues (although TEPCO was legally liable).
	September 3	Government decided upon a basic policy for the contaminated water issue at the site and announced decommissioning of the damaged nuclear reactors.

(Continued)

Table 3.4 (Continued) Sequence of Accident Events from June 2011 to May 2014

Year	Date	Events
	September 7	NRA initiated their own monitoring of the level of radioactivity leaked by the contaminated storage tanks that had spread to the bay area near the site.
	September 8	In an address inviting the 2020 Olympics to come to Tokyo, Prime Minister Abe declared that the water leakage issues at the Fukushima NPS were under control and pledged there would be no danger in Tokyo. (A few days later, a TEPCO official who was summoned to a televised Parliamentary session said that the water leakage issue was not under control.)
	September 13	NRA began to release information about the current situation at the nuclear power station, including the fact that contaminated water was still leaking and radioactivity had been detected in the seawater. Since then, at least once in a month, the release of information has continued.
	October 28	NRA chairman met with the TEPCO president concerning decommissioning of the damaged Fukushima reactors.
	November 6–12	IAEA experts visited Fukushima to monitor the radioactivity levels of the contaminated water leaking from the nuclear power station.
	November 18	Transfer of fuel rods from the Unit 4 spent fuel pool began.
	November 25 to December 4	IAEA experts visited Fukushima again and announced that the level of radioactivity was not hazardous to human health.
	December 20	Government adopted a new policy for additional support for TEPCO to facilitate the recovery process and decommissioning of the nuclear reactors (although TEPCO was legally liable).
2014	January 9	Media reported that TEPCO continued to construct additional water tanks without appropriate radioactivity countermeasures.
	February 15–16	TEPCO reported to NRA several incidents of water leakage.
	February 20	TEPCO reported to NRA that water leakage was found from the upper part of Tank C-1 in the H-6 tank area.
	April 11	Government decided upon a new national energy strategy that recognizes nuclear power generation as an important "base-load" energy source, such that nuclear power plant operation was to be resumed after strict review by NRA.
	April 13	TEPCO reported to NRA the inappropriate transfer of contaminated water at the Fukushima NPS.
	April 15	TEPCO opened the Fukushima NSP site to the press to show where additional water storage tanks were being built and new bypass facilities for underground water were being operated.

(Continued)

Table 3.4 (Continued)   Sequence of Accident Events from June 2011 to May 2014

Year	Date	Events
	May 13	TEPCO reported to NRA that 836 spent and new fuel assemblies out of 1533 were transferred from the Unit 4 spent fuel pool to the common spent fuel pool on site.
	May 27	NRA issued a press release on radioactivity levels in the seawater.

and private-sector companies. These reforms were based on the lessons learned from the Great Hanshin-Awaji Earthquake of 1995 and subsequent earthquakes. The well-respected emergency management system in place for the earthquake in 2011 itself provides the lesson that learning from previous disaster management cases can lead to better preparedness in the future.

Before the 3.11 disaster, the Japanese government had established a public safety-oriented governance system generally enjoyed by most of the citizens of Japan. The system was well known worldwide for the many examples of great longevity among the Japanese citizens, a national medical healthcare system, and strict water and food safety standards. Internationally, the country has been involved in and shared knowledge about building disaster governance capacity around the world, particularly since 1995 when the country contributed to the creation of a UN disaster governance international framework. Since the 3.11 disaster, various international meetings have been held in connection with the UN International Strategy for Disaster Reduction (UNISDR) program. The UNISDR World Conference on Disaster Risk Reduction was held at Sendai in 2015.

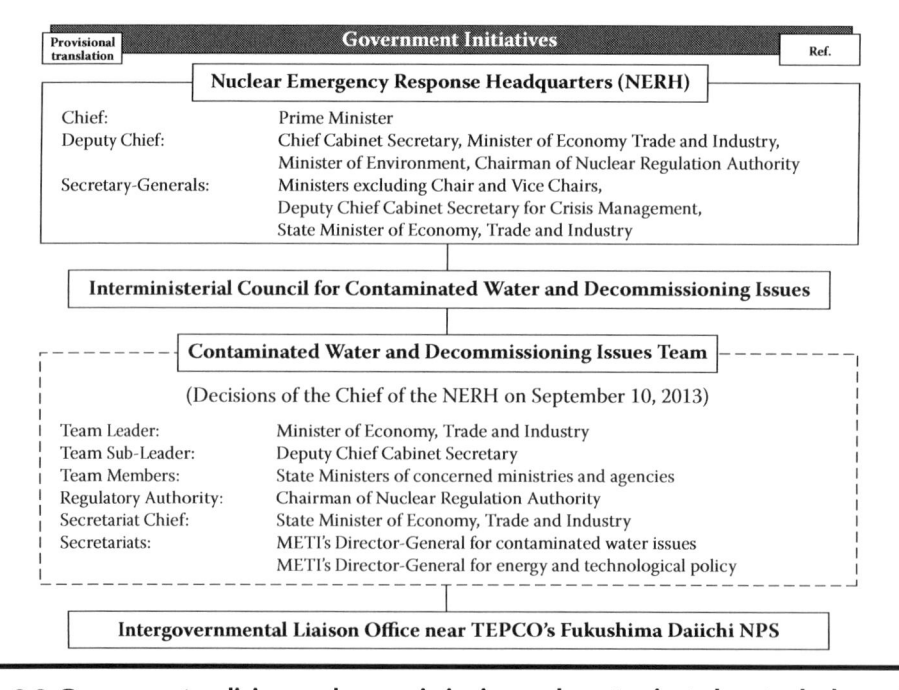

Figure 3.3 Government policies on decommissioning and contaminated water leakage. (From Government of Japan, *Information on Contaminated Water Leakage at TEPCO's Fukushima Daiichi Nuclear Power Station*, 2015, http://Japan.kantei.go.jp/ongoingtopics/waterissues.html.)

It was therefore a surprise for the majority of the citizens of Japan to discover during the 3.11 nuclear disasters that their lives were not as safe as they thought. It was then that the citizens of Japan and the world community learned that preparedness for nuclear power plants accidents had been grossly neglected, despite frequent alerts by professionals in Japan and overseas on the necessity of installing safety mechanisms at nuclear power stations. Local community evacuation drills had rarely been organized, and the lack of crisis preparedness resulted in the worst case of disaster management in Japan's history.

The Fukushima nuclear crisis may not be an exception to nuclear disaster preparedness worldwide, but it is difficult to compare Japan with other countries because nuclear crisis information can be a matter of national security that is not shared publicly. The Fukushima nuclear disaster is not yet over. During the long recovery process, the government has not yet shown to the public a valid ending scenario.

Lessons and Implications for NPS Crisis and Emergency Management

Establish Effective, Transparent, and Accountable System of Government Crisis Communication

For crisis and emergency management, preparedness is enhanced by learning from past lessons. The public should be made aware of the lessons learned through experience in order to better equip them with the knowledge necessary to deal with nuclear risks and have the greatest chance of survival. The roles of nuclear emergency managers and relief organizations must be clearly defined based on the lessons learned. It is crucial for the government to establish transparent and accountable government crisis and risk communication for all. The government should

- Improve the communication framework for public disclosure and sharing within several disaster management organizations.
- Strengthen public relations capability to promote information disclosure and sharing among relevant organizations.
- Prepare for worst-case scenarios to reduce the element of surprise in emergency and crisis management (GIC, 2012; NAIIC, 2012).
- Monitor parliamentary nuclear crisis and Fukushima disaster responses to ensure transparent and accountable government crisis and risk management (NAIIC, 2012).

Establish Accountable and Transparent Government Records Management to Facilitate an End to the Fukushima Nuclear Disaster and Mitigate Future Disasters

As described earlier, it was found that the government did not keep the records of meetings held at the Nuclear Emergency Response Headquarters or elsewhere during the emergency. A year later, the government reportedly assembled transcripts of emergency meeting records after the fact and released these to the public. These transcripts offered useful lessons for the emergency management system, particularly with regard to reorganizing the crisis and risk communication systems.

The as-yet-undisclosed transcripts of government managers and the local Fukushima NPS director at the time of the crisis are reportedly included in the government's investigation records (as of July 2014). These government records should be disclosed to the public according to a recently passed public records management law. Although the government is still resistant, it has been suggested that the government might consider disclosing them to the extent possible without jeopardizing national security or the privacy of the people involved. The Fukushima NPS director reportedly stated that it was difficult to gather crucial accident information at the damaged sites. Transparent and accountable records disclosure may provide useful lessons for better organizing nuclear accident risk and crisis management, as well as government crisis communication systems in particular. The implications of the lessons learned are that the following aspects must be strengthened:

- Public recordkeeping and disclosure by the central and local governments
- Utilization of public records to better prepare for possible future disasters and to more effectively disseminate crisis knowledge among both citizens and crisis managers

Resilient Capacity Building, Citizens' Rights, and Government Responsibility: Learning from the 3.11 Nuclear Disaster

In 2014, the Japanese government adopted a new energy policy that allowed for resumed generation of nuclear-energy-based electricity, although Japanese polls even now indicate that the majority of the Japanese citizens are against resumption of NPS operations. Following are some of their concerns:

- No practical decommissioning technology is available anywhere.
- Greater use of nuclear power stations is being promoted worldwide.
- Suitable sites to store radioactive nuclear wastes are difficult to find, in either Japan or anywhere else in the world.
- It is not possible to be perfectly prepared for a nuclear crisis that threatens the lives and safety of individuals and communities.
- The IAEA (2014) warned of the importance of better communication and the need to ensure that timely crisis and risk information is shared among the decision-makers and citizens.

In particular, the government of Japan must encourage resilient capacity building for nuclear disaster mitigation by

- Educating and training all of the professionals, bureaucrats, politicians, and citizens involved in disaster governance
- Emphasizing the importance of sharing nuclear crisis and risk information among all disaster stakeholders[*]
- Organizing drills for emergency evacuation
- Developing a valid plan to end the Fukushima nuclear disaster and eliminate further radiation risks, particularly now that the government is primarily responsible for facilitating decommissioning and reducing the spread of radiation from the nuclear debris
- Learning from the past experience, which is most essential for disaster mitigation and emergencies, and strengthening surprise management because any crisis situation always has surprises

---

[*] MEXT has proposed establishing a new focal research and training center in Fukushima in 2016 to develop safety decommissioning technologies. Innovations developed at the new center would be shared with professionals from around the world (*Yomiuri Shimbun*, June 20, 2014 issue, p. 1).

Conclusions

Disasters happen, particularly in natural-disaster-prone countries such as Japan. More than 3 years have passed since the 3.11 disaster, but the recovery process has been a slow one. Major earthquakes are predicted to occur in Japan in the future, so the lessons learned from the 3.11 disaster must be applied to building safety resilience capacity. Additionally, in Japan, the government needs to improve upon its accountable and transparent nuclear emergency management. Safety resilience capacity building needs to be aggressively pursued by the government of Japan, which has lost the trust of its citizens, and should seek the input of everyone involved. Some key lessons learned include the following:

- Nuclear crisis and risk information must be disclosed to all of those involved in a timely manner to ensure the citizens' rights and ability to choose the best course of action; such information would include evacuation routes and methods.
- Local municipal governments should hold drills for disaster emergency preparedness to help their citizens escape from danger.
- The central government should provide transparent and accountable nuclear risk and crisis information based on records from government or parliamentary investigative reports on the Fukushima nuclear disaster to local municipal governments, which are primarily responsible by law for planning disaster mitigation and emergency responses.
- The central government, through the passage of laws, should provide the necessary aid to local governments in support of their planning.

Questions for Discussion

1. Have you witnessed any type of government applying lessons learned from a crisis to improving their emergency and crisis management? If not, why do you think that hasn't happened?
2. How can a government ensure greater disclosure of accountable and transparent crisis and risk information to its citizens in this global communication era?
3. How can a government improve its records management in order to better assist both emergency managers and citizens and to enhance risk and crisis mitigation planning?
4. Informed, effective self-help and help provided by others are important elements in disaster mitigation. What should a government do to better prepare its citizens to survive a nuclear disaster emergency?

Additional Reading

Endo, K. (2012). *How the Media Communicated the Great Earthquake/Nuclear Power Plant Accidents: Examining Media, Press, Net News, and Documentary Write-Ups.* Tokyo: Tokyo Electricity University Publishing.

Government of Japan. (2013). *Government's Decision on Addressing the Contaminated Water Issue at TEPCO's Fukushima Daiichi NPS,* http://www.mofa.go.jp/policy/page3e_000072.html.

Horie, M. (2013). Introduction to the Symposium on Disaster Management: lessons from the Great East Japan Earthquake of 11 March 2011. *Asian Review of Public Administration*, 24.

International Atomic Energy Agency (IAEA). (2015). *Fukushima Daiichi Status Updates,* http://www.iaea.org/newscenter/news/2013/japan-basic-policy-full.html.

Morita, A. (2013). Lessons from the Great East Japan Earthquake and the safety and security of citizens and society. *Annals of the Japanese Society of Public Administration*, 48: 8–79.

Nuclear Emergency Response Headquarters, Japanese Government. (2013). *Preventive and Multilayered Measures for Decommissioning and Contaminated Water Management*, http://www.kantei.go.jp/jp/singi/genshiryoku/dai33/siryou1-2.pdf.

Nuclear Regulation Authority. (2013). *FY 2012 Annual Report*, http://www.nsr.go.jp/english/data/ar_0701.pdf.

Nuclear Regulation Authority. (2014). *NRA Library*, http://www.nsr.go.jp/english/library/.

Nuclear Regulation Authority. (2014). *Fukushima Daiichi NPS's Issues*, http://www.nsr.go.jp/english/f1issues/index.html.

Prime Minister of Japan and His Cabinet. (2014). *Information on Contaminated Water Leakage at TEPCO's Fukushima Daiichi Nuclear Power Station*, http://japan.kantei.go.jp/ongoingtopics/waterissues.html.

Suzuki, I. and Kaneko, Y. (2012). Overview of institutions for public policy making in Japan. In Kaneko, Y., Miyoshi, K., and Suzuki, I., Eds., *Public Administration Handbook of Japan*. Tokyo: Book Way Global.

Suzuki, I. and Kaneko, Y. (2013). Managing the Great East Japan earthquake emergency with emphasis on Fukushima nuclear crisis communication: best and worst practices. *Asian Rev. Public Admin.*, 24(1–2): 50–63.

References

Government Investigation Committee (GIC). (2012). *Final Report on the Accident at the Fukushima Nuclear Power Stations of TEPCO*, www.nirs.org/fukushima/SaishyuRecommendation.pdf.

Government of Japan. (2015). *Information on Contaminated Water Leakage at TEPCO's Fukushima Daiichi Nuclear Power Station*, http://japan.kantei.go.jp/ongoingtopics/waterissues.html.

International Atomic Energy Agency (IAEA). (2014). International Experts' Meeting on Radiation Protection after the Fukushima Daiichi Accident: Promoting Confidence and Understanding, Vienna, Austria, February 17–21, http://www-pub.iaea.org/iaeameetings/cn224Presentations.aspx.

Koide, H. (2012). *Fukushima NPS Accidents—What Should We Do with the NPS Now?* Tokyo: Kawai Publishing.

Ministry of Economy, Trade and Industry (METI). (2013). *Annual Energy Report FY2012*, http://www.enecho.meti.go.jp/about/whitepaper/2013html/3-3-2.html.

National Diet of Japan Fukushima Nuclear Accident Independent Investigation Commission (NAIIC). (2012). *Report on the Tokyo Electric Power Company Fukushima Nuclear Power Plant Accident*, from http://naiic.go.jp/report/.

Nuclear Regulation Authority. (2013). *Establishment and Operations: September 19, 2012–March 10, 2013*, http://www.nsr.go.jp/english/.

Rebuild Japan Initiative Foundation. (2012). *Investigation Report of the Independent Investigation Commission on the Fukushima Nuclear Accident*. Tokyo: Discover 21.

Reconstruction Agency. (2014a). *3.11 Progress Report*, www.tt.emb-japan.go.jp/Progress%20Report.pdf.

Reconstruction Agency. (2014b). *Report on the Indirect Deaths from the Great East Japan Earthquake*, http://www.reconstruction.go.jp/topics/main-cat2/sub-cat2-1/20140527_kanrenshi.pdf.

Suzuki, I. and Kaneko, Y. (2013). *Japan's Disaster Governance*. New York. Springer.

Chapter 4

Early Warning Success in Qinglong County, China, for the Magnitude 7.8 Tangshan Earthquake: Some Policy Lessons in Integrating Public Administration, Science, and Citizen Engagement

Jeanne-Marie Col

Contents

Chapter Goals	54
Introduction	54
Qinglong County and the Great Tangshan Earthquake	55
Lessons Learned from Analysis of Qinglong County Actions	57
Successful Disaster Reduction Lessons	61
Role of Best-Practices Case Studies in Emergency Management Analysis	63
Conclusion	63
Questions for Discussion	63
Practical Activities	63
Appendices	64
References	86

Chapter Goals

After studying this chapter, readers should be able to

1. Understand the role of public administrators in disaster anticipation, preparation, mitigation, response, and recovery.
2. Appreciate the role of scientists in understanding the scientific dynamics of major disasters.
3. Understand what citizens can do to increase their communities' resilience to major disasters.
4. Be able to map interrelationships among different levels of government and sectors in disaster cycles.
5. Understand how to practice developing policy statements for facilitating disaster planning.
6. Be able to define the characteristics of a disaster-resilient community.

Introduction

Critical analysis of disaster incidents seeks to discover factors whose understanding allows people to predict, prevent, or manage such incidents. The Qinglong County case study provides an example of a community that recognized an impending catastrophe and took actions to mitigate the negative effects of the disaster. More than 246,000 people were killed in the 1976 Great Tangshan Earthquake. In Qinglong County, despite the collapse of 180,000 buildings, no deaths were attributable to the earthquake and its aftershocks. This chapter describes Qinglong County's actions before and during the Great Tangshan Earthquake incident and presents an analysis of the public administration and emergency management lessons learned. These lessons include effective coordination among public administrators, scientists, and citizens and feature proactive policies, local government initiative, thorough implementation, delegation, information sharing, and citizen participation. These lessons are illustrated during all phases of the emergency management process: preparedness, mitigation, response, and recovery.

Most disaster incidents are negative experiences for people, institutions, and society. Following the standard operationalization of disaster incidents, one expects social panic and trauma, significant injury, loss of life and property, infrastructure damage, lack of coordination, and plenty of confusion, as well as a reduction of public trust in those institutions that are expected to take care of people and society. The case study of Qinglong County's official actions before, during, and after the Great Tangshan Earthquake in China in 1976 defies this stereotype of a disaster incident. Instead, the Qinglong County officials correctly predicted, widely prepared, mitigated against possible damage, responded to help people in surrounding areas, and rebuilt their infrastructure and buildings with cooperation and confidence. The actions of the officials and citizens of Qinglong County are even more impressive in contrast to the overall catastrophic consequences of the magnitude 7.8 earthquake, whose epicenter was in the city of Tangshan. More than 246,000 people were killed in this earthquake incident, the most devastating loss of life from a natural disaster of the 20th century. In Qinglong County, 115 km from the epicenter, despite the collapse of 180,000 buildings, no deaths were attributable to the earthquake and its aftershocks.

The methodology of data collection and analysis involved fieldwork in China over a period of 4 years. Most significantly, the author returned to Qinglong County five times, and many documents were translated into English. Each research visit permitted the author to dig deeper, peeling away the layers of the onion representing the roles and perceptions of the officials and citizens. Interviewing retired officials and the translation of more than 100 personal accounts written by the citizens on the 10th anniversary of the earthquake in 1986 assisted in confirming the sequence of official and citizen actions. The chronology of events in Qinglong County begins two years before the earthquake and continues through the short-term aftermath. The events are described according to who, what, and when and their impact on incident management (see Appendix 4A).

The overall experience of the Great Tangshan Earthquake was devastating to Tangshan, the surrounding area, and all of China. But, in the midst of all this destruction, the actions taken in Qinglong County serve to highlight the possibility of early warning and effective response to that warning, as well as the follow-up actions whereby the Qinglong County residents, who suffered damage but no loss of life, were able to respond to the medical, food, and shelter needs of Tangshan residents.

Qinglong County and the Great Tangshan Earthquake[*]

In the summer of 1976, an earthquake of magnitude 7.8 hit the Tangshan City region in northeastern China. Northeastern China is composed of four provinces (Hebei, Liaoning, Shanxi, and Shandong), one autonomous region (Inner Mongolia), and two special municipalities (Beijing and Tianjin). Within these jurisdictions, there are 431 counties (Anon., 2003). Qinglong County is one of these counties. More than 246,000 persons in the region died as a result of the 1976 earthquake and its aftershocks; however, no one in Qinglong County was included in this statistic (Col, 2007).

Several factors account for this seeming miracle in Qinglong County. One of the most important factors was the scientific understanding and preparatory actions of what was then called China's National Bureau of Earthquakes and is now the China Earthquake Agency (CEA). The CEA generates four types of earthquake predictions—long-term (more than 2 years), medium-term (1 to 2 years), short-term (few months), and imminent (1 to 14 days)—which are revised annually at the local, regional, provincial, and national levels. When the CEA gathers and analyzes sufficient data to indicate a coming earthquake, the CEA notifies the State Council (China's national cabinet), which in turn, issues an alert or a warning to the localities likely to be affected (Li, 1991).

With regard to the Great Tangshan Earthquake, the State Council issuing Document No. 69 in 1974 (see Appendix 4B) to warn the region of the increased risk of seismic activity in the coming decade (Col and Chu, 1999). This national policy document, an example of the CEA's long-term predictions, notified provincial and local governments in northeast China to prepare for the possibility of earthquakes. Specifically, Document No. 69 recommended that municipalities and provinces in the area, including Hebei Province in which Tangshan City and Qinglong County are located, prepare for earthquakes of magnitude greater than 6 on the Richter scale.

---

[*] Research for the Great Tangshan Earthquake was carried out under the auspices of the United Nations from 1995 to 2000, with multiple visits to Qinglong County. An initial familiarization visit was followed by a more intensive set of interviews, including those with retired public administrators. The then-State Science and Technology Commission (now the Ministry of Science and Technology) facilitated my visits to Qinglong County. The then-State Earthquake Bureau (now the China Earthquake Agency [CEA]) facilitated introductions to provincial, city, and county-level officials. Qinglong County officials opened their achives, including a unique collection of essays written by county residents recollecting their experiences on the 10th anniversary of the 1976 earthquake. These essays were translated into English by several Chinese colleagues and made possible comparison between interview comments and the statements written 10 years earlier. After two years of research and analysis, the chronology of Qinglong County events was translated back into Chinese and circulated among the interviewees in order to be certain of accuracy as seen through their eyes. Throughout this 5-year period, the Chinese Academy of Science (CAS) organized expert panels to explain the fine points of the science of earthquakes, and, for background understanding, the CEA and CAS arranged for additional interviews at earthquake epicenters throughout China.

Document No. 69 also called for increased local monitoring and public education and strengthening of the infrastructure, including buildings in the area. It also encouraged monitoring by citizens (i.e., lay monitoring) in factories, mines, and schools by local science volunteers. By 1976, most counties in Hebei Province had established an earthquake office and launched a variety of preparedness activities. Their proactive reaction to Document No. 69 reflected their knowledge of the 1975 earthquake experienced in nearby Haicheng. Based on the 1974 alert, several communities in the Haicheng area were evacuated before the 1975 earthquake.

In response to Document No. 69, the administrative leaders of Qinglong County, who were also political leaders of the county's Communist Party, established an earthquake office and hired a 21-year old graduate of a technical school as the earthquake disaster mitigation officer. He intensified public education by distributing thousands of copies of booklets and posters and presenting slide shows and movies in villages, towns, and cities, including a short earthquake preparedness film to be presented in movie theaters as a reminder before the main feature. He was also responsible for increasing the county's earthquake monitoring sites from 6 to 16, with 9 of them under the supervision of local middle schools and high schools.

At the same time, on the national level of government, CEA officials increased earthquake monitoring in northeast China and organized many regional training sessions for earthquake management professionals at which advice was given as to how to prepare for earthquakes. At one of the sessions, attendees, including the Qinglong County earthquake officer, were informed that professional earthquake monitoring teams and lay detection centers were reporting abnormal earthquake-related signals for the region comprised of Beijing, Tianjin, Tangshan, Bohai, and Zhangjiakou, thereby indicating the possibility of a significant earthquake during the period from July 22 to August 1976.

Session attendees were encouraged to examine readings from country-level earthquake monitoring equipment managed by the lay public. The officials were also encouraged to intensify earthquake preparation measures such as examining buildings and other public works in critical condition, conducting public education teach-ins, and promoting a general awareness of possible approaching earthquakes.

When the head of the earthquake office returned to Qinglong County on July 21, he learned that four sites were registering unusual earthquake-related signals. On July 23, a special evening meeting of the County's Standing Committee of the Chinese Communist Party (SC/CCP) was called to hear about the earthquake officer's findings and to discuss the significance of these findings. On July 24, 1976, the Qinglong County SC/CCP issued an "official alert" (see Appendix 4C) to all residents to evacuate buildings and to move to tents outdoors. It was decided that village officials should return with a leading county-level official to their communities immediately.

It is important to note that the social fabric was sufficiently strong, despite the overwhelming possibility of a catastrophe, that all officials continued their work, rather than checking on their families' well-being, in order to accelerate earthquake and flood preparation. Several photographs taken at the time depict schoolchildren sitting on benches and participating in outdoor classes and merchants selling their goods outdoors on makeshift shelves under plastic sheeting. Most residents of the county were also sleeping in tents outdoors.

On July 25 and 26, two and three days immediately preceding the earthquake, each community in Qinglong County held an emergency meeting to prepare villagers and instruct them in disaster damage reduction. Community leaders identified vulnerable buildings and reservoirs and assigned guards to report infrastructure failures. Most villages had overnight watch guards on duty circulating among the buildings to enforce the evacuation order. County and village broadcasts instructed people who were still in their houses not to close their doors and windows at night so that they could leave their homes as soon as they felt the ground shaking. Residents were also told to avoid being close to tall buildings and power lines. On July 27, 1976, one day before the earthquake hit, a leading county official gave a major talk at a countywide agricultural meeting on the earthquake situation and on mitigation measures.

At 3:42 a.m. on July 28, 1976, the Great Tangshan Earthquake struck. More than 180,000 buildings in Qinglong County were destroyed, but only one person died, and he died of a heart attack. In the city of Tangshan itself, and in all of its other surrounding counties, more than 246,000 people died. The seeming miracle of Qinglong County was the result of several factors: involvement of all levels of government, clear national policies, effective administration delegated to the lowest level, adaptation to changing conditions, open and operational channels of communication, and citizen participation.

Lessons Learned from Analysis of Qinglong County Actions

All levels of government were involved in disaster management and mitigation. In the Great Tangshan Earthquake of 1976, each level of government performed a critical role in earthquake management and mitigation. National-level officials aggregated data from stations throughout the region and made earthquake predictions. Ongoing monitoring of earthquake precursors by China's professional earthquake staff (the CEA) was shared in periodic regional meetings. In all communities, subject to earthquake risk, the CEA, through national, provincial and municipal officers, conducted emergency preparedness workshops. As mentioned earlier, Document No. 69, issued in 1974 for the northeast region, was part of a continuing national program of applied earthquake science maintained by the CEA. It regularly included outreach, training, and communication with subnational governments; made synthesized reports on risk and vulnerability; and promulgated official directions for earthquake mitigation to subnational administrators. The leader of the Northeast Analysis and Prediction Group sent teams, several of whom later died in the earthquake, into northeast China to gather additional information in July 1976. He attended a regional training meeting scheduled in Tangshan during which he reminded the county-level participants of the range of measureable precursors, illustrated his talk with current data on precursor signals, and encouraged them to check their local stations for unusual signals and anomalies. Although he could not make an official prediction, he encouraged local officials to check their locally generated data. The subtle message was to increase disaster preparations if local data indicated a likely coming event. On the subnational level, institutions in Qinglong County acted on local data, within the context of national policy. Led by the recommendations of Document No. 69 and further instructions from the CEA, Qinglong County officials added staff to disaster management, checked infrastructure for structural vulnerabilities, and increased the number of precursor monitoring stations—both professionally managed and citizen staffed.

National policies were proactive and widely shared and understood among administrative, scientific, and lay communities. By the 1970s, CEA had developed a vast network of precursor monitoring sites, employing a wide variety of scientific methods. These sites, with professional scientists, equipment, and communications systems, were supplemented by intensive lay monitoring by local volunteers who were assisted by the CEA but organized by local governments. Professional and lay monitors met annually under the auspices of the CEA in information-sharing meetings at local, provincial, and national levels. Out of these meetings emerged long-term, medium-term, short-term, and imminent predictions. Continuous monitoring and communications kept the entire network up to date on the probability of earthquake events, occasionally leading to imminent predictions.

Operational decision-making and organizing were delegated repeatedly to the lowest level of government possible. In 1976, earthquake alert warnings could emanate only from the national level, but they depended on information gathered locally. There were many recorded precursor signals, but no small preshocks. The national-level scientists could not agree on a definite prediction, and therefore did not issue an imminent warning for the Tangshan area. In contrast, Qinglong County officials, analyzing their locally generated data, observed that precursor signals were becoming increasingly strong and decided to issue a county-level warning. Strictly speaking, the county's earthquake warning was not allowable under national law at the time. Thus, the local officials circumvented national instructions and made a decision that they believed would be useful to their people. In interviews in 1996, the officials indicated that they were aware of the risks of disobeying national instructions but were convinced that they were taking a calculated risk for the sake of the well-being of the county's people (Col and Chu, 1999). In Qinglong County, many officials took extraordinary actions with an urgency that communicated seriousness to colleagues and community members. For example, the head of the Qinglong County science committee, when leaving for a meeting in Beijing, instructed his staff not to wait for his return for permission to act but rather to take action based on incoming local data. Despite the high regard for top-down hierarchical management, these Qinglong County officials delegated decision-making to the officials closest to the problem. During a telephone conference with the leading officials of all 23 towns, the head of Qinglong County administration emphasized that all officials would be responsible for preparing people in their areas and would be held accountable for their actions or inactions.

Local-level administrators adapted plans and mitigation strategies to meet changing conditions as the disaster developed. On July 24, without a specific national government instruction (but under the auspices of Document No. 69 of 1974), the County Committee declared an earthquake alert and a countywide evacuation of buildings, with special attention to auditoriums, cinemas, theaters, and schools. Aware that this alert would interrupt some economic and social activities, the committee decided to err in the direction of citizen safety, risking criticism if no earthquake occurred. In later interviews, these officials told the author that they relied on Document No. 69 to give them adequate "administrative cover" for their evacuation order, which was "not specifically authorized" (Col and Chu, 1999). The SC/CCP alert included specific instructions for public administrators and citizens to work side by side. The SC/CCP established a command center that was staffed around the clock. First responders and other officials were required to stay at their posts 24 hours per day. Some officials were assigned to work with citizens at monitoring stations and report daily to the command center.

County officials used existing and parallel mechanisms by shifting activities over to earthquake preparedness. On the morning of July 25, in order to intensify communications, the county took over a meeting of more than 800 agriculturalists, informed them of the earthquake risk, provided a "short course" on earthquake preparation and mitigation, and sent some of them home with materials to distribute to their towns and villages. Throughout the run-up to the earthquake event, there was inevitable tension between bureaucratic norms that encourage, among other things, stovepipe thinking and emergent norms that evolve from actual changing circumstances. In the case of Qinglong County, in every instance, emergency norms displaced bureaucratic norms. Official after official made decisions that were based on factual reality rather than theoretical manuals (Schneider, 1995).

All channels of communication—vertical and horizontal—were open and operational, thereby increasing community understanding, sharing of perceived risk, and ease of coordinating actions. On July 25 and 26, citizen meetings were held at the county and village level. All residents had the opportunity to contribute to the analysis of the situation and to decisions made about actions to be taken. The author's interviews in three villages, 20 years after the earthquake, revealed that each village had a forum in which people shared their understanding of the earthquake threat and the need for joint action (Col and Chu, 1999). Choices were made in the forum, and local officials and volunteers enforced those decisions, including evacuating buildings and living in tents. If the decisions had been made in a less open manner and citizens had been told to evacuate without communitywide discussion, some community members would no doubt have questioned the motives of the enforcers. With open discussion, even those in disagreement with the decision perceived the community consensus, and social pressure encouraged follow-through on disaster mitigation practices.

In order to facilitate interlevel coordination, teams dispersed throughout the county were each composed of one county-level official and one local-level official of the target community. Their goal was to inform every county resident within 36 hours (by the end of July 26). Each community was required to have a command center, 24-hour communications, and patrols to keep people from entering their homes and buildings. The communications system supported 24-hour communications so that each community would know every detail of trends in surrounding areas. By activating the countywide information network, county officials were able to broadcast announcements for mitigation activities, alert all precursor monitoring stations to report anomalous signals, and to maintain overnight watch duty until August 5 (the end of the prediction window). Furthermore, communication between national and local communities was maintained before and during the earthquake response. CEA professional scientists visited lay monitoring stations to discuss recorded precursor signals with the citizen monitors. Regional and national response units worked side-by-side with Qinglong County residents to assist the victims in Tangshan City.

Citizens participated in all stages of preparation and execution of emergency management measures. To the extent that citizens participate in the emergency management functions, especially preparation, mitigation, and response, they will embed "disaster awareness" into their everyday lives. Although it is common for citizens to help neighbors and victims in the aftermath of a major disaster, it is less common for citizens to participate directly in preparatory activities. For example, in Qinglong County in 1976, local citizens enthusiastically engaged in both precursor monitoring and emergency preparations with little sign of panic. More generally, vulnerability reduction is most effective and sustainable when accomplished by the vulnerable people themselves. From 1974, when the county was first notified about the possibility of earthquakes over the next few years, the citizens of Qinglong County received pamphlets, watched movies, read posters, participated in drills, and held community discussions about earthquake dynamics. The public learned about lay detection of precursors, such as anomalies in water level, color, temperature, chemistry, and quality; the release of gases such as radon; unusual animal behavior; and weather changes. Individuals in each jurisdiction accepted responsibility for participating in monitoring their environment over the coming years (Schneider and Ingram, 1993). Many institutions became involved. Employees in factories and mines were trained to monitor for earthquake precursors using instrument readings or observational data. In addition, students in schools became involved in operating simple scientific equipment and in interviewing neighbors on observable earthquake-related phenomena.

When Qinglong County declared the earthquake alert on July 24, local residents remained calm, but

- Schools moved furniture outside and held classes in the open air.
- Merchants constructed shelving outdoors under plastic sheets and continued selling their goods.
- Rural populations built makeshift tents and camped outdoors.

- Urban populations practiced exiting their homes and offices quickly and slept near exits at night.
- Citizens assembled teach-ins to share earthquake preparedness strategies.
- Communities established patrols to monitor preparatory activities.

Even schoolchildren contributed to successful community decision-making. Assisted by three physics teachers, a group of students in a secondary school developed a database on earthquake precursors. The students collected data from monitoring equipment and interviews with local people. They noted changes in water level, temperature, and chemistry. They also noticed that normally nocturnal yellow weasels were running around in large numbers in broad daylight. The weasel activity increased in number and frequency on July 27.

Although an earthquake teach-in was scheduled for the morning of July 28, the students, based on incoming data, convinced their teachers to hold the teach-in early in the evening of July 27, after which the school buildings were declared off-limits to everyone and patrols were set up to keep students from re-entering the school buildings. That the teachers followed the advice of the students resulted in the buildings being completely evacuated when the earthquake hit at 3:42 a.m. on July 28.

In situations where community members are passive and only tangentially hear about disasters, they are ill prepared to take action against the evolving natural phenomenon and are subject to rumors and panic. Partial citizen action involves those who read about natural disasters and respond to warnings. Such citizens are aware of the community's interest in being protected, and expect the government to warn them of danger from natural disasters. On the other hand, Qinglong County's citizens went far beyond relying on the government to take care of them. They were measuring changes in their environment and discussing the changes at the dinner table and at the workplace. Their involvement in daily monitoring of earthquake precursors led to a communitywide sense of risk awareness and joint community responsibility (Comfort, 1999).

The Activism Matrix provided in Appendix 4D illustrates the different levels of activism and consequences for each of three stakeholder communities: scientists, administrators, and citizens. Although these levels of involvement represent three points on an "activism" continuum, the categorization is not static. People can learn to be more active through experiencing natural disasters and through focused learning, such as public disaster education campaigns during a warning (prepare) or an alert (evacuate or take cover). The occurrence of dramatic natural disasters, though often hugely tragic, can make a lasting impression on community members and push disaster awareness and mitigation to the top of the policy agenda (Birkland, 2006).

During the Tangshan earthquake, Qinglong County officials and citizens achieved a significant success that was unpublicized in China and was unknown in the outside world. Within China, officials chose not to publicize the success because it was not sanctioned practice for local governments to declare their own earthquake alerts. The success was achieved by local people taking account of locally perceived precursor signals and acting on this information in a decisive and timely manner. Effective synergy between evolving conditions and administrative actions occurred because local organizations believed that they could deviate from national guidelines or that they could tolerate the consequences of sanctions against them for having deviated. Ten of the approximately 60 jurisdictions in the area were notified to check their precursor measurements. Of the 10 jurisdictions, only 2 followed through with collecting local data, making the leadership aware of the precursor signals and preparing the citizens to take action, including timely evacuation. Of these 2 counties, only Qinglong County completed its preparation and mitigation activities before the earthquake struck.

Successful Disaster Reduction Lessons

There is a positive slant to the Qinglong County incident analysis due to the fact that the incident was successfully resolved, despite incident management failure in surrounding areas. Much can be learned from a process in which useful decisions were made at every decision point. Although best-practices incident management processes are rare, they provide clues to more effective performance in urgent situations:

- *Time dimension*—Most critical incidents and natural disasters are time bound, and earthquakes are no exception. For a truly large earthquake (magnitude 6 or larger), there are the major earthquake and its aftershocks, as well as sometimes a series of foreshocks. The time span is usually a few weeks, but a truly large earthquake's aftershocks can continue for months. Generally, these aftershocks continue to destabilize buildings and infrastructure and make risky the tasks of response and recovery. The recovery stage can last for 10 or more years. Research visits 20 years after the event found the city completely rebuilt, except for the preserved sites, such as the epicenter, a large library building, and a heavy industrial site. The sites chosen for preservation were places where few people were killed; buildings such as university dormitories in which all the occupants were killed were built again from scratch.
- *Significant loss of life and injury*—The Great Tangshan Earthquake killed more than 246,000 people. More than 7000 families were completely obliterated. Hundreds of thousands were injured. About 1000 people were killed in Beijing, which is more than 300 km from the epicenter. Even today there are rehabilitation and assisted-living facilities for the many disabled victims. At the same time, in Qinglong County, no one was killed by the earthquake. The only death resulted from a heart attack. There were some injuries. Although the evacuation was complete, a few people had wandered back close to buildings and were injured.
- *Significant property damage*—Earthquakes are particular destructive of buildings and infrastructure. The Great Tangshan Earthquake leveled a city of 1 million people and left industrial plants producing railroad cars with twisted steel. For recovery, a public works specialist was brought in from another part of China, and the city was largely rebuilt within 10 years. As part of the recovery, Tangshan City preserved seven sites that illustrate the earthquake's destruction and built a large earthquake museum. This museum and the related sites serve as a reminder of the destructive power of large earthquakes. As schoolchildren and others visit these sites, they are reminded to be prepared for future earthquakes and to be vigilant in mitigation efforts, such as the enforcement of building codes. In Qinglong County, 180,000 buildings collapsed or were damaged. Also, the portion of the Great Wall of China in Qinglong County collapsed except for the towers. Most of Qinglong County is outside of the Great Wall and was not part of the old-time Chinese dynasties. Four days before the earthquake struck, the officials of the Qinglong County Administrative Committee sent two people to every village to enforce the evacuation. Tents were provided. Children attended school seated in chairs outdoors, and merchants sold their merchandise from tables under plastic tarps outdoors. The 180,000 buildings needed to be repaired and rebuilt, but all of the citizens were alive and able to participate in the reconstruction.
- *Declaration of state of emergency*—The declaration of a state of emergency was accomplished in two stages. First, the State Council (national-level cabinet) issued Document No. 69 in 1974, stating that northeastern China was likely to experience large earthquakes

in the next few years. Document No. 69, the national policy document, required local governments to prepare for a large earthquake (see Appendix 4B). These responsibilities were taken seriously in some locations but were neglected in other areas. Qinglong County took the responsibilities very seriously (see Appendix 4C). These preparations and mitigation strategies paid off with successful evacuation before the earthquake and no loss of life. The second important declaration of state of emergency was issued by Qinglong County on July 24, 1976, at 8:30 p.m. after an emergency night meeting of the administrative committee, 4 days before the earthquake hit. This document alerted the officials and citizens of the possibility of an earthquake very soon and an extremely large earthquake in the near future. The alert included specific actions that should be taken by various officials, organizations, and citizens. What is important about the Qinglong County alert is that it was not authorized by the national government. Although the national government had the same information as the county, the China Earthquake Agency determined that the information was not definitive and chose not to issue a warning to the people of the Tangshan area. Despite the silence of the national government, and the imperative of the Cultural Revolution to keep the economic sectors at high production levels, the Qinglong County officials risked their reputations, and perhaps their lives, to declare an emergency alert on their own at the local level. This position was vindicated more than 20 years later, when the State Council authorized local governments to declare earthquake alerts for their local levels.

- *Expectation and prediction*—The science of earthquake prediction is in a very preliminary stage. Earthquake science in China is multidisciplinary and relies on tracking macro and micro precursors that are associated with earthquakes. A characteristic of Chinese society is the strong alliance between professional scientists and the general public. Citizens in their communities are encouraged to participate in scientific data collection by tending professional monitoring equipment (sensing microprecursors) and watching for earthquake precursors in their environment. Scientists at all levels install equipment in localities and recruit volunteers to record and report the data. Moreover, some precursors, denoted as macro precursors, are perceptible to observant viewers. Ordinary citizens are generally aware of possible precursors and know whom to call to report anomalies. Sometimes referred to as *mass monitoring*, this citizen participation in perceiving risk and threats in their environment is viewed favorably by the current focus on governance and citizen engagement.

- *Emotional effect on people*—Qinglong County preserved its memories of the Tangshan earthquake through essays written by officials and citizens. Although the residents of Qinglong County were astonished by the earthquake's devastation, they were proud of their officials and their neighbors who took charge of prediction, mitigation, and preparedness. As they were already settled in their tents and had established schools and stores outdoors, they did not panic and were able to settle into response and recovery modes immediately.

- *Positive effects on societal norms and public trust*—In Qinglong County, there is widespread confidence that they can predict another earthquake. This confidence spills over into other areas, such as economic development. They do not feel immobilized, like many poor areas of developing countries. Local government officials are held in high esteem, and citizens continue to participate in lay monitoring for earthquakes.

Role of Best-Practices Case Studies in Emergency Management Analysis

Emergency management is overwhelmingly focused on negative incidents with negative consequences. Many case studies chronicle "what not to do." Analyses point to areas needing improvement, especially emergency management. It is rare to be able to research a case in which, at each decision point, officials and citizens and even children made correct decisions in the emerging context. Many case studies lead to one critical factor that, if handled correctly, would have avoided the incident or mitigated the incident's negative effects. In Qinglong County, there were several minor situations in which officials and citizens leaned in the wrong direction, as in trying to go back to their evacuated houses or businesses. County officials and neighbors patrolled their areas and maintained the evacuation. No detail was left uncovered.

Conclusion

The main lesson of Qinglong County and the Great Tangshan Earthquake is that it is possible to predict, prepare, and mitigate large disasters. The chronology shows no sloppy public administration and no one passing the buck. Every official and every citizen participated in the success. When a person was found dodging the evacuation, their neighbors intervened to correct their behavior. Furthermore, the case of Qinglong County is a ringing endorsement of citizen participation in civic society. Without the volunteers monitoring earthquake precursors there would have been no basis for making a decision. Without preparation and study, the officials would have been discouraged from making a prediction that was not directed from a higher level authority. Without citizens active in their communities, leaders would not have been able to enforce the evacuation, and without the success of Qinglong County it would have taken longer to get the first supplies of water, food, and medical care to the victims at the epicenter in Tangshan City.

Questions for Discussion

1. What is the role of local government in disaster preparedness and management?
2. How can citizens know about shared risks?
3. How can society integrate science, policy, and actions?
4. How do communities build institutions and procedures to mitigate risk and prepare for disaster events?

Practical Activities

1. Referring to Appendix 4A, identify five critical incidents that could have gone either way—success or failure—and analyze how the Qinglong County officials and citizens managed to avert disaster.
2. Map a local community's vulnerabilities and risks from natural disasters and other hazards.
3. Draft a sample emergency alert that is appropriate in scope and duration.

4. Co-create a sample disaster plan with an organization in your community (student–community activity).
 5. Review and report on the disaster plan of a local government in your area (check for personnel, finances, transportation, shelter-in-place, facilities, communications, relief supplies, mitigation strategies) or compare plans of various local governments.

Appendix 4A Events Analysis for Qinglong County and the 1976 Tangshan Earthquake: An Example of Best Practices in Public Administration

See Table 4A.1 beginning on next page.

Early Warning Success in Qinglong County, China ◼ 65

Table 4A.1 Events Analysis for Qinglong County

Public Administration Lessons	When	Who	What	Impact
Policy statements are essential.				
National earthquake (EQ) policy statement sets operational framework for later specific EQ disaster mitigation measures.	June 29, 1974	State Council, People's Republic of China	State Council orders Document No. 69 sent to seven municipalities and provinces: Beijing, Tianjin, Hebei, Shanxi, Inner Mongolia, Liaoning, and Shandong. Document No. 69 alerts public officials to the serious earthquake (EQ) situation; informs them of risk and advises region to prepare for EQs of magnitude greater than 6; magnitude 7 to 8 is also possible.	Document No. 69 alerts northeast China to the possibility of large earthquakes (EQs) within 2 years. Scientific information is shared openly with leading public administrators in the seven risk areas of North China and the Bohai Sea. EQ management offices are established, and top priority is placed on EQ preparedness. Cooperation between professional and lay detection teams is emphasized, and detection networks at regional, county, and village levels are set up and strengthened. Public education and EQ monitoring programs are intensified.
Counties intensify efforts in EQ preparedness: detection of precursors, public education, and review of infrastructure.	From 1974	Counties in the region affected by Document No. 69	EQ preparedness program is implemented, including monitoring, public education, and strengthening of structures. Lay monitoring in factories, mines, and schools is encouraged. EQ office for EQ preparedness activities is set up in most counties by 1976.	Public learns about EQs, the lay detection of precursors (anomalies in water level, color, temperature, chemistry, and quality; release of gases; animal behavior; weather changes), methods of preparing for disasters, and the need for heightened awareness.

(Continued)

Table 4A.1 (Continued) Events Analysis for Qinglong County

Public Administration Lessons	When	Who	What	Impact
Experience, interest, and responsibility spur top public administrators to strengthen scientific background.	From 1974	Ran Guangqi, Head of Chinese Communist Party (CCP) in Qinglong County	Alerted by Document No. 69 and recalling experience of the 1966 magnitude 7.3 Xingtai EQ, Ran Guangqi decides to learn about EQs from county's Science Committee's office and from textbook by Chinese geologist Li Siguang (J.S. Lee).	Through gradual self-training, the head of Qinglong County strengthens his disaster decision-making ability.
Energetic administrator increases county's EQ awareness and preparedness.	From November 1975	Wang Chunqing, a 21-year-old Qinglong County administrator	Wang Chunqing is placed in charge of Qinglong County's Science Committee's EQ disaster management program; he is appointed in June 1976 as head of the county's newly established EQ Office.	He increases the county's EQ monitoring stations/sites from 6 to 16 (9 of these lay monitoring sites are at schools). He intensifies public education by distributing thousands of copies of booklets and posters and presenting slide shows and movies in villages, towns, and cities, including a short EQ preparedness film before every cinema presentation (materials provided by the State Seismological Bureau [SSB]).
Delegation of authority creates conditions for greater efficiency.	Just before July 8, 1976	Wang Jinzhi, Head of Qinglong County's Science Committee, before leaving town for a meeting	Wang Jinzhi gives his deputy Zhang Hongjiu instruction to process urgent matters without waiting for his return.	County officials are able to take action quickly.

(Continued)

Early Warning Success in Qinglong County, China ◾ 67

Table 4A.1 (Continued) Events Analysis for Qinglong County

Public Administration Lessons	When	Who	What	Impact
Open channels allow for sharing information.	July 8	Wang Chunqing	Wang Chunqing attends Chengde District meeting on EQs.	Wang learns of the larger, regional meeting on EQs in Tangshan and proceeds there by July 14, 1976.
Administrators are trained to educate the public	July 14–19	State Seismological Bureau (SSB)	SSB holds regional conference in Tangshan City.	SSB trains administrators to educate the public on measures for EQ preparedness.
Conference organizers are quietly supportive of unplanned scientific presentation.	July 16 and 18	Wang Chengmin, head of the Beijing-Tianjin Section of the SSB's Analysis and Prediction Department	During Tangshan conference, Wang Chengmin holds two informal evening meetings (with only 2 hours' prior notice given) on intermediate- and short-term predictions of EQs.	He shows and discusses data regarding precursory signals, allowing participants to draw their own conclusions and to integrate these conclusions with past plus recent data and empirical trends.

(Continued)

Table 4A.1 (Continued) Events Analysis for Qinglong County

Public Administration Lessons	When	Who	What	Impact
Local administrators and scientists share EQ information, thus developing an interdisciplinary network of professionals who are knowledgeable about EQ preparedness and mitigation.	July 16	Wang Chunqing, administrator, attends scientist Wang Chengmin's presentation	Wang Chunqing takes detailed notes on presentation by Wang Chengmin.	Major points of presentation: (1) Many EQs of magnitude > 7 have occurred recently throughout the world. (2) Professional EQ monitoring teams and lay detection centers are reporting abnormal signals for the Beijing–Tianjin–Tangshan–Bohai–Zhangjiakou region that may relate to a possible EQ. (3) Analysis of scientific data acquired by seven major techniques, including stress and electrical measurements, indicate a good possibility that the region will be struck by a significant EQ. Data include the Sanhe monitoring team's prediction of an EQ of magnitude 5, between July 22 and August 5, 1976; the synthesis of data from field teams regarding dates, locations, and assessments of the situation; and comments on various EQs in northeast China and in Inner Mongolia: "From all the data and trends, we conclude that this area, within 1–2 years, may have a magnitude 8 EQ; the area should therefore actively prepare, widely circulate this EQ knowledge (especially to big factories and mines) and make plans and proper measures for EQ preparation."

(Continued)

Table 4A.1 (Continued) Events Analysis for Qinglong County

Public Administration Lessons	When	Who	What	Impact
Recent developments must be reported in a timely manner to county officials.	July 21	Wang Chunqing	Upon his return to Qinglong County, Wang Chunqing reports immediately to Zhang Hongjiu, Deputy Head of Science Committee, on EQ situation.	Zhang Hongjiu takes information very seriously and recommends county-wide preparations and education.
Senior officials recognize the significance of information reported by the junior official; leadership awareness of EQ risk increases.	July 21	Wang Chunqing and Zhang Hongjiu	Wang Chunqing and Zhang Hongjiu report to Yu Shen, the County's Associate Director in charge of supervising the County's Science Committee.	They tell Yu Shen of the danger of impending disasters (predicted EQ and possible flooding). Yu Shen recommends they make an appointment to report to leadership as soon as possible; he instructs Wang Chunqing to contact Ma Gang, county office administrator, to arrange an appointment with Ran Guangqi, Head of CCP in Qinglong County.
Science and administrative tasks are coordinated and integrated.	July 21–24	Wang Chunqing	Wang Chunqing participates in alerting top county administrators of EQ situation, while also contacting the county's 16 lay monitoring sites to obtain their latest readings. All 16 sites are linked by telephone to the county's EQ Office.	Wang Chunqing meets with Ma Gang on July 22. Ma Gang recognizes the significance of the EQ situation and the urgency of notifying County Head Ran Guangqi. He contacts lay monitoring sites for record updates to assess the immediate EQ situation in the county. Unusual changes are noted at four sites. Lay monitoring findings are integrated into report to county leadership.

(Continued)

Table 4A.1 (Continued) Events Analysis for Qinglong County

Public Administration Lessons	When	Who	What	Impact
Topmost official takes report seriously; priorities with regard to the EQ risk are crystallized.	July 23	Ran Guangqi, head of CCP in Qinglong County	Ran Guangqi says that the report should be made not only to him, but also to the entire CCP Standing Committee of Qinglong County.	Ran Guangqi calls a special meeting of the CCP Standing Committee to be held at 8:30 p.m. on July 24 to hear Wang Chunqing report on the EQ situation (even though the CCP and government leaders were busy preparing for a major agricultural conference).
Communication and information mechanisms aid mutual activities; information flows vertically and horizontally into EQ Office; protocols are set for rapid communication. Past and current EQ and flood data are integrated for decision-making.	July 24	Zhang Pingyi, Yu Shen, Chen Yongfu, Ma Gang, and Sun You	At the CCP Standing Committee meeting, there is a difference of opinion concerning the appropriate response to the EQ situation, the possibility of creating panic and loss of credibility, and the degree of popular knowledge and/or presence of superstitions about EQs. Ran Guangqi (absent at another meeting but kept fully informed) and Yu Shen, both of whom hold important posts, assert the wisdom of community preparation in view of Document No. 69 and information from Tangshan Conference.	An action plan is developed as follows: (1) Strengthen leadership at all levels. (2) Establish EQ Command Office, with Ran Guangqi as Head, Yu Shen as Executive Head, and Wang Chunqing as Associate Head. Keep it staffed for 24-hour communication. It is located for now in the Science Committee's office area. (3) Strengthen monitoring stations by assigning people to special 24-hour duty and by scheduling daily reports to EQ Office. (4) Place EQ equipment in air-raid-resistant structures (built for air defense concerns at the time). (5) Promote education on EQ detection and preparation.

(Continued)

Table 4A.1 (Continued) Events Analysis for Qinglong County

Public Administration Lessons	When	Who	What	Impact
Attention focused on EQ strengthens the power of officials to act without delay or top official approval. Senior officials take reports by junior officials seriously.	July 24	Zhang Pingyi, Yu Shen, Chen Yongfu, Ma Gang, and Sun You	Wang Chunqing reports on EQ situation and notes strong possibility of a magnitude 5 EQ between July 22 and August 5 in Beijing–Tianjin–Tangshan–Bohai–Zhangjiakou area. A magnitude 8 EQ is likely from the second half of 1976 to the beginning of the following year. Of the county's 16 monitoring stations, 6 have monitoring equipment installed.	(6) Instruct EQ Office to write up EQ preparation measures for county officials and the general public. Disseminate information county-wide by telephone and by public address system. (7) Emphasize that there may soon be an EQ, and that its effects can be mitigated. Give special attention to auditoriums, cinemas, and theaters. Strengthen safety measures at schools. (8) Instruct officials, civil workers, and citizens to be on alert. (Key officials go without sleep for 3 days.)
County alerts government officials at town and village levels.	July 24	Ran Guangqi, Head of Qinglong County CCP	Immediately after meeting, Ran Guangqi notifies by telephone leaders of all 43 towns in Qinglong County of possible disaster. (Note that the county was composed of towns and surrounding villages, known respectively as communes and brigades in 1976.)	Ran Guangqi discusses and arranges preparations for EQ (and flooding); he likens the urgent disaster situation to that of a fire alarm and emphasizes that every official is responsible for preparing people in their areas and that they are accountable for their actions or inaction.

(Continued)

Table 4A.1 (Continued) Events Analysis for Qinglong County

Public Administration Lessons	When	Who	What	Impact
Communication channel between counties are utilized; communication network is activated.	From July 24 onward	Wang Chunqing	Wang Chunqing contacts surrounding counties.	Wang Chunqing requests information on any anomalies recorded in neighboring counties, in accordance with periodic practice.
Public EQ announcement prepared for county-wide dissemination in anticipation of EQ risk.	Through night of July 24 and during day of July 25	Wang Chunqing and staff	Wang Chunqing and staff work 24 hours nonstop on providing detailed instructions to county officials and the general public on the EQ situation and preparation measures.	County-wide information network is activated; public is informed of EQ risk and of potential losses. Preparation measures include the following: (1) Broadcast lectures on EQs. (2) Alert EQ monitoring stations to pay particular attention, with overnight watch duty, between July 22 and August 5, 1976. (3) Assign officers to EQ preparation work on county, district, town, and village levels. (4) Inform by telephone the 22 factories, mines, schools, post offices, reservoirs, cinemas, auditoriums, etc., to prepare for a possible EQ.

(Continued)

Early Warning Success in Qinglong County, China ■ 73

Table 4A.1 (Continued) Events Analysis for Qinglong County

Public Administration Lessons	When	Who	What	Impact
County officials show flexibility by using an already-planned conference on another topic as the occasion to publicize the urgent EQ situation, demonstrating adoption of adaptive organizational behavior.	July 25 (morning)	Wang Jinzhi	County leadership has Wang Jinzhi report on EQ situation at county-level agricultural meeting of more than 800 county and town officials representing 43 towns, each composed of a cluster of contiguous villages (total of 404 organized villages, and 27,000 native places where government supervision is less).	At the agricultural meeting, a decision is made to send two officials (one county level and one local community level) to each town, with the following instructions: (1) Everyone must be informed by the end of July 26! (2) Officials must travel straight to their offices and go right to work, without stopping at home or for personal business (anyone negligent will be held accountable). (3) Immediately begin EQ and flood preparations and public education campaign. (4) Establish an EQ command office in each town and each village to transmit information throughout neighboring towns and city. (5) Set up 24-hour communications (e.g., reports, patrols) with nearby counties to share every detail of trends in surrounding areas. (6) Use various means to educate the people: broadcasting, workshops, blackboards, night schools, neighbors telephone calls to village offices, informing neighbors. (7) Keep windows and doors open; neither cook nor eat inside; where feasible, stay in sheds in the fields.

(Continued)

Table 4A.1 (Continued) Events Analysis for Qinglong County

Public Administration Lessons	When	Who	What	Impact
County Government alerts entire population.	July 25 (evening)	Broadcast Bureau	Broadcast Bureau begins broadcasting EQ information three times a day using a public announcement system that reaches all rural, residential, and business areas in the county.	The population is alerted to the most recent EQ situation, on the dangers of EQs, and how to make themselves safer before, during, and after an EQ.
A shared perception of emergency develops.	From July 25	Towns and villages	Emergency meetings are held at town and village levels.	Ability to spread the word is enhanced through this community-based network.
Leading public administrator sets example.	From July 25	Ran Guangqi, Head of Qinglong County	Ran Guangqi takes up residence in a makeshift tent made of poles and a plastic sheet.	Ran Guangqi encourages all county officials and residents to heed warnings to stay away from buildings.
Officials do not rest during the emergency preparations, working day and night; they intensify the investment of resources in preparedness.	July 24–27	Secretary of Dazhangzi Town (also a member of Qinglong County's CCP Standing Committee)	Secretary personally participates in town's EQ preparation activities; remains at town reservoir for 7 days and does not sleep for 3 days, eating only rice with salt.	Secretary instructs villages to set up own EQ offices with 24-hour monitoring. Pre-EQ conditions are hot weather, rains, and high humidity. There is an awareness of the 1975 magnitude 7.3 Haicheng EQ. Emergency broadcast on night of July 27 requests village officials to examine all buildings; every home is to have one person on watch (in shifts) throughout the night.

(Continued)

Table 4A.1 (Continued) Events Analysis for Qinglong County

Public Administration Lessons	When	Who	What	Impact
Top official integrates past and current information, goes to public to assess EQ preparations.	From July 25	Zhang Pingyi, Associate Head of CCP in Qinglong County	Zhang Pingyi visits 23 towns to examine EQ preparations.	Zhang Pingyi puts an emphasis on EQ preparation, because he remembers in a previous provincial meeting a discussion about disasters caused by EQs in Japan.
Officials work day and night, engaged in preparedness efforts.	From July 25	County engineer	County engineer sleeps outside for a month, maintaining a 24-hour watch before, during, and after the EQ main shock and aftershocks.	County engineer stays on alert to shut off power as soon as an EQ occurs; equipment is guarded 24 hours a day.
Village 1. Xia Dahudian				
Public behavior changes in response to reliable EQ risk data (scientific data from county level seen within context of earlier observations at grass-roots level).	From July 25	Village CCP and civil defense members are most responsible for carrying out EQ preparations. Xia Dahudian Village of Qinglong County is 90 km from Tangshan.	Broadcast EQ situation through loudspeakers at every home, factory, harvest field, and street corner. Alert people to build sheds in fields, move from homes into sheds, and avoid structures, including walls and power lines. Carry elderly out to sheds. By evening of July 26, everyone is relocated to sheds.	Most villagers believe EQ broadcasts because they are based on data from scientists. EQ warning corroborates lay monitoring evidence from two local sites. Strange animal behavior and changes in water level, color, chemistry, and gas release are observed. Since July 20, villagers had seen domestic animals behaving very strangely: pigs ran in circles and would not stay in pens; chickens refused to stay in their coops; yellow weasels left their hiding places and ran around unafraid of the villagers.

(Continued)

Early Warning Success in Qinglong County, China ■ 75

Table 4A.1 (Continued) Events Analysis for Qinglong County

Public Administration Lessons	When	Who	What	Impact
Villagers see county prediction as providing a framework for understanding already perceived sense-data.	From July 25	Village CCP and civil defense members are most responsible for carrying out EQ preparations. Xia Dahudian Village of Qinglong County is 90 km from Tangshan.		Village patrols (twice daily) are set up to prevent people from sneaking back into their houses (able-bodied people are fined if caught inside houses). Villagers learn techniques to detect EQs (e.g., balance an overturned, empty glass bottle in a metal wash basin so it will make a sound when it tips over in an EQ.
Village 2. Xia Baoyuhuai				
Grass roots response to reports by county officials occurs. Every family is taught to take responsibility for themselves.	From July 25	Village CCP and civil defense members are most responsible for carrying out EQ preparations. Xia Baoyuhuai Village of Qinglong County is 75 km from Tangshan.	Emergency meeting of leading officials and heads of production teams is held. Mass meetings of more than 300 people are held to inform villagers of possible EQ and of preparatory strategies. Sheds are built to provide shelter for people leaving their homes. By late July 26, everyone is out of their homes and buildings. Watch for precursors is intensified.	Chickens are flying high, and pigs are running into walls; well water is muddy and colder than normal on July 26 and 27; warm spring nearby used for washing clothes is usually 40°C but becomes colder 4 to 5 days before EQ; weather has been extremely hot and humid. Elementary school students put bottles upside down to detect earth shaking. Family members take shifts to stand guard and not sleep; families are instructed to take responsibility for their own survival and safety.

(Continued)

Table 4A.1 (Continued) Events Analysis for Qinglong County

Public Administration Lessons	When	Who	What	Impact
Village 3. Wen Quan				
Delegation and division of labor take place; diligence is maintained.	From July 25	Village CCP and civil defense members are most responsible for carrying out EQ preparations. Wen Quan Village of Qinglong County is 70 km from Tangshan.	Tasks are divided into building sheds, making sure people leave their buildings, and providing public education.	Tents and sheds from locally available materials are built. Large numbers of yellow weasels, nocturnal animals that normally hide and are afraid of people, are observed. Until the county EQ announcement, villagers had not realized the significance of this observation and other strange animal behavior seen 10 to 20 days before EQ.
EQ alert is intensified.	July 25–26	Town officials	Information is broadcast widely and to all levels to intensify EQ monitoring and preparations.	There is a heightened awareness that EQ could happen any day now due to the widespread dissemination of information on precursors.
Lay public in Qinglong City and throughout the county are educated with regard to the EQ.	July 27	Wang Jinzhi, Head of County Science Committee	At the request of county leadership, Wang Jinzhi gives a special talk on EQ situation and mitigation measures to more than 800 officials attending the agricultural meeting.	Attendees are informed of the EQ situation, advised to keep doors and windows open, and instructed as to how to get out and away from buildings should an EQ strike.

(Continued)

Table 4A.1 (Continued) Events Analysis for Qinglong County

Public Administration Lessons	When	Who	What	Impact
Schoolchildren participate in EQ science and public administration preparedness. Students are a major resource in preparedness activities.	July 24–27	Local middle school in Qinglong City has three teachers and a small group of students monitoring the situation. This monitoring site, one of nine in the county, was set up in December 1975.	The teachers and students collect data from local residents and record precursors; they note changes observed in the water and that normally nocturnal yellow weasels are running around in large numbers in broad daylight (especially large increase noted on July 27).	Symposium planned for July 28 is moved to earlier date of July 27 at the demand of the students who observed the large increase in yellow weasels running around in daylight. By the evening of July 27, school buildings are declared off-limits to everyone; students are not allowed to be inside the buildings.
Information is informally transmitted across county boundaries.	July 27	Dong Wu, physician in Qinglong County	Dong Wu goes to Tangshan and stays with relatives.	Dong Wu informs his relatives that Qinglong County is prepared for an EQ and warns them to prepare also; they listen in disbelief and tell him not to tell others to avoid panic. He puts his clothes by his bedside so he can leave the house quickly should the EQ begin. Relatives accept his advice to leave their doors and windows open, sleep lightly, and stand an empty bottle upside down on the edge of a table.

(Continued)

Table 4A.1 (Continued) Events Analysis for Qinglong County

Public Administration Lessons	When	Who	What	Impact
EQ warning data and actual experiences are reported by witnesses.	July 28 (just before EQ)	Residents of Qinglong County	Precursors immediately before EQ are observed.	Eye witnesses from villages of Xia Dahudian and Xia Baoyuhuai report: "Sky brightens momentarily with white light in direction of Tangshan City; ominous rumbling heard; ground vibrations begin." Dong Wu in Tangshan sees a flash of white light and hears the sound of ominous rumbling.
Lack of communication between public administrators and scientists leads to an unprepared public; great human suffering results. There is a generalized breakdown of the socio-technical connection.	July 28 at 3:42 a.m.	Magnitude 7.8 Tangshan EQ	The Great Tangshan EQ (GTE) occurs with an epicenter intensity of XI on the New Chinese Seismic Intensity Scale in the area with maximum damage. Trees lining the EQ fault surface rupture are burned on the side closest to the fault.	Over 240,000 people die, almost one quarter of Tangshan's population of 1 million, and 600,000 are seriously injured. At least 7000 families are completely obliterated, 10,000 Tangshan residents lose their spouses, 2652 children become orphans, and 3800 residents become handicapped by their injuries. The hypocenter was directly under the city of Tangshan at a depth of 11 km. People were fast asleep when the EQ struck. Lightning flashed across the sky and the earth rumbled seconds before the earth began to shake. In a matter of seconds an industrial city of a million people was reduced to rubble. This catastrophe not only shook China but also stunned the world.

(Continued)

Early Warning Success in Qinglong County, China ■ 79

Table 4A.1 (Continued) Events Analysis for Qinglong County

Public Administration Lessons	When	Who	What	Impact
Knowledge and preparation reduce loss of life; officials can empower the public to save their own lives.	July 28, 3:42 a.m.	Qinglong County	County residents are aware of the imminent danger and are prepared by the time GTE strikes. Qinglong County is located 115 km from Tangshan.	Only 1 death occurs, and that was due to a heart condition. Animals are safe. County sustains maximum damage of intensity VIII. Residents at Wen Quan Village hear and experience the destructive power of the EQ as large sections of the historic 1000-year-old Great Wall split and crash down from nearby hilltops. At least 7000 buildings collapse totally, and 180,000 buildings are damaged. At the county middle school, the roof shifts and walls collapse, but there is no loss of life. Some residents want to return to their homes to escape the heavy rains, but civil defense personnel insist on them staying in tents during the aftershock period.
Relevant knowledge aids mitigation of disasters.	July 28, 3:42 a.m.	Agricultural meeting in Qinglong City	More than 800 meeting attendees are able to exit the urban building complex, avoiding serious injury	One attendee misses the lecture on EQ safety held at county headquarters on the evening of July 27 and hence does not leave the building in the safest manner; he is cut by broken glass.

(Continued)

Early Warning Success in Qinglong County, China ■ 81

Table 4A.1 (Continued) Events Analysis for Qinglong County

Public Administration Lessons	When	Who	What	Impact
Survivors of disasters can play a significant role as rescuers.	July 28, 3:42 a.m.	Dong Wu	Dong Wu wakes relatives at the first rumbling and lifts two relatives out of their home through an open window before the building collapses.	Dong Wu saves himself and his relative's entire family. He drives 180 km to find a functioning hospital for an injured relative and stays to help the injured for 4 days. Qinglong County officials who had sent Dong Wu to Tangshan on medical business dispatches personnel to search for him. They find him on the 7th day and return him home to his much-relieved family in Qinglong.
Well-prepared local survivors can be the first to assist during a disaster.	July 28	Qinglong County	A rescue effort is immediately organized; within 5 hours after the EQ hit, medical teams are sent to the disaster zone.	In total, three rescue teams are sent. Injured residents are taken to county hospitals. Supplies, water, and food are sent to Tangshan and production is maintained.
EQs continue to wreak havoc after main shock; it is essential to maintain close cooperation and collaborative action among	July 28 onward, for 6 months	Aftershocks	Large aftershocks (magnitude 6.2 and 7.1) occur on July 28; many significant EQs occur for months after the main shock. Aftershocks define the EQ rupture zone; the region of damage is centered on Tangshan and stretches radially for 200 km. Heavy rains follow the main shock.	Magnitude 7.1 aftershock destroys almost all buildings left standing after the main shock. Survivors rebuild four times, with efforts often destroyed by aftershocks, which cause many more deaths and injuries. Heavy rains impede rescue efforts, adding to the death toll. As many as 400,000 are continuing to live outdoors. Careful questioning of the

(Continued)

Table 4A.1 (Continued) Events Analysis for Qinglong County

Public Administration Lessons	When	Who	What	Impact
public administrators, scientists, and the public to minimize loss of life and damages.				lay public by teams of scientists after the main shock provides invaluable data on EQ precursors, enabling rescuers to organize their efforts around the aftershocks. In the village of Yangguanlin, the observations of children later led scientists to predict the Ninghe magnitude 6.9 aftershock.
From the EQ ashes, a new city arises; public administrators, scientists, and the public continue to learn from GTE, a crisis that provides an opportunity for learning.	From 1976 to 1986	Recovery	Rebuilding begins in the damaged region almost immediately. New building codes protect to EQ intensity level VIII. Historic sites are designated to educate officials, scientists, and the public on EQs. A monument and museum are built by Tangshan City in memory of the GTE victims.	Some schools open and conduct classes in the streets after a month; some factories begin production within 2 weeks. One million sheds provide housing for survivors for 6 months after the EQ. After 7 years, people return to normal housing. After 10 years, all buildings are reconstructed except for seven historical sites that are preserved as examples of the destructive power of EQs.

Appendix 4B State Council Document No. 69, People's Republic of China June 29, 1974

State Council Endorses Chinese Academy of Sciences' Report on the Earthquake Situation in North China and the Bohai Sea Area

To the leading Public Administrators of Beijing, Tianjin, the provinces of Hebei, Shanxi, Shandong, and Liaoning, and the autonomous region of Inner Mongolia:

> Please pay close attention to the information and implement the recommendations in the attached Chinese Academy of Sciences Report on the Earthquake Situation in North China and the Bohai Sea Area. EQ work is an important mission that concerns the preservation of lives and property. We look to you to build and strengthen EQ management offices by implementing the national policy; that is, place top priority on EQ preparedness, integrate the efforts of professionals and the lay public, and combine Chinese and Western methods. Intensify EQ preparedness and mitigation efforts by mobilizing professional teams and organizing lay public monitoring and preparation. At present, the science and technologies to monitor and predict EQs are still in their early stages. Therefore, the large EQs forecasted in this report for this year and the next year are estimates only; they may or may not occur. However, we should operate on the assumption that there will be a large EQ and should therefore make preparations. At the same time, you must minimize the potential for public panic and social disarray that this alert may cause.

Report on the Earthquake Situation in North China and the Bohai Sea Area, Chinese Academy of Sciences, June 15, 1974

From June 7 to June 9, 1974, the State Seismological Bureau (SSB) held a conference on the EQ situation in the North China and Bohai Sea area. Representatives came from 20 units of EQ disaster management and research institutions of Beijing, Tianjin, Hebei, Shanxi, Inner Mongolia, Shandong, and Liaoning. The conference analyzed the EQ situation of the aforementioned areas. The majority opinion is that, within this year or the next year, EQs of magnitude 5 to 6 may occur in the Beijing–Tianjin area; north part of the Bohai Sea; Handan and Anyang in the border area between Shanxi, Hebei, and Henan; the Linfen Basin in Shanxi; the Linyi area in Shandong; and the central part of the Yellow Sea. EQs of around magnitude 5 may occur in Inner Mongolia in the area around Baotou and Wuyuan. The principle evidence for the previous condition is as follows:

Beijing–Tianjin area
- Recent frequent occurrences of small EQs
- Abnormal readings of crustal deformation
- Anomalous gravity measurements
- Unusual changes in radon content in groundwater

Northern Bohai Sea area
- Changes in water level in Jinxian County, which have been gradual over the past few years, at a rate of 0.11 mm/yr; however, the cumulative change in water level has already reached 2.5 mm (in 9 months)
- Geomagnetic anomaly of 22 gamma recorded in the Dalian area

- Six tide-monitoring stations in the northern Bohai Sea all reporting increases of 10 to 20 cm in sea level in 1973, a phenomenon that has not been seen for the past 10 to 20 years
- Marked increase in microseismicity

Linfen Basin in southern Shanxi
- Anomalies in seismic velocity in recent years in Shanxi, Henan, Hebei border area, and central part of the Yellow Sea
- Increase in microseismicity

Linyi area in southern Shandong
- Emergence of a pattern of high seismicity in the area peripheral to Linyi over the past few years, a pattern similar to the one that formed before the historic 1668 magnitude 8.5 EQ in the same area

In addition, based on the historical pattern of major EQ activity, the study of regional seismicity, the influence of the Western Pacific seismic belt, and those EQs with focal depths of 400 to 500 km in North China, some colleagues believe that North China has accumulated enough seismic energy for an EQ of magnitude 7 to 8. Furthermore, prolonged drought in the northern part of North China and abnormal meteorological conditions rarely seen since 1949—a warm winter, a cold spring, and imbalance in humidity during the past year—indicate the possibility of a major EQ of around magnitude 7 in North China.

In contrast, some colleagues have observed an increase in the Earth's rate of rotation over the last year, which from past experience indicates that large EQs are unlikely. An additional observation is that there is usually a long time period between large EQs in this region. They therefore believe that no EQ greater than magnitude 5.5 will occur in North China in the next few years.

Learning from the lessons of the successive devastating EQs in Liyang County in Jiangsu Province and Zhaotong County in Yunnan Province, the conference participants recommend that we should operate on the assumption that there will be a large EQ despite the inconclusive analysis. Therefore, we should heighten our alertness and prepare for the sudden strike of an EQ of magnitude greater than 6.

Our recommendations for strengthening EQ work in the risk areas are as follows:

1. *Strengthen leadership in EQ work.* Appoint at least one public official in each of the seven risk areas (Beijing, Tianjin, etc.) to take charge. Strengthen existing seismological bureau and EQ offices in Beijing, Tianjin, Hebei, Inner Mongolia, and Liaoning. In Shanxi and Shandong, where there are no established EQ offices or lay monitoring stations, such facilities should be set up immediately. Initiate EQ preparedness work at all regional and county levels and integrate the management of professional and amateur (lay public) monitoring teams.
2. *Develop lay public monitoring and preparation networks and mobilize the public in earnest.* In the seven risk areas, there are currently about 5000 people who participate in amateur monitoring teams, which is still inadequate. Experience has shown that in areas where good lay monitoring and preparation are implemented, it is possible to detect imminent precursors, thereby mitigating losses. Factories and major mining enterprises should take steps to organize amateur monitoring teams and to train volunteers. Villages should establish public education and monitoring programs and make effective use of meteorological stations, schools, and amateur science groups. At the same time, avoid panic by preparing the public psychologically for potential calamity.

3. *Professional teams should investigate fully all the areas in which anomalies have occurred, provide comprehensive analysis, and continue to monitor the EQ situation.* Raise the level of EQ prediction and strive for timely early warning. Ensure normal functioning of the 109 professional monitoring centers in the risk areas. New centers should be considered if necessary. Professionals should also work with the public and draw from their valuable experiences and consider development of lay monitoring and preparing a personal goal.
4. *Establish two regional groups.* One group—Beijing, Tianjin, Tangshan, and Zhangjiakou, headed by the SSB—should include EQ offices in Beijing, Tianjin, and Hebei; the Geophysics Institute; the Seismic Geology Group; and the Seismic Measurement Team. The second, the Bohai Group, should be comprised of the Liaoning, Tianjin, and Shandong EQ offices, headed by the Liaoning office. These two groups should cooperate closely and share all monitoring data in a timely manner.

Appendix 4C Qinglong County Administrators Issue Early Warning Four Days before Earthquake

Meeting of the Chinese Communist Party (CCP) Committee of Qinglong County

Attending members:	Zhang Pingyi, Yu Shen, Chen Yongfu, and Ma Gang
Other attendee(s):	Sun You
Chairperson:	Zhang Pingyi
Meeting date and time:	July 24, 1976, 20:30 (8:30 p.m.)
Minutes by:	Chai Wanhui
Meeting place:	Conference room at the County Committee
Meeting notes:	Wang Chunqing, of the Science Committee, reported on the main points of the earthquake conference:

- There may be, from July 22 to August 5, a magnitude 5 earthquake in the region of Beijing, Tianjin, Tangshan, Bohai, and Zhangjiakou, and from the second half of this year to the beginning of next year a magnitude 8 to 9 earthquake may occur.
- Our county has a total of 16 monitoring sites, of which 6 are equipped with instruments.
- The EQ office should write up information on earthquakes and send it to the broadcasting station for dissemination. The office should emphasize that there may soon be an earthquake, and that its effects can be mitigated.

Pay attention to the following tasks:

- Auditoriums, movie theaters, and other gathering places should receive special attention.
- Instruct each monitoring station to report relevant observations in a timely manner; personnel on duty must be on alert. Pay attention to safety measures at schools.
- Assign people to special duty at the monitoring sites for this period of time; the county EQ office should receive daily reports from these sites.
    1. Strengthen leadership at all levels to complete the tasks ahead.
    2. Promote dissemination of information and education on earthquakes.
    3. Strengthen work at the monitoring sites and improve timely communication.

- Place earthquake equipment in suitable air-raid-resistant shelters.
- Maintain EQ office location for now in the previous office space of the Science Committee. Reestablish telephone communications, with overnight duty personnel.

The early-warning document was sent out on July 24, 1976, by Qinglong County Public Administrators (http://www.globalwatch.org/ungp/). During a countywide telephone conference on the same day, County Secretary Guangqi Ran discussed earthquake and flood preparations.

Appendix 4D Activism Matrix: Public Administrators, Scientists, and Citizens Mitigate Natural Disasters

When public administrators, scientists, and citizens share perspectives with each other, they establish a basis for taking joint action and creating action networks throughout their communities. Intensified action enhances not only self-reliance, well-being, and orientation to the future but also community survival and development. See Table 4D.1, beginning next page.

References

Anon. (2003). Natural disasters cost China 100 billion a year. *China Daily*, October 8.

Birkland, T.A. (2006). *Lessons of Disasters: Policy Change after Catastrophic Events*. Washington, DC: Georgetown University Press.

Col, J.M. (2007). Successful earthquake mitigation in Qinglong County during the Great Tangshan Earthquake. *Chin. Public Admin. Rev.*, 4(1/2): 114–123.

Col, J.M. and Chu, J.J. (1999). Integrating public administration, science and community action: a case of early-warning success in Qinglong County for the magnitude 7.8 Tangshan earthquake. In Farazmand, A., Ed., *Handbook of Crisis and Emergency Management*, pp. 581–616. New York: Marcel Dekker.

Comfort, L.K. (1999). *Shared Risk: Complex Systems in Seismic Response*. New York: Pergamon Press.

Li, J.F. (1991). *Social Responses to the Tangshan Earthquake*, Preliminary Paper No. 165. Newark: University of Delaware Disaster Research Center (http://udspace.udel.edu/handle/19716/537).

Schneider, A. and Ingram, H. (1993). Social construction of target populations: implications for politics and policy. *Am. Polit. Sci. Rev.*, 87(2): 334–347.

Schneider, S.K. (1995). *Flirting with Disaster: Public Management in Crisis Situations*. Armonk, NY: M.E. Sharpe.

Table 4D.1 Activism Matrix

Attitude/Consequent Level of Participation	Citizens	Public Administrators	Scientists	Natural Disaster Outcomes
Unaware/little or no participation	"It will not happen here and not to me, my family, or my community." Citizens ignore disaster warnings or they panic.	Doing just enough work to hold the job; too busy with immediate daily priorities to consider the likelihood of natural disasters	Studying phenomena without considering their possible relationship to natural disasters and people	Total tragedy
Educated/moderate level of participation	"It might happen, but if it does then someone else will take care of the necessary preparations and relief."	Gathering and cataloging of information; developing natural disaster management plans; gathering statistics on the community, its vulnerabilities, and its disaster relief needs; lack of standards for evaluating accuracy of predictions and who can take responsibility for deciding accuracy or usefulness of predictions	Scientists noticing and recording correlation between natural phenomena and disasters, producing predictions with a degree of probability, but administrators and the public usually demand absolute accuracy	Tragedy; massive relief efforts; major impact on social and economic development

(Continued)

Table 4D.1 (Continued)   Activism Matrix

Attitude/Consequent Level of Participation	Citizens	Public Administrators	Scientists	Natural Disaster Outcomes
Aware and alert/high level of participation	Citizens accept the possibility of natural disaster occurrences. They educate themselves; prepare community-based plans; organize regular drills; circulate posters, pamphlets, school materials, videos, etc.; and participate in lay monitoring of disaster precursors. Schoolchildren participate in monitoring as part of science curriculum and community work. Citizens become aware of the immediate natural environment and its subtle shifts.	Organizing practice drills; establishing real-time information sharing; promoting disaster-related public education; involving mass media in dissemination of disaster-related information; reaching out to community groups, private sector NGOs, etc., for integrated public education, disaster preparedness, and response; developing an understanding of some basic dynamics of the Earth	Scientists sharing precursor signals with scientists of other disciplines, lay persons, and especially public administrators who can translate scientific observations into programs and actions likely to protect communities from natural disasters; scientists sharing their observations in ways that are comprehensible to administrators and the public	Early warning success; evacuations of communities where necessary; lives and property safeguarded; deaths and relief costs minimized; more resources still available for sustainable human development

Chapter 5

Emergency Management for Radiological Events: Lessons Learned from Three Mile Island, Chernobyl, and Fukushima Reactor Accidents

Frances L. Edwards

Contents

Chapter Goals	90
Introduction: Ubiquitous Radiological Materials	90
Existing Radiological Hazards to Communities	90
Accidental Exposure in Brazil	92
Nuclear Power	92
Nuclear Power Plants	92
Characteristics of Three Mile Island, Chernobyl, and Fukushima Compared	93
Emergency Planning for Radiological Events	95
Lessons Learned about Public Information	95
Medical Information and Misinformation	95
Chernobyl Medical Data	96
Three Mile Island Communication Failure	96
Chernobyl Communication Failure	97
Media Role	97
Lessons Learned about First-Responder Protection	98
Lessons Learned about Victim Care	99
Lessons Learned about Community Protection and Evacuation	100

Direct Site Remediation in Chernobyl 100
  Evacuation 100
 Lessons Learned about Psychological Impacts 101
Conclusion 102
Questions for Discussion 103
Additional Reading 103
References 103

Chapter Goals

After studying this chapter, readers should be able to

1. Understand the risks from radiological sources and the means of protection.
2. Recognize the different causes and effects of the accidents at the Three Mile Island, Chernobyl, and Fukushima nuclear plants.
3. Understand the medical consequences of a radiological event.
4. Understand the psychological consequences of a radiological event.
5. Know the key elements of a community emergency management plan for a radiological event.

Introduction: Ubiquitous Radiological Materials

Radiological materials are present in communities in many forms (see Table 5.1). Smoke detectors use americium-241, which emits alpha radiation (Health Physics Society, 2010). Tritium, a radioactive isotope of hydrogen, creates a steady supply of light for compasses, watch dials, and emergency exit signs. Ceramic mugs, compact fluorescent light bulbs, orange pottery, green depression glass, and potassium-containing foods such as bananas, oranges, and salt substitutes all emit low levels of radiation. Radon is a naturally occurring gas that decays into isotopes of lead and bismuth that emit beta radiation (Health Physics Society, 2010, 2012). Radiological materials may be just one of many hazardous materials found in a particular area. For example, Irvine, California, has over 1000 sites that store and use reportable quantities of various hazardous materials (Orange County Fire Authority, 2015); the city has a research reactor and several locations that store, ship, or use medical isotopes (e.g., for patient diagnosis, treatment with nuclear medicine). Medical tests and treatment represent 48% of human exposure to radiation (Health Physics Society, 2012). The University of California, Irvine, is also a receiving site for the potential evacuation of the southern portion of Orange County in the event of an accident at the San Onofre Nuclear Generating Station, adjacent to the Camp Pendleton Marine Corps Base. (Note that the San Onofre Nuclear Generating Station is currently being decommissioned.) For any hazardous material, it is important for the community in which it is located, or on which it may have an impact, to have a plan for dealing with an accidental release of or exposure to radiological materials.

Existing Radiological Hazards to Communities

Although many nuclear weapons have been decommissioned internationally and the Federal Emergency Management Agency (FEMA) no longer mandates specific community-level planning for nuclear war, communities must still prepare for the possibility of both accidents and the hostile

Table 5.1 Types of Radiation

Radiation Types	Examples	Characteristics	Protection
Alpha (ejected helium nucleus)	Radium, radon, uranium, thorium	Cannot penetrate skin but harmful if swallowed or inhaled	Inhalation protection; any skin barrier, including a sheet of paper or clothing
Beta (ejected electron)	Strontium-90, carbon-14, tritium, sulfur-35	Can penetrate a few layers of skin, can cause skin damage if allowed to remain on skin, harmful if swallowed or inhaled	Inhalation protection, clothing
Gamma and x-rays (highly penetrating electromagnetic)	Iodine-131, cesium-137, cobalt-60, radium-226	Penetrating radiation that can go through clothing, skin, and most materials	Dense materials such as lead and thick concrete

Source: Health Physics Society, *What Types of Radiation Are There?*, Fact Sheet, Health Physics Society, McLean, VA, 2011 (http://hps.org/publicinformation/ate/faqs/radiationtypes.html).

use of radiological materials and other chemical, biological, radiological, nuclear, or explosive (CBRNE) devices (FEMA, 2010). The location and management of Russian nuclear stockpiles continue to be a concern of counterterrorism programs (Zimmerman and Lewis, 2006), although experts do not believe that "suitcase nukes" (easily portable small nuclear bombs) actually persist as a threat (Vergano, 2007), as collecting the individuals and skills necessary to create a nuclear bomb would be a challenge (Goodrich, 2005), but fissile materials are part of a global supply chain that might be subject to a security breach. As Zimmerman and Lewis (2006, p. 8) stated, "Fissile material, including nuclear explosive material, is an item of commerce and moves from place to place. One of the side effects of our globalized economy is that opportunities for direct theft and bribing of nuclear custodians abound."

A more likely radiological scenario is the use of a "dirty bomb." This is a device that uses low-level radiological material found in the community as part of a conventional homemade bomb, or an improvised explosive device. Although the bomb would contaminate an area with radioactive dust, the addition of radiological material would not add to the number of deaths caused by the explosion. "Nonetheless, the area could be sealed off for months of decontamination, and hundreds of thousands of people could be expected to show up at hospitals for screening. Dozens of buildings might be razed because of the difficulty of decontaminating them" (Richter, 2002). Such devices would "exploit fears of radioactivity in a way that makes them a devastating terrorist weapon" and "there would be billions of dollars of economic damage" (Richter, 2002). Therefore, a community emergency plan should include procedures for managing the immediate response to a threatened or actual radiological release (FEMA, 2010).

Community-based uses of radiological material can be found throughout the country. There are 272 research reactors at universities and research laboratories that receive and store fuel and ultimately ship spent fuel for disposal, which can pose a security challenge (European Nuclear Society, 2015b). Radioisotopes used for medical treatments are moved from the manufacturer to medical facilities in lead-lined packaging within the normal package delivery supply chain. The European Commission (2009) estimates that 2.5 million packages of radioisotopes for medical purposes are shipped annually in its jurisdiction alone.

Accidental Exposure in Brazil

When medical equipment is decommissioned, the radiological sources are removed for reprocessing or are safely discarded; however, old medical equipment is sometimes improperly handled and can become lethal in the community. For example, in 1987 in Goiania, Brazil, a city of 1 million people, a radiotherapy machine was abandoned, stolen by two thieves, and sold for the scrap value of the shielding. A scrap yard dealer was able to open the protective capsule, leading to an uncontrolled release of cesium-137 that led to deaths and injuries throughout the community. People suffering from radiation sickness were initially misdiagnosed with infectious diseases and admitted to hospitals for treatment, thus contaminating five hospitals. In the 16 days that it took to discover the source of the radiation, 125,000 people were potentially exposed and had to be screened. Special precautions to prevent contamination were used when the 14 most seriously ill patients had to be moved to a specialized treatment facility. Of these patients, four ultimately died. Obtaining adequate medical care for the rest was difficult because there were few experienced caregivers. Seven areas of the city were heavily contaminated, two of which had to be evacuated. During the unknown exposure period the contamination spread outward to adjacent cities as far as 80 miles away (Edwards and Steinhausler, 2007).

Nuclear Power

Nuclear power is used in many nations to ensure a supply of relatively inexpensive and clean energy. For example, before being decommissioned, the San Onofre Nuclear Power Plant in San Diego County reported that they produced energy from a few-ounce pellet of uranium-236 equivalent to that produced by 140 gallons of oil, 150 gallons of gasoline, 2000 pounds of coal, or 17,000 cubic feet of natural gas. In 2013, nuclear power generation accounted for 20% of electricity production in the United States, where the goal of the Energy Policy Act passed in 2005 is to reduce the current annual emission of 5.8 billion tons of CO_2 from energy use. The use of nuclear power is one possible alternative to achieve that goal; however, the development of more nuclear generation plants is not without risks, as the movement of fuel to the plants and subsequent storage of spent fuel rods pose some security challenges (WNA, 2015b). Accidents at Chernobyl (Jarorowski, 1999) and Fukushima (Featherstone, 2012) have shown that fallout can travel around the world.

Nuclear Power Plants

For many years the nuclear power industry had an exemplary safety record. The American Nuclear Regulatory Commission has a safety goal of one accident for every 10,000 reactor years; however, "the world's fleet of light-water power reactors has racked up 11,500 reactor-years and counts five 'partial core melt' accidents," three at Fukushima, one at Three Mile Island, and one at Greifswald in East Germany (Featherstone, 2012, p. 11). Chernobyl, an older Soviet design, is the sixth reactor to release radiation, with the most devastating results. Fallout from Chernobyl was found around the world (Jaworowski, 2010), and iodine-131, a product of nuclear fission that was released at Fukushima, was detected in Chernobyl (Featherstone, 2012).

Table 5.2 Number of Nuclear Power Plants in 2014

Nation	Population	No. of Plants	Megawatts of Power Produced Annually
United States	313,858,000	100	99,244
France	63,605,300	58	63,130
Japan	127,587,800	48	42,388
Russia	143,165,000	34	24,654
Republic of Korea	48,906,300	23	20,717
India	1,259,721,000	21	5780
China	1,350,378,000	23	19,007

Source: Date from IAEA/PRIS, 2015.

The first electricity produced by nuclear energy was created in Acro, Idaho, on December 20, 1951. As of January 18, 2013, at least 437 nuclear power plant units were operating in 31 countries, and 68 plants were under construction in 15 countries. By 2011, the total electricity production since 1951 amounted to an estimated 69,760 billion kWh, and the cumulative operating experience added up to 15,080 years by the end of 2012 (European Nuclear Society, 2015a). Europe has the most nuclear power plants (186), followed by North America (125) (European Nuclear Society, 2015b). See Table 5.2 for the number of existing nuclear power plants in various countries around the world as of 2014.

Characteristics of Three Mile Island, Chernobyl, and Fukushima Compared

The three nuclear power plant accidents that provide the most evidence of impacts on a community are Three Mile Island in 1979, Chernobyl in 1986, and Fukushima in 2011. Two of the events—Three Mile Island and Fukushima—occurred in light water reactors where containment was relatively successful and the core remained intact and onsite. The Chernobyl event was the worst, having no containment and an explosion that dispersed the graphite core materials (see Table 5.3). Emergency planning for nuclear power plant accidents is a complex activity. According to Waugh (2000, p. 122), it can be characterized "as a kind of 'normal accident' that occurs in complex processes with 'tightly coupled' systems. A failure in one system affects others which, in turn, effects yet others." Howitt and Leonard (2009, p. 6) characterized the Three Mile Island accident as an "emergent crisis," an event growing "from ordinary circumstances … a simple pump failure out of which spun an escalating series of failures and mistakes until a major crisis was underway."

Although Three Mile Island resulted in little actual human harm or property damage, it was the source of many lessons learned about epidemiological tracking for potential injuries and the appropriate management of public information. Its system failures led to the creation of the Federal Emergency Management Agency (FEMA). Sylves (2008, p. 126) suggested that, "The Nuclear Regulatory Commission had managed public warning and evacuation so badly during the crisis that the President reassigned some of the commission's off-site radiological emergency

Table 5.3 Comparing the Three Nuclear Power Plant Accidents

Characteristic	Three Mile Island	Chernobyl	Fukushima
Date	March 28, 1979	April 26, 1986	March 11, 2011
Cause	Failure in the non-nuclear area led to the loss of coolant and a partial meltdown of about half of the core. It was attributed to inadequate instrumentation and inadequate emergency response training.	A sudden power output surge during a systems test caused a reactor vessel to rupture, leading to a series of blasts. An intense fire burned for 10 days.	A magnitude 9.0 earthquake and resulting tsunami damaged the plant's power systems, causing cooling systems to fail. A series of gas explosions followed.
Number of reactors	Two, but only one (TMI-2) involved	Four, but only one reactor involved	Six, but only three were of concern, plus pools storing spent fuel
Type of reactors	Light-water-fueled steam reactor; containment vessel remained intact, with only small releases of radioactive gas offsite.	Graphite-moderated boiling water reactor; the graphite made it highly combustible. The reactor had no containment structure, so nothing stopped the trajectory of radioactive materials into the air.	Boiling-water reactors; the containment vessels remained intact.
Radiation released	370 PBq of noble gases; HEPA and charcoal filters removed most radionuclides	5.2 million TBq	370,000 TBq
Deaths	None; no dose occurred above background levels.	UN report places total confirmed deaths from radiation at 64 as of 2008. How many will eventually die is disputed.	No deaths so far due to radiation but stress-related deaths occurred during evacuation.
Status	TMI-2 is permanently shutdown and defueled. TMI-1 will operate until the end of its license, which is currently set to expire in 2034. It is a top safety performer.	The damaged reactor is now encased in a concrete shell. A new containment structure is scheduled to be completed in 2017.	Engineers have brought the plant to a "cold shutdown condition," a key milestone in bringing it under control. It will take decades to dismantle it completely.

Sources: Anon., 2011; NRC, 2013; WNA, 2012, 2015a.

preparedness duties to FEMA." Chernobyl revealed the need for first-responder protective equipment and medical prophylaxis, carefully managed public education for evacuation, and international communication plans, as the residue from the plant traveled to Norway, Finland, and ultimately across the world. Fukushima demonstrated that natural hazards mitigation for nuclear plants cannot be expected to perform perfectly every time and reinforced the benefit of public communication plans, evacuation plans, and long-term relocation plans.

Emergency Planning for Radiological Events

Few local governments have had experience in managing accidental releases of radiological or nuclear materials, and potential sources of accidental catastrophic releases may remain unidentified in community risk analyses. Medical diagnostic equipment, medical isotopes, sterilizers in industrial facilities, and research reactors at university research centers may be overlooked. However, as the Goiania contamination in Brazil demonstrated, a small radioactive source can contaminate many people and a large area. Whereas military facilities do not pose an urban area threat (Nuclear Information Project, 2006), emergency planning coordinated with the military authorities is important for adjacent communities. Nuclear reactors used to generate power have mandatory emergency plans that may provide information useful in community planning for response to a radiological or nuclear incident, including a terrorist act. Events at Three Mile Island in Pennsylvania, Chernobyl in the Ukraine, and Fukushima in Japan may inform emergency planning efforts, including preparedness and post-event response and recovery issues. The exact location of a radiological event and the composition of the radiological material will affect the specific response plan. For example, the radionuclides may differ between a reactor accident and a terrorist release of radiological material, which will impact the immediate and long-term effects on the victims (Jarorowski, 2010) and the degree of damage to the physical plant of the community. The size of the deposition population may be different than that involved in the actual reactor events; however, the basic issues for emergency planning remain the same, regardless of whether the source of the radioactive or nuclear material release is a nuclear power plant reactor, a theft or mismanagement of radiological sources, or a terrorist device. The common issues for planning, response, and recovery among releases of radiological or nuclear material are public information, first-responder protection, victim care, community protection and evacuation, and psychological impact. These are discussed further in the following sections.

Lessons Learned about Public Information

Three nuclear power plants that have had significant accidents each demonstrate the crucial role played by good public information plans. Few communities have experience with large-scale exposure to radiological sources, so the three reactor accidents discussed here provide a paradigm for civilian exposure.

Medical Information and Misinformation

All radiological exposures are not the same. For many decades, the model of the impact of a nuclear release on a human population was the Japanese experience at the end of World War II (Sokolov et al., 1998). The bombs dropped over Hiroshima and Nagasaki exposed the victims to radiation from "plume shine" (Momeni, 1998), leading to exposure to x-rays and neutrons, which resulted in radiation burns and leukemia (Baverstock and Williams, 2006). The long-term findings from the Japanese bombings in 1945 may have led to overestimation of the long-term health consequences for the exposed populations. In 1965, at the 20-year point, medical researchers suggested that, "The only significant consequences … were increases in leukemia and thyroid cancer" (Baverstock and Williams, 2006, p. 1312). By 1974 a significant increase in solid cancers was found, and 50 years after the event "an unexpected incidence of non-cancer diseases was found" (Shimizu et al., 1990).

Chernobyl Medical Data

The data from Chernobyl contradict the assumption of heightened leukemias (Sokolov et al., 1998). In reactor accidents, radiation risks are principally from "inhalation of contaminated airborne radionuclides, ingestion of contaminated food and water, and external exposure to contaminated ground" (Momeni, 1998, p. 150). The results from these effects include thyroid cancer and specific types of tumors in higher than expected proportions, as well as gastrointestinal damage and skin lesions. "No consistent attributable increase has been confirmed either in the rate of leukemia or in the incidence of any malignancies other than thyroid carcinomas" (Crick, 1998, p. 2). Headaches, general disability, and a lower overall immune response form a syndrome that is being referred to as "Chernobyl AIDS" among those who received significant exposure to radiation (Allen, 1998). The lower dosage and ground-level deposition at Chernobyl make it a better model for planning for radiological and nuclear events in a non-war setting. The damage experienced by atom bomb blast survivors is not replicated with reactor accident victims and by extrapolation would not be a likely consequence of a radiological event (Momeni, 1998). Therefore, a communication plan must begin by providing accurate information about health risks to the affected public.

Three Mile Island Communication Failure

The Three Mile Island accident demonstrates that getting accurate information to the public quickly is important in managing a radiological accident. When the cooling system failure occurred, the Nuclear Regulatory Commission, Pennsylvania Department of Environmental Resources, Governor's Office, and President's Office all needed timely and accurate information to share with the media and in turn the public, but the utility that owned the facility had no emergency public information systems in place. According to Sylves (2012, pp. 58–59), "The slow response, miscommunication, lack of decisive leadership and poor coordination of the Nuclear Regulatory Commission with the utility, the state of Pennsylvania, and affected localities, demonstrated to policymakers the need to improve disaster response, coordination and planning." Well-meant but incomplete public information may lead to some inappropriate actions. For example, during the Three Mile Island event, which had no significant offsite release of radiological materials, the governor of Pennsylvania suggested that pregnant women and children under two within the immediate area of the reactor should leave as a precaution. The result was that people all over the state left for distant refuges in the homes of relatives or hotels (Behler, 1986). This created economic hardship, personal stress, and distrust of the government. Accurate information was not available to guide people's response to the invisible radiological threat that the public perceived. The World Nuclear Association (WNA, 2012) reported that hundreds of environmental samples were taken around Three Mile Island during the accident period but no unusually high readings were found, except for noble gases, and virtually no iodine. The readings were far below health limits, but a political storm raged based on confusion and misinformation.

Chernobyl Communication Failure

Chernobyl generally yields negative lessons for public information, as well. Little information was given to the affected populations in the first crucial hours, with people being told only that there had been an accident at the reactor and to be ready to evacuate within 2 hours (Kholosha, 1998). Therefore, individuals at most immediate risk did not know to shelter in place against immediate respiratory, ingestion, and injection exposure. One Norwegian leader has characterized the silence as causing "unnecessary harm to affected individuals, and a long heartbreaking and politically turbulent post-accidental situation" (Drottz-Sjoberg, 1998, p. 71).

A 2005 study of Chernobyl victims disclosed that people initially had no idea that exposure to the smoke from the burning reactor was dangerous. Even the children's outdoor May Day celebration was conducted as usual. The government information was optimistic, but it suddenly turned pessimistic when it informed people that 20% of the population would die as a result of the accident. "It was terror. It was terror," was the community's response to the inconsistent information (Abbott et al., 2006, pp. 110–111).

Unlike other disasters where the government is blamed, the fatalistic Chernobyl victims have not become activists on their own behalf. Researchers attribute this to the initial "optimistic misinformation" released by the government and the later "pessimistic misinformation" released by the media (Abbott et al., 2006). Havenaar and Rumiantseva (1994, p. 89) observed that "contradictory information about the accident in Chernobyl caused, and is still causing, 'cognitive dissonance'… most people think that radiation is an absolutely pathogenic factor and that it harms not only present but also future generations." Epidemiological studies of Chernobyl evacuees over the intervening 23 years demonstrated that the expected cancer rates did not occur (Jaworowski, 2010). Regardless, it was reported that "survivors have suffered a paralyzing fatalism due to myths and misperceptions about the threat of radiation, contributing to a culture of chronic dependency. Some 'took on the role of invalids.' Mental health coupled with smoking and alcohol abuse is a very much greater problem than radiation" (WNA, 2015a).

Early and honest information about self-protection must be an integral part of the emergency response and recovery plan for radiological events. City dwellers can more easily prevent ingestion of contaminated food than rural populations who live more directly off the land. Commercially prepared products can be evaluated by case lot and safe food rapidly restored to circulation in cities and towns. On the other hand, animals available to hunters and fishermen can only be evaluated after they have been caught. Unless evaluation stations are established in these remote areas, exposure through ingestion of contaminated game will continue, creating health effects even in distant populations.

Media Role

The Chernobyl experience demonstrates that immediate public information will come from the media. It is essential to have scientists with credibility and the ability to speak in simple terms to provide media briefings. Jaworowski (2010, p. 25) questioned the "radiophobia" that has developed as an offshoot of Cold War military strategies, noting that "natural background radiation in many parts of the world exceeds the dosage of those living near Chernobyl." Because most of the public has no knowledge about radiation exposure as it relates to health effects, it is important to use analogies for the press, such as comparing the radiation in a cigarette or banana or the background radiation in the high altitudes of Earth to the amount released in a specific event. The general public does not understand the implications of radiological measurements, so materials must be written in very simple terms and include such facts as symptoms, lengths of exposure, and specific areas where the population might be affected (Drottz-Sjoberg, 1998).

The emergency plan should include brochures for the media about radiological materials and related threats. Information about nuclear power plants is available on generating station websites, and the URL should be available for rapid dissemination to the media and community members in the event of an accident. EuroSafe has available a report of its work toward developing community radiological information, describing the variety of topics and pathways that it used to communicate during the Fukushima accident (Sentuc and Dokter, 2013).

Teachers, doctors, counselors, and health workers must be given continuous factual information about ongoing environmental effects so they can help calm community fears. For example, the Canadian government developed a coloring book for children to help them understand nuclear or chemical accidents and their potential effects on themselves and their communities (Becker, 1998).

Public education is essential to guiding the self-protective actions of the general population. After Chernobyl, when information was released that people were being given potassium iodide as protection against radiation effects, some parents administered tincture of iodine to their children, even though the iodine label clearly stated "poison." Any public information about medical care must detail not only the steps to take but also any obvious steps to avoid (Nauman, 1998).

As a critical link in community recovery, public information must be delivered in a culturally sensitive way by credible sources using the appropriate language and reading levels, as well as showing respect for local traditions. Information on where to get help should be featured prominently. Specific and practical information should be repeated frequently as public service announcements in electronic media and as advertisements in the press. If government agencies are blamed for the accident, other spokespersons with more credibility should be selected, such as university professors or medical professionals. A generalized hostile view of government may impact the ability of members of the public to actually hear the message about radiation and its effects (Flynn, 1998).

Lessons Learned about First-Responder Protection

Inhalation of radiological material is the greatest threat to first responders. Post-Chernobyl research demonstrated the benefit of respiratory protection. Any supplied-air system appears to provide adequate respiratory protection during acute exposure during an emergency response to a reactor site (Nauman, 1998). Overall the anticipated effect on first responders provided with reasonable shielding is minimal. Of the 800,000 Chernobyl responders, "237 were initially admitted to the hospital. Acute radiation syndrome was diagnosed in 134 cases, of whom 28 died from radiation injuries, all within the first three months" (Crick, 1998, p. 1). These findings suggest that proper training of emergency responders in the deployment and use of supplied-air systems is the key to minimizing health effects and lessening stress. Training on radiological scenarios in advance of an event is also a helpful mitigation tool. Potassium iodide administered to emergency responders immediately before exposure to the damaged reactor is beneficial (Momeni, 1998). Moreover, the Polish experience suggests that a single protective dose of potassium iodide would have only moderate and treatable unwanted side effects in the general population and would "significantly lower the thyroid burden of radioactive iodine-131 over time" (Nauman, 1998, p. 202). Psychosomatic responses, including a higher incidence of stress-related illnesses, were also related by first responders after Chernobyl. This suggests the importance of early psychological intervention, including critical incident stress defusing for all first responders after each shift (Winslow, 2000).

Lessons Learned about Victim Care

The general population in the area of the Chernobyl accident did not experience a measurable increase in any specific health affects. After 10 years, studies showed no consistent attributable increase in the rate of leukemia or the incidence of any malignancies in the general population (Crick, 1998). A small increase in the reported incidences of some nonspecific health effects may be due to the intense monitoring of the potentially affected population, rather than any increase in actual health-related affects. Minor illnesses that might never have been reported to medical authorities are now being picked up in the target populations due to the longitudinal study being conducted (Crick, 1998).

Notably, however, there was a highly significant increase in the incidence of thyroid cancer among children in the affected areas, notably children who were born less than 6 months after the accident and children who were less than 5 years old at the time. The papillary thyroid cancers in children were aggressive, but traditional treatment including removal of the thyroid was successful in most cases (Crick, 1998). Estimates for future thyroid cancers, as high as 72,000 cases by 2056, may be inaccurate because the post-Chernobyl damage was caused mainly by exposure to isotopes rather than x-rays and neutrons (Baverstock and Williams, 2006). Current studies of Chernobyl survivors suggest that the expected long-term medical impacts of elevated radiation are not occurring (Jarorowski, 2010).

Decontamination of the affected area is also critical for the long-term health of the general population. At Chernobyl, the radioactive materials were dumped into the ruins and a containment structure built around them. It is estimated that 50,500 km^2 were polluted by the accidental release of radionuclides. An area of 1000-km radius was checked for radiological emissions. Roadways were washed and fallen leaves and agricultural debris destroyed, which lowered the radiation exposure by 30%. Exposed foodstuffs, especially milk, were eliminated. Grazing lands and animal food were monitored, and soil modifiers were used to mitigate the radiation effects. Newly produced milk was filtered in an attempt to remove radiation (Kholosha, 1998).

Outside of the Ukraine, hot spots were found as far away as the mountain areas of Norway, where initially humans were exposed through external radiation from deposited radionuclides and inhalation of radionuclides from the air. After the first few months, however, the principal route of exposure was ingestion of contaminated foodstuffs. Sheep and reindeer were affected, principally through grazing. The human population ingested high levels of radiocesium through the consumption of reindeer meat, freshwater fish, and milk (Harbitz, 1998).

The government of Norway established intervention levels for contamination of the food supply; for example, about a third of all lambs were contaminated at levels above intervention levels at the time of slaughter due to eating contaminated pasturage. For the 10 years following the accident, over 1.5 million lambs and sheep were included in a special feeding program at a cost of over $23 million, representing a major economic burden for the government in affected areas (Harbitz, 1998).

Laplanders rely on reindeer for most of their protein, and the poor of many countries supplement their diets with wild game and fish. Because prohibiting hunting is unlikely to be successful, monitoring stations must be established where hunters and fisherman can have their game evaluated for safety (Drottz-Sjoberg, 1998).

The population of Belarus experienced a 53% contamination rate. The Chernobyl plume moved unexpectedly, and the population received their initial dose of radiation through "cloud shine" and inhalation. It was 8 days after the accident before the first protective actions were taken for the general population. The principal measure was to end the consumption of contaminated foodstuffs, which had yielded high doses of iodine-131 (Buglova and Kenigsberg, 1998).

Lessons Learned about Community Protection and Evacuation

Community protection includes direct site remediation and evacuation of those at long-term risk from radionuclide deposition.

Direct Site Remediation in Chernobyl

Direct site remediation in Chernobyl started with placing the debris in the ruins of the reactor and encasing it in a protective structure referred to as the "Shelter Object" (Rudenko, 1998). Intended to last for 10 years, it is only now being covered by a new steel sarcophagus that will shroud the reactor and allow it to be dismantled inside the protective structure. The project, costing 432 million euros, is not expected to be completed until 2017 (Anon., 2007b). Groundwater contamination may be resulting from the way the reactor building was constructed and then damaged. Coolant water and 200 tons of fuel remain in the ruined reactor. Strontium, cesium, plutonium, tritium, and americium can be found in groundwater, suggesting that internal shelter water is leaching out. The long-term health effects could be devastating if the contaminated water is used to irrigate field crops or for community drinking water supplied through wells. The new sarcophagus is intended to stop all offsite consequences from the reactor accident (Anon., 2007a).

The Chernobyl experience points out the importance of planning for effective remediation measures. A sealed environment must include a ground barrier. Based on contamination from an early nuclear reactor in Slavakia, remediation must include fencing off highly contaminated areas to limit population exposure and removal of affected soil or remediation through the addition of binders or modifiers. The environment should be cleaned up to background levels if possible, but to below levels of concern as a minimum (Slavik, 1998).

In the United States, the Environmental Protection Agency (EPA) has established recommended intervention levels: exposures of 5 REM require sheltering in place; 50 REM, a 1-week evacuation for remediation and dissipation; and over 100 REM, long-term relocation of the population (Meinhold, 1998). The principal public policy problem is to determine how safe is safe? Standards established by experts may provide some guidance that will be salient in political and legal arenas, but in the minds of the general public will the community ever be really safe?

Evacuation

Evacuation was also used as a protective measure in all three accidents. Evacuation is only needed when the reaction cannot be rapidly controlled so sheltering in place is not possible or when significant community remediation is required. Evacuees should be told how long they will be gone and given specific directions about what personal belongings and essential documents to take with them, such as medical, property, and personal information that victims will need at the evacuation point to receive financial and other assistance to resettle. The government must provide immediate emergency shelter, as well as relocation for long-term remediation (Kholosha, 1998).

Three Mile Island Evacuation

As noted earlier, at Three Mile Island there was no organized evacuation. A suggestion by the governor, combined with inadequate public information about the radiological threat, led to needless self-evacuation of people living many miles away from the damaged plant. As noted in Cantelon and Williams (1982, p. 50), "Garbled communications reported by the media generated a debate over evacuation. Whether or not there were evacuation plans soon became academic. What happened on Friday was not a planned evacuation but a weekend exodus based not on what was actually happening at Three Mile Island but on what government officials and the media imagined might happen. On Friday confused communications created the politics of fear."

Chernobyl Evacuation

During the Chernobyl accident people in adjacent Pripyat were given 2 hours to prepare to evacuate but no warning about the need to shelter in place to limit exposure to the airborne contamination from the burning graphite core or to avoid eating contaminated food (Barclay, 2011). Immediate evacuation included 100,000 people, with 350,000 ultimately being moved from contaminated areas in the Ukraine, Belarus, and Russia (Tran, 2011), where the evacuation of pregnant women and young children was very effective in lessening their exposure to iodine-131 (Buglova and Kenigsberg, 1998). In the Chernobyl area, people were evacuated the day after the event, but they were not offered shelter, which created new social and psychological problems for the victims (Kholosha, 1998).

Fukushima Evacuation

In Fukushima, the people living within a 12-mile radius were immediately evacuated, while 130,000 people living between 12 and 20 miles away were given the choice to shelter in place or evacuate (Tran, 2011). The Japanese government was also quick to remove contaminated food from the supply chain to limit exposure by ingestion (Barclay, 2011).

Lessons Learned about Psychological Impacts

At the 10th anniversary of the Chernobyl accident, experts concluded that "social and psychological effects were among the most prominent and lasting consequences" of the nuclear reactor accident (Drottz-Sjoberg, 1998, p. 73). The presence of the Shelter Object serves as a constant symbol of the accident and related losses. Birkland (1997) noted that symbols are shortcuts to understanding a disaster and gain their power from being recognizable. This readily recognizable symbol in Chernobyl keeps the sense of loss fresh for the survivors, with damaging psychological consequences (Drottz-Sjoberg, 1998). People fear radiation due to misinformation. One goal of post-event public information is the correction of Hiroshima stereotypes and the introduction of factual information about the actual event to ameliorate fear and psychosocial effects among the general public (Allen, 1998).

Most health effects take at least 5 years to appear, thus condemning survivors to anticipate the worst over a long period (Revel, 1998). The stress of the experience itself may induce psychological illness: "Psychological illnesses, changes in diet to avoid perceived food contamination, and the increased use of alcohol and cigarettes to cope with the anxiety all contribute to public health effects related to, but not caused by, the deposition of radiological materials in the community" (Baverstock and Williams, 2006, p. 1313). Furthermore, by 2002 in the areas around Chernobyl, people perceived themselves to be victims and expected to experience ill health, including feelings of anxiety, instability, and helplessness. They expressed a generalized fear about the future (Abbott et al., 2006).

Recent studies have suggested that the psychological effects of a terrorist radiological attack can be much stronger than reactions to natural events, which humans cannot control. Natural disasters occur quickly and are readily understood. A radiological or nuclear event is the result of human failure or human intention, magnifying the psychological stress and making it worse because the damage cannot be seen or fully measured in the early days after the accident. In Chernobyl, the true extent of the damage took months to evaluate, thus creating a "spreading catastrophe" (Havenaar and Rumiantseva, 1994). The emergency management plan for radiological events should include a psychological/mental health component, including pre-identified local or mutual aid resources. Potential counselors need to understand radiological risks and potential responses. They must be prepared to evacuate with the affected population and offer debriefings in the shelters. Long-term counseling will be needed by those who are permanently displaced, are bereaved as a result of the event, become ill, or have a close relative who becomes ill. The counselors may become a critical source of the information dissemination discussed earlier (Childs, 2006).

The community at large will also be disrupted and psychologically affected. Even those too far away to be contaminated may believe that they and their families are at risk. The Three Mile Island experience in Pennsylvania showed that unaffected people self-evacuated to distant points because of fear. Psychological counseling and aggressive public information campaigns must be directed at the unaffected portions of the community as well as the victims. The perceived failure of the government to act in a timely fashion in the Three Mile Island event resulted in high anxiety among the unaffected general public (Drottz-Sjoberg, 1998).

Terrorist events using radiological devices are likely to generate low radiation exposure levels for relatively short periods of time. It is critical that the emergency response be an appropriate reaction to the actual threat. Terrorists are anxious for their actions to be as disruptive as possible. Therefore, it is incumbent on the public officials to critically evaluate the actual threat to the population and draw the lines for evacuation and medical evaluation as narrowly as possible. Guidelines such as the *Principles for Intervention for Protection of the Public in a Radiological Emergency* (International Council on Radiation Protection, 1993) can guide realistic emergency plans, documenting what is prudent while protecting public officials from overreacting in response to political pressure, thus exacerbating public stress.

Conclusion

The nuclear reactor accidents in Pennsylvania and the Ukraine demonstrated the results of too little government action and delayed government action. Fukushima demonstrated better planning and a swifter response, even in the face of a much more widespread earthquake and tsunami "triple catastrophe." Public officials planning for the response to and recovery from radiological attacks can benefit from the lessons of these three nuclear power plant events. Illness and injury are most likely to be limited to those in immediate proximity to the site. Most injuries can be limited through sheltering in place, shielding, evacuation, respiratory protection, and avoiding contaminated food.

Communitywide impacts will be affected mostly by environmental factors: wind speed and direction, whether the release occurs outdoors or is contained in a building, whether or not groundwater is contaminated, whether the event occurs in a metropolitan area with little agriculture or in an area with animal agriculture or hunting and fishing resources. The socioeconomic factors in the community may make the response and cleanup easy because people trust the government and understand the information they are given. On the other hand, the situation may be made worse by low educational levels, language barriers, or an overall distrust of government.

Scenario-based advanced planning for any emergency will make a response more effective and efficient. The lessons learned from Fukushima, Chernobyl, and Three Mile Island can aid planners in developing workable and effective radiological incident plans for all potential hazards.

Questions for Discussion

1. What are the radiological risks in your community? What sources could you use to find them? Where are they located and who provides for their security?
2. Who would be the best media briefers if there were a release or theft at one of these facilities?
3. What are the common lessons from these three accidents and how would you incorporate them into a community emergency management plan?

Additional Reading

Birmingham, L. and McNeill, D. (2012). *Strong in the Rain: Surviving Japan's Earthquake, Tsunami, and Fukushima Nuclear Disaster.* New York: Palgrave.
Hernan, R. (2010). *This Borrowed Earth: Lessons from the Fifteen Worst Environmental Disasters around the World.* New York: Palgrave.
Sylves, R.T. (2008). *Disaster Policy and Politics.* Washington, DC: CQ Press.
Walker, S.J. (2006). *Three Mile Island: A Nuclear Crisis in Historical Perspective.* Berkeley: University of California Press.

References

Abbott, P., Wallace, C., and Beck, M. (2006). Chernobyl: living with risk and uncertainty. *Health, Risk Soc.*, 8(2): 105–121.
Allen, P.T. (1998). Modeling Social Psychological Factors After an Accident, paper presented at the International Radiological Post-Emergency Response Issues Conference, Washington, DC, September 9.
Anon. (2007a). Chernobyl to be encased in steel. *New Scientist*, 195(2622): 4.
Anon. (2007b). Steel tomb to shield Chernobyl wreckage. *Prof. Eng.*, 20(18): 9.
Anon. (2011). How does Fukushima differ from Chernobyl? *BBC News*, December 16 (http://www.bbc.co.uk/news/world-asia-pacific-13050228).
Barclay, E. (2011). Fukushima vs. Chernobyl: still not equal. *National Public Radio*, April 12 (http://www.npr.org/2011/04/12/135353240/fukushima-vs-chernobyl-what-does-level-7-mean).
Baverstock, K. and Williams, D. (2006). The Chernobyl accident 20 years on: an assessment of the health consequences and the international response. *Environ. Health Perspect.*, 114(9): 1312–1317.
Becker, S.M. (1998). Constructing More Effective Post-Emergency Responses: The Human Services Component, paper presented at the International Radiological Post-Emergency Response Issues Conference, Washington, DC, September 9.
Behler, Jr., G.T. (1986). *The Nuclear Accident at Three Mile Island: Its Effects on a Local Community*, Historical and Comparative Disaster Series No. 7. Newark: University of Delaware Disaster Research Center.
Birkland, T.A. (1997). *After Disaster: Agenda Setting, Public Policy and Focusing Events.* Washington, DC: Georgetown University Press.
Buglova, E. and Kenigsberg, J. (1998). Emergency Response After the Chernobyl Accident in Belarus: Lessons Learned, paper presented at the International Radiological Post-Emergency Response Issues Conference, Washington, DC, September 9.
Cantelon, P.L. and Williams, R.C. (1982). *Crisis Contained, The Department of Energy at Three Mile Island.* Washington, DC: U.S. Department of Energy.

Childs, J. (2006). *Critical Incident Stress Management in Disasters*. Santa Clara, CA: Bill Wilson Center.

Crick, M.J. (1998). EC/IAEA/WHO 1996 Conference One Decade After Chernobyl: Implications for Post-Emergency Response, paper presented at the International Radiological Post-Emergency Response Issues Conference, Washington, DC, September 9.

Drottz-Sjoberg, B.-M. (1998). Public Reactions Following the Chernobyl Accident: Implications for Emergency Procedures, paper presented at the International Radiological Post-Emergency Response Issues Conference, Washington, DC, September 9.

Edwards, F.L. and Steinhausler, F. (2007). *NATO and Terrorism—On Scene: Emergency Management After a Major Terror Attack*. Dortrecht, Netherlands: Springer.

European Commission. (2009). *Preliminary Report on Supply of Radioisotopes for Medical Use and Current Developments in Nuclear Medicine*. Luxemburg: European Commission (http://ec.europa.eu/health/healthcare/docs/radioisotopes_report_en.pdf).

European Nuclear Society. (2015a). *Nuclear Power Plants Worldwide*. Belgium: European Nuclear Society (http://www.euronuclear.org/info/encyclopedia/n/nuclear-power-plant-world-wide.htm).

European Nuclear Society. (2015b). *Research Reactor Fuel Management*. Belgium: European Nuclear Society (http://www.euronuclear.org/events/rrfm.htm).

Featherstone, S. (2012). Chernobyl now: are nuclear disasters the new normal? *Popular Science*, July 17 (http://www.popsci.com/science/article/2012-06/chernobyl-now?single-page-view=true).

FEMA. (2010). *Developing and Maintaining State, Territorial, Tribal and Local Government Emergency Plans (CPG101)*, Version 2.0. Washington, DC: Federal Emergency Management Agency (http://www.fema.gov/pdf/about/divisions/npd/CPG_101_V2.pdf).

Flynn, B.W. (1998). Emergency Events Involving Radiation Exposure: Issues Impacting Mental Health Sequelae, paper presented at the International Radiological Post-Emergency Response Issues Conference, Washington, DC, September 9.

Goodrich, D.C. (2005). Implosion device. In Croddy, E.A., Wirtz, J.J., and Larson, J.A., Eds., *Weapons of Mass Destruction: An Encyclopedia of Worldwide Policy, Technology, and History*. Vol. 2. *Nuclear Weapons*. Santa Barbara, CA: ABC-Clio.

Harbitz, O. (1998). Consequences of the Chernobyl Accident and Emergency Preparedness in Norway, paper presented at the International Radiological Post-Emergency Response Issues Conference, Washington, DC, September 9.

Havenaar, I.M. and Rumiantseva, G.M. (1994). Mental health problems in the Chernobyl area. *Russ. Soc. Sci. Rev.*, 35(4): 87–95.

Health Physics Society. (2010). *Consumer Products Containing Radioactive Materials*, Fact Sheet. McLean, VA: Health Physics Society (http://hps.org/documents/consumerproducts.pdf).

Health Physics Society. (2011). *What Types of Radiation Are There?*, Fact Sheet. McLean, VA: Health Physics Society (http://hps.org/publicinformation/ate/faqs/radiationtypes.html).

Health Physics Society. (2012). *Background Radiation*, Fact Sheet. McLean, VA: Health Physics Society (http://hps.org/documents/background_radiation_fact_sheet.pdf).

Howitt, A.M. and Leonard, H.B., Eds. (2009). *Managing Crises: Responses to Large-Scale Emergencies*. Washington, DC: CQ Press.

IAEA/PRIS. (2015). *Nuclear Share of Electricity Generation in 2014*. Vienna, Austria: International Atomic Energy Agency/Power Reactor Information System (https://www.iaea.org/PRIS/WorldStatistics/NuclearShareofElectricityGeneration.aspx).

International Council on Radiation Protection. (1993). *Principles for Intervention for Protection of the Public in a Radiological Emergency*, Publ. No. 63. Ottawa: International Council on Radiation Protection.

Jaworowski, Z. (1999). Radiation risks and ethics. *Phys. Today*, 52(9): 24–29.

Jaworowski, Z. (2010). Observations on the Chernobyl disaster and LNT. *Dose Response*, 8(2): 148–171.

Kholosha, V.I. (1998). Managing the Immediate and Long-Term Response to the Chernobyl Accident: Problems and Perspectives, paper presented at the International Radiological Post-Emergency Response Issues Conference, Washington, DC, September 9.

Meinhold, C.B. (1998). Philosophical Challenges to the Establishment of Reasonable Clean-Up Levels, paper presented at the International Radiological Post-Emergency Response Issues Conference, Washington, DC, September 9.

Momeni, M.H. (1998). A Discussion of Public Health Issues from a Severe Nuclear Reactor Accident, paper presented at the International Radiological Post-Emergency Response Issues Conference, Washington, DC, September 9.

Nauman, J.A. (1998). Potassium Iodine Prophylaxis in Case of Nuclear Accident; Polish Experience, paper presented at the International Radiological Post-Emergency Response Issues Conference Meeting, Washington, DC, September 9.

NRC. (2013). *Three Mile Island Accident*. Washington, DC: Nuclear Regulatory Commission (http://www.nrc.gov/reading-rm/doc-collections/fact-sheets/3mile-isle.pdf).

Nuclear Information Project. (2006). *Where the Bombs Are*. Washington, DC: Federation of American Scientists (http://www.nukestrat.com/us/where.htm).

Orange County Fire Authority. (2015). www.ocfa.org.

Revel, J.-P. (1998). Red Cross Programme Responding to Humanitarian Needs in Nuclear Disaster, paper presented at the International Radiological Post-Emergency Response Issues Conference, Washington, DC, September 9.

Richter, P. (2002). Studying "dirty" bomb scenario—terrorism: an Al Qaeda leader's warning that his group has the know-how to build a radioactive device exploits fears, experts say. *Los Angeles Times*, April 24 (http://articles.latimes.com/print/2002/apr/24/news/mn-39653).

Rudenko, Y.F. (1998). Radio-Hydrogeochemical Monitoring of Area Adjacent to the Shelter Object, paper presented at the International Radiological Post- Emergency Response Issues Conference, Washington, DC, September 9.

Sentuc, F.-N. and Dokter, S. (2013). *The GRS Emergency Centre During the Fukushima NPS Accident: Communicating Radiological Information to the Public*. Cologne, Germany: EuroSafe (http://www.eurosafe-forum.org/sites/default/files/Eurosafe2011/2_4_paper_Sentuc_GRS_Emergency_Centre_final_20111027%281%29.pdf).

Shimizu, Y., Kato, H., Schull, W.J., and Hoel, D.G. (1990). Studies of the mortality of A-bomb survivors. 9. Mortality, 1950–1985: Part 3. Noncancer mortality based on the revised doses (DS86). *Radiat. Res.*, 130(2): 249–266.

Slavik, O. (1998). Clean-Up Criteria and Technologies for a Cs-Contaminated Site Recovery, paper presented at the International Radiological Post-Emergency Response Issues Conference, Washington, DC, September 9.

Sokolov, V.A., Khoptynskaya, S.K., and Ivanov, V.K. (1998). Five Years' Experience in Publishing the Bulletin Radiation and Risk, paper presented at the International Radiological Post-Emergency Response Issues Conference, Washington, DC, September 9.

Sylves, R.T. (2008). *Disaster Policy and Politics*. Washington, DC: CQ Press.

Sylves, R.T. (2012). Federal emergency management comes of age: 1979–2001. In Rubin, C.B., Ed., *Emergency Management: The American Experience 1900–2010*, pp. 115–166. Boca Raton, FL: CRC Press.

Tran, M. (2011). Nuclear crises: how do Fukushima and Chernobyl compare? *The Guardian*, April 12 (http://www.theguardian.com/world/2011/apr/12/japan-fukushima-chernobyl-crisis-comparison).

Vergano, D. (2007). Experts close the lid on "suitcase nukes." *USA Today*, March 10 (http://usatoday30.usatoday.com/tech/science/2007-03-12-suitcase-nuclear-bombs_N.htm).

Waugh, W. (2000). *Living with Hazards, Dealing with Disasters*. Armonk, NY: M.E. Sharpe.

Winslow, F.L. (2000). The first-responder's perspective. In Drell, S. and Sofer, A., Eds., *The New Terror: Facing the Threat of Biological and Chemical Weapons*. Stanford, CA: Hoover Institution Press.

WNA. (2012). *Three Mile Island Accident*. London: World Nuclear Association (http://www.world-nuclear.org/info/inf36.html).

WNA. (2015a). *Chernobyl Accident 1986*. London: World Nuclear Association (http://www.world-nuclear.org/info/chernobyl/inf07.html).

WNA. (2015b). *U.S. Nuclear Power Policy*. London: World Nuclear Association (http://www.world-nuclear.org/info/inf41_US_nuclear_power_policy.html).

Zimmerman, P.D. and Lewis, J.G. (2006). The bomb in the backyard. *Foreign Policy*, October 10 (http://foreignpolicy.com/2009/10/16/the-bomb-in-the-backyard/).

II

GLOBAL CASES OF BEST AND WORST PRACTICE IN CRISIS AND EMERGENCY MANAGEMENT

Chapter 6

Hurricane Katrina and the Crisis of Emergency Management

Carole L. Jurkiewicz

Contents

Chapter Goals 109
Importance of Ethical Leadership 110
Portrait of Unethicality in Crisis Management 112
Ethical Culture 113
Manifestations of Louisiana's Ethical Culture 114
Consequences of Unethical Leadership 116
Post-Crisis Performance Review 117
Questions for Discussion 120
Additional Reading 120
References 120

Chapter Goals

By the end of this chapter, readers will be able to answer the following questions:

1. How do existing ethical standards affect community response to crisis situations?
2. What is the role of the community leader in establishing the ethical standards that guide behavior during a crisis?
3. How can character mapping be utilized to assess a leader's ethical ability to manage crises?
4. What role does culture play in shaping a community's ethical response to crisis situations?
5. What are some clues to a community's ethical culture that we can use in advance of a crisis to anticipate response in an emergency situation?

Crises, whether imposed from external events such as natural disasters, economic shocks, or political upheavals, evoke a set of behaviors that can determine whether or not a community will successfully weather the events. In the absence of planning and clearly articulated policies to address such circumstances, individuals are likely to respond in idiosyncratic ways specific to their personal concerns and priorities. Such unfocused responses can be chaotic and detract from the organization's function and its responsiveness to the needs of the environment in which it operates. They also create opportunities for unethical behavior that is harmful to organizations and the community. Hurricane Katrina provided an unfortunate example of an externally imposed crisis in a community lacking clearly developed models for dealing with such emergencies, and within a culture widely considered one of the most corrupt in the United States, led by an elected official whose unethical behavior would eventually lead to a federal conviction and incarceration (Johnson and Robertson, 2014). Although New Orleans has not yet fully recovered from the crisis, it does provide an excellent learning model of the importance of ethics in crisis management.

When crises occur, the preeminent concerns are saving lives, damage assessment, communication systems, and emergency relief. Simultaneously, the media converge upon the affected area and begin to establish their own infrastructures. Concomitant to and directive of how these initiatives are instituted and progress is an ethical filter. Whether it be questions of resource distribution, triage, media coverage, funding, or political expression, each emerges from a perspective of what is right and what is wrong and what is excusable, rationalizable, obscurable, opportunistic, or untrackable; all factors dictate ethical behavior in crisis management. Some ethical elements of crisis response are planned in advance, such as media protocol on reporting and the degree to which they will immerse themselves in rescue operations and individuals who are on the ready to personally reap profits from the disaster, such as false nonprofits and sham relief organizations. These are premeditated, intentionally ethical, or unethical choices. Other response initiatives flow organically from the established cultures in both the responder organizations and the community of the affected. Emergent from the culture, they reveal the ethical framework of the unit, but actions are taken without ethical review, with a general understanding of right and wrong.

Whereas much can and has been written about unethical behavior committed with intent and premeditation, the focus here will be on how organizational and community ethics emerge in crises and how this information can be used to assess whether ethics interventions are needed once the crisis itself has passed. The key influencer on organizational and community ethics is ethical leadership. This element establishes the norms of how the crisis is managed and to a great extent what is done or not done. Without time for reflection, external input, or careful consideration, leader behavior during the crisis is the ethical role model for what the citizens should do and rationalizes what they in effect actually do. The immediacy of the actions necessitated by crises removes the intellectual debate that may restrain such behaviors if more time was allowed for reflection. Thus, the actions reflect the values inherent in the community or organization existent at the time of the crisis and for which the leader holds direct ethical responsibility. The actions of the leader of New Orleans, Mayor Ray Nagin, following Hurricane Katrina are used here to illustrate this social–behavioral mechanism.

Importance of Ethical Leadership

Any discussion of a manifestation of an ethical framework through behavior evinced at the group level must necessarily begin with a review of the role of a public leader. A centuries-old phrase ascribed to the Chinese encapsulates its importance: "The fish rots from the head down." It is used to mean that an unethical leader is a causative factor that leads to unethical followers, and, conversely, that if the top person exhibits a higher level of ethical behavior then followers will model their behavior accordingly. Leaders establish the culture of an organization or a city, state, or country through their actions even more so than their words (Jurkiewicz, 2000, 2002, 2006) and are accountable for the culture they create. Foucault (1984) asserted that normalized values as articulated by those in authority lead to dominant and unquestioned institutional practices, which in turn define acceptable behavior and restrict individual autonomy. He described it as an involuntary, often unconscious, submission to the power of institutional authority, a view expanded upon by Bourdieu (1990) to describe how individuals create and maintain commonplace practices and adopt expected roles even when these practices are oppressive and marginalizing and are in contrast to one's previously held ethical beliefs. Kohlberg (1976, 1981, 1985) emphasized the point that leaders have a profound effect on the level of ethicality employed by their subordinates in deciding on which action is ethically right or wrong. Trevino (1990) asseverated that cultures such as that found in Louisiana and most particularly New Orleans and cultures that encourage, celebrate, and reward pushing the limits of legality to achieve personal gains exert a powerful influence on creating and sustaining unethical behavioral patterns. Ethical, or unethical, behavior is thus learned from those in positions of authority over us. This is a key element in the woefully ineffective and inefficient recovery efforts in New Orleans following Katrina. A cursory review of just a few of the thousands of reports of unethical behavior in the wake of Katrina, accompanied by the charges of ethical violations against Mayor Nagin, provides a clear example of this top-down ethical relationship. The head of the fish can claim to have no knowledge of the rot occurring further down the body, but it is neither possible nor true as the head is the standard bearer. Whereas both state- and federal-level administrations share the responsibility in part for either contributing to the cultural ethic in the New Orleans area or failing to intervene, both also have within their power the ability to rectify ethical violations. Of course, the federal level can be said to affect Mississippi as well as Louisiana, and the state level can be said to affect other Louisiana parishes beyond New Orleans, so again the focus returns to local leadership.

Unethical behavior from citizens, businesses, and public employees in the wake of Katrina has been well documented. Numerous false claims for Federal Emergency Management Agency (FEMA) funds have been widely reported, although false claims for funds from the Red Cross have not been so broadly publicized (Salmon, 2005). Insurance companies have been and are being sued for alleged contract violations, unethical business practices, and fraud (CNN, 2005d). Additionally, police officers reportedly stole luxury vehicles during the chaos following Katrina landfall (Gyan, 2006), were captured on video looting (CNN, 2005f), and were recorded stealing luxury items from storm-ravaged boutiques and department stores (CNN, 2005a,b). Documented reports of unwarranted killings by Blackwater operatives in the days following Katrina about which local law enforcements were aware and did nothing, in addition to Blackwater personnel commandeering citizens' property for their own use (Scahill, 2008), are further examples. One representative case of ethical malfeasance in the healthcare sector was a nursing home whose owners were charged with negligent homicide for abandoning elderly and infirm clients during the storm, 34 of whom drowned (CNN, 2005c). An example of egregious political behavior is that reported by the Louisiana National Guard regarding Representative William Jefferson, who requested two National Guard heavy trucks and a helicopter, along with military support personnel, to escort him to his family home in New Orleans where he allegedly retrieved documents and a computer relevant to 16 criminal charges on which he has been indicted while others were waiting for emergency rescues from their rooftops, a trip during which personnel waited over an hour (Tapper, 2005). These are but a few illustrations of the scope and seriousness of the many ethical violations that occurred in post-Katrina New Orleans. The focus now shifts to the leader of the city.

Portrait of Unethicality in Crisis Management

New Orleans' Mayor Ray Nagin gained international renown for his role in Katrina and his behavior in its aftermath, and the ethically charged issues surrounding him and his administration are viewed by many as one of the roadblocks to recovery in New Orleans. He has been widely criticized for the lack of planning despite clear scientific and weather reports, his actions during the hurricane (e.g., taking control of key top floors of a downtown hotel, evading calls for leadership and emergency decision-making), incendiary comments he made, and the initiatives he enacted during the recovery period that followed (Russell, 2005). His lack of definitive leadership in calling for an evacuation of New Orleans following the National Hurricane Center's August 26, 2005, prediction that Katrina would reach Category 4 status has been attributed to his concerns for the city's liability for closing hotels and other businesses (Russell, 2005). Finally, announcing the evacuation on August 28, less than 24 hours before landfall, was a direct cause of increased hardship for the 90,000 citizens (mostly impoverished and infirm) left in the city as 80% of it went under water (Parry, 2005). Looking to the federal government for relief, Nagin stated in his own news conference that, "I don't want to see anybody do anymore goddamn press conferences ... until the resources are in this city ... now get off your asses and let's do something, and let's fix the biggest goddamn crisis in the history of this country" (Robinette, 2005). Michael Chertoff, then Secretary of Homeland Security, responded with, "The way the emergency operations act under the law is, the responsibility and the power, the authority, to order an evacuation rests with the state and local officials. The federal government comes in and supports those officials" (Nagourney and Kornblut, 2005). This exchange is illustrative of the battles that permeated various government levels over coordination of relief efforts. Former FEMA Chief Michael Brown stated that his biggest failure was "not recognizing ... that Louisiana was dysfunctional" (CNN, 2005e).

Nagin's conflicts with state and federal officials, as well as special interest groups, have also been widely reported. Nagin's order to seize firearms sparked immediate litigation by the National Rifle Association and the Second Amendment Foundation (GPO, 2008), resulting in a court ruling on contempt of court violations and issuing a permanent injunction against Nagin. Nagin was deeply distrustful and did not want to relinquish control when former Federal Deposit Insurance Corporation (FDIC) head Donald Powell was originally appointed to oversee recovery efforts. Powell was met with suspicion and administrative power struggles, as Nagin warned Powell he was not the *federal mayor of New Orleans* (Roig-Franzia, 2005). He complained he was only allowed to spend $15 million of the $27 billion budget, although his initial plan to invest these funds to create a casino district as a recovery tool was quickly abandoned, and post-Katrina analyses outlining what is needed to rebuild New Orleans remain absent from Nagin's reported initiatives. Favoritism in appointments to recovery committees and political battles with the governor as well as key business people continued to fuel the area's long-standing reputation for dysfunction and corruption (Roig-Franzia, 2005).

Conflicts of this nature continued into the initial stages of recovery, with Nagin stating at a town hall meeting in October 2005, "I can see in your eyes, you want to know, 'How do I take advantage of this incredible opportunity? How do I make sure New Orleans is not overrun with Mexican workers,'" a comment widely criticized, most vocally by the U.S. Hispanic Chamber of Commerce (Anon., 2005). This was followed by Nagin's comment on the Tavis Smiley show (Stevens, 2006) that he hoped New Orleans would emerge as a "chocolate city," referring to its future demographics. He further inflamed ethnic tensions with claims that he knew the will of God (Sublette, 2006) and that the city "will be a majority African-American city. It's the way God wanted it to be" (CNN,

2006). He disparaged "uptown" folks, his previously strong white, affluent base (Amrhein, 2005), by proclaiming that, "God is mad at America. He sent us hurricane after hurricane … he is upset at black America. … We're not taking care of ourselves" (Martel, 2006).

Some of the reasons why funding authorities refused his monetary requests and hampered recovery efforts and why controversy continued to surround him when he finished his last term as mayor include the controversy surrounding his election, when ethnic activists bused in evacuees from other states to vote, giving Nagin a slim margin of victory in the election; his failed 100-day plan; a lawsuit by a contractor alleging Nagin was given gifts in exchange for preferential treatment; and his widely publicized view that record murders in New Orleans held positive consequences for New Orleans as it "keeps the New Orleans brand out there" (Bohrer, 2007). The Metropolitan Crime Commission called upon the State Ethics Board to investigate Nagin's alleged acceptance of vacation trips paid for by a company awarded contracts by the city, the same company involved in a lawsuit of cost overruns to the city for a crime camera system (Bohrer, 2009).

The annual quality of life poll for New Orleans (Johnson, 2009) reported approval ratings for Nagin at 29%, the lowest since the poll began, with Nagin tied for third place in a listing of the biggest problems facing the city. Later surveys by the University of New Orleans showed an even lower 24% approval rating (Bohrer, 2009). A website was established to count down the days to the end of Nagin's term in May 2010, which was viewed as a significant opportunity for advancing recovery efforts in New Orleans. Of course, this success depends, in no small part, on the ethics and political leadership of the individual elected to replace him, Mitch Landrieu.

Ethical Culture

While the reputation of the state is overwhelmingly one of rife corruption, and deservedly so, Louisianians are by and large genuinely proud of that heritage. An oft-repeated phrase is that Louisiana is no more corrupt than any other state, and its citizens are simply more proud of the fact. To natives, it's a compliment that the state, which generally appears last among all the desirable measures of health and human progress and at the top of lists of dysfunction, can outwit all those policymakers and know-it-alls who think they can bend Louisiana to be like everyone or every place else. It may be that if the standards followed elsewhere were acknowledged as ones Louisiana should emulate, then they would have to contend with a view that the way things are may not be the ideal after all. Pride in being unique, even if with a negative connotation, runs deep and wide here. If there is anything native Louisianians know for sure, it's that they are indisputably the best when it comes to the things that matter most to them: family, heritage, food, faith, and fun.

Viewed as a parochial culture separate from the demands imposed by crises, Louisiana can appear to be a comfortable place to live and visit, as many tourists, convention goers, and revelers have known for centuries. What makes the state remarkably warm and inviting, however, is also that which, in the face of catastrophe, renders it effectually incapable of recovery. In the immediate aftermath of the hurricane, when government at all levels seemed incapable of action, individuals who would come to be known as the Cajun armada took the initiative to use their own pirogues and motorboats and whatever other floatable device they had on hand to rescue stranded survivors. This provincialism was viewed as enviable and heroic as were the selfless acts of individuals and institutions across the state who opened their homes, hearts, and wallets to help those in need. It is hard to imagine any other state whose citizens could exhibit such genuine altruism and sincere desire to forsake personal safety and comfort to assist others. Yet, when the immediate crisis of saving lives concluded and it came time for a professional public administration to step in and establish order and rebuild the infrastructure of a decimated society, the vacuum of professionalism and leadership in state and local administrations was glaring, accentuated by partisan and ill-functioning federal, state, and local administrations.

Louisianians were calling out for help that could not or would not come. For the most part, they placed their hopes on the rhetoric of politicians and disaster profiteers and longing for the good ol' days of Huey Long or Edwin Edwards, some even calling for an early release from prison of the former governor in time to save the republic. It was expected and accepted that he would skim some off the top of the pile for himself, but the people felt sure there would still be enough resources left for them and that was better than what they were getting. For those interested in understanding a system of ethics and moral standards that not only accepts but facilitates and protects an administration and politic that by most any measure is unprofessional and inept, the question of why citizens do not demand fiscal, environmental, educational, and demonstrable competence begs for an explanation.

Manifestations of Louisiana's Ethical Culture

It would be neither fair nor accurate to characterize the entire state in the same manner. Northern Louisiana is much more socially, religiously, and culturally conservative than the areas directly affected by Katrina. As this discussion focuses on the aftermath of Katrina, the focus is necessarily on the southern part of the state. Cultural anthropologists, while not of one mind on the epistemological questions of measuring culture, agree that it is a body of learned behaviors common to a given society that shapes behavior and cognitive preferences (Bodley, 1994). Essentially, it is a system of (1) shared meaning that distinguishes one group from another (Schein, 1985), with language being the most important; (2) ways of organizing society such as kinship groups, organizational processes, and politics; and (3) distinctive techniques and characteristic products. Strauss and Quinn (1998) classified these cultural properties as durability of the individual, motivation force, historical durability, thematicity, and sharedness. Although cultural study can include surveys, demographic profiles, and population movement, culture is most commonly recorded through quasi-constructivist observation and reporting (Sewell, 1992; Spillman, 1995; Eliasoph, 1996).

When applying this model to Louisiana's ethical culture, it can be characterized by a unique patois of English, French, and Cajun and peppered by idioms that appear to serve both as native identifiers and as exclusionary cues to non-natives. Humor is an important aspect of the Louisiana culture and illustrates the ethical culture relevant to this discussion. The majority of the humor involves an element of sexuality, which is predictable given the economic profile of the state (Jurkiewicz, 2007), and the jokes tend to feature people using wiles to (1) outsmart another to gain an advantage, (2) outsmart an educated authority to prove common sense trumps formal learning, or (3) allow the joke recipient to feel superior to those in the story. A predominant theme is to use language to gain an advantage such as in the following examples.

> A lawyer and a Cajun are sitting next to each other on a long flight. The lawyer asks if the Cajun would like to play a fun game. The Cajun is tired and just wants to take a nap, so he politely declines and tries to catch a few winks.
>
> The lawyer persists that the game is a lot of fun. "I ask you a question, and if you don't know the answer, you pay me only $5; you ask me one, and if I don't know the answer, I will pay you $500."

This catches the Cajun's attention, and to keep the lawyer quiet, he agrees to play the game.

The lawyer asks the first question. "What's the distance from Earth to the moon?" The Cajun doesn't say a word, reaches in his pocket pulls out a $5 bill, and hands it to the lawyer.

Now, it's the Cajun's turn. He asks the lawyer, "What goes up a hill with three legs and comes down with four?"

The lawyer uses his laptop and searches all references. He uses the Airphone; he searches online and even the Library of Congress. He sends e-mails to all the smart friends he knows, all to no avail. After an hour of searching, he finally gives up. He wakes up the Cajun and hands him $500. The Cajun pockets the $500 and goes right back to sleep.

The lawyer is going nuts not knowing the answer. He wakes the Cajun up and asks, "Well, so what goes up a hill with three legs and comes down with four?"

The Cajun reaches in his pocket, hands the lawyer $5, and goes back to sleep.

Boudreaux and Tuseau got married in Jeanerette. On their honeymoon trip, they were nearing New Orleans when Boudreaux put his hand on Tuseau's knee. Giggling, Tuseau said, "Boudreaux, ya can go a little farther now if ya want to." So Boudreaux drives to Mobile.

A Cajun was stopped by a game warden in Southern Louisiana recently with two ice chests of fish, leaving a bayou well known for its fishing.

The game warden asked the man, "Do you have a license to catch those fish?"

The Cajun replied, "Naw, ma fren, I ain't got none of dem, no. Dese are my pet fish."

"Pet fish?!" the warden replied.

"Ya. Avery night I take dese here fish down to de bayou and let dem swim' round for a while. I whistle and dey jump rat back into dere ice chests and I take dem home."

"That's a bunch of hooey! Fish can't do that!" said the game warden.

The Cajun looked at the game warden for a moment and then said, "It's de truth ma' fren, I'll show you. It really works."

"Okay, I've GOT to see this!" The game warden was curious now.

The Cajun poured the fish into the bayou and stood and waited. After several minutes, the game warden turned to him and said, "Well?"

"Well, what?" said the Cajun.

"When are you going to call them back?" The game warden prompted.

"Call who back?" the Cajun asked.

"The FISH!"

"What fish?" the Cajun asked.

Kinship groups, organizations, and political offices are highly protective of their traditions, are insular, and are fueled by patronage. Louisiana natives rarely relocate away from families except under extreme circumstances, which of course intensified the personal tragedies of families scattered to various U.S. locales after Katrina. Most native families know each others' histories for multiple generations with many across the state sharing the same surnames. Frequently, the family reputation from centuries past is attributed to the decedents living today, whether warranted by observable circumstances or not. Individuals cannot overcome their ancestral reputations and are often referred to as being just like a Thibodeaux or a Robichaux or a LeJuene. Newcomers are greeted with repeated queries regarding one's ancestry, and cool familial relations are met with disbelief followed by opprobrium. Extramarital affairs are common and various crimes are easily forgiven, with extended families encircling the wrongdoer and standing resolute regardless of the circumstances. Distinctive traditions and products abound—state-observed holidays such as the week-long elaborate observance of Mardi Gras, celebrations such as Easter crawfish boils and early autumn Cochon de Lait, and foods and cuisines globally renowned for their ingredients, spice blends, and cooking techniques. Applying the measures of cultural anthropologists, Louisiana possesses a unique and clearly defined culture that exerts a strong and dynamic influence on behavior and cognitions (Rosenthal and Masarech, 2003), as well as ethical frameworks. To reiterate an earlier point, researchers have indicated that strong cultures that encourage, celebrate, and reward pushing the limits to achieve personal gains exert a powerful influence on creating and sustaining unethical behavioral patterns (Trevino, 1990).

Consequences of Unethical Leadership

One can build a persuasive argument to join the overwhelming collective voice lamenting the wasteful, unfocused, and inefficient recovery of New Orleans after Katrina. Unlike Mississippi, Texas, and Florida, which routinely suffer the effects of hurricanes, New Orleans has failed to thrive, and most fingers point to the lack of ethical and effective leadership at the local level. Although certainly not the totality of the problem, when the focus is solely on the issue of ethical leadership the buck stops in exactly this place. The ethical culture of South Louisiana is what supported Nagin's election and it can be said that he is representative of that culture. Perhaps that culture is determinant, and he was unable to rise above the tradition of corruption and selfishness characterizing Louisiana politics, as discussed in the previous section. A leader, however, is called upon to rise to the responsibilities given them, to communicate a vision for a greater public good than what preceded that individual's term in office. A leader does not use the cultural history of an area as an excuse for poor, even egregious, performance nor a "he did it so I can, too" mentality, nor the dirty hands argument. A fish rots from the head down, but it can also thrive in the same directional manner if the leader at the top sets the example for all those who follow.

Knowing the effect that leader ethicality has on the effectiveness of crisis management efforts, what can be done to improve this aspect of those in charge? Certainly, electing ethical individuals from the start is the easiest route, but determining a candidate's ethicality when only a carefully edited version of the true individual is displayed during the campaign makes such judgments nearly impossible. Ongoing ethics training based on sound scholarly research is one approach that has demonstrated effectiveness, but one cannot force individuals to be ethical if they do not want to do so. For those who have the intent but lack the tools to fully assess and articulate their ethical frameworks, and thereby act as a moral leader, two assessment tools come immediately to mind. The first is Foucault's (1984) key question set for leading an individual to systematize his or her ethical theory. The second is the Rubel character map (Rubel, 2010), a diagnostic tool to engage the leader on aspects of their character that require further development. Used in conjunction with one another, they offer insight and prescriptives to enhance leader ethicality.

Table 6.1 Foucault's Assessment of Ethicality

1.	*Ethical substance*—Which part of myself or my behavior is influenced or concerned with moral conduct? What do I do because I want to be ethical?
2.	*Mode of subjection*—How am I being told to act morally? Who is asking? To whose values am I being subjected?
3.	*Ethical work*—How must I change myself or my actions in order to become ethical in this situation?
4.	*Ethical goal*—Do I agree with this definition of morality? Do I consent to becoming this character in this situation? To what am I aspiring when I behave ethically?

Foucault's four questions are intended to help an individual understand how ethical intent is motivated and influenced by the self-interests of other organizations and persons. With Foucault, as with many others, reality is viewed as socially constructed; thus, one's ethicality is subject to cultural forces such as organizational images, the media, religious beliefs, compelling ideologies, heroes, cultural figures, and parents (Simons, 1995). Becoming aware that one's ethicality is thus defined by others allows an individual to consider how she or he might resist adopting an ethical framework that is reactive in nature and defined by an external authority. Such a self-examination leads individuals to understanding and accepting responsibility for their own actions separate from the influences of others. These questions are listed in Table 6.1. Essentially, by objectively addressing this question set, individuals can enhance the complexity of their ethical frameworks, much as suggested by Kohlberg's (1981) hierarchical model of moral development. From least to most complex, the model can be understood as illustrated in Table 6.2 (Crain, 1985).

The Rubel character map is comprised of a list of 25 virtues essential for leadership against which the individual is self- or other measured on a scale from 1 to 9. A score on the lower end of the continuum demonstrates a deficiency; at the other end, an excess. Thus, each virtue can be an advantage or a detriment to ethical character when taken to an extreme. Individuals' virtues identified on the scale as being detrimental to leader effectiveness suggest areas for needed improvement. Development in areas where an individual needs work is a protocol of action, habituation, evaluation, corrective measures, and reassessment. The virtues that comprise the Rubel character map are detailed in Table 6.3. The user circles the degree to which each virtue is exhibited by the leader in his or her observable actions, writings, and verifiable reports of behavior. What that person says about him- or herself, or what others with a particular bias may say, is not considered; instead, rely on objective data and assessment are relied upon in determining the absence of these virtues in the person's character.

Post-Crisis Performance Review

Leaders are the indisputable role models for ethical behavior in their organizations and their electorate. Although leaders generally emerge from the culture they are elected to serve, it is incumbent upon them and the responsibilities they hold to exemplify an ethical culture that elevates the community, rather than represents its lowest common denominator. The ethical impact of a leader under normal circumstances is evinced in the manner by which business is conducted, how people interact with one another, how highly education and the cultural arts are valued, the level of crime, and the environmental policies supported, as well as politics. This

Table 6.2 Kohlberg's Hierarchy of Moral Development

Stage		Description
Stage 1	Heteronomous morality	To avoid breaking rules backed by punishment, obedience for its own sake, and avoiding physical damage to persons and property.
Stage 2	Individualism, instrumental purpose, and exchange	Following rules only when it is to someone's immediate interest; acting to meet one's own interests and needs and letting others do the same. Right is also what's fair, what's an equal exchange, a deal, and an agreement.
Stage 3	Mutual interpersonal expectations, relationships, and interpersonal conformity	Living up to what is expected by people close to you or what people generally expect of people in your role as son, brother, friend, etc. Being good is important and means having good motives, showing concern about others. It also means keeping mutual relationships, such as trust, loyalty, respect, and gratitude.
Stage 4	Social system and conscience	Fulfilling the actual duties to which you have agreed. Laws are to be upheld except in extreme cases where they conflict with other fixed social duties. Right is also contributing to society, the group, or institution.
Stage 5	Social contract or utility and individual rights	Being aware that people hold a variety of values and opinions, that most values and rules are relative to your group. These relative rules should usually be upheld, however, in the interest of impartiality and because they are the social contract. Some nonrelative values and rights such as life and liberty, must be upheld in any society and regardless of majority opinion.
Stage 6	Universal ethical principles	Following self-chosen ethical principles. Particular laws or social agreements are usually valid because they rest on such principles. When laws violate these principles, one acts in accordance with the principle. Principles are universal principles of justice: the equality of human rights and respect for the dignity of human beings as individual persons.

impact is revealed in both the short and long terms. In a period of crisis, the ethicality of a leader is immediately apparent, his or her motives and intents communicated without the buffer of time to obfuscate, if indeed that is the usual *modus operandi*. Highly ethical leaders prosper during this period, demonstrating their focus on the public good, their integrity, and their effectiveness in rallying resources and organizing people to action. The unethical leader hides, vacillates, makes excuses, blames others, makes statements that engender scorn, and ultimately fails to put the safety and future of citizens first. Both the ethical and the unethical leader can have the same budgetary acumen, the same number of years of service, and same education, but it is that person's ethical character that makes the difference, most acutely in times of crisis, as to whether or not the community will prosper. Although it would be ideal to have foreknowledge of a leader's

Table 6.3 Rubel Character Map: List of Virtues

Virtue	Deficit				Average				Excess
Perseverance	1	2	3	4	5	6	7	8	9
Pride	1	2	3	4	5	6	7	8	9
Wisdom	1	2	3	4	5	6	7	8	9
Curiosity	1	2	3	4	5	6	7	8	9
Ingenuity	1	2	3	4	5	6	7	8	9
Spirituality	1	2	3	4	5	6	7	8	9
Perspective	1	2	3	4	5	6	7	8	9
Judgment	1	2	3	4	5	6	7	8	9
Open-mindedness	1	2	3	4	5	6	7	8	9
Critical thinking	1	2	3	4	5	6	7	8	9
Justice	1	2	3	4	5	6	7	8	9
Loyalty	1	2	3	4	5	6	7	8	9
Compassion	1	2	3	4	5	6	7	8	9
Courage/bravery	1	2	3	4	5	6	7	8	9
Emotional intelligence	1	2	3	4	5	6	7	8	9
Gratitude	1	2	3	4	5	6	7	8	9
Love	1	2	3	4	5	6	7	8	9
Self-control	1	2	3	4	5	6	7	8	9
Humility	1	2	3	4	5	6	7	8	9
Forgiveness/mercy	1	2	3	4	5	6	7	8	9
Honesty/integrity	1	2	3	4	5	6	7	8	9
Prudence	1	2	3	4	5	6	7	8	9
Humor	1	2	3	4	5	6	7	8	9
Optimism/hope	1	2	3	4	5	6	7	8	9
Patience	1	2	3	4	5	6	7	8	9

ethical character, a post-crisis review using the instruments discussed here as well as data assessed from his or her words and actions will provide a clear profile on which the leader and the electorate can take action. As Martin Luther King axiomatically stated in 1963, "The ultimate measure of a man is not where he stands in moments of comfort and convenience, but where he stands at times of challenge and controversy."

Questions for Discussion

1. How can an electorate assess the ethical character of a leader prior to election? How reasonable is it to expect citizens to undertake this process? If they do not, is there a basis upon which they can rightfully complain or litigate when faced with ethical transgressions of the individual whom they elected without fully vetting that individual's character?
2. How can a community's ethical culture be changed? Whose role is it to undertake such changes? How can you assess when such a change process has been successful? What does a positive ethical culture look like in a community?
3. In a crisis situation, when it is clear that the ethical leadership and ethical culture are exacerbating the problem rather than facilitating a solution, whose responsibility is it to step in and correct the problem? When is the right time for this to happen?

Additional Reading

Brinkley, D. (2007). *The Great Deluge*. New York: Harper Perennial.
Eggers, D. (2010). *Zeitoun*. New York: Vintage.
Fink, S. (2013). *Five Days at Memorial: Life and Death in a Storm-Ravaged Hospital*. New York: Crown.
Robinson, D. (2005). *Hurricane Katrina: The Destruction of New Orleans*. Seattle, WA: BookSurge.
Rose, C. (2005). *1 Dead in the Attic: After Katrina*. New York: Simon & Schuster.
U.S. Senate. (2005). *Hurricane Katrina in New Orleans: A Flooded City, A Chaotic Response*, Hearing Before the Committee on Homeland Security and Governmental Affairs, U.S. Senate, 109th Congress, First Session. Washington, DC: U.S. Government Printing Office.

References

Amrhein, S. (2005). In Big Easy cleanup, us vs. them. *St. Petersburg Times*, October 23.
Anon. (2005). USHCC deplores remarks by New Orleans Mayor Ray Nagin regarding Mexican workers and the rebuilding of New Orleans. *HispanicPRWire.com*, October 19 (http://hispanicprwire.com/en/ushcc-deplores-remarks-by-new-orleans-mayor-ray-nagin-regarding-mexican-workers-and-the-rebuilding-of-new-orleans/).
Bodley, J.H. (1994). *An Anthropological Perspective from Cultural Anthropology: Tribes, States, and the Global System*. Mountain View, CA: Mayfield.
Bohrer, B. (2007). News of killings keeps "New Orleans brand out there," *Associated Press*, August 10.
Bohrer, B. (2009). Popularity plummeting, Nagin caught in vacation controversy. *Boston Globe*, May 17.
Bourdieu, P. (1990). *The Logic of Practice* (R. Nice, trans.). Stanford, CA: Stanford University Press.
Crain, W.C. (1985). *Theories of Development*. Upper Saddle River, NJ: Prentice Hall.
CNN. (2005a). The latest on Katrina's aftermath: evacuees say Gretna police blocked access to river's west bank at gunpoint. *CNN.com*, September 13 (http://www.cnn.com/2005/US/09/07/news.update/).
CNN. (2005b). Reaction to Katrina split on racial lines. *CNN.com*, September 13 (http://www.cnn.com/2005/US/09/12/katrina.race.poll/).
CNN. (2005c). Nursing home owners charged. *CNN.com*, September 14 (http://www.cnn.com/2005/LAW/09/13/katrina.nursinghome/).
CNN. (2005d). The latest on Katrina's aftermath: Mississippi attorney general files lawsuit against insurance companies. *CNN.com*, September 15 (http://www.cnn.com/2005/US/09/15/news.update/).
CNN. (2005e). Brown puts blame on Louisiana officials. *CNN.com*, September 28 (http://www.cnn.com/2005/POLITICS/09/27/katrina.brown/).

CNN. (2005f). Witnesses: New Orleans cops took Rolex watches, jewelry. *CNN.com*, September 30 (http://edition.cnn.com/2005/US/09/30/nopd.looting/).
CNN. (2006). Nagin apologizes for 'chocolate' city comments. *CNN.com*, January 18 (http://www.cnn.com/2006/US/01/17/nagin.city/).
Eliasoph, N. (1996). Making a fragile public: a talk-centered study of citizenship and power. *Sociol. Theory*, 14(3): 262–289.
Foucault, M. (1984). On the genealogy of ethics: an overview of work in progress. In Rabinow, P., Ed., *The Foucault Reader*, pp. 340–372. New York: Pantheon.
GPO. (2008). *National Rifle Association of America (NRA), Inc. and Second Amendment Foundation, Inc. v. C. Ray Nagin and Warren Riley*, No. 05-4234 (E.D. LA 2008). Washington, DC: U.S. Government Printing Office.
Gyan, Jr., J. (2006). Ex-N.O. officer charged in post-Katrina theft. *The Advocate*, January 21, p. B5.
Johnson, Jr., A. (2009). Survey: N.O. mood better. *The Advocate*, April 7, p. 9A.
Johnson, Jr., A.M. and Robertson, C. (2014). 10-Year term on graft charges for C. Ray Nagin, former mayor of New Orleans. *The New York Times*, July 9, p. A14.
Jurkiewicz, C.L. (2000). The trouble with ethics: results from a national survey of healthcare executives. *HEC Forum*, 12(2): 101–123.
Jurkiewicz, C.L. (2002). The phantom code of ethics and public sector reform. *J. Public Affairs Issues*, 6(3): 1–19.
Jurkiewicz, C.L. (2006). Soul food: Morrison and the transformative power of ethical leadership in the public sector. *Public Integrity*, 8(3): 245–256.
Jurkiewicz, C.L. (2007). Louisiana's ethical culture and its effect on the administrative failures following Katrina. *Public Admin. Rev.*, 67(6): 57–63.
Kohlberg, L. (1976). Moral stages and moralization: the cognitive–developmental approach. In Lickona, T., Ed., *Moral Development and Behavior*, pp. 170–205. New York: Rinehart & Winston.
Kohlberg, L. (1981). *Essays on Moral Development*. Vol. 1. *The Philosophy of Moral Development*. San Francisco, CA: Harper & Row.
Kohlberg, L. (1985). A current statement on some theoretical issues. In Modgil, S. and Modgil, C., Eds., *Lawrence Kohlberg: Consensus and Controversy*, pp. 485–546. Philadelphia, PA: Falmer.
Martel, B. (2006). Storms payback from god, Nagin says. *Associated Press*, January 16.
Nagourney, A. and Kornblut, A. (2005). White House enacts a plan to ease political damage. *The New York Times*, September 5.
Parry, R. (2005). Mississippi burning: pollution hell as fires, explosions and oil spills follow the hurricane. *Mirror Online*, September 3 (http://www.mirror.co.uk/news/uk-news/mississippi-burning-556039).
Robinette, G. (2005). Mayor to feds: "Get off your asses." WWL-AM Radio, September 2 (www.edition.cnn.com/2005/US/09/02/nagin.transcript/).
Roig-Franzia, M. (2005). Who's in charge of rebuilding New Orleans? *Washington Post*, November 4, p. A03.
Rosenthal, J. and Masarech, M.A. (2003). High-performance cultures: how values can drive business results. *J. Org. Excel.*, 22(2): 3–18.
Rubel, R. (2010). *Rubel Character Map*. Annapolis, MD: U.S. Naval Academy.
Russell, G. (2005). Nagin gets mixed reviews: evacuation plans, Superdome use criticized. *The Times Picayune*, October 23, p. 1.
Salmon, J. (2005). Fraud alleged at red cross call centers. *Washington Post*, December 27, p. A02.
Scahill, J. (2008). *Blackwater: The Rise of the World's Most Powerful Mercenary Army*. New York: Nation Books.
Schein, E.H. (1985). *Organizational Culture and Leadership*. San Francisco, CA: Jossey-Bass.
Sewell, W. (1992). A theory of structure, duality, agency, and transformation. *Am. J. Sociol.*, 98(1): 1–29.
Simons, J. (1995). Transgression and aesthetics. In Simons, J., Ed., *J. Foucault and the Political*, pp. 68–80. London: Routledge.
Spillman, L. (1995). Culture, social structure, and discursive fields. *Curr. Perspect. Social Theory*, 15: 129–154.

Stevens, A. (2006). Ray Nagin: former mayor of New Orleans. *CityMayors.com*, May 28 (http://www.citymayors.com/mayors/new_orleans_mayor.html).

Strauss, C. and Quinn, N. (1998). *A Cognitive Theory of Cultural Meaning*. Cambridge, MA: Cambridge University Press.

Sublette, N. (2006). P-Funk politics. *The Nation*, June 5.

Tapper, J. (2005). Amid Katrina chaos, congressman used National Guard to visit home. *ABC News*, September 13 (http://abcnews.go.com/US/HurricaneKatrina/story?id=1123495).

Trevino, L.K. (1990). A cultural perspective on changing and developing organizational ethics. In Pasmore, W.A. and Woodman, R.W., Eds., *Research in Organizational Change and Development*, Vol. 4, pp. 195–230. Greenwich, CT: JAI Press.

Chapter 7

Katrina: A Case of Manmade and Natural Disaster

Steven G. Koven

Contents

Chapter Goals 123
Introduction 124
Hurricane Katrina and the Readiness of New Orleans 124
    The Storm and Its Impact 124
    Hurricane Studies and Preparedness..125
Critique of the Emergency Management Response 126
    Failure of Initiative.. 126
    Systemic Failure of Institutionalized Patronage 127
    Individual Failure of Patronage Appointees 129
Lessons from Hurricane Katrina 131
Conclusions 132
Questions for Discussion.. 132
Additional Reading 133
References 133

Chapter Goals

1. Provide a better understanding of the dichotomy between merit and patronage hiring.
2. Highlight the need for basic competence in emergency management.
3. Discuss the highly visible role played by emergency managers during crises.
4. Describe the need for coordination in emergency management.

Introduction

Widely perceived as "a disaster within a disaster," Hurricane Katrina revealed the extent to which serious positions within the federal bureaucracy are filled by persons with questionable qualifications. The storm exposed the consequences of such policies, as the emergency response was marked by a lack of coordination, callousness, delay, and transferring blame. Images of residents trapped on their roofs, pleading for assistance, were quickly imprinted on the minds of the American public. Officials were widely castigated for incompetence as well as their callous disregard for the suffering of their fellow citizens. Commentators in the media asked how this could happen in America, a nation that prides itself not only on its wealth but also on its "can do" attitude. This case study describes the devastation of the hurricane, how prepared New Orleans was for the storm, the incompetence of people in charge, the mistakes that were made, and the key lessons learned from the crisis. The damage attributed to incompetence is highlighted as well as how unqualified managers can exacerbate problems. A crisis demands swift and effective action, which, as this case demonstrates, was not present as the devastating hurricane ravaged the states along the Gulf of Mexico in August of 2005.

Hurricane Katrina and the Readiness of New Orleans

The Storm and Its Impact

Hurricane Katrina made landfall southeast of New Orleans on August 29, 2005. Katrina brought severe winds, rainfalls of up to 14 inches, and catastrophic flooding. Katrina was the costliest and one of the five deadliest hurricanes in American history (Kates et al., 2007). The high winds (reaching 175 miles per hour at sea) created a powerful storm surge that led to the collapse of three major levees in the city (van Heerden and Bryan, 2006). When the levees were breached, a wall of water surged out, eventually occupying approximately 80% of the city. The deputy director of the Louisiana State University Hurricane Center reported that 87% of all the water that flooded the greater New Orleans metro area was caused by levee failure rather than rainfall. Water poured out of the breached levees for more than 60 hours, after which the city's water level equaled the water level in adjoining Lake Pontchartrain (van Heerden and Bryan, 2006).

As a result of Katrina, most of the city of New Orleans was inundated with water approximately 6.5 to 10 feet (2 to 3 meters) deep; in some areas, the depth of the water was more than 16 feet (5 meters). Immediately health concerns were raised about the "toxic gumbo" of water contaminated by pollutants such as hydrocarbon fuels (from fuel storage units) and chemicals from commercial chemical storage units. There were also fears expressed about elevated levels of metals such as lead and arsenic. Other sources of contaminants included gasoline from automobiles and herbicides found in home gardens (Reible, 2007).

The psychological impact of Katrina is also apparent. Researchers at the University of New Orleans, the University of Southern Mississippi, Stanford University, and Arizona State University queried residents of the areas affected by Katrina. They found that over 50% of the those surveyed reported that they experienced symptoms of general distress, including upsetting memories, trying to avoid conversations about the hurricane, increased irritability, increased anger, worries about recurring storms, and tense feelings (Weems et al., 2007).

According to an official government report, Hurricane Katrina caused 1326 deaths, displaced more than 700,000 people, and destroyed or damaged an estimated 300,000 homes. Disaster declarations covered over 90,000 square miles (Office of Inspector General, 2006). Monetary costs associated with Katrina were enormous. Some estimates put the cost of the storm's property damage at about $97 billion: $67 billion from housing damage, $7 billion from damage to consumer durables, $20 billion from damage to business property, and $3 billion from damage to government property (Koven, 2008). Estimates of property damage ranged from $20 to $22 billion (Kates et al., 2007) to as high as $81 billion (Tate, 2011). Some of the total damage estimates ranged from $125 to $150 billion. These figures surpassed costs associated with the 9/11 attack in inflation-adjusted dollars (Tate, 2011).

Katrina had a scarring impact, particularly on the elderly, the poor, and minorities. In the state of Louisiana, about 71% of those who died from Katrina were older than 60 years of age, and 47% were older than 75. Some of the dead were found in nursing homes allegedly abandoned by their caretakers (Office of Inspector General, 2006). More than 100,000 residential structures were flooded. Of those structures, about 78,000 were severely damaged or completely destroyed. Of the 126 public schools in New Orleans, only 7 had no damage and in more than half damage exceeded 25% of replacement value. In July 2007, nearly 2 years after the storm, New Orleans had an estimated 300,000 residents, only two thirds of its estimated 452,000 pre-hurricane total (Nelson et al., 2007).

Hurricane Studies and Preparedness

A major storm that would hit New Orleans was not unexpected. Officials from Louisiana State University's Coastal Studies Institute had been warning people all over the world that New Orleans was a "nightmare" waiting to happen. This nightmare hit on August 29th, 2005. Although the nightmare of the storm was expected, the seeming inability of officials to directly deal with the crisis came as a surprise to many who watched on television as stranded citizens pleaded for help.

These citizens deserved better, and given the history of New Orleans (replete with natural disasters) the city should have been better prepared. From its founding by the French in 1718, municipal leaders were well aware that much of city sat below sea level. The response from the French founders and later settlers was to build levees. Following floods, levee heights were raised approximately a foot higher than the last high-water level. This strategy provided some safety but also led to future catastrophes. In the 4 years preceding Hurricane Katrina, there were extensive warnings from scientists that the "big one" would eventually hit (Kates et al., 2006).

As New Orleans grew in population, responsibility for levee construction shifted to the state and eventually the federal government. Incremental improvements in the levees were made on the basis of the size of the last storm. In addition to increasing the height of levees, two major floodways were built to divert waters. This diversion appeared to enhance protection from river flooding but did little to shelter the city from hurricanes.

Over time, Congress passed flood protection legislation. Following the great floods of 1927, the Flood Control Act of 1928 supplemented the levee system with reservoirs, channel improvements, and floodways. The Flood Control Acts of 1936 and 1938 continued to make improvements. In 1968, the Federal Insurance Administration and the National Flood Insurance Program were created. These initiatives encouraged communities to explore different approaches to flood management, such as land use planning and flood-proofing buildings (Hauber and Michener, 2006).

The city of New Orleans did possess an emergency management plan (i.e., Comprehensive Emergency Management Plan) to deal with the destruction of a major storm. This plan was included in the Flood Control Act of 1965; however, it was not adequately implemented. Implementation was hindered by delays, cost overruns, legal challenges, local opposition, environmental concerns, and other issues (Carter, 2005; GAO, 2005). Between 1996 and 2005, government funding for natural disasters declined despite warnings from the U.S. Corps of Engineers about the need to invest in aging infrastructure (Carter, 2005). Faced with difficult budget choices, both Republican and Democratic administrations ignored the threat posed by a Katrina-sized hurricane.

Prior to 2005, a variety of studies were conducted by the U.S. Army Corps of Engineers. These studies estimated that improvements in the levee system could be made to protect against a major Category 5 storm. It was estimated that improvements would cost at least $2.5 billion and take 10 to 20 years to complete. Funding, however, did not materialize, and in Fiscal Year 2005 Congress appropriated only $100,000 toward a feasibility study (Carter, 2005). There was little sense of urgency in Congress, and the recommended $2.5 billion that would have provided added protection for residents of the city of New Orleans was not allocated. In hindsight, this money would have been very well spent.

On paper, New Orleans was not totally unprepared for the hurricane. In July 2004, federal, state, and local officials as well as leaders from volunteer organizations participated in a mock hurricane exercise. This drill (Hurricane Pam Exercise) was designated to equip officials with the ability to respond to a Category 3 hurricane making a direct hit on New Orleans (Glasser and Grunwald, 2005). Under this scenario, it was anticipated that more than 1 million residents would have to be evacuated from the city (Hurricane Pam Exercise Concludes, 2004). The exercise predicted that a Category 3 hurricane would require about 1000 shelters to be open for 100 days. A hurricane plan called for the state of Louisiana to supply the shelters for the first 3 to 5 days, after which the federal government and other providers would replenish supplies. The hurricane plan also provided for search and rescue of stranded residents (FEMA, 2004). Officials expected that about 300,000 people would be trapped in the city if a Category 3 storm hit the area (Anon., 2005b). The White House was informed of the possible damage that a powerful hurricane could produce but took no action (Glasser and Grunwald, 2005).

The levee and floodwall system in New Orleans was not designed to protect the city against the unusual occurrence of a slow-moving Category 4 or 5 storm (Carter, 2005). Furthermore, a study conducted by a team of Louisiana investigators indicated that the levee system in New Orleans was flawed. They concluded that sheet piles (the interlocking sheets of steel driven into the soil to anchor the levees and prevent water from flowing underneath) were too shallow. The U.S. Army Corp of Engineers agreed that problems with piling depth were present but concluded that the problem represented only one of numerous factors that contributed to the disaster (Schwartz and Drew, 2005).

Despite exercises and the existence of a disaster plan, public officials seemed ill prepared. The police department drew special criticism. Officers did not seem to know about contingency plans, hundreds of police patrol cars were either flooded or stranded, the police department's primary radio system did not function, the exchange that handled the New Orleans cell phone area code was inoperative, and many of the existing police cars were either running out of gas or had flat tires from running over debris (Baum, 2006). The American media displayed pictures of desperate people sitting on roof tops, surrounded by water and holding up handwritten signs that pleaded for help.

Critique of the Emergency Management Response
Failure of Initiative

As the images of Katrina victims appeared on television, Americans asked how such a calamity could occur. Blame was heaped on the professional planners as well as state, city, and federal officials who seemed to be incapable of addressing a natural disaster of such magnitude. Few focused on the fact that the seeds of the city's destruction had been building for decades. The erosion of wetlands, inadequate design of levees, confusion over responsibility for levee maintenance, a poorly designed navigation canal, and insufficient funding to update the levee system all were cited as factors contributing to the catastrophe (Carter, 2005; Reible, 2007).

A U.S. House of Representatives report, titled *A Failure of Initiative*, concluded that numerous levels of government failed to meet their obligations and that the response to Hurricane Katrina constituted "a litany of mistakes, misjudgments, lapses, and absurdities all cascading together, blinding us to what was coming and hobbling any collective effort to respond" (Ink, 2006, p. 800). According to the Congressional Report, the inadequate response to Katrina was primarily the result of a failure of policy implementation, not a failure of public policy. The report was critical of the Department of Homeland Security (DHS), citing (1) poor movement of information across departments and between jurisdictions; (2) poor coordination among the Defense Department, DHS, and state of Louisiana; (3) a lack of joint training with other groups; (4) government red tape that delayed needed medical help; and (5) a failure of initiative (Ink, 2006).

In retrospect, many things could have been done differently. The mayor of New Orleans waited until Katrina escalated to a Category 5 storm before ordering a mandatory evacuation. Michael Brown, the director of the Federal Emergency Management Agency (FEMA), waited until 5 hours after Katrina hit land to request additional Homeland Security employees. Brown did not allow fire and emergency service personnel to respond to calls for help unless they were lawfully dispatched by state and local authorities. Municipal and school buses were flooded and were inoperative. New Mexico's governor, Bill Richardson, offered the governor of Louisiana (Kathleen Blanco) the assistance of his state's National Guard, yet the paperwork needed to implement the plan was delayed for 4 days (Brinkley, 2006; Dyson, 2006; Koven, 2008).

Offers of help for hurricane victims were not given adequate attention. For example, the head of the American Bus Association volunteered to assist in an evacuation. FEMA, however, did not accept the offer and did not order buses until 18 hours after the hurricane made landfall. Assets from an 844-foot ship with helicopters, marines, physicians, hospital beds, food, and the ability to make 100,000 gallons of water a day were underutilized. Only the helicopters were used to rescue stranded citizens (Dyson, 2006). Airboat pilots volunteered to rescue storm victims and transport supplies but were prevented by FEMA from entering the city. The Red Cross was denied entry to the city because FEMA claimed the city was not safe. FEMA rejected assistance from the city of Chicago and blocked a 500-boat citizen flotilla that tried to deliver aid. FEMA also kept the Coast Guard from delivering diesel fuel, turned back a German plane that was carrying rations, failed to properly utilize hundreds of volunteer firefighters, and wasted the efforts of about 1000 firefighters from other communities when they were given the task of distributing flyers (Koven, 2008).

Systemic Failure of Institutionalized Patronage

The hapless response to Hurricane Katrina is at least indirectly linked to patronage. More than 100 years ago, revulsion about the abuses of spoils produced an outcry that led to the creation of a politically neutral civil service system. The ethos that spurred this reform, however, has been undermined since the 1980s, spurred by the image of lazy incompetent public officials. If competence is not assumed or demanded then, in theory, it is not a long way down the slippery slope to assume that unqualified people can be appointed to positions of authority without doing much damage. The limits of antigovernment positions, though, were revealed in Hurricane Katrina. Media portrayals of helpless citizens and self-centered government officials seemed too much for the American people, who began to look for answers.

One answer to Katrina's "disaster within a disaster" can be traced to blatant disregard for the ethos of merit. This ethos stands at the heart of the discipline of public administration. The genesis of public administration can be traced to Woodrow Wilson's appeal for separating day-to-day administration from the "rough and tumble" of politics. For Wilson, government employees could be more businesslike and more efficient if they were allowed greater autonomy from the pressures of politics (Wilson, 1887). This insight later became codified in the infamous "politics–administration dichotomy." Under the framework of the "politics–administration dichotomy," day-to-day decisions should be placed under the domain of "businesslike" professionals. Wilson called for Americans to learn about efficiencies of governance from Europeans but to still remain aware of the differences between autocratic (European) and democratic (American) societies. Wilson stated that there needed to be a "science of administration which shall seek to straighten the paths of government, to make its business less unbusinesslike, to strengthen and purify its organization, and to crown its dutifulness" (as quoted in Shafritz and Hyde, 1992, p. 13). Furthermore, Wilson stated that public administration must be "Americanized" by embracing the "good" of efficiency while at the same time rejecting the "bad" of centralized power (as quoted in Shafritz and Hyde, 1992, p. 23).

City managers as well as other government officials are trained professionals in contrast to elected officials whose decisions may be swayed by powerful voting blocks. The advantage of having professionals in place in positions of authority (rather than unqualified cronies of powerful politicians) was highly evident in the emergency response to Hurricane Katrina. In the immediate aftermath of Katrina, the inadequacies of the unqualified director of FEMA could not be hidden.

The German scholar Max Weber also supported the idea of separating politics from administration. In Weber's view, politicians give direction to policy and passionately express values. In contrast, bureaucrats impartially administered the law. This neutral application of rules, according to Weber, constitutes legal–rational authority that is a hallmark of modern societies. Weber contended that administration under legal–rational authority produced organizations that were fairer and more efficient than those governed by charismatic or traditional forms of authority (Fry, 1989).

In contrast to the ethos of neutral competence, the ethos of patronage maintains that winners in electoral contests should receive their "spoils." In accord with an ethos of spoils, political parties are able to reward their follower with jobs and contracts. Political appointments follow the logic that for elected officials to be representative of the people that voted for them they should be able to exercise greater control over the permanent bureaucracy through appointments (Goodnow, 1900). The concept of spoils or merit, however, is not an either/or proposition but one of degree. The question that arose in the aftermath of Katrina concerns the proper balance between patronage and merit. Insights from Katrina suggest that hiring practices in the George W. Bush administration tilted too strongly in the direction of spoils.

Spoils or patronage can be a double-edged sword. It can enhance representation but at the same time undermine competence (Kaufman, 1956). From the time of Andrew Jackson, spoils expanded representation and allayed fears of elitism. These fears have a long traditional in American politics. James Madison wrote in the *Federalist No. 39* that those who administer government should be chosen from the society at large, not from a favored class. An extension of this principle would allow elected officials to have broad discretion and the freedom to appoint officials who shared their values.

The danger of patronage, however, is evident. During the time of the George W. Bush administration a director of FEMA was appointed who clearly lacked any experience in emergency management but possessed strong political connections. The background and behavior of this political appointment are described below in detail. This appointment unambiguously identifies the damage patronage can inflict on citizens who expect a minimal level of service from their public officials.

Patronage abuse was identified in a 2008 report prepared by the U.S. Justice Department's Inspector General. The report found that senior aides to former Attorney General Alberto Gonzales broke civil service laws by using politics to guide hiring decisions. The report singled out Monica Goodling, a young lawyer from the Republican National Committee, for inappropriate actions. In May 2007, at the height of an uproar over the firings of U.S. Attorneys, Goodling admitted that she may have crossed the line at times in using politics to influence hiring (Lichtblau, 2008).

The Department of Justice investigation revealed that Ms. Goodling and other Justice Department officials used personal interviews and Internet searches to screen out candidates who might be "too liberal" and identify candidates who were supportive of President Bush. The Department of Justice investigation indicated that one candidate was rejected for a job in part because she was thought to be a lesbian. A Republican lawyer received high marks on his job interview because of his conservative views about "god, guns, and gays." A highly regarded prosecutor was passed over for an important position because his wife was active in Democratic politics (Lichtblau, 2008).

The New York Times reported that the White House was also involved in decisions to dismiss federal prosecutors. White House officials consulted with the Justice Department in preparing a list of prosecutors for removal. Seven prosecutors were forced out. In one case, a U.S. Attorney was removed to make room for an adviser to Karl Rove, a close associate of President Bush. Rove also passed on complaints about a U.S. Attorney who had failed to indict Democrats in a voter fraud scandal. This attorney, along with six others, was dismissed on December 7, 2006 (Johnson and Lipton, 2007).

Individual Failure of Patronage Appointees

After Hurricane Katrina, FEMA Director Michael D. Brown became a poster child for the incompetence of political appointees. Numerous accounts cast serious doubt on his truthfulness and ability to manage; for example, his biography posted on the FEMA website revealed that Brown served as an assistant city manager in Edmond, Oklahoma, with emergency services oversight. When questioned about Brown's position, however, a representative from Edmond stated that Brown had no authority over other employees and was more like an intern.

An article in *Time* magazine observed that Brown listed under the "Honors and Awards" section of his profile, "Outstanding Political Science Professor, Central State University," although Brown was only a student at Central State. Under the heading of "Professional Associations and Memberships," Brown stated that he had been director of a nursing home in Edmond. An administrator with the home, however, reported that Brown was "not a person that anyone here is familiar with." His padded résumé apparently went undetected when he was appointed head of FEMA in 2003. Brown claimed that the *Time* article distorted his record but he did not provide proof to refute the story (Fonda and Healy, 2005; Brinkley, 2006; Koven, 2008; Anon., 2015).

Brown's work prior to joining FEMA was uneven at best. In the 1980s, he worked for an attorney in Oklahoma who described him as "not serious and somewhat shallow." Brown was one of the two attorneys (out of 37) who were terminated when the firm split up. Brown ran for Congress in 1988 against a Democratic incumbent and lost by a wide margin. From 1999 to 2001, Brown was the Judges and Stewards Commissioner for the International Arabian Horse Association (IAHA). Some members of the IAHA nicknamed him "The Czar" for his imperious attitude. After numerous lawsuits were filed against the IAHA by its own members, Brown resigned from his position (Koven, 2008).

The history of FEMA sheds some light into how someone such as Brown could be appointed its director. FEMA was created in 1979 by President Jimmy Carter but was held in low regard by the incoming Reagan administration. Tulane Professor Douglas Brinkley noted that, by 1981, the agency already smacked of patronage, and appointing a person as director of FEMA was "akin to giving a donor or friend the ambassadorship to Luxembourg—a cushy, largely honorary position." FEMA was perceived as a joke. When Hurricane Hugo hit the Carolinas in 1989, South Carolina senator Fritz Hollings called FEMA employees "the sorriest bunch of jackasses I've ever known" (Brinkley, 2006).

Brown's appointment can be attributed to the fact that he was an old college friend of Joseph Allbaugh, a fellow Oklahoman and chief of staff under Texas governor (and later president) George W. Bush. Allbaugh served as Bush's campaign manager during the 2000 presidential election. After Bush was elected, Allbaugh was appointed director of FEMA. Although Allbaugh excelled at raising money and troubleshooting, he knew almost nothing about disaster relief. Allbaugh retired from FEMA, in 2002, after FEMA was absorbed into the new Department of Homeland Security. After retirement, Allbaugh was replaced by his old friend, Michael Brown.

From a public relations perspective, Brown's performance in the Katrina spotlight was an unmitigated disaster. Faults with Brown's management are well documented. Among the more egregious of Brown's actions are the following:

- On August 29, 2005, 5 hours after the hurricane hit land, Brown made his first request for Homeland Security rescue workers. He requested that rescue workers should not be deployed to the disaster area until they completed 2 days of training. This significantly slowed down the response at the time of greatest need.
- Brown instructed fire and rescue departments outside of the affected areas to refrain from providing trucks or emergency workers without a direct appeal from state or local governments. The intent was to avoid coordination problems and the accusation of overstepping federal authority. This again slowed down the government response.
- Regarding how he might be perceived on television, Brown discussed whether he should roll up his shirt sleeves.
- On August 31, FEMA's key employee in New Orleans e-mailed Brown, stating, "Sir, I know that you know the situation is past critical. … Estimates are many will die within hours. … We are out of food and running out of water at the dome, plans in works to address the critical need." Brown responded, "Thanks for the update. Anything specific I need to do or tweak?" This response suggested a complete inability to adequately perform assigned responsibilities as well as an official totally out of his depth and unprepared to assume his responsibilities.
- When Brown received the above-mentioned e-mail, his press secretary wrote that, "It is very important that time is allowed for Mr. Brown to eat dinner." This e-mail is indicative of Brown's imperious nature reminiscent of when he was the commissioner for the International Arabian Horse Association.
- On September 1, 2005, Brown told Paula Zahn of CNN that he was unaware that New Orleans' officials had housed thousands of evacuees, who ran out of food and water. Major news outlets had been reporting this for at least a day. It was apparent that Brown seemed to know less about what was going on in New Orleans than the media and media watchers.
- On September 2, 2005, Mayor of Chicago Richard M. Daley stated that he pledged firefighters, police officers, health department workers, and other resources on behalf of the city, but he was asked to send only one tank truck. This suggested that Brown was either insensitive to victims or unaware of the seriousness of the situation.

- An e-mail from a New Orleans congressional representative offering medical equipment went unanswered for 4 days, again suggesting serious incompetence on the part of Brown.
- On the morning of the hurricane, Brown asked the deputy director of FEMA, "Can I quit now?" A day later, he asked an acquaintance to "please rescue me." This displayed a jocular demeanor that was ill fitted for the gravity of the situation.
- In the midst of the crisis, Brown wrote about his "problems finding a dog-sitter."
- In an e-mail to his deputy public affairs director, Brown joked that he was a "fashion god" and that his clothes came from Nordstrom. Such a narcissistic demeanor at the time of emergency represented the height of arrogance that reinforced the negative stereotypes of public officials (Anon., 2006; Koven, 2008).

On September 9, 2005, the head of the Department of Homeland Security Michael Chertoff relieved Brown of all onsite duties along the Gulf Coast. On September 12, 2005, Brown announced his resignation as the director of FEMA. Chertoff, however, granted Brown two 30-day contract extensions and Brown continued to receive his $148,000 annual salary until November 2, 2005. Brown was viewed by some as a scapegoat; however, a more reasonable explanation is that he was representative of a patronage system run amok.

In spite of these events, following his dismissal, Brown seemed unrepentant. In testimony before a U.S. House of Representatives investigative panel, Brown blamed the Louisiana governor, the mayor of New Orleans, the military, and Department of Homeland Security officials for the problems of Katrina. He admitted to making only two mistakes: not holding regular media briefings and not being able to persuade the governor of Louisiana and the mayor of New Orleans to "get over their differences." Brown concluded that he was happy to be a scapegoat if it meant the FEMA he knew could be "reborn" and "get back to where it was" (Hsu, 2005). Brown became the butt of jokes for popular comedians. Comedian Jon Stewart stated, "No word yet on Mr. Brown's future plans, though sources say he does want to spend more time doing nothing for his family." Jay Leno observed, "This is very exciting. You may have heard today President Bush announced a plan to put a man on Mars—the head of FEMA." Damning references to Brown also came from elected leaders. The president of Jefferson Parish near New Orleans pleaded for Brown's replacement, stating, "Take whatever idiot they have at the top of whatever agency and give me a better idiot. Give me a caring idiot. Give me a sensitive idiot. Just don't give me the same idiot" (Anon., 2005a; Kurtzman, 2006).

Lessons from Hurricane Katrina

Hurricane Katrina exposed the soft underbelly of American disaster preparedness. It helped reveal the extent to which public organizations are suffused with political cronyism as well as the consequences of patronage hiring. The behavior of Michael Brown indicates that essential government services are undermined by the clueless behavior of political appointees at the top of large public organizations. Brown's actions during the response to Hurricane Katrina serve as a sober reminder of the negative consequences of patronage.

One lesson of Katrina is that clear lines of authority should be determined in reactions to emergencies. In the case of Katrina, too many decisions seemed to be postponed. Needed aid was rejected because of confusion over who had responsibility for what. The insensitivity and incompetence of patronage officials were glaringly revealed. High-ranking officials should be given at least minimal instruction on how to respond to crisis situations or they should totally delegate authority to lower level officials who are better able to handle emergency situations.

Emergency management plans should not be ignored. Expenditures for proper construction and upkeep of levees would have been cost effective. Ignoring safety concerns with regard to the levees in New Orleans was penny wise but pound foolish.

The concept of basing responsibility on competence linked to testing, experience, education, and capabilities should be revisited. These ideals were espoused by supporters of the Progressive Movement in the early 20th century. The ideals of merit and neutral competence in government, however, fell out of favor in the latter part of the 20th century as critics of government castigated caricatures of the lazy, incompetent, underworked, overpaid, and nonresponsive civil servant. Hurricane Katrina reinforced this stereotype and, at the same time, exposed the need to instill confidence in government.

Dealing with natural disasters is a key governmental responsibility. In order to fulfill this responsibility it is incumbent upon government leaders to appoint people capable of carrying out their assigned duties. Katrina exposed the dirty secret that many jobs are filled because of party loyalty or political ideology. These features trump the requisite for even minimal levels of competence in appointed positions.

A final lesson of Katrina is to pay more attention to warnings of engineers and other professionals. Louisiana State University researchers issued a report in 2007 stating that Katrina was largely a "manmade" catastrophe and that citizens were denied the protections mandated by Congress in the 1965 Flood Control Act. An official of the American Society of Civil Engineers termed Katrina the worst engineering catastrophe in U.S. history borne out by a failure to recognize the fragility of the levees and how destructive the consequence of levee failure would be (Tate, 2011).

Conclusions

The implications of Katrina for emergency management are profound and highlight the dangers of patronage and potential embarrassment for the government. The ethos of patronage, however, appeared to be alive and well during the Bush administration. This case study highlights missteps that occurred during one of the largest natural catastrophes in the nation's history. Missteps were exacerbated by officials who appeared to be ill informed and out of their depth. Patronage, lack of coordination, and neglect of infrastructure all played a role in the poor response or exacerbation of the damage. Finally, Hurricane Katrina reinforced various maxims: (1) there is a legitimate role for government in American society; (2) citizens demand at least a minimal level of competence; (3) excessive cronyism can cause political embarrassment; (4) rather than concerning itself with writing reports, emergency management instead should be actively involved in ensuring proper implementation of plans; and (5) establishing standard operating procedures for emergencies will go a long way toward reducing confusion. Patronage at a minimum can act as a burdensome weight on government effectiveness. Costs of political appointments may be bearable as long as appointees are not faced with responsibilities of any magnitude. Once faced with such responsibilities the inadequacies of political selections can be quickly exposed. These costs might literally have deadly consequences. The damage to governance that emanates from appointments such as FEMA Director Brown is real.

Questions for Discussion

1. What role should political appointees play in running organizations? Should they be largely ceremonial or should they have real responsibility? How can the potential damage from political appointees be mitigated?

2. What differences may have occurred in the Katrina response if a merit employee headed FEMA rather than Michael Brown?
3. Would the public be better served by limiting the number of patronage appointments?
4. What would it take to restore faith in government organizations?
5. Do you think disaster response has improved since Katrina? How so?

Additional Reading

Brinkley, D. (2006). *The Great Deluge*. New York: Harper Collins.
Dyson, M. (2006). *Come Hell or High Water: Hurricane Katrina and the Color of Disaster*. New York: Basic Books.
Ink, D. (2006). An analysis of the House Select Committee and White House reports on Hurricane Katrina. *Public Administration Review*, 66(6): 800–807.
Kates, R.W., Colten, C.E., Laska, S., and Leatherman, S.P. (2007). Reconstruction of New Orleans after Hurricane Katrina: a research perspective. *Cityscape: A Journal of Policy Development and Research*, 9(3): 5–22.
Kaufman, H. (1956). Emerging conflicts in the doctrines of public administration. *The American Political Science Review*, 50(4): 1057–1073.
Van Heerden, I. and Bryan, M. (2006). *The Storm*. New York: Viking Press.
Wilson, W. (1887). The study of administration. *Political Science Quarterly*, 56(4): 481–506. (Reprinted in Shafritz, J. and Hyde, A., *Classics of Public Administration*, 3rd ed., Brooks Cole Publishers, Pacific Grove, CA, 1992.)

References

Anon. (2005a). FEMA director bears the brunt of Katrina anger. *Associated Press*, September 8 (www.msnbc.msn.com/id/9244682).
Anon. (2005b). LSU researchers assist state agencies with hurricane response plans. *LSU Highlights*, Summer.
Anon. (2015). Michael D. Brown. *Wikipedia*, http://en.wikipedia.org/wiki/Michael_D._Brown.
Baum, D. (2006). Deluged. *The New Yorker*, January 9, pp. 50–63.
Brinkley, D. (2006). *The Great Deluge*. New York: Harper Collins.
Carter, N.T. (2005). *New Orleans evees and the Floodwalls: Hurricane Damage Protection*, Congressional Research Service Report for Congress RS22238. Washington, DC: Library of Congress.
Dyson, M. (2006). *Come Hell or High Water: Hurricane Katrina and the Color of Disaster*. New York: Basic Books.
FEMA. (2004). Hurricane Pam Exercise Concludes [press release]. Washington, DC: Federal Emergency Management Agency (http://www.fema.gov/news release/2004/07/23/hurricane-pam-exercise-concludes).
Fonda, D. and Healy, R. (2006). How reliable is Brown's resume? *Time*, September 8 (www.time.com/time/nation/article/0,8599,1103003,00.html).
Fry, B. (1989). *Mastering Public Administration: From Max Weber to Dwight Waldo*. Chatham, NJ: Chatham House.
GAO. (2005). *Army Corps of Engineers: Lake Pontchartrain and Vicinity Hurricane Protection Project*, Testimony before the Subcommittee on Energy and Water Development, Committee on Appropriations, House of Representatives, statement of Anu Mittal, Director, Natural Resources and Environment. Washington, DC: Government Accountability Office (www.gao.gov/new.items/d051050t.pdf).
Glasser, S.B. and Grunwald, M. (2005). The steady buildup to a city's chaos. *Washington Post*, September 11, p. A1 (http://www.washingtonpost.com/wp-dyn/content/article/2005/09/10/AR2005091001529.html).
Goodnow, F.J. (1900). *Politics and Administration: A Study in Government*. New York: Russell & Russell.
Hauber, R. and Michener, W. (2006). Natural flood control. *Issues Sci. Technol.*, 15(1): 74–80 (http://issues.org/?s=Natural+Flood+Control).

Hsu, S. (2005). Brown defends FEMA's efforts. *The Washington Post*, September 28 (http://www.washingtonpost.com/wp-dyn/content/article/2005/09/27/A).

Ink, D. (2006). An analysis of the House Select Committee and White House reports on Hurricane Katrina. *Public Admin. Rev.*, 66(6): 800–807.

Johnston, D. and Lipton, E. (2007). White House said to prompt firing of prosecutors. *The New York Times*, March 13 (http://query.nytimes.com/gst/fullpage.html?res=9A0DE3DE1131F930A25750C0A9619C8B63).

Kates, R.W., Colten, C.E., Laska, S., and Leatherman, S.P. (2006). Reconstruction of New Orleans after Hurricane Katrina: a research perspective. *Proc. Natl. Acad. Sci.*, 103(40): 14653–14660.

Kaufman, H. (1956). Emerging conflicts in the doctrines of public administration. *Am. Polit. Sci. Rev.*, 50(4): 1057–1073.

Koven, S.G. (2008). *Responsible Governance: A Case Study Approach*. Armonk, NY: M.E. Sharpe.

Kurtzman, D. (2006). *Hurricane Katrina Jokes: Late-Night Jokes about the Botched Response to Hurricane Katrina*, http://politicalhumor.about.com/od/hurricanekatrina/a/katrinajokes.htm.

Lichtblau, E. (2008). Report faults aides in hiring at Justice Department. *The New York Times*, July 29 (http://www.nytimes.com/2008/07/29/washington/29justice.html?pagewanted=all&_r=0).

Nelson, M., Ehrenfeucht, R., and Laska, S. (2007). Planning, plans, and people: professional expertise, local knowledge, and governmental action in post- Hurricane Katrina New Orleans. *Cityscape*, 9(3): 23–52.

Office of Inspector General. (2006). *A Performance Review of FEMA's Disaster Management Activities in Response to Hurricane Katrina*, Report OIG-06-32. Washington, DC: U.S. Department of Homeland Security.

Reible, D. (2007). Hurricane Katrina: environmental hazards in the disaster area. *Cityscape*, 9(3): 53–68.

Schwartz, J. and Drew, C. (2005). Levee break blamed on design flaw. *Louisville Courier Journal*, December 1, p. A3.

Shafritz, J. and Hyde, A. (1992). *Classics of Public Administration*, 3rd ed. Pacific Grove, CA: Brooks Cole Publishers.

Tate, K. (2011). Hurricane Katrina history and numbers (infographic). *LiveScience*, January 27 (www.livescience.com/11235-hurricane-katrina-history-numbers.html).

Van Heerden, I. and Bryan, M. (2006). *The Storm*. New York: Viking Press.

Weems, S.F., Watts, S.E., Marsee, M.A., Taylor, L.K., Costa, N., Cannon, M.R., Carrion, V.G., and Pina, A.A. (2007). The psychosocial impact of Hurricane Katrina: contextual differences in psychological symptoms, social support, and discrimination. *Behav. Res. Ther.*, 45: 2295–2306.

Chapter 8

Managing at the Edge of Chaos: Lessons Learned from the 2006 Bam Earthquake in Iran

Ali Farazmand

Contents

Chapter Goals	136
Introduction: Managing at the Edge of Chaos	136
2003 Iranian Bam Earthquake	137
Crisis Management and Emergency Governance	138
Response System	138
Crisis Leadership and Command Structure	139
Managing Chaos	140
Organization and Management	141
Lessons Learned	143
Leadership	143
Chaos, Crisis Management, and Emergency Governance	143
Organization and Coordination	144
Policy and Administrative Lessons	144
Dealing with Public Health Challenges	144
Post-Disaster Recovery and Return to Normalcy	145
Popular Volunteer Response	145
Mistakes to Avoid	145
Managing on the Edge of Chaos	146
Conclusion: Best or Worst Practice?	146
Questions for Discussion	147
Additional Reading	147
References	147

Chapter Goals

The goals of this chapter are to

1. Identify crisis and emergency management situations.
2. Explain the differences between emergency governance and crisis management.
3. Describe linear and nonlinear models for chaos and crisis management.
4. Discuss Iran's Bam earthquake and its implications.
5. Highlight the lessons learned from the Bam earthquake as a global case in crisis and emergency management.

Introduction: Managing at the Edge of Chaos

Managing crises and emergencies has been a central concern and function of governments throughout history. How much we have learned from the great ancient empires (such as Persia and Rome, which had the best organized and managed systems) and smaller, self-managed communities, cities, and towns is an important topic beyond the scope of this short chapter (e.g., Olmstead, 1948; Cook, 1983; Farazmand, 2009). Despite much progress in human development and management of natural resources, along with the application of more advanced technologiesI, we have now come to realize that managing on the edge of chaos is a subject of study that has advanced considerably but still has a long way to go. Indeed, some of the best governed and managed empires of the ancient world had good ideas on how to anticipate, plan and prepare for, and mitigate large-scale crises borne out of chaos and disasters. No doubt, advances in crisis management and emergency governance have led to significant improvements and offer increased sophistication in an age of rapidly growing information and communication technologies (Farazmand, 2017). Knowledge of chaos and transformation theories is thriving, thanks to research by an increasing number of scholars ranging from the natural to social sciences (Jantsch, 1980; Prigogine and Stengers, 1984; Loye and Eisler, 1987; Kiel, 1994; Gleick, 1997). Today, advances in crisis and emergency management have led to the development of finely calibrated capacity building in governance and public administration (Farazmand, 2004, 2009).

On the surface, chaos denotes disorder, or a lack of organization, cohesion, and orderliness—the opposite of order, stability, and smooth functioning of phenomena, systems, and organizations (Farazmand, 2003). Closer examination and study of chaos and chaotic situations, however, may reveal how wrong we may be in our conception of external phenomena and how we, confined within the prisons of our own thinking, may misread and misunderstand the dynamics of chaos and chaotic phenomena and developments. The dynamics of a dialectical relationship require closer examination of the forces seeking maintenance of stability and the *status quo*, on the one hand, and the forces seeking change and innovation, on the other. The relationship between order and chaos is often manifest through social changes or alteration of physical environments over time and climatic or manmade changes (Farazmand, 2003). Managing chaos is different from managing regular emergencies, even most crises. What makes it so different is that chaos-driven crises often display properties unique to chaotic situations, so unique that the capacity to manage the chaos would be overkill if applied to regular crises and emergencies (for more on this, see Chapter 1).

2003 Iranian Bam Earthquake

Iran is one of the few countries in the world prone to frequent earthquakes. The country covers an area of 1,648,000 km² in southwest Asia and has a population of over 75,000,000, primarily concentrated in urban areas. Iran has almost every natural resource any country needs for industrialization and technological advancement (Farazmand, 1989). The country is bordered by Pakistan and Afghanistan on the east; Turkmenistan, the Caspian Sea, and Azerbaijan on the north; Turkey and Iraq on the west; and the Persian Gulf littoral in the south, where several major Iranian islands are located. Iran is highly vulnerable to natural disasters, most notably earthquakes, due to its location in the active Alpine–Himalayan seismic belt. Over 300 Iranian cities are located within the earthquake areas. The number of people killed as a result of the many earthquakes since the mid-20th century has been estimated to be over 126,000, third after China and Japan and possibly fourth after Mexico, as well. Given the fact that the country is rich in oil (one of the top five oil-producing countries of the world) and gas reserves (second after Russia), casualties due to earthquakes can and often are more devastating than elsewhere in the world.

At about 1:56 a.m., on December 26, 2003, a devastating earthquake measuring 6.3 on the Richter scale struck the ancient city of Bam in the southeast province of Kerman, some 1250 km away from the national capital of Tehran. Although the center of the earthquake hit Bam, it devastated the entire province of Kerman, destroying every highway, road, and type of infrastructure it touched. A rich agricultural area, Bam has many natural resources, but the city is most famous for its political history and its many landmarks, including the world's first and largest mud brick fortification, the Bam Citadel (*Arg-e Bam*), an international treasure that attracts millions of visitors per year—foreign as well as domestic. The Bam Citadel is over 2700 years old, dating back to the early Median and Persian empires and even the earlier Elamite Empire. The city of Bam rivaled the Burned City, located in the next border province of Sistan and Baluchistan in the southeast region of Iran.

The earthquake destroyed almost the entire city proper of Bam, including its government infrastructure, roads and highways, commercial buildings, public and private facilities, houses, and livestock. Only a few modern buildings survived, including a local export bank, Bank Saderat. The casualties included the loss of 40,000 to 50,000 of the city's population of 120,000 and almost all of the city's livestock. About 70 to 80% of the Bam Citadel, a magnificent landmark structure that had survived for 2700 years old, was destroyed. This historical landmark, a UNESCO World Heritage Site, had withstood many prior earthquakes, wars, and invasions. The Bam Citadel fortification had sheltered thousands if not millions of people fleeing invasions and raids for thousands of years. Extensive damage was done to the Citadel's beautiful exterior facade and expansive interior structure, with its many ancient *caravanserais* (roadside inns) that used to house thousands of travelers on the ancient Silk Road that stretched from China to Europe through Persia and Iran. The Bam Citadel is currently being restored, a process that may require many years of painstaking efforts to complete.

The earthquake hit the region after midnight, when most people were asleep in both the city and its suburbs, representing another 130,000 people, many of whom also died. The destruction extended well beyond the city limits of Bam—all highways as far as 100 miles away were destroyed. The provincial capital of Kerman city, about 125 miles away, was also affected, and transportation systems to and from the capital were disrupted. A truly chaotic crisis hit the city, its survivors, government officials, and the governance system in the aftermath of the earthquake.

However, several days later, when international relief teams arrived, including the International Federation of Red Cross and the U.S. Federal Emergency Management Agency (FEMA), the situation in Bam was already returning to relative normalcy. The author traveled with the FEMA team returning back from Bam and was told by the team leader that, "Things are under control and we have nothing to do."

How was the earthquake disaster operation managed? How was the rescue and response effort organized and managed? How did the emergency management system work? How was the crisis governed and managed? What organizational structure was instituted in the wake of nearly total collapse of the city? What strategic and operational lessons can be learned from this global case of crisis and emergency management for the future? These and other related questions are important not only for the fields of crisis and emergency management but also for chaos-based crisis management. Following are brief responses to some of the above questions, followed by a short list of additional reading. Data used for this chapter were collected from the following sources: interviews conducted with the victims and witnesses of the Bam earthquake; with some of the officials directly involved in the crisis and emergency and crisis management of Bam; with officials who participated in a workshop in Tehran on crisis and emergency management that this author conducted the following year, with a focus on the Bam earthquake as a case study; and with some scholars studying and reporting on the earthquake, as well as published and unpublished materials.

Crisis Management and Emergency Governance

Response System

The response to the Bam earthquake came in three forms: unofficial, official, and a combination of the two. The unofficial response was quick and immediate but unorganized, desperate, problematic, chaotic, and haphazard. This was the immediate response of people who had survived the earthquake, who had sustained injuries, who had lost loved ones and friends or neighbors. In such situations it is common to see people rushing to the rescue, helping to recover bodies and belongings, or simply surviving by fleeing the scene of the crisis and seeking safety elsewhere, which is a very natural response in times of danger. In the case of Bam, few who survived fled; most stayed on and helped. They actively searched for victims, both human and animal. There was not much in the way of belongings to recover, as almost the entire city was destroyed. Remarkably, some people were still found alive after days and nights of cold winter weather. The problems associated with this response were manifold; for example, people used every means possible to dig through the ruins to find their loved ones, but doing so risked causing harm to injured survivors buried a few feet away. The response was chaotic, unorganized, and uncoordinated but demonstrated what can be accomplished when people unite for a common cause.

The official response, too, was problematic for the first 24 hours, as the entire city infrastructure was destroyed, including all government buildings, hospitals, emergency vehicles, and any means of providing relief. Roads and highways were damaged within a 100-mile radius of the city, limiting immediate access to the disaster scene. The only access was by air or by ground transportation provided by nearby military bases. Two major crisis centers were set up, one at the provincial/regional capital city of Kerman and another in Tehran, Iran's capital. Airborne emergency services arrived in Bam shortly after. It wasn't until the third day after the earthquake that comprehensive response services were able to arrive at the scene. The volunteer forces were comprised of local and regional civilians, professionals and nonprofessionals, and technically equipped teams from other provinces all over the country. Because of the severity of the disaster situation, Iran declared a national disaster emergency, and international aid organizations sent in emergency teams, including the International Federation of Red Cross and FEMA.

Crisis Leadership and Command Structure

The Bam earthquake created a sudden crisis of vast proportion requiring a national response. In addition to being a strategic ancient city with many historical landmarks, Bam is also a bridge stone on the ancient Silk Road that connects China and the Far East to the Mediterranean and Europe via Iran. Further, Bam is a strategic communication link between eastern and southeastern Iran and the rest of the country. Finally, Bam is a popular tourist destination that draws millions of visitors from all over the world. Thus, addressing the Bam disaster was too important to be left to regional crisis and emergency management.

An immediate national response to the Bam earthquake crisis was the formation of a central crisis management center in Tehran under the leadership of the Office of the President and the National Emergency Management Agency (often referred to as a crisis management center or office), the highest national office coordinating and offering leadership to crises and emergency situations. Two parallel crisis centers were also set up at the same time in Kerman and in Bam. The field command center in Bam began immediately coordinating and providing emergency services to those in need, coordinating rescue and lifesaving operations, and managing the collection and distribution of relief supplies as well as food and warm clothing (with the aid of numerous official and unofficial local and national volunteer services). Make-shift tents were spread out throughout the area in anticipation of possible aftershocks that could cause significant damage if the tents were set up in a central area. The center also helped facilitate transportation systems by repairing roads and highways, erected temporary hospital and health clinics in tents to avoid potential disease outbreaks, and coordinated security efforts. Along with the local crisis management command system in the field, a host of other organizations were mobilized and engaged, including the Revolutionary Guards' Corp, Special Elite Forces, the military, and numerous volunteer organizations.

The immediate task of the crisis management command centers in Tehran, Kerman, and Bam was to address the chaos created by the disaster. The three words of utmost importance in Bam's crisis management were disaster, chaos, and crisis. One citizen said, "Initially, we the survivors were so mentally and physically shocked and exhausted that we couldn't see what was going on. I wondered if there was anyone in my family alive, even though I could see my grandson crying and walking around." A key health worker observed that, "The situation on the first and second day was so chaotic and desperate that even the best organized and equipped clinical services were helplessly unutilized due to most survivors' and their outside relatives' interfering with the relief efforts. This is a collective culture with full traditions of volunteering, selfless support mentality, and give-it-all-you-have norms of national character. People tend to forget their own self-interest and jump in to sacrificing efforts to help others." This, she continued, was both good and bad—good because everyone helped, but bad because in doing so they contributed to the chaos and disorder.

The arrival of the regiments of national and regional organizational forces of the Revolutionary Guards as well as "chaos control forces" to the field subdued the chaos, and crisis management proceeded smoothly. Yet, several challenges remained to be managed: public health issues, continued search-and-rescue operations, the cold weather of December, and the cultural and religious belief systems.

Security was an issue that clearly fell under the control of special forces. Iran's paramilitary forces (Basij) were present from the first day but were better prepared on the second and third day. It was against the people's cultural and religious beliefs to use machines to dig in the rubble and bring out humans—dead or alive. Further, these beliefs also ran counter to the mobilization of search-and-rescue dogs. Many people believed that dogs are not clean and should not be welcomed inside houses, certainly not living as pets as elsewhere in the world. Also, drug dealers and users feared the use of dogs that could locate drugs and lead police to those possessing drugs, resulting in incarceration. "Some dogs disappeared during the operation, because some traditional people and some drug dealers and users didn't want them there," commented a former official in charge of a subfield command center on the eastern side of Bam.

Normally, chaos begets chaos, complicating emergency rescue and relief operations, but this did not happen in Bam. The multidimensional chaos that had prevailed the first day or two was quickly and effectively arrested, but the crisis remained and had to be managed. Particularly critical issues were sheltering people in an organized fashion, providing food and clothing, and ensuring sanitary services to prevent a potential epidemic. Bam's 95 health clinics, 14 rural health centers, 10 urban health centers, 5 health posts, public and private hospitals, nursing centers, and almost any facility providing any type of health services were damaged, with the extent of damage ranging from 40 to 100% (Jahangiri et al., 2012). There was no shortage of medical and food supplies, as they were shipped in by air and over newly opened roads, but the distribution and effective management of medical supplies and health services remained a major problem. Tent hospitals were erected in every corner and neighborhood of the city, guarded by security and neighborhood watch committees, as well as the police and Revolutionary Guards.

Chaos was arrested, and the crisis was brought under control, but managing on the edge of chaos was an interesting challenge that tested the ability and capacity of the both government and volunteer organizations in Bam. The national government had a reputation for being able to navigate through the high seas of crises; in fact, managing at the edge of crisis is and always has been an exceptional capacity of Iranian post-revolutionary institutions.

Managing Chaos

How was the crisis managed and how was the chaos tamed? The leadership of this national disaster addressed the task of chaos management at three levels: a centralized national command center, a regional provincial command center that oversaw various local service providers and command centers, and a field command center in Bam, which coordinated various official and unofficial organizations, mostly civilian. The Revolutionary Guards and special task force units followed their own commend structures in concert with the central command center.

A key feature of any major disaster is a tendency for chaos to ensue; in fact, chaos is a normal development. One must expect the unexpected, anticipate the unanticipated. A problem with many modern managers is that they often think linearly (Weick and Sutcliffe, 2001) and forget that the world does not always operate on a linear path (Farazmand, 2009, 2014a). The ability to think outside of the box, to anticipate the unanticipated, or to expect the unknown builds the capacity necessary to govern and manage (Farazmand, 2009, 2014b).

The three levels of command structures maintained contact with each other and provided essential feedback that contributed to making decisions. The experiences of the 8-year war with Iraq provided Iranian crisis management systems ample opportunities to learn and relearn, to retool their capacities as the dynamics of the war changed and unfolded. No one took any moment of stability for granted; no one anticipated anything other than unknowns and the unthinkable, ranging from unexpected ambushes to the use of chemical weapons by Saddam. The Bam earthquake disaster was another testing ground for the government's capacity to operate on the edge of chaos. Various organizations helped the government with its central command in Tehran. A multitude of government agencies were involved in taming the chaos on the ground in Bam and managing crises as they arose. These agencies included the Ministry of Roads and Transportation, Ministry of Communications and Information Technology, Ministry of Intelligence and National Security, and Ministry of Health and Medical Education. These and other national agencies worked at a horizontal level with the agencies that moved, transported, and delivered supplies from Tehran and other national centers to Bam, where local agencies then distributed supplies to those who needed them within and around the city.

These local agencies provided a direct link to the people—both surviving victims and service providers, including volunteers, official organizations, international aid teams, and regional emergency service teams. Conflict would sometimes arise as to who was responsible for what, but at the end of the day it was always clear that the local agencies were in charge. Chaos occasionally intensified as opportunists and criminal elements from nearby cities descended on Bam in hopes of stealing food, clothing, and shelter materials. Most of these criminals were caught right away, and those who got away were usually caught miles away by undercover security and intelligence officials. Local field coordinators played a very significant role in building and maintaining credibility and trust among Bam's citizens and surviving victims, thus reinforcing a positive attitude toward government and the Revolutionary Guard forces, as well as the popular people-organized mobilization forces known as Basij. The Guards and the Basij provided constant vigilance against potential terrorism from outside and perhaps even inside, against the potential threat of secret foreign military operations, and against disturbances that could serve as a prelude to further chaos. They also maintained law and order along with newly installed or transplanted local police.

The National Intelligence and Security Agency operated overtime on a 24-hour basis to make sure that accurate intelligence was gathered and accurate information was provided to the central command center, while maintaining the security of communication lines and coordinating with the local and provincial information centers. The provincial command center was an important link between the central and local command centers and performed horizontally with other provinces engaged in crisis and emergency management of the disaster.

Organization and Management

The people of Bam and surrounding areas were initially placed in various housing shelters. Tents were erected throughout the city in a number of neighborhoods. Large concentrations of tents were avoided in anticipation of possible aftershocks. These tents were helpful in alleviating the immediate hardships endured by the survivors. Regionalized areas were designated for service delivery and management, and provincial support systems served as both suppliers and back-up service providers. Erecting tents throughout the city within the first few days of the crisis was a temporary measure designed to deal with the immediate disaster and emergency or crisis management issues. Development of the regionalized service delivery and management areas progressed over time as the crisis was brought under control and order was restored, although emergency management challenges were still enormous. To make the crisis more manageable, the city of Bam and its surroundings were initially divided into 6 districts; this number was then increased to 10 and then to 13 after 15 days. Two districts were outside of the city, in Khajeh Asghar and Bravat. Government intervention and public management of the post-quake disaster were organized around these districts to maximize efficiency and effectiveness.

The provincial command center assigned 13 major provinces to serve as support systems based on their proximity to Bam and resource capacities. Each of these provinces provided support services and was charged with the responsibility of providing various services to one of 13 designated districts. These services included providing food, shelter, human resources, and medical services; removing debris; cleaning up; and transporting waste. The governor of each province was charged with leadership responsibility for the Bam district to which the province was assigned, along with the Red Crescent Society, the municipality, and the medical university of the province. These provincial institutions and organizations had the mission and responsibility to make sure all necessary services were provided to the districts in Bam. The 13 provinces involved in this effort were (1) Yazd, (2) Khorasan, (3) Isfahan, (4) Hormozgan, (5) Tehran, (6) Gilan, (7) Fars, (8) Central (Markazi), (9) Azarbaijan Sharghi (Eastern Azarbaijan), (10) Qom, (11) Mazandaran, (12) Azarbaijan Gharbi (Western), and (13) Sistan and Baluchestan (Jahangiri et al., 2012). Other provinces were assigned to provide additional support to help the assisting provinces perform their tasks more efficiently and effectively; for example, the Kashan province was assigned to support Isfahan province, and Chaharmahal Bakhtiyari was assigned to support the Qom province.

Medical universities in the assisting provinces were assigned the responsibility of providing healthcare services to their designated districts in Bam. The responsibilities of each medical university included providing the following (Farazmand, 2012; Jahangiri et al., 2012):

1. *Physical space*—At least four distinct places (i.e., tents) set up to provide medical examinations, vaccinations, family planning and obstetrician services, and first aid services
2. *Equipment and facilities*—Bedding, desks, chairs, coolers, refrigerators, vaccine carriers, stethoscopes, flashlights, and more
3. *Drugs and medications*—Antibiotics, oral rehydration solutions, serums, sedatives, contraceptive pills, and more
4. *Human resources*—At least 11 staff members for each unit, including one or two doctors, a pathologist, an environmental health expert, two environmental health technicians, two disease diagnosis and prevention specialists, an obstetrician or midwife, and a healthcare assistant

According to eyewitnesses on the scene, about an hour after the earthquake struck the area, Iran's mental health administration agency dispatched to Bam several psychologists and mental health professionals who provided emergency mental support services to the survivors. The agency had recently held a workshop for healthcare workers, officials, and administrators that were sponsored by the medical universities, social welfare organizations, University of Social Welfare and Rehabilitation Sciences, Red Crescent Society, Ministry of Education, and National Youth Organization.

This discussion has revealed only the tip of the iceberg with regard to the services offered to Bam and the surrounding districts in the province of Kerman; for example, the Bam Citadel was immediately put on UNESCO's agenda for restoration, a process that continues as of today. Most if not all survivors of the earthquake disaster have returned to the city and surrounding areas. The economy of the city is picking up and has been doing well. The residents of Bam have tended to put their sad memories behind them and have moved forward. The city of Bam is vibrant again, and tourists are returning for traditional sightseeing purposes and to assess the impact of the earthquake.

Lessons Learned

Institutions can survive massive disasters if the response is immediate and effective. The Bam disaster was a unique case of emergency and crisis management in action. It provides a good case study to demonstrate that, despite an initial delay of 24 hours due to massive logistic obstacles (e.g., destruction of roads and airfields), the organization and management of the crisis and emergency management can be remarkably well done.

The historic disaster that struck the ancient city of Bam caused massive destruction and will be remembered for a long time to come. However, despite the nearly total destruction of the entire city of 120,000, the deaths of over 50,000 people, and 50,000 survivors in need of serious medical care, and despite total destruction of the area's infrastructure within a 100-mile radius, the disaster was managed effectively. Studies and reports may vary due to the investigators' expectations, criteria, and other assumptions, but the fact is that, despite the many odds faced, deficiencies encountered, and shortcomings experienced, the crisis was managed well. The chaos was subdued immediately, no public health crisis was allowed to develop, no rioting occurred, no looting took place, no security breaches happened, and no conflicts got out of hand. Also, no further loss of lives occurred because emergency services were provided within 24 hours. So, what lessons can be learned from this global case for the future of crisis and emergency management? At least nine major lessons may be drawn from this case for the study and practice of crisis and emergency management.

Leadership

The massive earthquake of Bam challenged leadership functions at local, provincial, and national levels. This was a huge challenge that the national political leadership had to shoulder for a variety of reasons: political demands to do something and to do it very quickly, the need to utilize effective crisis management and emergency governance to bring the situation under control quickly, the need to maintain national and regional security to forestall any foreign opportunistic aggression, and having the greatest capacity to respond to the crisis at hand. The leadership challenge was met effectively, although it perhaps could have been accomplished in less time. The Revolutionary Guards and Basij responded immediately, along with a nationally dispatched health service response to deal with the mental and basic health needs of the survivors. The national leadership setting up a crisis command center was a step in the right direction that helped subdue the immediate chaos and deal with the crisis that lie ahead. The provincial leadership under the command of the Kerman governor, as well as parallel command centers in Kerman, provided ample leadership support to manage the disaster in Bam.

Chaos, Crisis Management, and Emergency Governance

Not all disasters and emergency situations cause crises, but almost all crises create a sense of urgency and demand emergency responses. The massive earthquake in Bam caused an emergency situation that quickly turned into temporary chaos with crisis dynamics that were changing and unfolding by the hour. Chaos is inevitable and expected in most emergency and crisis situations, but the dynamics and indicators vary from situation to situation. The chaos in Bam was primarily caused by the lack of available resources due to the destruction of almost all of the infrastructure, facilities, and food and drinking water supplies, in addition to the cold conditions of winter. The ability of the central command center to airlift tents, supplies, food, water, and medical necessities within 24 hours was remarkable and served to arrest the chaos. Chaos can quickly turn into a crisis situation of many dimensions. Anticipating the unexpected was a key feature of the national and regional crisis command centers that helped bring chaos under control. The implementation of crisis management and emergency governance was declared not only for Bam but also for areas hundreds of miles away from the earthquake center. Emergency governance can take military, security, political, and managerial measures as needed; such governance was shown to be effective and timely in Bam. Similarly, crisis leadership took measures to manage the crisis through both vertical and horizontal functions, as noted earlier.

Organization and Coordination

Another lesson learned from Bam disaster management was the importance of organization and coordination. Dividing the city of Bam and its surrounding into 13 districts was an innovative approach to managing the emergency situation at hand. In addition, gathering supplies from around the country and delivering them to Bam for distribution by local command systems were major tasks that required careful organization. The designation of assisting and supporting provinces to come to the aid of fellow citizens in Bam and its surroundings was a remarkable achievement, an idea that can be applied almost anywhere in the world.

Policy and Administrative Lessons

The policy and administrative lessons are clear in that, without a sound national policy on crisis and emergency management, many functions and efforts can be wasted and without result, thus failure will almost certainly follow. Having a clear policy is essential in guiding swift actions, but that requires strong leadership and capacity building capable of responding to all crisis situations. The national government had in place such a capacity to respond, and all key elements of the national policy were put into action immediately after the disaster, including military and security functions; providing health care, food, and shelter; and initiating search-and-rescue operations. Critical to the success of crisis management in Bam was the implementation of policy decisions coming from command centers at both national and provincial levels, as well as dividing the disaster areas into 13 districts and assigning assisting and supporting provinces to provide aid to those districts.

Dealing with Public Health Challenges

Another key lesson to be drawn from this example is the issue of public health and healthcare service delivery. In most large-scale disaster situations, a major challenge is preventing or controlling the spread of disease among the survivors. Providing immediate healthcare services for the injured and survivors and providing the necessary sanitary facilities, immunizations, medical supplies, hospital bedding, and medical staff to arrest potential public health crises are critical, requiring effective and efficient emergency leadership and management. In Bam, the immediate healthcare service response was remarkable, despite the delay caused by impassable roads and inoperable communications systems. The assignment of assisting provinces and additional supporting provinces to aid the 13 designated districts of the disaster area ensured the timely provision of healthcare services under the leadership of the various provincial medical universities, a remarkable achievement. The multi-organizational and multi-institutional healthcare service response was extremely well coordinated and implemented, a lesson that can be applied to all crisis and emergency situations worldwide.

Post-Disaster Recovery and Return to Normalcy

Space limitation forbids extensive discussion of this lesson, but suffice it to say that the challenge of post-disaster recovery and a return to normalcy was effectively met. This was accomplished by transferring the surviving population to designated areas where shelter was provided, by rebuilding housing for those who had lost their homes, by offering national and provincial aid to citizens to help them recover from their losses, by providing compensation and subsidies to affected business owners, and by rebuilding the public facilities and infrastructure, including hospitals, roads, street lights, electric power stations, schools, playgrounds, tourist centers, commercial and banking services, security and police stations, cultural centers, mosques, and more. The city of Bam recovered fairly quickly and returned to partial normalcy in less than a year. Today, though, more work remains to be done, such as restoring the Citadel and other major tourist spots, as well as the development of a more modern and quake-proof infrastructure to protect the city from future disasters.

Popular Volunteer Response

Another lesson to be learned from this case was the role that volunteers played in the response and recovery stages of this national disaster. The people of Iran are very collectively minded, and their concern for others in times of crises and disasters is a very strong public service motivational force. People responded from all over the country by rushing to the site to help with the search-and-rescue operations (although at times they became obstacles to professional emergency responders), offering material and monetary aid, making themselves available to carry out any and every task they could be assigned, cleaning up streets and roads, helping with transportation, cooking hot meals for the survivors, helping with orphaned children and trying to find relatives or caregivers, taking care of livestock, and more. The response of the Iranian people to the Bam earthquake was outstanding and was a response that one should hope for all over the world.

Mistakes to Avoid

Still another lesson to be learned from this disaster is that mistakes are inevitable but can be avoided. These mistakes may be categorized as cultural, personal, or organizational and managerial. An example of a cultural mistake in this case is the many people who, based on traditional and religious grounds, displayed little appreciation for the efforts of the search-and-rescue dogs that were brought in to help. Dogs are certainly among the best friends of people, and the value of their services cannot be overstated. Security and neighborhood watch committees failed to safeguard against the actions of drug users who sought to kill the rescue dogs so their drug supplies would not be revealed. A program to raise awareness of the value of these precious animals must be launched nationally so their extremely important services are helped rather than hindered during times of disaster.

With regard to personal mistakes, people need to be trained, through community education, neighborhood training events, and periodic drills, on how best to respond in disaster situations so their volunteer assistance is not wasted. Similarly, professional disaster and emergency managers need to receive adequate training on how best to utilize the free and valuable support services volunteers provide. Clearly stated policies, guidelines, procedures, and rules of conduct should be developed so volunteers do not risk getting hurt. In the case of the Bam earthquake, there were reports of individual volunteers being treated improperly and who were hurt due to a lack of proper coordination and backup services.

Organizational and managerial mistakes will be made but are not acceptable. A rush of various types of aid pouring in during all stages of disaster management can be expected, but the failure to coordinate activities on the ground can be a fatal mistake, as has happened in many disaster situations around the world. The potential for corruption and the abuse of monetary and materials resources is growing. It is not uncommon for thieves to enter a disaster area, such as Bam, to steal whatever they can get their hands on. There must be a system in place to prevent this from happening. According to one official at Bam, "One hundred sixty blankets, over fifty tents, and medical supplies were stolen during the third and fourth days of disaster management in Bam." It is necessary to have safeguards in place against such theft.

Managing on the Edge of Chaos

Finally, managing at the edge of chaos is a capacity not many organizations have, but it is a capacity all modern organizations and governments must build and develop. The last lesson learned from how the Iranian Bam earthquake disaster was managed is how important it was to have effective authorities in Tehran and on the ground to manage at the edge of chaos. Iran developed this ability during and after the Revolution and refined it during the 8-year war with Iraq. Iran's effective chaos management has been further refined by the constant challenges and threats the country has faced from within by terrorists and abroad by foreign adversaries. Managing at the edge of chaos is supremely important for survival. It is not a luxury but a necessity.

Conclusion: Best or Worst Practice?

Was the Bam disaster management a best or worst practice? A key conclusion that can be drawn from this case study is that it was a best practice, even though a number of deficiencies were revealed. Given the lessons outlined above, the case of Bam disaster management should be considered a best practice in a country that has been facing a multitude of challenges, including economic and political sanctions, external military threats, flight of massive amounts of capital during and after the Revolution, and the need to rebuild the country and advance to the status of a "developed" nation by 2020. Much has been accomplished toward achieving this goal, particularly in science and technology, space, nuclear energy, manufacturing and export of vehicles and heavy machinery, petrochemical production and export, pharmaceuticals, and attaining not only self-sufficiency in but also the capacity to export agricultural and industrial goods.

Yet, many challenges still face the nation in its quest to achieve the goal of being a "developed" nation that can influence not only regional but also international affairs and politics, as the recent successful nuclear negotiations among the world's most powerful nations—the P5 + 1 (United States, France, Britain, China, Russia, and Germany)—demonstrated globally. Was the response to the Bam disaster a "perfect" practice? No, but this case study provides another case of successful management at the edge of chaos, a capacity that all modern organizations and governments must develop, a capacity that utilizes in practice that has been called *surprise management theory*, which is "adaptive, collaborative, and citizen engaging and draws on chaos and complexity theories to cope with hyperuncertainties and unknowns" (Farazmand, 2014, 2017).

Questions for Discussion

1. What is meant by "managing at the edge of chaos"?
2. What is the difference between chaos-driven crises and non-chaos-driven crises and emergencies?
3. Where in Iran is Bam located, and why is this ancient city so important in history?
4. What are some other countries prone to constant earthquakes?
5. What is meant by the "surprise management theory," and what are its key characteristics?
6. Why was the Iranian earthquake in Bam so important and considered a global case of best practice in crisis and emergency management?
7. What were the organizational features of crisis and emergency management in the Bam earthquake?
8. What were the key leadership features of the Bam earthquake crisis management?
9. What lessons can be learned from the Iranian earthquake and Bam crisis and emergency management?
10. What mistakes were made that should be avoided in future crisis and emergency management?

Additional Reading

Farazmand, A. (2001). *Handbook of Crisis and Emergency Management.* New York: Marcel Dekker.
Haddow, G.D., Bullock, J.A., and Coppola, D.P. (2011). *Introduction to Emergency Management*, 4th ed. Boston: Butterworth-Heinemann.
Kaneko, K. (1995). Chaos as a source of complexity and diversity in evolution. In Langton, C., Eds., *Artificial Life: An Overview*, pp. 163–177. Cambridge, MA: MIT Press.
Murphy, P. (1996). Chaos theory as a model for managing issues and crises. *Public Relations Rev.*, 22(2): 95–113.
Pinkowski, J., Ed. (2008). *Disaster Management Handbook.* Boca Raton, FL: CRC Press.

References

Conner, D. (1998). *Leading at the Edge of Chaos.* New York: Wiley.
Cook, J.M. (1983). *The Persian Empire*, New York: Schocken Books.
Farazmand, A. (1989). *The State, Bureaucracy, and Revolution.* New York: Praeger.
Farazmand, A. (2002). *Modern Organizations: Theory and Practice.* Westport, CT: Praeger.
Farazmand, A. (2003). Chaos and transformation theories: a theoretical analysis with implications for organization theory and public management. *Public Organ. Rev.*, 3(4): 339–372.
Farazmand, A. (2004). Learning from Katrina crisis: a global and international perspective, with implications for future crisis and emergency management. *Public Admin. Rev.*, 67(s1): 149–159.
Farazmand, A. (2009). Building administrative capacity for the age of rapid globalization: a modest prescription for the twenty-first century. *Public Admin. Rev.*, 69(6): 1007–1020.
Farazmand, A., Ed. (2014a). *Crisis and Emergency Management: Theory and Practice*, 2nd ed. Boca Raton, FL: CRC Press.
Farazmand, A. (2014b). Learning from the Katrina crisis: a global and international perspective with implications for future crisis management. In Farazmand, A., Ed., *Crisis and Emergency Management: Theory and Practice,* 2nd ed., pp. 461–476. Boca Raton, FL: CRC Press.
Farazmand, A. (2017). *Advances in Crisis and Emergency Management: Theory and Practice.* Boca Raton, FL: CRC Press.
Gleick, J. (1997). *Chaos: Making a New Science.* New York: Random House.

Jahangiri, K., Danaeefar, H., and Farazmand, A. (2012). Lessons Learned from Iran's 2006 Bam Earthquake Catastrophe: The Case of Post-Earthquake Public Health Interventions in the Ancient City of Bam, unpublished paper prepared by Jahangiri, translated into English by Danaeefar, and edited by Farazmand.

Jantsch, E. (1980). *The Self-Organizing Universe*. New York: Pergamon.

Kiel, D.L. (1994). *Managing Chaos and Complexity in Government: A New Paradigm for Managing Change, Innovation, and Organizational Renewal*. San Francisco, CA: Jossey-Bass.

Loye, D. and Eisler, R. (1987). Chaos and transformation: implications of nonequilibrium theory for social sciences and society. *Behav. Sci.*, 32(1): 53–65.

Olmstead, A.T. (1948). *History of the Persian Empire: The Achaemenid Period*. Chicago, IL: University of Chicago Press.

Prigogine, I. and Stengers, I. (1984). *Order Out of Chaos*. New York: Bantam.

Weick, K. and Sutcliffe, K. (2001). *Managing the Unexpected: Assuring High Performance in the Age of Complexity*. New York: Wiley.

Chapter 9

The United States: Emergency Management and the September 11, 2001, Terrorist Attacks

William L. Waugh, Jr. and Christine Allison Canavan

Contents

Chapter Goals 149
Introduction 150
Counterterrorism Policy before 9/11 151
Emergency Management on 9/11 152
Impact of 9/11 on American Emergency Management 153
FEMA and Creation of the Department of Homeland Security 154
FEMA, DHS, and the President's Management Agenda 157
Conclusions 158
Questions for Discussion 158
Additional Reading 159
References 159

Chapter Goals

The goals of this chapter are to

1. Provide an overview of counterterrorism policy before September 11, 2001.
2. Describe the role of emergency management agencies on September 11, 2001.
3. Describe the changes to American emergency management following the September 11, 2001, attacks.
4. Relate the formation of the Department of Homeland Security and its impact upon American emergency management.

Introduction

As the saying goes in the United States, the world changed on 9/11. Perhaps more correctly, *our* world changed. As the Executive Summary of the 9/11 Commission Report termed it, the United States became "a nation transformed" (9/11 Commission, 2004a). The nation was unprepared for the attacks and scrambled to create a coherent mechanism to prevent future attacks. The attacks on the World Trade Center towers in New York City, the attack on the Pentagon in Washington, DC, and the abortive attack that ended when the airplane crashed in rural Somerset County, Pennsylvania, led to a "war on terrorism" that has profoundly changed American politics. The pursuit of the perpetrators of the attacks, members of al-Qaeda, required massive investments in security and counterterrorism, two wars (although one was not linked to the attackers), and billions of dollars spent to recover from the physical, social, economic, and cultural effects of the attacks. The response to the attacks did not end with the capture and killing of the terrorist leader, Osama bin Laden, in 2012. The response also did not stop with the implementation of enhanced border and civil aviation security. Life changed. It is not possible to sort out the direct effects of the attacks from costs that may be associated with new threats and other kinds of disasters, but some say that these actions were necessary after the attacks on the United States.

The attacks on the morning of September 11, 2001, directly resulted in the deaths of 2977 people, including 2753 killed in the collapses of the World Trade Center towers. International attention focused on the rescue operations at Ground Zero in Lower Manhattan, at the Pentagon, and around the crash site of United Airlines Flight 93. The operation at Ground Zero lasted months, although Mayor Rudolph Giuliani announced a transition from rescue to recovery on September 24 because there was little expectation that additional survivors would be found. Nonetheless, fire department personnel continued to search for survivors even though the rescue operation had formally ended. Only 18 people had been rescued from the rubble. On December 19, New York Governor George Pataki announced that the fires at Ground Zero had been extinguished, and on May 30, 2002, the recovery effort formally ended (9/11 Memorial, 2014). It can also be argued that the disaster is still not over in the sense that we have fully moved on to other issues. Many 9/11 responders were exposed to hazardous materials and there are still people dying from their effects.

The attacks revealed serious national vulnerabilities that resulted in a radical reordering of national priorities and a restructuring of the nation's defenses against terrorist attack. The nation had felt somewhat safe from international threats, although domestic terrorism had shaken that feeling of safety more than once in recent decades. The bombing of the Murrah Federal Building in Oklahoma City in 1995 by domestic antigovernment terrorists that resulted in the deaths of 168 people certainly had such an impact upon the security of government facilities.

Following the attacks, American emergency management also changed. The focus on natural disasters that led to the creation of the Federal Emergency Management Agency (FEMA) in 1979 was replaced by a singular focus on the perceived weaknesses that left the nation vulnerable to international terrorist attack, most notably the security of the national borders and of civil aviation. Policymakers switched their focus to the unsecured borders that made it possible for terrorists to enter the United States undetected, the gaps in civil aviation security that permitted terrorists to take over aircraft, and the maze of anti- and counterterrorist agencies that failed to identify the terrorists and uncover their plot. However, it must also be noted that American emergency management changed again in 2005 when Hurricane Katrina made landfall on the Gulf Coast and governments at all levels were found to be ill-prepared to deal with its impact. American emergency management agencies had to respond to new demands, and conflicts arose over national priorities and Homeland Security investments. The threat of terrorism was certainly a compelling issue for the nation, but the threat of hurricanes along the Gulf and the threat of earthquakes on the Pacific coast were more certain for state and local governments (Waugh, 2007a). The focus here is on the national emergency management system leading up to and during the 9/11 disaster and the system that emerged in the aftermath of the attacks.

It is an understatement that the impact of the attacks on September 11, 2001, was profound. The economic losses have been estimated to be in the billions of dollars. Entire corporate headquarters staffs died in the collapse of the World Trade Center towers. Local businesses were destroyed. The social and economic life of New York City and Washington, DC, was disrupted (e.g., Chernick, 2005; Foner, 2005). The Pentagon was severely damaged. Hundreds of people died in aircraft, in buildings, and on the ground. It can also be said that the economic impact of the events is also still being felt even after much of the physical damage has been repaired. And, certainly, great damage was done to the American psyche; indeed, the psychological impact of the attacks is still significant.

Counterterrorism Policy before 9/11

There is a disparity in how counterterrorism in the United States was conducted before and after the September 11 attacks. Compared to after the attacks, the counterterrorism policies before were minimal. The Federal Bureau of Investigation (FBI) was responsible for addressing internal threats, and the Central Intelligence Agency (CIA) was responsible for addressing international threats. Coordination among law enforcement and intelligence was problematic, as the response to the 9/11 attacks demonstrated. Their roles and responsibilities were clarified in 1995 when President Clinton signed Presidential Decision Directive 39 (PDD-39), which identified specific roles with regard to counterterrorism activities and during a potential terrorist attack. The Department of State was responsible for terrorist incidents that affected American citizens outside of U.S. territory. The Federal Aviation Administration (FAA) addressed air piracy, and the Department of Justice, through the FBI, determined procedures with the Departments of Defense, Transportation, and State in the event of a hijacking. The FBI was also responsible for reducing vulnerabilities of any domestic terrorist attacks, and the Federal Emergency Management Agency (FEMA) was in charge of a response plan in the event of a terrorist attack on U.S. soil.

Counterterrorism activities in the United States were conducted primarily by the FBI. The main goal of this organization was to take a "traditional law enforcement approach" to thwarting and capturing terrorists. Efforts to capture and charge terrorists were more those of individual agents and branch offices rather than a collective endeavor on the part of the entire agency. The FBI was intent on foiling potential terrorist attacks and developing investigations after attacks occurred to convict those responsible, as seen with the World Trade Center bombing in 1993, the plot to bomb the Manila airport in 1995, and the bombing of the U.S. embassies in Tanzania and Kenya in 1998 (9/11 Commission, 2004b).

After the 1993 bombing of the World Trade Center, the FBI shifted their focus from solving crimes of terrorism to trying to mitigate potential attacks. Some examples of the major changes that occurred within the FBI include creation of the National Counterterrorism Center, as well as the establishment of a unit whose only goal was to pursue Osama bin Laden. The FBI also began to collect data on counterterrorism, trained agents in counterterrorism techniques, and created counterterrorism sections in individual field offices (9/11 Commission, 2004a). Before the FBI took on greater responsibility in preventing and mitigating against terrorist attacks, "the Bureau devoted significantly more special agent resources to traditional law enforcement activities such as white collar crime, organized crime, drug, and violent crime investigations than to domestic and international terrorism issues" (OIG, 2003). The 9/11 Commission Report (2004a) described a terrorist threat that went unheeded. In the words of its authors, "The system was blinking red."

Emergency Management on 9/11

The 9/11 attacks occurred 8 months into the administration of President George W. Bush. Joe Allbaugh, former chief of staff for Governor Bush and a manager of the Bush presidential campaign, was the appointed head of FEMA. Michael Brown, who succeeded Allbaugh as head of FEMA in 2003, was brought in to be FEMA counsel and was involved in FEMA's 9/11 response in New York. Prior to the attacks, the focus of FEMA and its state and local counterparts was on natural disasters, but with some antiterrorism responsibilities. The consolidation of federal resources to deal with natural disasters was the reason why the agency had been created by President Jimmy Carter in 1979. There had been a number of FEMA directors without disaster or hazard management experience prior to 2001, but the director who served in the previous administration had had such qualifications. James Lee Witt, a former local emergency management director in Arkansas, was appointed by President Clinton. In other words, the agency had come far since its problems with Hurricanes Hugo (1989), Andrew (1992), and Iniki (1992) and a congressional reauthorization process that might have abolished the agency. The Witt years are still described as the "Golden Age" of FEMA. Witt was an administrator respected by both Democrats and Republicans. When asked by President Bush to remain as head of FEMA in 2001, Witt declined.

The emergency management operation in New York, in particular, is well documented. A less known aspect of the response is that the Bush administration considered taking over the New York operation. A continuing issue among federal officials was whether what came to be known as "incidents of national significance" should be managed by the federal government rather than by state and local governments. There was some discussion of that possibility during the Hurricane Katrina disaster in 2005, as well. As it worked out, New York City, with the support of federal, state, and other local agencies, managed the event. Although there were problems, the emergency management system already in place was up to the task of coordinating the response and recovery operations and integrating outside resources into those operations. There were serious problems that had to be addressed, including the lack of interoperable communications that would facilitate communication among the responders and emergency operations centers. FEMA was also criticized for being slow to respond. The city emergency operations center (EOC) itself was destroyed in Tower 7 and a new facility was cobbled together at Pier 92 on the Hudson River. That temporary EOC operated for 12 weeks and housed approximately 150 representatives from federal, state, and city agencies and from private and nonprofit sector organizations (Rotanz, 2007). FEMA provided material and financial support and utilized an Air Reserve Base outside of the city to serve as a marshaling area. The State of New York also provided support, and hundreds of nongovernmental organizations filled the need for everything from support for responders at Ground Zero to pet rescue and apartment cleaning for residents in the surrounding neighborhoods. Emergency managers from around the country took turns at Ground Zero, in the EOC, and in other parts of the operation. Tens of thousands of volunteers were used to support the operations, as well.

Impact of 9/11 on American Emergency Management

In the immediate aftermath of the attacks, Public Law 107-40 authorized the President "to use all necessary and appropriate force against those nations, organizations, or persons he determines planned, authorized, committed or aided the terrorist attacks that occurred on September 11, 2001, or harbored such organizations or persons, in order to prevent any future acts of international terrorism against the United States by such nations, organizations or persons" (U.S. Congress, 2001a). The U.S. government radically changed its counterterrorism policy. The Bush administration announced the implementation of the Office of Homeland Security, which was to be headed by Tom Ridge, the Pennsylvania Governor (PBS, 2004). By October 2001, the USA PATRIOT (Uniting and Strengthening America by Providing Appropriate Tools Required to Intercept and Obstruct Terrorism) Act was introduced. This act widened the powers of intelligence agencies and law enforcement to investigate potential threats of terrorism. The PATRIOT Act allowed the government to search through telephones, e-mails, and health records of people in the United States in return for their safety against terrorism (U.S. Congress, 2001b). Soon after September 11, troops were deployed to the Middle East and the war on terrorism began in Afghanistan (PBS, 2004).

The focus on protecting the United States against terrorism continued to grow, particularly with regard to air travel. In November 2001, the government was given responsibility for airport screenings through the Aviation and Transportation Security Act, and planes flying in the United States were required to have resistant cockpit doors. In the years to come, the Transportation Security Administration (TSA) set up explosives detection systems, implemented a program for volunteer aviators to be armed and to assist in the event of acts of violence or air piracy, screened all cargo on domestic flights, and initiated other changes to security on airlines including the removal of shoes during security checks and a limitation on the amount of liquids in carry-on bags (TSA, 2014).

The switch in focus of emergency management from natural disasters to terrorism after September 11 brought one document to the forefront, NFPA 1600: Standard on Disaster/Emergency Management and Business Continuity Programs, which focuses on emergency management, communication, business progression, and recovery from disasters (NFPA, 2009). The 9/11 Commission's report recommended that NFPA 1600 be used in the event of a disaster and also proposed readiness for both the private and public sectors in the event of a disaster. NFPA 1600 is also currently being used by the U.S. Department of Homeland Security. Since its inception in 1991, NFPA 1600 has been revised a few times. Some of the changes of this document specifically after September 11 have addressed improved alarm systems, preparedness for building emergencies, utilization of elevators during emergencies, developing evacuation plans for people with disabilities, and studying the safety of high-rise buildings for occupants (NFPA, 2006). The changed in the NFPA 1600 has shown the evolution of the focus of emergency management since the 9/11 attacks.

The attacks of September 11 radically changed the way emergency management and counterterrorism efforts are dealt with in the United States. Since 2001, the protection of U.S. citizens from terrorism has been on the forefront of people's minds. The creation of the Department of Homeland Security was one of the actions designed to assist in mitigating future terrorist attacks on U.S. soil. The legislation and related actions taken in the immediate aftermath of the attacks are listed in Table 9.1. The actions taken in 2001 include passage of the Aviation and Transportation Security Act, which initiated airport screening and created the Transportation Security Administration (TSA, 2014).

Table 9.1 Legislation Passed and Related Actions in the Immediate Aftermath of the 9/11 Attacks

Year	Legislation Passed and Actions Taken
2001	Supplementary Act for Response and Recovery Executive Order 13224—Blocking Property and Prohibiting Transactions with Persons Who Commit, Threaten to Commit, or Support Terrorism Authorization for the Use of Military Force Airport Transport, Safety, and System Stabilization Act Executive Order 13231—Critical Infrastructure Protection in the Information Age Executive Order 13228—Establishing the Office of Homeland Security and the Homeland Security Council U.S. Patriot Act Aviation and Transport Security Act
2002	Victims of Terrorism Tax Relief Act Executive Order 13254—Establishing the U.S.A. Freedom Corps Executive Order 13253—Ordering the Ready Reserve of the Armed Forces to Active Duty and Delegating Certain Authorities to the Secretary of Defense and the Secretary of Transportation Executive Order 13260—Establishing the President's Homeland Security Advisory Council and Senior Advisory Committee for Homeland Security Enhanced Border Security and Visa Reform Public Health Security and Bioterrorism Preparedness International Convention for Suppression of Bombings Executive Order 13267—Establishing a Transition Planning Office for the Department of Homeland Security Within the Office of Management and Budget National Strategy for Homeland Security National Money Laundering Strategy Supplemental Appropriations for Further Recovery from and Response to Terrorist Attacks in the U.S. National Security Presidential Directive 17/Homeland Security Presidential Directive 4—National Strategy to Combat Weapons of Mass Destruction Authorization for Use of Military Force Against Iraq—Resolution National Military Strategic Plan for the War on Terrorism—Northern Command, Department of Defense Cyber-Security Research and Development Act Intelligence Authorization Act Maritime Transportation Security Act Homeland Security Act

Source: Rubin, C.B., Cumming, W.R., and Renda-Tanali, I. (2003). *Terrorism Time Line: Major Focusing Events and U.S. Outcomes (1993–2003),* http://www.disaster-timeline.com/TTLJune1204Irmak_smaller.pdf.

FEMA and Creation of the Department of Homeland Security

The Department of Homeland Security (DHS) was created in 2003 under a reorganization that brought 22 agencies and offices and labs under the DHS umbrella. DHS was created on November 25, 2002, with the signing of the Homeland Security Act. Homeland defense had been the province of the Departments of Defense and Justice, and there had been turf wars over

Table 9.2 Agencies and Offices Added to the Department of Homeland Security

Origin	Agency
U.S. Department of Agriculture	Animal and Plant Health Inspection Service Plum Island Animal Disease Center
U.S. Department of Commerce	Critical Infrastructure Assurance Office
U.S. Department of Defense	National Biological Warfare Defense Analysis Center National Communications System
U.S. Department of Energy	Lawrence Livermore National Laboratory Nuclear Incident Response National Infrastructure Simulation and Analysis Center
U.S. Department of Health and Human Services	Chemical, Biological, Radiological, and Nuclear Response Assets Civilian Biodefense Research Programs
U.S. Department of Justice	Immigration and Naturalization Service Office of Domestic Preparedness (FY03 part of FEMA) National Infrastructure Protection Center (from FBI) National Domestic Preparedness Office (from FBI)
U.S. Department of Transportation	U.S. Coast Guard Transportation Security Agency
U.S. Department of the Treasury	Customs Service Secret Service
General Services Administration	Federal Protective Service Federal Computer Incident Response Center

counterterrorism programs and funding. The new organization, with its roughly 170,000 employees (not counting the addition of 25,000 to 30,000 federal passenger screeners), did not include the intelligence agencies with responsibility for monitoring terrorist activity. The design of DHS was a direct response to the September 11 attacks, and its counterterrorism mission included both civil aviation and border protection. The challenge was to integrate the 22 agencies into one. Table 9.2 shows the organizations that became part of DHS.

From the beginning, problems were encountered. The new organization did not resemble the organization recommended by the 9/11 Commission in its review of the attacks and recommendations made to prevent future attacks. *Intraorganizational problems* were expected, as the 22 agencies and programs involved had diverse missions and cultures. *Interorganizational problems*, too, were expected with regard to coordinating policies and programs among the estimated 100 agencies in 12 departments outside of DHS that were involved in Homeland Security. Certainly conflicts arose due to external competing missions, given that the nation's intelligence agencies (namely, the CIA and FBI) were not part of DHS but were critical to security. *Political problems* occurred due to turf battles among the 88 separate congressional committees having oversight. *Internal mission problems* were expected in reconciling DHS counterterrorism and non-terrorism-related missions, especially for FEMA and perhaps the U.S. Coast Guard. FEMA was essentially put on the back burner because of the size of the agency. *Intra-agency problems* arose because some of the agencies had been identified by the Government Accountability Office as being "problem" agencies, especially the Border Patrol, Immigration and Naturalization Service, Customs Service, and U.S. Coast Guard (U.S. GAO, 2000). Resources were shifted to the counterterrorism effort at the expense of FEMA's and other agencies' non-terrorism missions. FEMA was relegated to a support role in consequence management and was tasked with supporting the counterterrorism effort. FEMA had little role in mitigating the effects of terrorist acts. As a result, the nation's capacity to deal with large natural disasters, such as Katrina, shrank (Waugh, 2009).

Little or no consideration was given to how the focus of DHS should transition to mitigation, preparedness, and recovery when the prevention of terrorist acts does not succeed. In fact, emergency managers considered mitigation not to be a priority, and it was left out of the new approaches developed for both natural and manmade disasters. The all-hazards approach that had been the core of emergency management since the 1970s seemed to have been lost in the shuffle. That concern was evident in the development of new national response plans—first the National Response Plan and later the National Response Framework. The administration's approach was top-down, and state and local officials were seldom part of the discussion. The development of the Homeland Security Advisory System, the color-coded threat advisory, did not include alert and warning experts from the National Weather Service and other agencies that do issue warnings to government agencies and the general public (PPW, 2002). Concerns were expressed about the need to improve intra- and interorganizational information sharing. The 9/11 Commission noted that a lack of information sharing was a problem associated with the failure to identify and apprehend the 9/11 attackers. Although U.S. agencies had pieces of information related to the planned attack, that information was not shared among law enforcement and intelligence agencies in such a way that the pieces could be put together. Greater information sharing became a major goal in the creation of a new counterterrorism program and, later, in the development of fusion centers to bring agencies together to encourage communication.

At the time, social scientists were anxious to examine how DHS was planning to integrate agencies and programs into the department. This was the biggest federal reorganization since the creation of the Department of Defense in 1946, and that department still experiences serious problems arising from internal rivalries and competition over missions, budgets, space, and resources. There were and still are cultural change issues ranging from changes in the patches and badges worn by uniformed officers to the openness of decision-making processes. Career ladders, incentive systems, and other personnel system attributes changed due in part to the integration of agencies, such as the Customs Service and the Immigration and Naturalization Service, which became Immigration and Customs Enforcement (ICE), and to the administration's push for executive-centered management. President Bush's Management Agenda also influenced the limitations put on unions representing personnel in DHS (Moynihan, 2005).

Little mention was made of the issue of how to shrink the top-heavy administrative structure. There were too many layers of bureaucracy, including several layers of political appointees who came to DHS from its constituent programs. Witt's FEMA had cultivated strong relationships with its state and local counterparts, and those connections seemed to be lost in the centralization of decision- and policymaking in the new DHS. Relationships with nongovernmental organizations and volunteers were vaguely mentioned in the National Response Framework. Turf battles, poor coordination with state and local agencies, and inadequate information sharing plagued the large-scale Top Officials (TOPOFF) counterterrorism program.

FEMA, DHS, and the President's Management Agenda

Up to this point, the picture has been one of an emergency management system adapting to the nature and scale of the 9/11 attacks. Resources were mobilized, albeit sometimes very slowly. City, state, and federal officials improvised when necessary and, for the most part, addressed pressing needs. There were some obvious missteps early on, such as the failure to ensure that responders adequately protected themselves from the hazardous conditions around Ground Zero. As a consequence, there continue to be casualties of the attacks as 9/11 responders die of cancer and related causes.

Another impact of the attacks has been the centralization of authority in federal agencies, particularly in the Department of Homeland Security. Soon after taking office in 2001, President Bush's Management Agenda was published by the Office of Management and Budget (OMB). The focus ostensibly was on expanding managerial flexibility in personnel, budgeting, and property disposal, and, according to OMB (2001), the intent was that "hierarchical 'command and control' bureaucracies will become flatter and more responsive." Agencies were to focus on results rather than process, and actions were to be based upon evidence. The stated goal was to reduce overlap in functions and turf wars over jurisdiction. Bills to implement the agenda were proposed and found little support in Congress. The Bush administration clashed with the unions representing public employees over the issue of giving administration officials greater flexibility to hire and fire civil service employees (Moynihan, 2005). The Comptroller General testified that the proposed "Freedom to Manage Act" had "profound implications for the relative role that Congress plays in developing legislation and conducting oversight to enhance the performance and ensure the accountability of the executive branch. … The proposed bill, by design, would provide significant new power to the President to not only initiate changes, but also to affect the ultimate debate and outcome" (U.S. GAO, 2001). In other words, executive-centered management was the broad goal and it would be at the expense of Congress.

Although the President's Management Agenda found little purchase prior to 9/11, the atmosphere following the attacks and the creation of the Department of Homeland Security offered opportunity to pursue that agenda under the guise of security (Moynihan, 2005). As a result, DHS was created with a much more top-down orientation and with greater executive discretion in personnel, budgeting, and other functions than other federal agencies. The arguments for the changes were couched in terms of national security and necessary flexibility, rather than in terms of the President's Management Agenda. DHS was to be a nimble organization.

Interestingly, the assessments of the 9/11 and Katrina responses by the Bush administration called for greater centralization of decision making even when serious problems were caused by too much reliance on decisions made in Washington rather than onsite. Concerns were expressed, during the short-lived debate over whether FEMA should be included in the new DHS, about the impact on the relatively decentralized management approach in FEMA and the very centralized approach in DHS. FEMA had relied on its regional offices to work with state and local officials during major disasters. The relationships generally were close; however, in 2005, DHS dispatched its own agent to Louisiana during the Katrina disaster despite FEMA having a federal coordinating officer onsite. Much has also been made of the failure of FEMA leadership in Washington to understand what was needed in Mississippi and Louisiana, despite the extensive media coverage (Waugh, 2006). DHS has had a serious morale problem and, consequently, has had a difficult time keeping experienced personnel. The point is simply that the new management approach that the Bush administration incorporated into DHS may have created decision-making and coordination problems that continue today.

Conclusions

The Pentagon Memorial opened on September 11, 2008; the Flight 93 National Memorial and National Park opened in Pennsylvania on September 10, 2011; and the National September 11 Memorial at Ground Zero was dedicated on September 11, 2011, and opened the next day. The recovery process has been slow and contentious (9/11 Memorial, 2014). It is the custom to build memorials to the victims of terrorist attacks and aviation disasters to give some closure to those who survive. September 11 was a particularly traumatic event for Americans, and our grief has been shared by many around the world. To be sure, not all of the victims were American, but the attacks were on our soil and we were the targets. Lessons were learned, and, as too often happens, some have been relearned in subsequent attacks. Memories fade with time. Within a few years, the 9/11 attacks came to be seen as New York and Washington events by many Americans. This amnesia happens with natural disasters, as well. What it means in policy terms is that there is a flurry of activity in the immediate aftermath of a disaster because it represents a "focusing event" that affords opportunity and impetus for action.

The Department of Homeland Security was created hurriedly without following the recommendations of the 9/11 Commission. The new department did not include the intelligence agencies charged with gathering information on threats and potential threats. There was little planning for the integration of the department's components and little study of the effects of reorganization. There were pundits who suggested that FEMA not be included in the new department because its culture was so different from that of the law enforcement and military agencies that comprise the core of DHS. Conflicts continue, but the Katrina experience may have sufficiently demonstrated that FEMA needs to be more directly linked to the President rather than buried under bureaucratic layers that inhibit clear communication and close cooperation. Nonetheless, it is uncertain whether DHS officials appreciate the collaborative nature of FEMA and the necessity of transparency in working with the public. In a department where information sharing is problematic, open communication with the public would seem alien.

The creation of DHS presented an opportunity for President Bush to implement his executive-centered management agenda. It remains to be seen whether that kind of management will be effective as the focus on natural and unnatural disaster risk reduction shifts to community resilience. In many respects, terrorism is a hazard like other hazards, and an emergency management approach may be more effective than a command-and-control approach (Waugh, 2005, 2007b). Engaging the public in Homeland Security efforts will require trust and transparency.

Questions for Discussion

1. Are there any additional changes that should have been made to the Federal Emergency Management Agency and the role of emergency management in the United States after September 11, 2001?
2. What changes in emergency management after September 11 do you believe caused the greatest impact to the United States? Consider political, economic, and social implications.
3. Briefly describe the formation of the Department of Homeland Security.
4. What can be done to give the Department of Homeland Security less of a "top-down" approach and more of an emphasis on its relationships with local and regional governments and with nongovernmental organizations?

Additional Reading

Hernandez, R. (2002). FEMA's pace on 9/11 aid is criticized. *The New York Times*, June 14 (http:/www.nytimes.com/2002/06/14/nyregion/fema-s-pace-on-9-11-aid-is-criticized.html).

Katz, E. (2015). The five agencies where morale is dropping the most. *Government Executive*, October 2 (http://www.govexec.com/pay-benefits/2015/10/five-agencies-where-morale-dropping-most/122510/).

Markon, J., Nakashima, E., and Crites, A. (2014). Top-level turnover makes it harder for DHS to stay on top of evolving threats. *Washington Post*, September 21 (https://www.washingtonpost.com/politics/top-level-turnover-makes-it-harder-for-dhs-to-stay-on-top-of-evolving-threats/2014/09/21/ca7919a6-39d7-11e4-9c9f-ebb47272e40e_story.html).

U.S. GAO. (2003). *Disaster Assistance: Information on FEMA's Post-9/11 Public Assistance to the New York City Area*, GAO-03-926. Washington, DC: U.S. Government Accountability Office.

Waugh, Jr., W.L. (2003). Terrorism, Homeland Security and the National Emergency Management Network. *Public Org. Rev.*, 3: 373–385.

Waugh, Jr., W.L. and Sylves, R.T. (2002). Organizing the war on terrorism. *Public Admin. Rev.*, 62(s1): 145–153.

References

9/11 Commission. (2004a). *The 9/11 Commission Report: Final Report of the National Commission on Terrorist Attacks Upon the United States*. New York: St. Martin's Press.

9/11 Commission. (2004b). *Law Enforcement, Counterterrorism, and Intelligence Collection in the United States Prior to 9/11*, Staff Statement No. 9, 10th Public Hearing, http://www.9-11commission.gov/staff_statements/staff_statement_9.pdf.

9/11 Memorial. (2014). *9/11 Interactive Timeline*, http://timeline.911memorial.org/#Timeline/3.

Chen, D. (2003). Report criticizes FEMA's handling of 9/11 economic claims. *The New York Times*, January 8 (http://www.nytimes.com/2003/01/08/nyregion/08FEMA.html).

Chernick, H., Ed. (2005). *Resilient City: The Economic Impact of 9/11*. New York: Russell Sage Foundation.

Foner, N., Ed. (2005). *Wounded City: The Social Impact of 9/11*. New York: Russell Sage Foundation.

Moynihan, D.P. (2005). Homeland Security and the U.S. public management policy agenda. *Governance*, 18(2): 171–196.

NFPA. (2006). *Changes to NFPA Documents: Changes Made or Pending to NFPA Documents or Programs Relating to Some Aspect of the September 11, 2001, Terrorist Attacks*. Louisville, KY: National Fire Protection Association (www.nfpa.org/safety-information/for-consumers/emergency-preparedness/homeland-security/changes-to-nfpa-documents).

NFPA. (2009). DHS Announces Intent to Adopt NFPA 1600 for the Voluntary Private Sector Preparedness [press release]. Louisville, KY: National Fire Protection Association (http://www.nfpa.org/press-room/news-releases/2009/dhs-announces-intent-to-adopt-nfpa-1600-for-the-voluntary-private-sector-preparedness).

OIG. (2003). *Federal Bureau of Investigation Casework and Human Resource Allocation*, Report No. 03-37. Washington, DC: Office of the Inspector General (www.justice.gov/oig/reports/FBI/a0337/exec.htm).

PBS. (2004). *Flashpoints USA: Post-9/11 Timeline*. Arlington, VA: Public Broadcasting Service (http://www.pbs.org/flashpointsusa/20040629/infocus/topic_01/timeline_sep2001.html).

PPW. (2002). *Effective Hazard Warnings Report*. Emmitsburg, MD: Partnership for Public Warning.

Rotanz, R.A. (2007). Applied response strategies. In Waugh, Jr., W.L. and Tierney, K., Eds., *Emergency Management: Principles and Practice for Local Government*, pp. 143–157. Washington, DC: International City/County Management Association.

TSA. (2014). *TSA Evolution Timeline*. Washington, DC: Transportation Security Administration (http://www.tsa.gov/video/evolution/TSA_evolution_timeline.pdf).

U.S. Congress. (2001a). Authorization for Use of Military Force (AUMF), Public Law 107-40. Washington, DC: U.S. Congress.

U.S. Congress. (2001b). *Uniting and Strengthening America by Providing Appropriate Tools Required to Intercept and Obstruct Terrorism (USA PATRIOT) Act of 2001.* Washington, DC: U.S. Congress.

U.S. GAO. (2000). *High Risk Series: An Update*, GAO-01-263. Washington, DC: U.S. Government Accountability Office.

U.S. GAO. (2001). *Government Management: Observations on the President's Proposed Freedom to Manage Act*, GAO-02-2412. Washington DC: U.S. Government Accountability Office.

Waugh, Jr., W.L. (2005). Terrorism and the all-hazards approach. *J. Emerg. Manage.*, 4(2): 8–10.

Waugh, Jr., W.L. (2006). The political costs of failure in the responses to hurricanes Katrina and Rita. *Ann. Am. Acad. Pol. Soc. Sci.*, 604: 10–25.

Waugh, Jr., W.L. (2007a). Local emergency management in the post-9/11 world. In Waugh, Jr., W.L. and Tierney, K., Eds., *Emergency Management: Principles and Practice for Local Government*, 2nd ed., pp. 3–23. Washington, DC: International City/County Management Association.

Waugh, Jr., W.L. (2007b). Terrorism as disaster. In Rodríguez, H., Quarantelli, E.L., and Dynes, R.R., Eds., *Handbook of Disaster Research*, pp. 388–404. New York: Springer.

Waugh, Jr., W.L. (2009). FEMA in shambles. In Morgan, M.J., Ed., *The Impact of 9/11 on Politics and War: The Day that Changed Everything?*, pp. 61–74. New York: Palgrave McMillan.

Chapter 10

Wilma and Sandy: Lessons Learned from Public Servants

John J. Carroll

Contents

Chapter Goals 161
Introduction 162
Hurricane Wilma: October and November 2005 163
Hurricane and Post-Tropical Cyclone Sandy: October to November 2012 167
    Town of Hempstead Senior Council Member Anthony J. Santino: "On Being a Conduit" 168
    Village of East Rockaway Vice Mayor Bruno Romano: "It Took a Village" 169
    East Rockaway Schools Superintendent Roseanne Melucci: "We'll Make It Work" 170
    Rhame Avenue Elementary School Principal Laura Guggino: "Home for the Holidays" 172
Lessons Learned: Collaborative Emergency Management 173
Implications for Public Administration and Crisis and Emergency Management 175
Conclusion 176
Questions for Discussion 176
Additional Reading 177
References 177

Chapter Goals

The goals of this chapter are to

1. Review response to 2005 Hurricane Wilma.
2. Review response to 2012 Superstorm Sandy.
3. Identify lessons learned for future responses.
4. Discuss the implications of Wilma and Sandy for crisis/emergency management and public administration.

Introduction

"46 West" is what we called the very modest two-bedroom, one-bath, single-story house that served as our family's home from 1961 to 1984. The 750-square-foot wood frame structure sits atop a 2100-square-foot lot on a narrow and crowded suburban street in Bay Park—a small unincorporated area on the south shore of Long Island. For 23 years, in a house where we barely had enough room to change our minds, our parents raised their kids and sent us to the local village public schools. We visited with friends and relatives, played in the nearby county park, and generally lived our lives like so many other lower middle class, blue-collar families. Looking back, it was a fairly idyllic place, even antiseptic, when contrasted with the colossus of New York City looming just to our west. In 1984, with the kids in various stages of moving on with their own lives, the family decided to take advantage of opportunities elsewhere and became part of the great migratory outflow from the Northeast to South Florida—leaving behind life-long friends, extended family, and 46 West.

Almost 30 years later, on October 29, 2012, a tremendous storm surge washed over the barrier islands of Western Long Island, into the bays, inlets, channels, creeks, canals, and other waterways in the Greater New York Metropolitan Area. An 8-foot storm surge, compounded by an almost 3-foot astronomical (full moon high) tide, inundated Bay Park (NOAA, 2014). 46 West was among those houses flooded and severely damaged by Sandy. Since then, the roof, doors, and windows have been replaced and the interior stripped down to the frame. 46 West was like many houses on the street that could be saved, nestled among others boarded up and abandoned or simply bulldozed over into empty lots. Perhaps, like the countless human victims of disasters everywhere, from the outside 46 West looked a lot like it was keeping up appearances but inside it would have to struggle mightily to start over again.

This chapter originally was to have been a recounting of the lessons learned by a former public safety executive who responded to many large-scale events, but it then grew to include very different public servants. The intent of this chapter is to compare the experiences of public servants in positions of leadership during the preparation and subsequent recovery of two major natural disasters. In late October 2005, Hurricane Wilma struck South Florida—the last of the many storms to directly strike Florida over the busy 2004 and 2005 seasons. Seven years later, almost to the day in late October 2012, Superstorm Sandy came ashore in coastal New Jersey, but not before impacting a wide swath of the Northeastern and Mid-Atlantic/Midwestern United States with storm surges, hurricane-force winds, rain, and—most unbelievably—a substantial blizzard (NOAA, 2013).

It became clear in the research how essential it is for local officials to work together as well as across levels of government and with the private and nonprofit sectors. The author was a long tenured public safety executive tasked with managing command posts during agency responses. Each response provided learning opportunities to address the challenges of working in subsequent events. The author depended on relationships built over time in order to inform decision makers and guide responses leading up to Hurricane Wilma.

To broaden the comparison of experiences with a more recent event, the author interviewed public servants outside public safety to gauge lessons learned in other forms of government. The author elected to focus on his hometown as the point of comparison. Local officials had to contend with a complex recovery across multiple jurisdictions. This chapter will show the lessons learned, even over time, and the implications for the disciplines. Hurricane Wilma in 2005 and Superstorm Sandy in 2012 will be referred to by the names assigned by the National Hurricane Center, especially as there is conflict over exactly what type of storm Sandy was—it depends on the sources. The research also became a personal introspective on recovery in places long since left behind.

Hurricane Wilma: October and November 2005

Wilma was a late-season tropical cyclone that formed in the Gulf of Mexico. It developed quickly, as many storms had done in the 2004 and 2005 seasons, becoming one of the most dangerous storms ever recorded in the Atlantic and Gulf of Mexico basins. Wilma had the lowest barometric pressure ever recorded in the Atlantic Basin, with 185-mile-per-hour sustained winds. Wilma did not come ashore at this strength, instead making landfall on the extreme southwest portion of the Florida peninsula as a Category 3 storm with sustained winds of 120 miles per hour. Wilma made a track northeast across the peninsula, exiting into the Atlantic Ocean (NCDC, 2005).

The hurricane-force winds (above 74 miles per hour sustained) extended about 90 miles from the center of the storm. There were some other unusual aspects to Wilma, all of which helped to reduce the potential impact of the storm. The forward speed of the storm was 23 miles per hour and the "eye," or center of circulation, was 45 miles wide. The event lasted about 6 hours, and only about 4 to 6 inches of rain fell. There was no storm surge effect on the east coast of Florida (NCDC, 2005).

Wilma is considered to be the strongest storm to strike the Fort Lauderdale metropolitan area since 1950 (Lagorio, 2005). Wilma caused about $29 billion in damage, making it the fourth most costly natural event in the United States. In its wake, Wilma left 6 million people without power, widespread water and sewer service outages, no traffic control lights to move vehicles, and major transportation hubs (rail, airport, and seaport) out of commission (Carroll, 2006). Southeast Florida (or more commonly referred to as "South Florida") is comprised of three counties: Miami-Dade, Broward, and Palm Beach. The population of this region in 2005 was over 5 million people. Broward County is geographically between Miami-Dade and Palm Beach counties and at the center of the population region. In 2005, Broward's population was over 1.7 million people.

Broward County has a multilayered government structure. This includes the constitutional elected offices of sheriff, supervisor of elections, property appraiser, clerk of court, state attorney, and public defender. The county government is overseen by an elected commission, which does not include jurisdiction over the municipalities. There are 31 municipalities and a separately elected countywide school board. There are also numerous other special districts that serve as their own taxing authorities, such as the South Florida Water Management District and North Broward Hospital District.

The Broward County Sheriff, as a state constitutional officer, is charged with law enforcement responsibility in all of the unincorporated areas of the county, including serving the court's papers and providing security for the courthouses and county and circuit court judges. Whereas the Broward County Sheriff is considered the "chief law enforcement officer" of the county, the authority of the office does not generally include jurisdictions with their own policing agencies. The government of Broward County assigned responsibility for the county jail to the Broward County Sheriff's Office, as well as some elements of public safety communications. The Broward County Sheriff's Office is also permitted (with concurrent approval by the County Commission) to contract with other governments for services.

In 2005, the Broward County Sheriff's Office was under contract to provide law enforcement services to 14 of Broward's 31 municipalities (each through an independent agreement). The government of Broward County contracted with the Sheriff's Office to provide services to the county's airport and seaport and to manage the county's fire rescue services. By 2005, the Broward County Sheriff's Office had become the largest public safety agency of its kind in the United States and was the nation's second largest sheriff's office, behind Los Angeles County. At the time, the Sheriff's Office was responsible for patrolling about one third of the Broward County population and providing call-taking and dispatch services to about half of the population (Carroll, 2005).

The day-to-day operations of the Broward County Sheriff's Office in 2005 were divided into five basic functions: (1) law enforcement; (2) detention/county jail; (3) fire rescue; (4) administration (e.g., budget, finance, human resources, information technology); and (5) community services (e.g., media relations). Crisis and emergency management functions at the Sheriff's Office were internally maintained, with a control center being centrally located in the agency's headquarters. The Sheriff's Office also provided representatives to act as liaisons to the contracted municipalities and county command centers. Each operational command in the Sheriff's Office had to establish its own command post in their respective geographic service areas. All of these locations were coordinated through redundant lines of communications (satellite, cellular, and landline telephones; computers; direct-connect hotlines; radios; runners; and, frankly, anything else that could be thought of at the time), with clear instructions that if all else fails then individual commands would have to make their own operational decisions when needed (Carroll, 2008).

Hurricanes were historically the "main event" in Florida. The terrorist attacks on September 11, 2001, changed everything. A senior law enforcement command meeting was being held that morning, when the news broke that a plane had crashed into one of the towers of the World Trade Center. The projection screen in the room was shifted from budget and crime statistics to the images of a burning tower. In the end, thousands perished, including hundreds of first responders. Over the coming days, we would learn that, if anything, our response plans needed immediate attention. A week later, the wheels fell off our wagon.

Beginning on September 18, a series of letters containing anthrax were sent to government and media offices. We were to learn later that these letters were not related to the terrorist attacks the week before, but the public and first responders were still very much on edge from 9/11. One of those letters landed at the office of the *National Enquirer* (AMI Media, Inc.) in Boca Raton, Florida (just north of Broward County), fatally affecting a man and setting off something like a panic across South Florida. Call-taking and dispatch centers across Broward County for both police and fire were swamped with "white powder" calls.

Public safety had no procedures or practices at the time to handle these types of calls, as they could be both a rescue situation and a criminal investigation. Broward County Fire Rescue was a separate county agency operating out of the same headquarters building as the Sheriff's Office. The leadership of both agencies decided to create joint teams of deputies and firefighters to respond to these calls, with a Fire Rescue Battalion Chief and Deputy Sheriff Major (your author) to coordinate activities and (literally) write procedures and protocols on the fly as the calls multiplied. This relationship, and the 9/11 response, became the nexus for both agencies to begin working more closely together and the eventual contract-enabled merger.

The years 2002 and 2003 were very active in absorbing the lessons of 9/11 and realigning response relationships (Jackson et al., 2001). McKinsey & Company (2002a,b) concurrently released two informative and candid after-action reports critiquing the actions of the City of New York Police and Fire Departments to the World Trade Center. Titan Systems Corporation (2003) also released an after-action report on the Arlington County (Virginia) police and fire department responses to the Pentagon. We saw stark differences in command and control, communications, coordination, and results. Arlington County benefited from clear lines of authority and first responders who actually practiced together prior to 9/11.

We realized we had to make substantial changes in our plans and response structure. Our first test working together followed the disastrous 2000 general election, when Broward County became the focus of international attention for botching the elections process and leaving an entire presidential election hanging in the balance. Broward County Constitutional Officers pulled together with county government, municipalities, school boards, and other entities to jointly assist the Supervisor of Elections Office with the 2002 general elections. The county's new Emergency Operations Center was used for this task and a plan was designed around the election as if it were an emergency/disaster event.

In 2003, after numerous public hearings, commission meetings, proposals, negotiations, countless hours, and sleepless nights, the Broward County Commission approved a contract that merged the County's Fire Rescue (and Emergency Medical Services) with the Sheriff's Office. This was a truly unique partnership in local government and public safety (Carroll and Taylor, 2014). The 2004 hurricane season would prove to be very active (Smith and McCarty, 2006). The first storm, Hurricane Charley, landed around Port Charlotte on the southwest coast of Florida on August 13. Charley gained strength suddenly as it came ashore as a Category 4 storm, wreaking havoc as it crossed the state from west to east. The second storm to make landfall was only 3 weeks later, just north of West Palm Beach (in Palm Beach County, north of Broward). Hurricane Frances came ashore as a Category 2 storm on September 4, entering the state from the Atlantic side. Three weeks after Frances, a third and stronger storm made landfall in almost the same location as Frances. Hurricane Jeanne came ashore as a Category 3 storm on September 25.

The Sheriff's Office activated every time a storm threatened the region. The 2004 hurricanes provided opportunities to deploy joint public safety teams that had been practicing together since the merger. As soon as each hurricane was no longer a threat in Broward, self-sustaining teams were formed to respond to stricken areas—meaning the teams had to carry all of their supplies (e.g., food, fuel, bedding) and had to be able to get down to work as soon as they arrived. Support staff were also deployed with teams to perform maintenance, set up work areas, establish communications, and provide supplies to the teams. All responses in affected areas were coordinated with their local counterparts.

The final preparation for the approaching 2005 hurricane season occurred June 5 to 7 with participation in the largest planned event in the history of Broward County. The Organization of American States (OAS) held its General Assembly meeting in Fort Lauderdale, the first such meeting held in the United States since 1989. Delegations from the 34 member nations, including their leaders, came to Broward County for the event. This would require an unprecedented multijurisdictional, multiagency response to address a host of security and safety issues. Fortunately, most of the players from the federal, state, and local agencies had been working together since 9/11 and spent much time seemingly in conclave during the 2004 hurricane season. Extensive planning, training, command and control, communications, and redundant features were assembled for this event. In the end, there were no reported incidents. There was not much time to recover after the OAS meeting, as the 2005 Atlantic hurricane season was already underway. It would become the busiest in recorded history. There were 28 storms, of which 5 became Category 4 hurricanes and four reached Category 5 strength (Pesaturo, 2006). Two of those Category 5 storms, Katrina and Wilma, would actually make landfall in South Florida—though, thankfully, neither at full strength. Before Hurricane Katrina went on to make its historically destructive path along the Gulf Coast (Townsend, 2006), the storm came ashore along the border of Broward and Miami-Dade Counties on August 25. This event proved to be fairly minor for Broward County.

Wilma came in late October. Law enforcement managers were responsible for overall command of the response. Senior-ranking deputy sheriffs acted as the Incident Commander and Deputy Incident Commander. The author filled the latter role and was primarily responsible for coordinating the Sheriff's Office centrally located Unified Command Post (UCP). This coordination included staffing and contact with the Broward County Emergency Operations Center and the Florida Department of Law Enforcement's Multi-Agency Command (FDLE, 2005). The UCP tracked personnel, equipment, and incidents throughout all of the Sheriff's Office commands.

The primary roles for law enforcement were to initially restore order when the storm passed, to provide traffic control and escorts during daylight hours, and to suppress crime at night. Restoring order began with assessing damage and deploying as many marked police vehicles into the community as possible to reassure citizens. As the response continued to unfold, law enforcement had to contend with multiple curfews (every municipality decided to enact their own). The curfews, in addition to unnecessarily taxing the already stressed jail system, unintentionally were preventing delivery of much-needed supplies (such as gasoline) during the night when it was most opportune to move such goods.

The county jail system had a myriad of responsibilities. Detention personnel had to provide security for the evacuation shelters, which were set up in public schools. Detention was holding approximately 6000 inmates and overseeing another 5900 offenders on community supervision. The system had to contend with damage to each of its facilities, as well as providing food, water, medication, and health care to the inmates and staff. Fire Rescue personnel were responsible for the initial medical, fire, and rescue calls but also played a significant role as the "heavy lifters" of the Sheriff's Office response. Fire Rescue had extensive experience with the Incident Command System, mobilizing unique equipment, and, of course, demobilization. Paramedics were deployed to the evacuation shelters. Fire Rescue vehicles helped moved essential supplies around the county and took the lead in keeping vital communications equipment functioning.

The administrative and community support teams did everything else. They had to make sure that all items were accounted for, the all-important reimbursement forms were completed, and supplies were acquired. This staff was the "mortar between the bricks," so to speak. For example, deputy sheriffs and select fire rescue personnel were issued "take home" vehicles, and they had access to fuel throughout the response. The remaining employees—all essential to the response—such as communications, detention, and other support personnel, did not have such access, and fuel shortages in communities were evident immediately following the storm. The administrative team took proactive action by storing as much fuel in as many Sheriff's Office facilities as could be done safely before the storm (even being accused by other agencies of hoarding). Fuel was released from this supply in order to get employees back and forth to work.

The Chaplain's Office was tasked with the welfare of Sheriff's Office employees. The UCP had to account for all employees, many of whom were also storm victims. It was a policy of the agency to expend public resources for the employees to ensure they could get to work and then once they arrived to attend to employees' emotional and mental needs. Among the many things the Chaplain's Office did to help employees was to bring in several members of the same team used to debrief first responders at the World Trade Center site. The Chaplain's Office brought in a mobile dry-cleaning and laundry center for employees and even brought in massage and aroma therapists—whatever worked to reduce stress. The Media Relations Office worked into a cycle of repetitive messaging and frequent briefs, as it was unknown when people were able to tune in.

There were surprises and unanticipated activities—every response has them. With electric out in almost all of Broward County, there were no traffic control devices operating, including railroad crossings. No commercial service stations could provide fuel, nor were the water pumps available to move water and sewage through the system. Installation of generators at these businesses and key infrastructure sites would be required by ordinance *after* the 2005 hurricane season. The sanitary implications of a lack of water are obvious, but it was learned that potable water also had to be pumped through coolers in the Public Safety Building to support communications and computer equipment. Also out of service was the Fiveash Water Treatment facility in the City of Fort Lauderdale which provided water to the Public Safety Building, as well as fire hydrants and fire suppression systems at the airport and Port Everglades, meaning the two transportation hubs could not operate.

Port Everglades was the transfer point for petroleum products to all of South Florida. Even if service stations could open, there would be no fuel for them or for generators. One response was to begin running the trains again, to bring in supplies and chlorine to purify water. Southeast Florida has two major commercial freight lines, the CSX and Florida East Coast railroads. None of the literally dozens of crossings had traffic control. Some of those crossings required four personnel to direct traffic.

When the response routine had settled in and schedules were set, employees who worked nights were extremely exhausted due to the lullaby of chainsaws and generators keeping them awake during the day. Liberalized rest periods were added for those employees. When the supply and volunteer spigots opened, they could not be turned off. We had to learn how to manage those arriving to help and find places to safely store supplies. Many of those involved unofficially measured the success of the response by the lack of interest by the national media. The catastrophe that followed Katrina on the Gulf Coast and decidedly poor response in and around New Orleans provided a great deal of fodder for the media. None of that was present in Broward County. In addition, the response had to include ensuring that the 2005 general election, to be held the week following Wilma, was properly administered. The relationships and collaboration built following 9/11 (Raymond et al., 2005), the number of actual events occurring prior to Wilma, the regular updating of response plans, and exceptional coordination among many players contributed to the success of the response.

Hurricane and Post-Tropical Cyclone Sandy: October to November 2012

There is still much debate about the type of storm Sandy was, other than a major disaster. To put it in perspective, Sandy was over 1150 miles across. When the storm came up the East Coast of the United States, about 66.5 million people were in its path. Twenty-four states would be impacted, including West Virginia, where 24 inches of snow came down (Masters, 2012). Flood warnings were issued as far west as Chicago. At its height of intensity, Sandy reached Category 3. When Sandy made landfall just northeast of Atlantic City, New Jersey, on October 29 (7 years to the week after Wilma struck South Florida), sustained winds were below the hurricane threshold (FEMA, 2013).

The winds and rain were to play a role, but it was the widespread storm surge that devastated so many areas. With Sandy, there was nowhere for the water surging ahead of the storm to dissipate—water was forced to go inland, made worse by the storm coinciding with an astronomical high tide. When it was over, over 8 million people were without power, at least 55 people died, and scores were injured (Masters, 2012), although these figures vary widely depending on the source. Sandy would quickly move into second place among the most expensive storms in American history (behind Katrina).

Transportation systems and infrastructure were inundated. The New York Metropolitan Area airports were under water. Water and sewer facilities were knocked offline; for example, the Bay Park Sewage Treatment Plant in New York's Nassau County was swamped in the storm surge. This plant was responsible for treating the sewage of about 40% of the county's population. The plant was completely out of service for 44 hours and released over 100 million gallons of untreated sewage into surrounding neighborhoods and waterways. During the recovery, it took over 6 weeks to fully restore service to the plant, and ultimately about 2.2 billion gallons of partially treated sewage were released into adjoining waterways (Spychalsky, 2013). This type of ecological and sanitary disaster occurred at plants throughout the Northeast (Anon., 2013; Croce, 2013; Kenward et al., 2013).

Then it snowed. As if to add insult to injury, the temperatures dropped each day. Prior to and during the storm, the temperatures peaked in the mid-60s but dropped steadily each day, reaching lows in the low 30s. The response was further complicated from November 7 to 8 when over 4 inches of snow fell on top of storm-stricken areas. Many victims of Sandy had endured no electricity, no water and sewer, major supply interruptions (like gasoline), and now the addition of cold and snow.

New Jersey and New York City have received ample and much deserved coverage following Sandy. This section focuses on local jurisdictions on the south shore of Nassau County (Village of East Rockaway, Town of Hempstead, and East Rockaway School District). The local government structure is layered, with independent villages, townships, cities, and county governments. The townships and county governments divide responsibilities for the unincorporated areas. School districts have separately elected boards at the village or city level. The bulk of public safety responsibilities fall to the Nassau County Police Department, which provides law enforcement services in all unincorporated areas and in 45 of the county's 64 incorporated villages. The vast majority of fire and emergency medical responses are handled by the 71 volunteer fire departments located throughout the county. Volunteer fire rescue is very highly regarded in Nassau County.

Town of Hempstead Senior Council Member Anthony J. Santino: "On Being a Conduit"

The Town of Hempstead (www.toh.org) proclaims itself as the largest township in the United States. It is a separate taxing authority located entirely within Nassau County and comprises most of the county's South Shore. Its boundaries encompass 22 villages (including East Rockaway), 50 unincorporated areas, 36 school districts (including East Rockaway School District), and approximately 756,000 residents. Hempstead maintains roadways, operates public spaces, collects refuse, and provides water and sewer services. It has a Public Safety Department, but the personnel are not sworn nor have arrest powers. Hempstead's elected board is comprised of a town supervisor and Council members; its FY2013 budget was $414.4 million. The town supervisor acts as both the town's chief executive officer and chief financial officer.

Council member Anthony J. Santino is the longest serving member of the board, thus the moniker "senior." The author has known Tony for more than 40 years and cannot recall a time when Tony did not want to be a public servant. During discussions for this research, he said that he feels very lucky to be able to continue serving the public after so many years. He related that he still finds it interesting, fresh, and new every day, that each day brings another challenge to his job as a Council member. He sincerely believes he has been making a difference in the lives of others and wants to continue to do so. There have been other tests and obstacles to overcome before and since, but none like Sandy.

As an elected Council member, Tony functions as a legislator, not as an executive or administrator; therefore, his tasks and responsibilities are different from those of an appointed official. After the initial shock of the storm settled into the post-storm recovery phase, he went out into the streets of stricken neighborhoods in his district to act as a "conduit" (his term) to those in need. He saw his role primarily as a facilitator between his constituents and the assistance being provided by the government. This is a critical point in the research and discussion, because his actions were not limited to his capacity as an elected representative from the Town of Hempstead; rather, they extended to coordinating recovery efforts with other public entities at the village, school district, county, state, and even federal levels—often working through the offices of other elected officials and their staffs.

His district was hit very hard, including the Village of East Rockaway, where he resides. He recalled that simple things such as recharging a cellular telephone or refueling a vehicle could not be done, nor could personnel readily gather and disseminate information among the damaged areas. A major concern was similar to one that arose in Florida following Hurricane Wilma (October 2005)—the ability to administer the polling process for Election Day—albeit on a different scale. Tuesday, November 6, 2012, was a general election with a presidential race at the top of the ballot. Shortly after Sandy struck, preparations for the upcoming election process had to include checking every polling place for serviceability. Council member Santino coordinated with the Nassau County Board of Elections Office and other government agencies to relocate polling stations as necessary and ensure that notices of the changes went out to voters. He related that there were no reports to his knowledge of any Sandy-related problems at the polling places on Election Day.

In all, Tony estimates that he spent about 6 months serving as a conduit for the public to other service and business providers. He attended many community forums to hear from constituents. He believed his most important contribution was helping people get answers when there were often none to be had, whether they came from other government agencies, private insurers, or nonprofits. In his opinion, Hurricane Irene in 2011 did not provide any guidance for the response to Sandy, because Irene came and went and nothing substantial happened. Unfortunately, for this reason, people did not take Sandy as seriously as they should have as it approached Long Island.

Village of East Rockaway Vice Mayor Bruno Romano: "It Took a Village"

It was a warm but pleasant mid-July evening to spend at the Village Council meeting. After the formalities of calling the meeting to order, individual awards were presented to members of the East Rockaway High School girls varsity softball team. Despite being out of their damaged school from the time Sandy struck until April 2013 (during their softball season), the team was being honored by the Village as Nassau County Class B Champions. Once the handshakes and photographs with elected officials were completed, the chambers emptied out, with only six audience members remaining, several of whom were Village employees giving their respective department reports to the Council.

The Village of East Rockaway (www.villageofeastrockaway.org) is an approximately 1-square-mile incorporated village within the Town of Hempstead. According to the 2014 Bureau of Census, the population was 9854 residents. This is a real-life example of small-town America that has changed little over the years. The elected Village Council consists of a mayor, a vice mayor, and three trustees. The Village government includes a clerk (parking permits, business licenses, permits), building department, public works department (sanitation, street lights), recreation department, auxiliary police, library, emergency management, code enforcement, and a volunteer fire department. All other local services are provided by the Town of Hempstead or Nassau County.

The author has known Vice Mayor Bruno Romano for over 40 years. In his full-time life, he works in the freight and travel businesses. He was elected in 2002 and has served on the Village Council in consecutive terms since then. Coming from the private sector, Vice Mayor Romano brings a different career perspective to elected office. He says he genuinely loves doing his "part-time job" and has "learned an awful lot" about public service since his first election. A recurring theme in East Rockaway was how the efforts of volunteers and professional staff combined to deal with Sandy, as well as how the Village government worked across boundaries in the recovery effort. Vice Mayor Romano said the intensity of Sandy upon impact took them by surprise, because of the "hype" behind Irene the previous year. Village employees and volunteers assisted in conducting evacuations, using their own private boats to do rescues.

Because Village heavy equipment (such as garbage trucks) was stored in garages and facilities near waterways, the decision was made during pre-storm preparations to pull everything possible back inland to open areas in the park space adjacent to Village Hall. In retrospect, Vice Mayor Romano believed that was one of the best decisions made. All of the equipment, though staged outside and exposed to the elements, survived intact and could be deployed right away for rescue and recovery. An emergency management operations command center was established on the second floor of Village Hall. As the recovery unfolded, this command center also functioned as a distribution control point for other contiguous communities. FEMA personnel were later integrated into the command center for more direct contact with local governments.

Electric, water and sewer, and other utilities were out of service in the Village, which established a "code red" system for getting important information out to residents, including printing flyers for door-to-door distribution. The "code red" system has since been integrated into Village services (Lenahan, 2013). Vice Mayor Romano praised the working relationships between the elected and appointed officials in the adjacent villages as well as with the Town of Hempstead. The Village got a great response from its volunteer auxiliary police and volunteer firefighters. Nonprofits and religious groups (St. Raymond's Roman Catholic Church and East Rockaway Nazarene Church among them) all came together to help with the recovery effort. He said it was remarkable the way in which people adapted to performing tasks manually. Vice Mayor Romano said he was genuinely impressed with the way volunteers and professionals worked together throughout the recovery.

East Rockaway Schools Superintendent Roseanne Melucci: "We'll Make It Work"

The East Rockaway School District (www.eastrockawaschools.org) is a public education entity and a separate jurisdiction with taxing authority that serves most of the Village of East Rockaway and adjacent unincorporated areas. An elected board that oversees the school district is comprised of five officials—president, vice president, secretary, and two trustees—and is responsible for presenting the budget for a public ballot and approval each year, managing the district, and selecting appointed officials. The FY2014 budget was approximately $36.8 million, including capital expenditures. The district has about 200 teachers and staff for almost 1300 students attending two elementary schools and a junior/senior high school (Ochtera, 2013).

School Superintendent Roseanne Melucci was responsible for administering the school district, its facilities, employees, and, of course, students. The position of school superintendent is an appointed one and serves at the will of the elected school board. Each of East Rockaway's three schools is led by its own principal and staff, who report to the superintendent. The high school complex is located on the Mill River waterway, and Rhame Avenue Elementary School has waterways approximately 1000 feet away both to the east and south of the school building. These waterways have continuous flow access to bays, channels, and eventually the ocean. According to U.S. Geological Survey gauges (NOAA, 2014), East Rockaway experienced a 10.8-foot maximum water level (combined 8.08-foot storm surge and 2.72-foot astronomical high tide) at 8:42 p.m. Sandy overflowed these waterways and surrounding areas, flooding the grounds and first floor of the high school, as well as the grounds and first floor of Rhame Avenue Elementary School.

The immediate major concerns were tracking down school district employees and students, assessing and repairing damaged facilities, and resuming instruction. School Superintendent Melucci's team fanned out into the community to track down and hear from every district employee. She personally drove through the district to meet parents and children. Although many families were made homeless by Sandy, the school district circulated flyers in addition to using existing contact information to reach students. Social workers assisted by looking for displaced students in temporary housing. The school district also partnered with the fire department to distribute water and supplies to the community.

In assessing facilities, it was determined that the high school and Rhame Avenue buildings were not serviceable. Flooding from the storm surge had rendered both inoperable. The high school was substantially damaged and would remain closed for months. The waterline in the auditorium (at ground level) was 5 feet high. Water flooded the basement where the electrical mains and boiler were located. It was initially estimated that the building might not be ready for classes again until the following school year. All vehicles and equipment on ground level were lost in the storm surge. As the recovery got underway, the staff had to deal with commutes complicated by gasoline shortages, and cellular telephones were undependable.

The school district's finance and facilities staff had to find restoration companies. The business office's work with FEMA involved many, many meetings and rotations of FEMA teams. The curriculum and technology office worked on restoring connectivity via telephone and Internet. The pupil personnel office kept track of the students living in temporary housing and how they were being transported to school. The elected school board met regularly to review the progress and offer assistance. The parent–teacher associations (PTAs) were there to assist each step of the way.

School Superintendent Melucci praised the working relationships among other units of government and local elected officials. She noted that local politicians were visible and came to the school for briefings. Elected officials, she felt, took a personal interest because these were "their schools." The Board of Cooperative Educational Services (BOCES) of Nassau County served as an example for the role of intergovernmental cooperation within East Rockaway School District. Nassau County's BOCES is a unique public entity within education. It is a group funded by all of the county's 56 school districts to provide educational services at a county level that might be deemed too costly or complex at the individual district level. It is governed by a nine-member board elected by the members of the 56 school boards.

Superintendent Melucci communicated with BOCES to find vacant schools that would be suitable temporary replacements. No one wanted to split up the student body into different schools and locations. The school district of nearby Village of Baldwin had closed two elementary schools in June 2012, and these were selected as the temporary schools. Because the school district did not own or use school buses, the staff also had to procure buses to get the students from East Rockaway to the two schools in Baldwin. Many school buses in the county were damaged and unavailable, which only increased the level of difficulty for obtaining any.

The student body was divided by grade between the two schools, with junior high/middle school students located in one school and high school students in the other. Staff and teachers, as well as state-mandated onsite positions (nurses, principals, etc.), were then assigned where needed. Superintendent Melucci noted there was very little drop-off in enrollment, absenteeism was low, and the school spirit was great. The athletic director kept the intermural athletic teams active by coordinating activities with the coaches and other districts. Everyone involved refused to cancel any season or any part of a season, despite the recovery efforts. The school district of nearby Village of Malverne permitted East Rockaway students to use their facilities for the annual Rock Rivalry competition.

This is not to say that this recovery was one big group hug. Successful leaders have to play both "bad cop" and "good cop." Superintendent Melucci, who was responsible for managing the recovery activities and restoration of facilities, did not like to see workers who were hired to repair facilities standing idle or failing to do the work for which they were contracted. She rode herd on workers to "get the kids home." Much behind-the-scenes hustling and follow-up were necessary to make sure tasks were properly completed.

It was important to keep the recovery story in the public eye. Superintendent Melucci said the good deal of positive media coverage resulted in $20,000 being raised to replace the high school band's musical instruments. A dress rental company, Rent the Runway, sponsored a dream prom, which included donating all of the girls' prom dresses and paying for the event for the entire junior and senior classes. Men's Wearhouse donated all of the boys' tuxedos.

Superintendent Melucci emphasized that the recovery and its success were a team effort. She believed that members of her team worked well together because they had been doing so for some time. They had established mutual respect, collaboration, trust, and cooperation, all before Sandy occurred. Finally, she effusively praised the students: "And the children … they were amazing!" This narrative only scratches the surface of the amount of work and coordination that went into getting the high school reopened, keeping the student body whole, and aiding in the healing process. On April 29, 2013, the high school building reopened ahead of schedule.

Rhame Avenue Elementary School Principal Laura Guggino: "Home for the Holidays"

The sign in front of Rhame Avenue Elementary School reads, "Established in 1926." The original three-story brick structure was the elementary school the author attended. On January 19, 1986, and despite the efforts of 12 volunteer fire companies from East Rockaway and surrounding villages, the building burned down (Anon., 1986). It was replaced with a two-story structure that opened in 1990. It is the current home to 23 teachers and staff, and about 330 students in kindergarten through sixth grade.

Principal Laura Guggino leads her teachers and staff and manages the school as its chief administrator, but she is also absolutely committed to the entire education experience: her students, their families, and the community she serves. One of the county's youngest principals, she became principal at Rhame Avenue in 2001—just in time for 9/11. She believed that event helped her to grow in her role and earn the respect of her colleagues. Sandy was an emotional time, because the families of many of her students became homeless. She knew that it was necessary to take care of the immediate needs of families first but also to find an alternative for the Rhame Avenue building. Because Irene proved to be of little consequence in 2011, no one expected the type of event that Sandy became. The storm surge poured about 2 feet of water into the first floor of the school building, damaging classrooms, equipment, and cabinetry. The waterline on the outside of the building was close to 4 feet high.

The brief safety plan for the building called for it to be secured for the storm. The post-storm plan was more of a daily proposition, with two basic priorities: (1) account for students and employees to get them back into instruction, and (2) get the building back in service before the winter holiday break in December. It was going to be a day-by-day struggle, with almost no reference point. Such a task had never been undertaken before.

To keep all of the school district's students together, it was decided to double-up the classrooms at Centre Avenue Elementary School, which was inland and largely undamaged. This move essentially merged two schools into one building. Both school staffs helped move chairs and tables to Centre Avenue, with the Rhame Avenue students being officially welcomed by the Centre Avenue students. The effort was termed "CARE," for Centre Avenue/Rhame Elementary, and received positive media attention.

When the Rhame Avenue students first relocated to Centre Avenue, about 200 students initially reported, with more filtering back in as time went on. Principal Guggino adapted a registration system to account for the students and get them back in the system. She sat with social workers to develop status checklists for parents to determine what they had and if they were able to meet basic family needs. The staff formed a post-incident response team to evaluate the needs of the parents and assist in getting supplies to the families. These activities went well beyond the scope of their educator roles. Principal Guggino related that she clearly had a number of students who experienced trauma. Social workers were brought in to augment the work of the in-house psychologist. They developed role-playing scenarios for the staff to alert them to what behaviors they should look for in the students (and to some extent, other employees) and offered guidance on how to respond to such behaviors. Students were encouraged to tell their stories as part of the healing process.

Five weeks later, on December 13, the Phillip Phillips song "Home" could be heard playing on the school loudspeakers at Rhame Avenue Elementary for the grand return of its students, who could now start back on the path to reconnect with the building and the community. Just in time, they were home for the holidays. This was a great story of a small suburban school district working across boundaries to recover from a disaster.

Lessons Learned: Collaborative Emergency Management

The research and experiences of Wilma and Sandy revealed numerous lessons learned. The following is by no means all inclusive or in priority order:

- *Value of teambuilding and experience*—This was an important aspect of both responses. Even though the public servants in New York did not necessarily have emergency event experience, all credited the lengthy and often close working relationships already established among their own teams or other players through day-to-day functions. The Broward County Sheriff's Office already had much experience in forming relationships, assembling teams, and accumulating real-world knowledge about emergency responses. In both cases, when the time came, public servants knew each other, had worked together, and were ready to shift into response mode.
- *Assessing damage*—Once the storm has passed, restoring order and determining those requiring assistance are the most important initial activities. An assessment will determine the extent of the damage and the scope of the response. Damage assessment should include public and private property, prioritized for the recovery effort.
- *Communications* It is essential to build in redundant and layered communications in order to keep the recovery effort progressing. When teaching public safety executives, the author often recommended that they build their communications plans based on "medieval" conditions (meaning no modern conveniences) and work their way up from there. Such plans may include runners or couriers, point-to-point radios, "two if by sea" communications, or any other methods limited only by the imagination of those managing the recovery.
- *Fuel, fuel, fuel*—Without it, the entire response comes to a standstill. Vehicles will not move and generators cannot be replenished. A hurricane or tropical storm is the only natural event that gives ample warning. There should be no excuse for failing to stockpile, hoard, or whatever one wants to call it a supply of fuel that will suffice until supplies flow in from outside the affected area.
- *Damage to infrastructure*—Roads, bridges, rail lines, runways, and other vital transportation infrastructure may be damaged or become nonfunctional. Such infrastructure must be made serviceable as soon as practicable to facilitate the recovery.

- *Loss of utilities*—It is likely that electricity, water, sewer, telephones, and other utilities will be offline. This could mean no traffic lights, no toilets, no cellular telephones, or other deficits complicating recovery efforts. Plans have to include contingencies for working without utilities.
- *High visibility of elected officials*—The author has stressed the point in every single class ever taught that somewhere along the line all public servants work for elected officials. They may serve the public, but they also report to those who have stood for and won elections. Those elected officials, in the author's experience, do not require coaxing to be seen during a recovery effort. In fact, they need to be seen by constituents as a measure of their leadership and their ability to reassure and help their constituents. Ensuring high visibility for elected officials, ranging from village council members to the president, should be included in any preplanning.
- *Media relations*—The word has to get out; the public has to be informed. In any recovery effort, the media must be able to perform their jobs. The public sector must work with the media beyond the usual website postings, citizen e-mails, and door-to-door flyers. Information that has to be disseminated to the public generally goes through the media. Because it may not be known how much access members of the public have to the media, messages should be repetitive and accurate. Media releases and interviews should be timed to permit news outlets to broadcast on time.
- *Managing volunteers and supplies*—Volunteers and supplies will come, and there could be many more than may be needed. Neither can be turned away, though, and both have to be effectively managed as part of the recovery effort. In the preplanning or review phase, locations where volunteers and supplies could be marshaled during a recovery effort should be identified.
- *Employees as victims*—Depending on the scope of the event, many public servants and their loved ones could also be victims of the event. This was evident in the responses to both Wilma and Sandy, although the Broward County Sheriff's Office developed procedures and set aside specific resources to support this effort. Public agencies must have their employees back as part of the recovery effort, but it would be both immoral and irresponsible to overlook the welfare of those employees.
- *Elections*—Hurricane season, spanning 6 months per year, may affect primary and general election cycles, as happened with the late-season storms Wilma and Sandy. Governments have to work together to ensure that registered voters can exercise their right on the appointed day. There have to be adequate polling places and information disseminated so people know what to do.
- *Continuity of Operations (COOP) planning*—Whether it involves providing for the care and custody of 6000 inmates or getting hundreds of students back into their classrooms, the public sector must have procedures in place for the business of government to continue, as well as safeguarding vital information that will be needed when the recovery is completed. Public service may be disrupted, but it must continue and be seen by the public as continuing.
- *Surprises*—Anticipate surprises. No matter how well prepared one may be, how comprehensive the response plan, or how complete the checklists, at least one thing will occur that was unplanned and unexpected. This has happened in every event in which the author has participated or has studied. The lesson here is to be flexible enough in staffing, resources, and capabilities to respond to the inevitable surprise when it does occur—and it will.

Implications for Public Administration and Crisis and Emergency Management

Public safety and elected officials tend to attract the lion's share of attention during rescue and recovery efforts following a disaster. Education also plays a vital day-to-day role for local government services in a community, a role that was vital in the Sandy recovery effort. If the activities of public safety after a storm can be described in brightly colored broad brushstrokes, then those of education would be more of nuanced hues and shades. We can readily accept the importance attached to repairing damaged facilities, to getting students back into classrooms to continue their studies, and to reducing any disruptions in their education. We may not realize the less easily quantified importance of schools providing a sense of normalcy for children traumatized by disaster or serving the need to have a home for many who were driven from their own.

The stories of the local jurisdictions in New York are remarkable tales of courage and persistence, intergovernmental coordination, and, frankly, unconditional love. They were what really made the whole recovery effort work. As a public safety executive with hands-on experience in large-scale events, the author can readily recount the logistical aspects of rescue and recovery. The number of personnel can be tallied, as can the equipment deployed, debris moved, dollars spent, meals served, bags of ice distributed, blankets issued, and the like (Carroll and Taylor, 2008). However, it is difficult to measure the unquestioned reciprocal trust between elected and appointed officials and the community stakeholders.

The research that was conducted in New York revealed additional implications for event response not necessarily indicated by the Broward County Sheriff's Office experiences. These may be the product of the types of positions held by the interviewees, the culture of a very small village such as East Rockaway, or other factors. One very critical mistake made, and this seemed to be a regionwide issue in the Northeast, was terming Hurricane Irene in 2011 a "non-event." People seemed to collectively let their guard down and did not take seriously the approaching Sandy in 2012.

Many displaced families took refuge at shelters, relatives' homes, or other locations all over Long Island. Yet, even with elementary school children being doubled up in one building, with junior high/middle school children in one school and high school children in another, the parents brought the children to their own district to attend classes. The parents and the greater community trusted their district employees. "Unconditional love" may be the best way to describe this bond. This description is not the author's; rather, it was offered in separate interviews by both educators, who ardently believed it was present. The notion of unconditional love in the context of event response is worth exploring in future research.

Disaster and emergency management response is still viewed through a fairly masculine lens. Public safety, despite advances over the years, remains male dominated; however, the author was afforded the opportunity to head out on a different path of discovery when he looked beyond the traditional knowledge base and sought the views of the opposite gender. The author met both of the East Rockaway educators for the first time during the interviews. In the interviews, it became apparent that terms such as "nurturing" and "our kids" were integral to their take on the recovery effort. Their distinctly feminine standpoint rounded out the findings and emphasized aspects of the community not usually studied alongside public safety and emergency management.

There seemed to be a stronger emotional attachment to the response by the interviewees in New York compared to those in Broward. They saw themselves as integral players in the healing process for the people they served. There was an effort to celebrate small victories along the path to the healing. Despite having no real detailed plans to work from or previous event experiences, all of the interviewees were satisfied with their responses and less critical of others. I could never say the same of the Broward County Sheriff's Office, where criticism of others was something of an art form. All of the interviewees said they felt lucky to serve, that it was where they belonged, and that they were fortunate to be able to help.

Conclusion

The tiny house Barbara Shovlin lived in for more than 60 years was inundated by Sandy's 14-foot storm surge in Brooklyn. It was in this house, as a young widow, where she raised six of the author's cousins in the small shoreline community of Gerritsen Beach. In just a few hours, she lost a lifetime's worth of belongings and memories. She was out of her home for many months as she and her family worked to repair the damages. During a visit to conduct the interviews for this chapter, the author saw her at a family gathering. It was unsettling to see how frail she had become and how deeply Sandy affected her life. Apparently, the toll would prove to be too much for her, and she passed away on October 9, 2013, just shy of the first anniversary of Sandy and her 84th birthday. Aunt Barbara may not be officially listed among the dead and injured from Sandy, but she was just as much a victim. This is why it is so essential for all first responders to remember that, no matter the type of event, to the victim it is a disaster.

There is a greater narrative here about those who not only choose public service but also take on a leadership role. Day-to-day leadership is challenging enough, but it is when confronted by crisis that we are truly tested. The elected and appointed officials interviewed in New York were examples of what is right about public service. Event responses occur across time, jurisdictional borders, cultures, and public career paths. At the time this chapter was written, there had not been a direct strike in Florida from a storm in almost 9 years. The distance between events will certainly impact the next response. The leadership team of the Broward County Sheriff's Office has changed twice since 2005, which could also affect response relationships.

To be learned properly, the lessons taught by such events have to be cumulative. We should be able to gain experiences from events, both positive and negative, that we can apply to the next one. The lessons learned here may not fit neatly into a standard format. Collaboration among the players (formally or informally) is a key to success, and public servants should be recognized for their unswerving desire for wanting to make it work—no matter what difficulties they encounter. When the response comes to an end, public servants simply shift gears from one mode to another and continue to serve in their regular day-to-day roles.

Questions for Discussion

1. What is collaborative emergency management and why does it matter?
2. If you were tasked to present a new or revised hurricane plan to your community leaders, what would be your priorities (and why)?
3. Public safety tends to attract a much larger portion of attention and responsibility in the response to an event; how do we avoid overlooking the other services that must be provided?
4. When the author argues that, in an emergency or disaster event, to the victim it is always a disaster, what does this mean?

Additional Reading[*]

Farazmand, A., Ed. (2014). *Crisis and Emergency Management: Theory and Practice*, 2nd ed. Boca Raton, FL: CRC Press.
FEMA. (2011). *National Disaster Recovery Framework: Strengthening Disaster Recovery for the Nation*. Washington, DC: Federal Emergency Management Agency.
Haddow, G.D., Bullock, J.A., and Coppola, D.P. (2011). *Introduction to Emergency Management*, 4th ed. Boston: Butterworth-Heinemann.
Pinkowski, J., Ed. (2008). *Disaster Management Handbook*. Boca Raton, FL: CRC Press.
Waugh, W.L. and Tierney, K., Eds. (2007). *Emergency Management: Principles and Practice for Local Government*, 2nd ed. Washington, DC: International City/County Management Association.
Zelikow, P. (2003). *9/11 Final Commission Report*. Washington, DC: U.S. Government Printing Office.

References

Anon. (1986). School destroyed by fire on Long Island. *The New York Times*, January 20.
Anon. (2013). Study: Sandy dumped 11 billion gallons of sewage into surrounding waters, mostly in NYC and NJ. *Associated Press*, April 30.
Carroll, J.J. (2005). Consolidation, Coordination, and Communication: A New Model for Public Safety, paper presented at the 15th World Conference on Disaster Management, Toronto, Canada, July 10–13.
Carroll, J.J. (2006). Hurricane Wilma and One Agency's Unified Command Experience, paper presented at the National Hurricane Conference, Orlando, FL, April 10–14; Governor's Hurricane Conference, Fort Lauderdale, FL, May 8–12.
Carroll, J.J. (2008). Strategic Planning in a Complex Multi-Jurisdictional Political Environment, paper presented at the Law Enforcement Planning and Research Directors' Forum Meeting, Miami, FL, April 23.
Carroll, J.J. and Taylor, L.E. (2008). Regionalism in the States: Lessons Learned for Florida's State-Local Model of Strategic Interaction and Emergency Management in Homeland Security, paper presented at the American Society for Public Administration (ASPA) National Conference, Dallas, TX, March 7–11.
Carroll, J.J. and Taylor, L.E. (2014). Collaboration, consolidation, and coordination in the Broward Sheriff's office: a new paradigm in public safety and emergency management? In Farazmand, A., Ed., *Crisis and Emergency Management: Theory and Practice*, 2nd ed. Boca Raton, FL: CRC Press.
Croce, B. (2013). Outage at Bay Park sewage plant dumps 3 million gallons of waste into channel. *LIHerald*, May 15 (http://liherald.com/stories/Outage-dumps-3-million-gallons-of-waste-into-channel,47708).
FDLE. (2005). *Annual Statewide County Reports*. Tallahassee: Florida Department of Law Enforcement (http://www.fdle.state.fl.us/Content/FSAC/UCR/Annual-UCR.aspx).
FEMA. (2013). Six Months after Sandy, New York Communities in Recovery [press release]. Washington, DC: Federal Emergency Management Agency (http://www.fema.gov/disaster/4085/updates/six-months-after-sandy-new-york-communities-recovery).
Jackson, B.A., Peterson, D.J., Bartis, J.T., LaTourette, T., Brahmakulam, I., Houser, A., and Sollinger, J. (2001). *Protecting Emergency Responders: Lessons Learned from Terrorist Attacks*. Santa Monica, CA: RAND Corporation (http://www.rand.org/pubs/conf_proceedings/CF176.html).
Kenward, A., Yawitz, D., and Raja, U. (2013). *Sewage Overflows from Hurricane Sandy*. Princeton, NJ: Climate Central (www.climatecentral.org/pdfs/Sewage.pdf).

---

[*] Refer to anything written by William L. Waugh, Louise K. Comfort, Christine Gibbs Springer, Beverly A. Cigler, and many of the other giants of the growing discipline of crisis response and emergency management. Federal, state, and local government websites are a veritable treasure trove of information, and video sites, such as YouTube, have terrific videos of events and the television shows that cover them. Seek out material and read it.

Lagorio, C. (2005). Millions powerless in Florida. *CBS/Associated Press*, October 25 (http://www.cbsnews.com/news/millions-powerless-in-florida/).

Lenahan, F.T. (2013). Emergency Preparedness Bulletin from Village Hall, flyer produced by Village of East Rockaway, New York.

Masters, J. (2012). Sandy by the numbers: trying to comprehend a stunning disaster. *Weather Underground*, November 1, www.wunderground.com/blog/JeffMasters/comment.html?entrynum=2284.

McKinsey & Company. (2002a). *Improving FDNY Emergency Preparedness and Response*, consultant report commissioned by the Fire Department of the City of New York.

McKinsey & Company. (2002b). *Improving NYPD Emergency Preparedness and Response*, consultant report commissioned by the New York Police Department.

NCDC. (2005). *Hurricane Wilma*. Asheville, NC: National Climatic Data Center (www.ncdc.noaa.gov/extremeevents/specialreports/Hurricane-Wilma2005.pdf).

NOAA. (2013). *Service Assessment: Hurricane/Post-Tropical Cyclone Sandy, October 22–29, 2012*. Silver Spring, MD: National Oceanic and Atmospheric Administration.

NOAA. (2014). *Hurricane Sandy*. Upton, NY: National Weather Service (www.weather.gov/okx/Hurricane Sandy).

Ochtera, K. (2013). 2013–14 Proposed Budget for East Rockaway schools. East Rockaway, NY: East Rockaway School District.

Pesaturo, C. (2006). Records set in Atlantic hurricane season of 2005. *Weather Underground*, www.wunderground.com/hurricane/record2005.asp.

Raymond, B., Hickman, L.J., Miller, L., and Wong, J.S. (2005). *Police Personnel Challenges After September 11: Anticipating Expanded Duties and a Changing Labor Pool*. Santa Monica, CA: RAND Corporation.

Smith, S.K. and McCarty, C. (2006). Florida's 2004 Hurricane Season: Demographic Response and Recovery, paper presented at the Southern Demographic Association Annual Meeting, Oxford, MS, November 3–5.

Spychalsky, A. (2013). Mangano: we need money for Bay Park. *LIHerald*, May 15 (http://liherald.com/islandpark/stories/Mangano-We-need-money-for-Bay-Park,47720?page=2&content_source=).

Titan Systems. (2003). *Arlington County After-Action Report on the Response to the September 11 Terrorist Attack on the Pentagon*. Washington, DC: U.S. Department of Justice, Office of Justice Programs, Office of Domestic Preparedness.

Townsend, F.F. (2006). *The Federal Response to Hurricane Katrina: Lessons Learned*. Washington, DC: Executive Office of the President of the United States.

Chapter 11

Lessons Learned from Managing Governance Crises in the Arab States

Jamil Jreisat

Contents

Chapter Goals 179
Introduction..180
Governance in the Arab States..181
Dilemma of Choice..182
Resurgence of Political Islam 186
Lessons Learned 190
Questions for Discussion..192
References 193

Chapter Goals

1. Focus on governance and public policies in the Arab states as determinants of societal development and stability, and analyze recent experiences that demonstrate many common attributes, although each state is distinct.
2. Emphasize the point that Arab societies have been enduring systems of governance that are largely autocratic, nonrepresentative, corrupt, and with modest records of social and economic achievements.
3. Address the fact that, even after the nominal end of colonialism, Western countries continued to interfere, invade, occupy, and exert influence over most Arab states.
4. Discuss the changes in demography, technology, and popular attitudes among the Arab people that generated forceful new demands for reform of governance, which escalated to popular revolutions in certain countries, referred to as the *Arab Spring*, that did not achieve all their demands; in some cases, they deteriorated into civil wars manipulated by external interference.

5. Highlight the lessons learned from the search for reform, including demonstrable resilience of public resistance to autocratic and corrupt governance, crucial role of competent and transformative leaders, and centrality of a widely supported reform doctrine with competent structures to articulate and implement visionary ideas.

Introduction

For centuries, philosophers, political scientists, historians, and reformers have sought to determine what constitutes good governance and how to achieve it. Many Arab and Islamic thinkers throughout the centuries have attempted to answer the same question. One, in particular, was Abu Nasr al-Farabi, who lived in the ninth century and is considered to be one of the greatest Arabic–Islamic philosophers of all times. A philosopher and logician, al-Farabi was also a major political scientist and is often referred to as the "Second Teacher," Aristotle being the first. The father of Islamic Neoplatonism, al-Farabi was absorbed by Aristotelianism. His most famous work, *al-Madina al-fadila* ("The Virtuous City") was not a clone of Plato's *Republic*, but some of its politics were in harmony with Platonism (Netton, 1998). Plato's *Republic* and al Farabi's *al-Madina al-fadila* were both profound inquiries into the essential elements of good governance.

Governance of contemporary societies has attracted wide interest from scholars, practitioners of public affairs, and citizens (Rosell, 1999; Ahrens, 2002; Donahue and Nye, 2002; Hyden, 2002; Jain, 2002; Farazmand, 2004, 2009; Klingner, 2006; Doeveren, 2011; Jreisat, 1997, 2011). Conceptual models and definitions of governance are many. As an inclusive function, governance encompasses, in addition to the central authority, players who share the responsibilities, such as local authorities, businesses, voluntary organizations, and a variety of civic associations (Klingner, 2006). Effective governance is a universal pursuit of societies, developed and developing alike. In Africa, for example, it has been suggested that the Prime Minister of the Democratic Republic of the Congo, Augustin Matata Ponyo, has revolutionized governance in this resource-rich country; his recipe includes the "golden trilogy" of leadership, good policies, and good governance. The Prime Minister believes that his country can illustrate to the world "how good governance can change the perception of Africa" (Trustfull, 2012). The recent uprisings in the Arab countries, referred to as the *Arab Spring*, are primarily attempts to change and to remedy past flaws and failures of governance.

As observed in Pierre (2000, pp. 3–4), "In much of the public and political debate, governance refers to sustaining co-ordination and coherence among a wide variety of actors with different purposes and objectives such as political actors and institutions, corporate interests, civil society, and transnational organizations." Fundamental change of governance can prove to be challenging, often marred by internal and external obstacles that impede development of the necessary political and administrative institutional capacities for action. As the exercise of accountable and effective political and administrative authority to manage a country's public affairs, systemic governance requires appropriate instruments, processes, and institutions in order to exercise its authority.

Ineffective and corrupt governance has been blamed for conditions of poverty, economic stagnation, lack of political stability, confused priorities, and impeded sustainable development and modernity. Similarly, the ability of a society to prosper in a world of rapid change will largely depend on its ability to develop a more participatory and effective governance system (Rosell, 1999). Since the collapse of the colonial order over six decades ago, developing participatory and effective governance has become more of a vision than a reality in many developing countries.

Governance in the Arab States

Since independence, most Arab states have been weighed down by autocratic and ineffective governance structures and processes. In addition to the occasional traumatic succession of rulers, people have endured restricted freedom, mediocre results of socioeconomic development, and failed attempts to build representative political and administrative public institutions (Jreisat, 1997). Although many of these governments have been dominated by autocratic rulers, countries formally regarded as republics have also been most abusive of the succession process. To stay in power, leaders often have managed fraudulent elections and leveled specious charges against their opponents in order to prosecute them and remove them from competition. As a result,

- For 42 years (1969 to 2012), Libya was ruled by one man, Muammar Gaddafi, until a popular revolution resulted in his murder.
- For 55 years after gaining independence from the French, Tunisia was ruled only by two men.
- Since 1970, Syria has been ruled by a father and his son.
- Egypt was ruled for 30 years (1981 to 2011) by one man, Hosni Mubarak.

In other Arab countries, whether ruled by monarchs or presidents, longevity has been ensured in both success and failure. Except for Lebanon, Arab leaders have proven that only death can separate them from office. No Arab country has experienced a current and a former head of state living or interacting concurrently. Moreover, these regimes have consistently ruled in a highly centralized and autocratic mode that has earned them various negative characterizations, such as autocratic, corrupt, inept, wasteful, and relying on nepotism and favoritism in appointments to public positions. The dilemma is that, by the end of the 20th century, Arab societies and people had changed dramatically in demography, education, use of technology, and expectations from their governments. Also, public policies and the performance of public authorities have been blamed for the disparity of income, low economic growth, increasing poverty, high unemployment, and a deepening sense of insecurity.

The mounting incongruity between the rulers and the ruled has generated untenable negative conditions that ultimately threaten the political and social stability of many Arab countries. Dissatisfaction with the political leaders has ignited public explosions demanding removal of many of these leaders, even by force, as in the brutal ending of the Libyan dictator Gaddafi. The initial uprising began in Tunisia in 2011 to force out of office the top autocratic leader and to replace him with a new governance system more representative of citizens' preferences. Within a few months, similar uprisings followed in Egypt, Libya, Bahrain, Yemen, and Syria. Although many of these uprisings began peacefully, in some cases violence followed that exacted enormous human and material costs, such as in Libya, Yemen, and Syria. In the case of Syria, the revolution against an autocratic rule has evolved into a brutal war between two determined and armed camps. The popular rebellion has been transformed into an international struggle where the rebels are armed, trained, and funded by foreign countries. Thus, the Syrian case has evolved into a different and tragic struggle.

A significant dimension of governance is public administration institutions and their employees. Over recent decades, several Arab states have allocated huge financial resources to expand public employment and to create vast bureaucracies, but they did not achieve the needed levels of performance or professionalism of public management. In addition to political obstacles and incongruity of methods and values, public sector reforms in general have been the result of a complex combination of historical traditions, efforts of political leaders to pursue new goals, and pressure from domestic and international environments (Pollitt and Bouckaert, 2004; Christensen and

Dong, 2012). In the Arab states, early assessments concluded that bureaucratic performance in several Arab countries offered "little hope that Middle Eastern bureaucracies will serve as positive forces of economic and social development in the region" (Palmer et al., 1987, p. 241). Consistently, criticisms of Arab bureaucracies have identified many deficiencies including apathy, corruption, insensitivity to citizens, incompetence, and a lack of innovation (Palmer et al., 1987; Jabbra, 1989).

Rigid governance that centralized all important decisions in the hands of an autocratic ruler, unrepresentative processes of policymaking, and poor results of public policies created unsustainable governance systems. The crisis became more threatening and public dissatisfaction was rising as failures of economic development policies resulted in expanded unemployment and poverty. The Arab Spring is the popular designation for the citizens' revolutions in 2011 against unpopular autocratic rulers, demanding a more representative, competent, and ethical governance. The uprisings in various states created opportunities for change as well as risks and challenges. Until recently, initiatives to change Arab politics and administration came primarily from outsiders. The underlying values of governance reforms continued to be mostly foreign reformers' conceptions, which limited theoretical and intellectual thinking beyond the inherited tradition of colonial roots. Any conceptualization of "emancipatory politics," as Neocosmos (2012) referred to it in the African context, was consistently excluded. It is widely acknowledged that the Arab Spring changed the process by effectively bringing in local interests and demands, reviving the potential of reflecting liberating intellectual thoughts, particularly those rooted in Arab culture and history. The strength of the revolutions in Tunisia and Egypt is that they have been almost entirely home grown. In comparison, a decade of U.S. hard power in Iraq (leading to thousands of American and tens of thousands of Iraqi deaths) has been less effective than a few months of peaceful protests in setting countries on the road toward representative governments (Anon., 2011a).

Western governments have been apprehensive about new and more assertive Arab politics that will be more resistant to dictation by foreign powers. As U.S. Secretary of State Hillary Clinton reportedly acknowledged, "We are facing an Arab Awakening that nobody could have imagined and few predicted just a few years ago" (Myers, 2011). In a very short time, Arab uprisings swept aside lots of the prevalent old conceptions. Through its ties to Arab dictators, the West had great clout in the Middle East. With power shifting to new, more representative systems of governance, the spirit and methods of future interactions remain uncertain. The transition in Tunisia has been fairly tame and peaceful, but it differs from the rest of the Arab countries.

In the end, a most compelling issue may be explained this way: "If the idea behind the thinking of politics is to overcome the subjective and objective limits of our current world … it is imperative to develop concepts and categories which make alternatives thinkable and thereby possible" (Neocosmos, 2012, p. 465). The search for alternatives by the Arab post-revolution reformers has to answer basic questions such as what system of governance to construct that can overcome past limits and deficiencies as well as promote principles of freedom, dignity, justice, equity, and accountability. Similarly, the new system must be competent and effective in managing public services, implementing strategies of social and economic development, and translating emancipating revolutionary objectives and values into realistic actions.

Dilemma of Choice

Reform is the highest priority in the states that have experienced revolutions and successfully deposed their autocratic leaders: Tunisia, Egypt, Libya, and Yemen. The discourse on reform evokes models and alternatives ranging between utopia and repackaged and recycled traditional thoughts and experiences. Modernity, reform, or development is not a uniform concept or process; it is beset by certain impreciseness (Paolini, 1999). For few years, *SPIEGEL*, a German research publication, sought answers to the perennial question: "Of all the governing styles in the world, does one country stand out as more successful than the others?" (Zand, 2012). Western democracies consider themselves to be efficient, farsighted, just, and prime examples of "good governance," but in recent years the euro and debt crises, along with wars in Iraq and Afghanistan, have shattered faith in the reliability of Western institutions. In 2008, when *SPIEGEL* published a series of articles on the future of democracy, the concept was at the center of a philosophical and even moral debate. According to Zand (2012), "U.S. President George W. Bush had declared the democratization of the world a political objective he was prepared to push through militarily, if necessary, just as he had in Iraq," but most governments, including Germany's, refused to follow him down this path. The claim of democratization was followed by a global economic crisis that undermined many claims of established democracies, and, based on achieved results, questioned the competence of many Western leaders in mastering their craft in governing (Zand, 2012). Thus, for Arab Spring countries, the overall performance of leaders of Western democracies and their claims of "good governance" require careful assessment before emulation.

The continuing debate among Arab pundits, politicians, academicians, newspaper columnists, and others over what kind of governance is needed and can be implemented is vital and historical. The *SPIEGEL* article (Zand, 2012) pointed out that Brazil and China may provide no less relevant models than the United States or Europe. The political systems in the United States, Europe, and Japan are all showing their limitations and their failures. Different tools, different objectives, and varying levels of leadership competence all indicate a loss of power by their institutions as well as a lack of will to deal with global financial and other problems. Western democracies no longer see eye to eye on how to solve many of these serious global problems (Zand, 2012). Furthermore, domestic considerations and power politics by vocal interest groups often stand in the way of making appropriate policy decisions on domestic as well as international problems such as trade, environment, and regulations.

For the Arab world, successful translation of the broad concepts and high principles of democracy into concrete actions and processes has its own prerequisites. For example, in a public opinion poll conducted by the Al-Ahram Center for Political and Strategic Studies (Anon., 2011b), the percentage of Egyptians who were "doubtful of their society's readiness for democracy" decreased from 67.7% in August 2011 to 59% in October 2011. More than a year after the first stirrings of the Arab Spring, a Pew Research (2012) public poll revealed a strong desire for democracy in Arab countries. Solid majorities in Lebanon, Egypt, Tunisia, and Jordan believe that democracy is the best form of government. The Pew Research poll also reported that "nearly three-quarters in Egypt and seven in-ten in Tunisia" believed that the 2011 popular uprisings will lead to more democracy in the Middle East.

But, a governance system is not a mechanical or a static construct; it is a continually evolving and adapting process. As Lynch (2012) argued, the fall of particular leaders is but the least of the changes that will emerge from the unrest. The far-ranging implications of the rise to power of a new generation of interconnected communities are not well understood, particularly when a continuous tide of events seems to change the outlook almost on daily basis.

Constructing a governance system is far more complex than simply searching for the ideal model to be cloned or emulated. Among the many preconditions of reform is the presence of leaders with unambiguous intentions and goals, clear definitions of problems and solutions, and insights into the possible effects of reform (Christensen and Dong, 2012). Former U.S. President Jimmy Carter observed that three decades of experience confirmed that "democracy … is a process that needs to be learned and perfected over time" (Carter Center, 2012). Preliminary pronouncements by elected and appointed leaders of the Arab Spring countries promise commitment to combating corruption, openness to citizens' input, and compliance with provisions of accountability and transparency. The problem is whether such policies and objectives are determined through deliberative and openly participatory processes, are adopted in accordance with preordained precepts, or are mere responses to dominant public sentiments. Actual application of the democratic model varies among countries, but it remains the most idealized model by its advocates, beyond its practical capacities. Universal democratic politics, even those that have roots within singular locations, simultaneously transcend location (Neocosmos, 2012). Still, critics of Western democratic practices evoke major reservations.

During and after the 1980s, the power of the state in industrialized countries and its ability to address societal issues was challenged from within. The rapid ascendance of neoliberal regimes in several advanced democracies has led to the state being regarded not as a source of collective action or as a base for solutions but rather as the main source of many societal problems (Pierre, 2000). The thrust of this political thinking, referred to as the Washington Consensus, is an ideology forced on many countries that relies on a monetarist economic policy supported by deregulation, privatization, drastic reductions of civil service, and a push to "reinvent government" and manage it more as a business (Falk, 1999). In the United States, an assertive neoconservative group with their own particular agenda gained prominence and was able to influence public policy. The neoconservative ideas and doctrine of military preemption often provided the rationale for greater military spending and frequent military interference in foreign countries, all while demanding restrictive domestic government initiatives. In 2002, the U.S. administration published *The National Security Strategy of the United States of America* (White House, 2002), a report described as "enshrining the doctrines of preventive war and overwhelming U.S. military superiority" (Prestowitz, 2003, p. 22). Skeptics of globalism encouraged the United States to walk away from international agreements and to undermine the concept and practice of multilateralism that has been "an underpinning of the global system since the end of World War II" (Prestowitz, 2003, p. 22).

The invasion of Iraq in 2003 can be considered to be a heavy-handed decision strongly supported and rationalized by neoliberals and special interest groups in the United States. The decision to invade Iraq was based on false premises and fabricated excuses and destroyed Iraq's infrastructure, deepened sectarian schisms, inflamed Arab and Muslim anti-American feelings, and resulted in huge losses of life and property for both the United States and Iraq. For many people in the Arab region, the U.S. claim to respect human rights and international laws, while repeatedly violating them, seemed hypocritical and deceptive.

The United States is viewed in the Middle East and in many other countries as the main obstacle to implementation of international law and United Nations resolutions for solving the Israeli–Palestinian conflict. In the words of an American career diplomat, "The American government also works hard to shield Israel from the international political and legal consequences of its policies and actions in the occupied territories, against its neighbors, or, most recently, on the high seas. The nearly 40 vetoes the United States has cast to protect Israel in the U.N. Security Council are the tip of the iceberg" (Freeman, 2010, p. 14). Many public opinion polls over several years indicate that most Arabs view U.S. policies as the major obstruction to realization of the human, legal, and political rights of the Palestinian people: "Israel's 45-year-long oppression of the Palestinians—the cruel siege of Gaza, the relentless land-grab on the West Bank—remains a major source of humiliation and rage. The United States bears the prime responsibility because, having sustained Israel in every possible way, it has failed to persuade it to give the Palestinians a fair deal" (Seale, 2012, p. 12). The Western world has not yet comprehended the psychological and emotional anger of the millions of Arabs and Muslims throughout the region for the injustice inflicted on the Palestinian people, particularly the continuation of the occupation since 1967. As Alterman (2012, p. 9) pointed out: "Few issues are as crucial to the future of the human race as the dynamics of the Israeli–Palestinian conflict, and few are as misunderstood in American politics."

Emerging hard-right nationalist political groups have passed specific laws to regulate the clothing of Muslims and restrict the building of more minarets, laws that were supposedly aimed at integrating Muslim minorities into Western culture. "To the extent these laws have integrated Muslims into their place in the new hierarchy of European racism—a toxic blend of traditional fascism and Western bigotry posing as secular liberalism—they've been successful" (Younge, 2012). Other covert and overt discriminatory practices have regularly been reported in the areas of immigration, employment, and various depictions and portrayals of Arab and Muslim cultures. All such policies and actions have had the effects of deflating claims by Western countries about fairness, equal employment opportunities, and freedoms within their societies.

Parenti (2010, p. 2) observed that the U.S. government "represents the privileged few rather than the needy many and that elections, political parties, and the right to speak out are seldom effective measures against the influence of corporate wealth." This was most evident in the general election of 2012, for which corporate funding was the largest in history (exceeding $2 billion). This was 2 years after the U.S. Supreme Court ruled in *Citizens United v. Federal Election Commission* that corporations have First Amendment right to spend large sums of money to outside groups (e.g., political action committees) to influence elections. In 2014, the Supreme Court decided that limits on aggregate donations violated the constitutional right to free speech: "In this decision, the court found no risk of corruption from the corporations, unions, millionaires, and billionaires that bankroll a candidate's election through a third-party group, even if the candidate attends the group fundraisers … and the group explicitly makes decisions based on the candidate's public statements" (Scherer, 2014, p. 14). Based on data released by the Election Commission, an article in the *Tampa Bay Times* observed that 18 donors gave $1 million or more to the Tampa Republican National Convention (Danielson, 2012). One corporate donor, under investigation for violation of the law, spent over $50 million in support of his Republican candidate for President.

Unlimited campaign contributions to political committees of both Democratic and Republican parties have the potential to become legal bribes that influence policymaking, thus distorting the functioning of democracy. Not surprisingly, a recent Gallup poll reported that the U.S. Congress has hit an all-time low approval rating. A mere 10% of Americans think members of Congress are doing a good job; a similar rating was reported a year earlier (Kim, 2012). Based on a list of corporate contributions, cases of conflict of interests, and various corrupt practices committed by members of the Congress, a journalist (Collins, 2013) wondered whether Congress could get worse. Hence, a recurring theme in the discourse of the 2012 election was how to break the deadlock and tame a dysfunctional political system (Zakaria, 2012).

Finally, history shows that democratic elections do not always produce democratic governance. Autocracy of the majority is more than a potential outcome. Historically, it has also become a reality. Specifically, in Europe free elections produced Nazi and Fascist governments before World War II. Religious and patriotic zeal mixed with glorification of the "great hero" can and did produce a Hitler, a Mussolini, and other leaders with similar views within Western-type democracies.

The perceived failings and shortcomings of Western systems of governance, in addition to the colonial legacy, are often cited by traditionalists and revolutionaries in the Middle East to disparage and to oppose the transfer or adoption of Western models in current Arab governance. Such conclusions would be a misinterpretation of evidence, confusing the behavior and actions of political leaders (unprincipled as they often have been) with the systems they lead. With reference to a popular metaphor, "Driving recklessly is not the fault of the vehicle." Arab reformers and intellectuals, looking beyond the confines of domestic autocratic rule and colonial relations, need to separate utilitarian and effective use from the misuse of democratic governance. Despite its failings and abuse under certain leaders, democratic systems epitomize the principles of freedom, representation, equality, and public participation. These values remain essential aspects of the desired reforms of Arab governance. Unfortunately, reinterpretation and evaluation of Western political and administrative practices and values often elicit ambivalence or their reflexive removal from consideration in the grand designs of future governance. Experiences with colonialism, invasions, and occupation still have considerable influence on the public choice and may have been a factor in the ascent of political Islam in recent elections in Arab states.

The values hoped for in good governance, such as checks and balances, accountability, ethics, equality, and representation, remain aspirations for many Arab states. It is clear by now that the reconstruction of governance involves far more than conducting elections. Understanding historical experiences and influences on Arab governance is necessary for societies inheriting laws, political relationships, management systems, and cultural norms (Pollitt, 2008). The influence of historical experiences on the current political and administrative structures and functions in the Arab states has been particularly enduring (Jabbra and Jreisat, 2009). Today, religious and tribal groups and the growing powers of the military and security apparatus contribute methods and attitudes that facilitate centralization of power in governance. The development of certain political–administrative institutions has also been associated with particular traditional authoritarianism that is inconsistent with the values of freedom and equality.

Resurgence of Political Islam

The struggle to build representative governance in the Arab world is continuing. Early indications are that the new governance will be different from the former; the uprisings promote a more assertive regime in foreign affairs and greater action taken to fight corruption. On the economic front, the new governance will have to be focused on economic revival and the alleviation of poverty, but these attributes do not include a critical challenge that seems to defy a reasonable resolution—namely, the role of religion in governing the Arab states. We know from history that the 16th- and 17th-century perception of political order as divine, natural, hierarchical, and beyond human control has been replaced by a conception of governance that is political, secular, and based on human choice and consent (March and Olsen, 1995). Divisiveness and distrust between religious and secular political groups in Arab societies are deep rooted and often confrontational, impeding the search for a satisfactory resolution.

The influence of political Islam within Arab societies grew as rulers failed to meet their responsibilities and serve the needs of the population. The popular appeal of the Islamists has many aspects: They offered a new identity to alienated individuals in the urban and modern society. They capitalized on the failures of secular and socialist political parties and on the dominance of corrupt regimes throughout the Arab world since independence. Islamists effectively utilized their assets such as mosques, schools, charities, and mass media to mobilize the poor and to organize opposition and protest movements against ineffective rulers. A paradox from the Cold War years, however, is that the West, the United States in particular, fomented Islamist activism against communism. Many Islamic organizations were created at the behest of the United States, utilizing Saudi Arabia's amenability, to form a buffer against communism and to check the Arab nationalist movement in Egypt and elsewhere (Jreisat, 1997).

The cases of Egypt and Tunisia illustrate, persuasively, the processes employed and the choices made in transitioning to post-Arab Spring governance. Egypt, the largest Arab state, has significant cultural influence over the region. The experience of Egypt after the uprising demonstrates success in the creation of a new constitution, holding elections, and selecting a new president. The first free election in Egypt, after the autocratic president was forced out of office, resulted in governance dominated by the Muslim Brotherhood. In the first legislative election in 2011, 33 political parties competed for seats in the Parliament (Anon., 2011c). Not surprising, the non-religious parties had modest results, and the Muslim Brotherhood, with its superior organization and resources, won both legislative and presidential elections. The Muslim Brotherhood soon revealed excessive zeal in their quest to monopolize power and reshape governance into their own image. On November 22, 2012, the new president of Egypt, Mohamed Morsi, previously a senior operative of the then-outlawed Muslim Brotherhood and subsequently head of the Brotherhood's subsidiary political party Freedom and Justice, made decisions that incensed his opponents. He issued a presidential edict that gave him unchecked authority, exempted from legislative or judicial review. This action, the opposition charged, meant that Morsi was reclaiming dictatorial powers, which sparked massive protests across Egypt. Liberal and secular leaders expressed a rare unity that belied a record of divisiveness that had earlier rendered them incoherent and ineffective. The crisis deepened after President Morsi decided to move on with the referendum on the new constitution that had been hastily drafted during the chaotic political transition. The document that Egyptians voted on was a rushed revision of the old charter, infused with religious precepts and pushed through an Islamist-dominated assembly in an all-night session, after liberal and secular representatives quit in protest.

The vote in December 2012 on the new constitution for Egypt was 63.8% in favor and 36.2% opposed, but the problem extends beyond the recorded numbers. Those who voted "yes" accounted for only about 20% of eligible voters. This means that about 80% of the voters were opposed or did not vote. Careful reading of the numbers indicates that support for the new constitution, and for President Morsi, represented neither an incontestable mandate nor an absolute victory. In a society with a culture of traditional deference to authority, the negative votes are significant. The day after the new constitution was inaugurated, the following appeared in an editorial in *The New York Times* (Anon., 2012a):

> Ideally, a new constitution in Egypt would unite citizens around a consensus vision for their country and set a firm foundation for a democratic transition. The Islamist-backed constitution that took effect this week has only exacerbated divisions and left millions of non-Islamists feeling disenfranchised, angry and determined to force changes in the document.

The up-or-down vote on a new constitution was an easy win for the Brotherhood, but the opposition parties (liberals, nationalists, and seculars) protested the outcome and warned of a protracted struggle to prevent an "Islamic dictatorship" from taking hold in the society. The divided opposition parties became more allied and joined in a "National Salvation Front" after a period of fragmentation and incoherent messages. A major casualty of the rivalry in Egypt between religious and non-religious political parties was the economy. Violence and paralysis of the government triggered serious negative economic consequences in employment, growth, budget deficits, and dwindling foreign-currency reserves.

Finally, the military moved against the Muslim Brotherhood regime in 2013, nullified the newly declared constitution, arrested President Morsi, and appointed a non-military interim president and new cabinet. The military revealed their strategic "road map," with the first major step being implemented in January 2014: a new constitution, written and approved by 98% of voters. A vote on president and parliament members followed shortly thereafter. The return of the military to politics raises questions regarding their role in governance in Egypt. The most memorable military takeover in Egypt was that of Abdel Nasser, who was an exceptional leader and became a world political figure despite ruling over tired institutions and unreliable associates. Nasser was succeeded by Sadat (killed in office) and Mubarak (thrown out of office). Overall, the record of military rule in the rest of the Arab world has been undistinguished.

A new cabinet was sworn in on March 2, 2014, and newly appointed Prime Minister Ibrahim Mahlab urged a halt to protests and strikes to allow the nation a breather to rebuild after more than 3 years of turmoil. Egypt experienced bloodshed and mass detentions as authorities staged a massive crackdown on supporters of ousted Islamist President Morsi who opposed the military, often with the use of violence. The turmoil sweeping Egypt since the 2011 uprising had a devastating effect on the economy, particularly the tourism sector. Former Army General Abdel Fattah al-Sisi won the presidential election held June 8, 2014, and the list of problems he faces is daunting. Addressing them will require exceptional leadership skills and dedication to restore stability and bring about a successful transition to democracy.

The transition in Tunisia illustrates a different path than that seen in Egypt. Decades of corrupt and oppressive rule in Tunisia have been replaced by coalition governance, with a constitution ratified by an elected National Assembly (200 votes out of 216 members). After the vote on January 26, 2014, political leaders declared the approved constitution by the Assembly as "one of consensus." Thus, Tunisia proclaimed its governance a democracy, with a civil state and a constitution dedicated to protection of citizens' rights, including protection from torture, the right to due process, and freedom of worship. The new constitution also guarantees equality between men and women before the law and the right to free health care and free education. The process of writing a new constitution for Tunisia was open and welcomed diverse political views. The new constitution received broad support and was genuinely celebrated. Tunisia's exceptional success is helped by the fact that it has never drawn the same degree of attention from the outside world as most of the other countries of the region (Ryan, 2014). Whereas the uprisings in Libya and Syria were quickly internationalized, Tunisia's uprising and subsequent political transition have been overwhelmingly domestic. Tunisia's success in transitioning to democracy can be attributed to the fact that the country "has neither vast amount of oil or gas, nor a shared border with Israel" (Ryan, 2014). It was further observed in Ryan (2014) that "the West has shown incredible double standards in the way it's said it has tried to promote democracy in the Middle East."

The Tunisian experience indicates that integrating Islamists into the political spectrum of Arab societies is possible. In Egypt, the policy followed the path of ignoring and eliminating the political weight of the Muslim Brotherhood, causing excessive violence throughout the country. In Tunisia, a general agreement was reached among religious and secular political parties to work together in a coalition that serves common objectives. The head of the Tunisian religious party Ennahda expressed his enthusiastic approval of the coalition governance and endorsed a "marriage between the two models," Islamists and seculars (Ryan, 2014). So far, trying to establish such common ground in Egypt and other Arab countries has been a futile endeavor. In Egypt, Libya, and Yemen, the crisis of governance continues with the lines of separation intensifying between the Islamists and seculars.

In April 2014, Tunisia's interim prime minister claimed that the government at last had a handle on extremism and the transition to democracy was back on track: "It's time to fix the faltering economy." He emphasized that Tunisia had learned how to confront the extremists and that the new Tunisian constitution was progressive and written by Islamist, left-wing, and liberal parties: "The country is now looking forward to new elections by the end of the year, after a transition that has been marked by terrorist attacks, political assassinations and widespread social unrest" (Anon., 2014a). It is important to point out that Islamists, like most large political associations, are not one voice but include moderates and extremists. Actually, in most Arab states, moderate Islamist parties were hurt by tensions and confrontations between elected governments and opposition fundamentalist Islamist groups known as Salafis. In Tunisia, the Salafis demanded closing bars, banning liquor sales, and observing their version of the Islamic faith. They have been described as a fringe of political Islam who disdain modernity and development and prefer going back to the ancient methods of conduct and living just as in the days of the founders of Islam (the literal translation of Salafi in Arabic is "predecessor" or "forerunner"). The views of former Prime Minister Moncef Marzouki are indicative of the depth of hostility (Ghosh, 2012): "We are dealing with a real danger, a threat. [Salafism] is like a cancer. The more we wait, the more it becomes extremely difficult to cure." The rigid Salafi dogma and tendency to resort to violence have become more pronounced after expansion of the space for free expression inaugurated by the Arab Spring. The Salafis have generated deep apprehension among Arab societies, as they are viewed as the spoilers of victorious revolutions: "The demonstration of Salafi street power set off alarm bells in Muslim countries, nowhere more than in those liberated by the revolutions of 2011, where the fundamentalists seem determined to drown out all other voices in the political conversation" (Ghosh, 2012).

In addition to developments in Egypt and Tunisia, the rest of the Arab states are taking small timid steps toward more effective governance (Morocco and Jordan); are still in a state of disorder with unpredictable results (Libya and Yemen); or are immobilized in a grim battle between determined opponents (Syria). As to Syria, unexpectedly, in early April 2014, Murtada Mansour, who had just declared his candidacy for the upcoming presidential election in Egypt, offered a frank perspective on the crisis in Syria, widely shared in the region. He said: "Syria is enduring a conspiracy not a revolution. I am surprised about the so-called Syrian Free Army receiving weapons to fight their own people" (Mansour, 2014). Thus, resolution of the governance crisis in the Arab world is not complete. Hard choices are slowly evolving. The dissension and political disagreements have caused many premature judgments to be made, voicing the death of Arab Spring or associating violence and instability with endogenous Arab or Muslim culture. Such prejudicial or misinformed judgments ignore the fact that the current turmoil is largely indicative of public determination to resist difficult internal and external oppressive influences. An article written for *Bloomberg Businessweek* included the headline "The Awakening: The Arab Spring was a victory for Islam. Should that scare us?" (Goldberg, 2011). The public pronouncements of the Islamists, however, in both Tunisia and Egypt were unequivocal. They declared adherence to democratic principles of equality, acceptance of existing laws and international agreements, support of individual freedoms, and commitment to ethical and accountable governance. In comparison, it is noted that no similar alarm has been expressed in the West over Israel's radical religious groups in government, ruling in a coalition of rigid doctrinal politics. Attitudes in the West seem quite different when "the spectrum of political Judaism is as wide as political Islam's" (Anon., 2011a). An Israeli activist offered this opinion about the January 2013 election in Israel: "People here think all extremists are in the Arab world, but there are plenty in every religion, including here" (Cohen, 2013). Similarly, not much alarm was voiced when policies expressed by some Republican Party candidates in the primary debates for the 2012 U.S. presidential election sounded indistinguishable from evangelical Christian preachers. In Western societies, cultural bias and objectivity often collide when debating political Islam, as if it cannot be granted meanings already conceded to other faiths as democratic with secular values even if they are not.

Lessons Learned

The development of effective governance is a universal objective. The problems and challenges faced by contemporary Arab societies in attempting reform of their governance systems are not unique. The experiences of some Arab states and the wide range of events they have dealt with offer valuable lessons relevant to countries seeking changes in governance. The public uprisings introduced new political forces that altered the traditional balance of power in societies. The broad participation in the revolutions brought together Islamists, fundamentalists, secularists, socialists, labor unions, students, farmers, and others who may have experienced their first involvement in political activism. On the other hand, such a combination of participants, in the absence of prior agreement on a plan or a strategy of action in the transition following ousting the despot, resulted in turmoil, diffusion of the revolutionary political thrust, and contradictory objectives among participants. Following are the particularly manifest lessons, out of many, that may be derived from the experiences of the revolutionary states.

First, the Arab uprisings demonstrated the remarkable resilience of people resisting despotism and demanding legitimization of governance. The ousting of dictators from power by massive public demands is unprecedented in modern Arab history. The Arab Spring exposed and threatened the underlying power structure in each society that served mainly the privileged few. In essence, the Arab Spring represented empowerment of the people in their vigorous demand for economic justice. The uprisings emphatically called for accountability of governance, inspiring "people's power" everywhere. This is significant because past initiatives to change Arab politics and administrations were primarily by outsiders, reflecting foreign values and foreign reform concepts. The Arab Spring changed that by effectively bringing in the local side, the demand side, with the potential for reflecting refined traditional cultures and contextual influences. Initially, the revolutions in Tunisia, Egypt, Libya, and Yemen were almost entirely home grown. The public uprisings added new forces to the political equation, generating additional pressures to contend with during the transition. The range of participants in the revolutions has been broad and has expanded representation, enhancing the power of the revolutionaries. People from the left and from the right of the political spectrum, religious and non-religious groups, found themselves in the same fold. The uprisings demonstrated the power of the people, succeeded in their immediate goal of forcing the dictators out of office, and spurred other Arab countries to seriously consider change.

Second, after ousting dictators, the revolutionary forces faced the difficult challenge of building a just society and representative governance. The big question after the uprisings became what form and what alternative governance should be adopted. No clear vision or prior plan of action was established and disseminated among the revolutionary groups, which made it difficult to construct a governance system responsive to public demands. The absence of an agreed-upon and integrated strategic vision to bind together the huge public participation after a dictator was ousted was a serious flaw. As a result, conflicts emerged that hindered future political action. As the veteran revolutionary Mao Tse-Tung observed in his 1948 *Revolutionary Forces of the World Unite: Fight Against Imperialist Aggression!*, "If there is to be revolution, there must be a revolutionary party. Without a revolutionary party, without a party built on … revolutionary theory … it is impossible to lead."

Revolutionary zeal alone cannot promptly erase various aspects of autocratic rule or build democratic culture on demand. So far, the transition has been protracted and contentious with the exception of Tunisia. The Tunisians are making significant progress as politicians with vastly different agendas have managed to come together to approve a new constitution and find common grounds on policy within a democratic means of governing (Ryan, 2014). In most Arab states, however, claims of democratization remain muddled, and a genuine infrastructure of openness, transparency, and political culture to intensify democratic values remains lacking. Political Islam emerged as the winner in the initial elections in Tunisia and Egypt. Pronouncements by leaders in Libya, Yemen, Bahrain, Morocco, and Jordan indicate a willingness to improve policies and support reforms that ensure fundamental freedoms, fight corruption, and improve accountability. Implementation of these reforms, however, has been either too slow or still mired in internal disagreements. The perilous deterioration of political authority in Libya left armed militias able to dictate to the central authority; some tribal forces even assumed local autonomy. The constant battling among these armed groups for turf and power is creating political chaos. The conclusion is that the revolutionary forces that toppled the dictators lacked a coherent, integrated, and agreed-upon vision and plan for what was to follow. Such a serious flaw had many negative consequences and crippled the implementation of reform policies.

Third, competent and committed political and administrative leaders are the imperative and the epicenter of a revolutionary change of governance. Effective leaders provide clear goals and problem-solving skills, they know how to organize and control the reform, and they understand what is required in the implementation processes (Aberbach and Christensen, 2014). The Arab Spring revolutions lacked experienced leaders with strategic vision, commitment, and professional competence to manage the change and to harmonize conflicting values. One cannot emphasize enough the necessity of having leaders with unambiguous intentions and goals, clear definitions of problems and solutions, and insights into the possible effects of reform (Christensen and Dong, 2012). The central role of leadership is particularly crucial for managing societal change. The systems that experienced popular uprisings needed leaders who were skillful in negotiation, reconciliation, and consensus building rather than leaders relying on the traditional methods of command and control, reminiscent of the former autocratic leaders who excelled in forcing compliance. An important lesson from the Arab revolutionary experience is that political and administrative leadership is vital for achieving common objectives.

Fourth, a valuable finding is that despotic rulers do not usually build an institutional infrastructure that respects competing decision-making powers. Arab governance in general is notoriously personalized and limits decision-making power to the top person. Institutional roles and responsibilities, therefore, are weak, undefined, and often ignored altogether. Thus, when an autocratic ruler is removed, a vacuum of governance is formed that causes inflexible competition among political groups seeking to fill the power space. This has been demonstrated in all of the countries that experienced uprisings that removed the ruling dictator. Each country has had to write a new constitution, elect a new representative council, and elect a new head of state. The governance vacuum may not be filled smoothly or peacefully. Extremism clashes with middle-class values, and violence, even chaos, becomes a real menace to society. Libya is an illustration of such a condition.

The type of governance in place is reflected in the administrative, political, and economic actions and policies. Political events in the Arab states at this time seem to dominate all other concerns. No administrative reform programs produced in any country have extended beyond general expressions of intention to act against corruption and to initiate administrative reform measures, but change requires processes that incorporate expert knowledge, consensus within the political leadership, and consideration of cultural and historical influences. Traditional bureaucratic behavior that perpetuates traditional organization and management practices and requires blind obedience to authority does not readily respond to change requiring creative and risk-taking performance. Cultural norms and habits such as nepotism and favoritism in appointments to senior government positions have penetrated the processes of recruitment and appointment in all types of organizations. The end result is an autocratic political structure that relies on obedient and loyal public service, staffed through non-merit considerations; administrative competence and discretion remain limited.

Efficient and effective civil service requires a serious effort to promote professionalism and to end the practices of nepotism, cronyism, or religious loyalty in appointments to senior public administration positions. Reforms have to emphasize alternative models of management that do not assume autocratic political authority and command but are based on cooperation, negotiation, and better horizontal coordination instead of the usual hierarchical patterns. Reliance on the power of persuasion and effective communication of facts and evidence has to supersede the norms of a personal central command of superiors (Hertog, 2011). Growing corruption endangers the effectiveness of governance, promotes mismanagement, and deepens a culture of administration and politics that retards all efforts for reform. Reform is always difficult within such an environment. All of these effective managerial and organizational concepts can only be realized with the appropriate leadership and by investing in the training and education of public employees. The significant growth in public employment and its cost did not translate into improved administrative performance or meeting expanded responsibilities (Jreisat, 2006).

Fifth, when the politics of fragmentation lead to a paralysis of governing, economic deterioration follows. Such a reality often creates a temptation for military intervention. In Egypt, a new system of governance has been installed with the help of the military. In January 2014, a new constitution was written and approved by 98% of voters. A new president and parliament members were elected later that year. A widespread concern is that the new governance in Egypt will apply restrictions and an authoritarian method that will not produce the necessary stability, economic growth, or wide public support. A root problem in Egypt that contributes to political and social instability is the poverty that has been growing for the past four decades. It has led to the deterioration of public services and the development of misguided public policies that serve the few who created a state within the state. Experts from within and from outside of the country have warned of the need for a strategy to fight poverty but have gone unheeded. Egypt's poverty poses a threat to national security due to the increased crimes, violence, and religious extremism. The inescapable connection among poverty, security, and politics demands a solution to the poverty problem; 54% of Egyptians are living on less than $2 a day (Anon., 2014b). Winning the war against poverty in Egypt is the most important job for the new governance system and for the future of the country.

Syria remains in a proxy war of enormous complexity that involves many foreign parties, including Arab rulers. Diplomacy and military force have failed to achieve peace, and foreign fighters from half a dozen countries are at war not only with the Syrian regime but among themselves as well. As these atrocities continue and leaders on both fronts refuse to reason and to negotiate, Syria is systematically being destroyed and its people are suffering. The Arab world has had a long history of military rule. A *coup d'état* led by Husni al-Za'im in 1949 was followed by others. Iraq, Yemen, Libya, Algeria, and Sudan all have had their own experiences with military takeovers. The most memorable military takeover was that of Abdel Nasser in Egypt. He was an exception because he was competent and committed, and he became a world political figure despite ruling over tired institutions and unreliable associates. Nasser was succeeded by Anwar Sadat, who was killed in office, and by Hosni Mubarak, who was thrown out of office. Overall, the record of military rule in the Arab world generally has not been an inspiring or illustrious one.

Questions for Review

1. What common attributes of governance contributed to public dissatisfaction and distrust of governance in the Arab States that experienced revolutionary uprisings since 2010?
2. What are the catalysts of the social movements in the Arab States that stimulated the uprisings referred to as the Arab Spring?

3. Selecting a governance system that represents reform, what method has been dominant in terms of collaborative, participatory, hierarchical, centrally dictated, or other?
4. What is the most important lesson in governance learned from the public uprisings in these states?

References

Aberbach, J.D. and Christensen, T. (2014). Why reforms so often disappoint. *Am. Rev. Public Admin.*, 44(1): 3–16.
Ahrens, J. (2002). *Governance and Economic Development*. Northampton, MA: Edward Elger.
Alterman, E. (2012). Shut up about the Jews already … . *The Nation*, October 22, p. 9.
Anon. (2011a). Political Islam everywhere on the rise. *The Economist*, December 10, http://www.economist.com/node/21541440.
Anon. (2011b). Public poll. *Al-Ahram*, November 5.
Anon. (2011c). Commentary. *Al-Ahram*, November 5.
Anon. (2012a). Egypt's flawed constitution. *The New York Times*, December 27, p. A26.
Anon. (2012b). The rise of state capitalism. *The Economist*, January 21 (http://www.economist.com/node/21543160).
Anon. (2014a). AP interview: Tunisia premier wants to fix economy. *Associated Press*, April 3 (http://www.dailymail.co.uk/wires/ap/article-2595803/AP-Interview-Tunisia-premier-wants-fix-economy.html).
Anon. (2014b). Editorial. *Al-Ahram*, April 14.
Bouckaert, G. and Halligan, J. (2008). *Managing Performance: International Comparisons*. London: Routledge.
Carter Center. (2012). *Celebrating 30 Years: A Letter by Jimmy Carter*, October 2, p. 2.
Christensen, T. and Dong, L. (2012). Imitating the West? Evidence of administrative reform from the upper echelon of Chinese provincial government. *Public Admin. Rev.*, 72(6): 798.
Cohen, R. (2013). Israel's Mr. Normal. *The New York Times*, February 2 (http://www.nytimes.com/2013/02/03/opinion/sunday/cohen-yair-lapid-israels-mr-normal.html).
Collins, G. (2013). Looking forward. *The New York Times*, January 2 (response in *Tampa Bay Times*, January 8).
Danielson, R. (2012). Fundraising success for RNC host committee came from small number of big checkbooks. *Tampa Bay Times*, October 18, p. 6A.
Doeveren, V. (2011). Rethinking good governance. *Public Integrity*, 13(4): 301–317.
Donahue, J.D. and Nye, Jr., J.S. (2002). *Visions of Governance in the 21st Century*. Washington, DC: Brookings Institution Press.
Falk, R. (1999). *Predatory Globalization: A Critique*. Cambridge, UK: Polity Press.
Farazmand, A. (2004). Sound governance in the age of globalization: a conceptual framework. In Farazmand, A., Ed., *Sound Governance: Policy and Administrative Innovations*, pp. 1–23. Westport, CT: Praeger.
Farazmand, A. (2009). Building administrative capacity for the age of rapid globalization. *Public Admin. Rev.*, 69(6): 1007–1020.
Freeman, C.W. (2010). The big lie: that Israel is a strategic asset for the United States. *Washington Rep. Middle East*. XXIX(7): 14–15.
Ghosh, B. (2012). The rise of the Salafis. *Time*, October 8, http://content.time.com/time/magazine/article/0,9171,2125502,00.html.
Goldberg, J. (2011). The Awakening: the Arab Spring was a victory for Islam. Should that scare us? *Bloomberg Businessweek*, December 22, http://www.bloomberg.com/bw/magazine/the-awakening-12222011.html.
Hertog, S. (2011). *Princes, Brokers, and Bureaucrats*. Ithaca, NY: Cornell University Press.
Hyden, G. (2002). Operationalizing governance for sustainable development. In Jreisat, J.E., Ed., *Governance and Developing Countries*, pp. 13–32. Boston, MA: Brill.
Jabbra, J. and Jreisat, J.E. (2009). Administration of the Arab state: synthesizing diverse traditions. In Pagaza, I.P. and Argyriades, D., Eds., *Winning the Needed Change: Saving our Planet Earth*, pp. 112–126. Amsterdam: IOS Press.

Jain, R.B. (2002). Globalization, liberalization, and human security in India: challenges for governance. In Jreisat, J.E., Ed., *Governance and Developing Countries*, pp. 111–126. Boston, MA: Brill.
Jreisat, J.E. (1997). *Politics Without Process: Administering Development in the Arab World*. Boulder, CO: Lynne Reinner.
Jreisat, J.E. (2006). The Arab world: reform or stalemate. *J. Asian African Stud.*, 41(5-6): 411–438.
Jreisat, J.E. (2009). Administration, globalization, and the Arab states. *Public Org. Rev.*, 9(1): 37–50.
Jreisat, J.E. (2011). Governance: issues in concept and practice. In Menzel, D.C. and White, H.L., Eds., *The State of Public Administration: Issues, Challenges, and Opportunities*, pp. 424–438. New York: M.E. Sharpe.
Kim, S.M. (2012). Congress rating drops to new low. *POLITICO*, February 8, http://www.politico.com/story/2012/02/congress-rating-drops-to-new-low-072625.
Klinger, D.E. (2006). Building global public management governance capacity: the road not taken. *Public Admin. Rev.*, 66(5): 775–779.
Lynch, M. (2012). *The Arab Uprising: The Unfinished Revolutions of the New Middle East*. New York: Public Affairs.
Mansour, A. (2014). Presidential election. *Al-Ahram*, April 7, p. 1.
March, J.G. and Olsen, J.P. (1995). *Democratic Governance*. New York: The Free Press.
Myers, S.L. (2011). Hillary Clinton issues blunt warning to Pakistan. *The New York Times*, October 20.
Neocosmos, M. (2012). Political subjectivity and the subject of politics: thinking beyond identity from the south of Africa. *J. Asian African Stud.*, 47(5): 465–481.
Netton, I.R. (1998). al-Farabi, Abu Nasr (c. 870–950), http://www.muslimphilosophy.com/ip/rep/H021.htm.
Palmer, M. et al. (1987). Bureaucratic rigidity and economic development in the Middle East: a study of Egypt, the Sudan, and Saudi Arabia. *Int. Rev. Admin. Sci.*, 53: 241–257.
Paolini, A.J. (1999). *Navigating Modernity: Postcolonialism, Identity and International Relations*. Boulder, CO: Lynne Reiner Publishers.
Parenti, M. (2010). *Democracy for the Few*. New York: St. Martin's Press.
Pew Research. (2012). *Pew Global Attitudes Project: Spring Survey Topline Results*. Washington, DC: Pew Research.
Pierre, J. (2000). Introduction. In Pierre, J., Ed., *Debating Governance*, pp. 1–10. New York: Oxford University Press.
Pollitt, C. (2008). *Time, Policy, Management: Governing with the Past*. Oxford: Oxford University Press.
Pollitt, C. and Bouckaert, G. (2004). *Public Management Reform: A Comparative Analysis*. New York: Oxford University Press.
Prestowitz, C. (2003). *Rogue Nation: American Unilateralism and the Failure of Good Intentions*. New York: Basic Books.
Rosell, S.A. (1999). *Renewing Governance*. Toronto: Oxford University Press.
Ryan, Y. (2014). How one country emerged from the Arab Spring with a democratic state. *Nation*, February 12 (http://www.thenation.com/article/how-one-country-emerged-arab-spring-democratic-state/).
Scherer, M. (2014). Money talks. *Time*, April 3, p. 14.
Seale, P. (2012). Why do Arabs and Muslims hate America? *Washington Rep. Middle East Affairs*, XXXI(8): 12–14.
Trustfull, P. (2012). The best of Africa: a remarkable Renaissance. *Forbes*, September 24 (www.forbescustom.com/SectionPDFs/092412AfricaSection.pdf).
White House. (2002). *The National Security Strategy of the United States*. Washington, DC: U.S. Government Printing Office (http://georgewbush-whitehouse.archives.gov/nsc/nss/2002/).
Younge, G. (2012). Europe: hotbed of Islamophobic extremism. *Nation*, June 14 (http://www.thenation.com/article/europe-hotbed-islamophobic-extremism/).
Zakaria, F. (2012). Breaking the deadlock: taming a dysfunctional political system will be the next president's first priority. *Time*, November 12, p. 28.
Zand, B. (2012). The craft of ruling: which country has the best government? *SPIEGEL Online*, August 10, http://www.spiegel.de/international/world/good-governance-series-which-goverment-is-best-a-845170.html.

III

MITIGATION CAPACITY BUILDING FOR CRISIS AND EMERGENCY MANAGEMENT: LESSONS FROM GLOBAL CASES

Chapter 12

Resilience Capacity Building for Global Crisis and Emergency Management

Clifford R. Bragdon

Contents

Chapter Goals	198
Introduction	198
Global Trends	200
Population Growth, Distribution, and Urbanization	201
Transcommunication and Intermodalism	202
Congestion and Gridlock	203
Natural and Manmade Threats	205
Economic Costs	207
Resilience Capacity Building	210
Combined Physical and Electronic Terrorism	210
Neoteric Planning	210
Resiliency: A Comprehensive and Balanced Approach	212
Resilience-Based Attributes and Applications	214
Kinetic Energy Harvesting	215
Advanced Telematics	216
Shrinkable Cars	216
Vertical Farming	216
Biomass Production for Energy	217
Diet-Resilient Cities	217
Advancing Sustainability in the Area of Energy Technology	217
Global Applications of Resilience: U.K. Department for International Development	218
Lessons Learned	219
Questions for Discussion	219
Additional Reading	220
References	220

Chapter Goals

The objectives associated with this chapter address resiliency and its importance for understanding and protecting the global biosphere and our physical, social, and economic well-being. Specific chapter objectives for the reader include being able to

1. Define and describe the global trends that are a challenge to the survival of our planet and its resiliency for protecting its 7 billion inhabitants.
   a. Population growth if uncontrolled and unplanned could reach over 11 billion population by the end of this century.
   b. Further encroachment of the population into the coastal zone along with the climate changes occurring could result in threatened coastlines, rising sea levels, and a growing population at risk.
   c. Mobility and logistics are increasingly impaired due to congestion and gridlock, resulting in the lack of an intermodal integrated system of transport that logistically affects the efficient movement of people, goods, and information.
   d. The number of both natural and manmade disasters is rapidly rising, along with a major increase in terrorism, especially related to cybersecurity and cybercrime.
2. Delineate the neoteric planning principles that will enhance resiliency capacity building.
   a. Three-dimensional (3D) planning allows the earthscape to be observed and utilized in three planes—aerial, surface, and subsurface—so as to optimize their potential and effectively apply these spatial dimensions to crisis management
   b. Time is a 24/7 resource to be both optimized and utilized for crisis management
   c. The five senses that we possess (sight, hearing, touch, smell, and taste) can be optimized and their potential incorporated in planning for crisis management.
3. Present the four attributes of resilience, describing their importance and the need for them to be collectively integrated in a holistic manner to protect our biosphere.
   a. The concept of *sustainability* contributes to protecting the physical attributes of our biosphere and addresses environmental protection, balanced environmental resources, balanced economic growth, and the integration of both natural and social resources.
   b. *Safety* is essential because it addresses accident reduction and social institutional awareness, enhances worker productivity, and interactively supports community preparedness.
   c. *Security* focuses on terrorism prevention, risk reduction, and protection for all information technologies utilized in communication and secure access control.
   d. *Health* is necessary because it addresses both physical and mental parameters, including ensuring survival, preventing injury, reducing stress, and enhancing enjoyment.
   e. No one attribute should dominate the others, thereby diminishing or excluding another attribute or attributes to the point where the biosphere and resilience capacity building become vulnerable.

Introduction

The world's growing population is now 7.25 billion and is projected to exceed 11 billion by 2100. Demographers previously thought the world's population was going to level off; however, the United Nations Population Division along with a cadre of university scientists now predict world

Resilience Capacity Building for Global Crisis and Emergency Management ■ 199

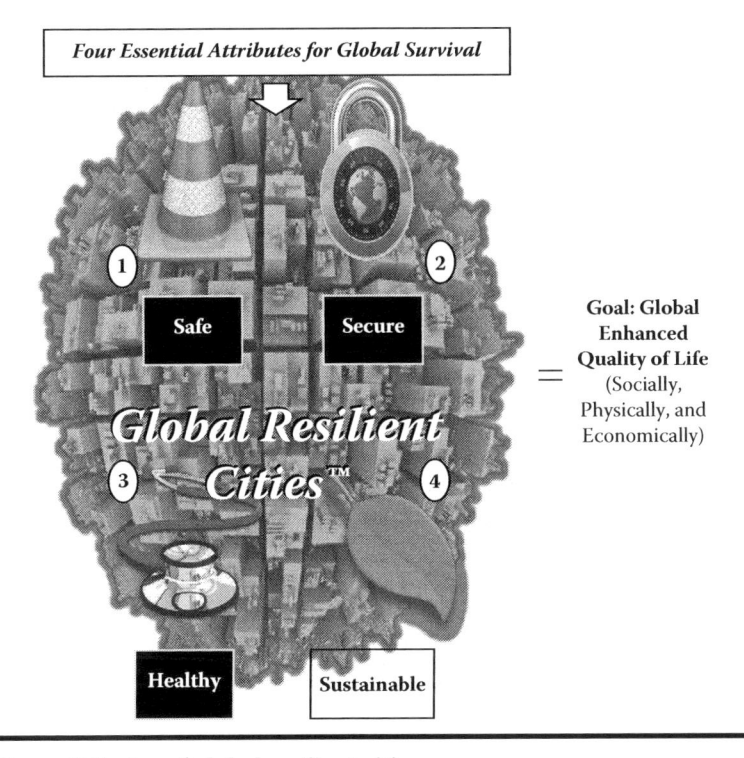

Figure 12.1 Four attributes of global resilient cities.

population stabilization is unlikely to occur in this century (Gerland, 2014). Resilience is an absolute necessity for addressing the associated global crises and emergency management. A sustainable or green environment alone will not provide comprehensive protection for our biosphere and all of its inhabitants. Resilience addresses the four interrelated attributes necessary to effectively protect and manage our planet: sustainability, safety, security, and health (Figure 12.1). By considering all four of these attributes in an integrated manner, communities can more effectively address natural and manmade disasters impacting our physical infrastructure, including such issues as cybersecurity and cybercrime. The global infrastructure must collectively support the resilient movement of people, goods, and information (both physically and electronically) by air, land, sea, and space. Our mobility-based global society requires resilient logistics utilizing an integrated intermodal system of transportation.

A climate positive community, with onsite CO_2 emissions near zero, represents a sustainable condition, but it does not mean its population is totally protected in perpetuity from both natural and manmade disasters, as evidenced by Japan's earthquake and tsunami that occurred March 11, 2011. As a country, Japan was ranked number one in terms of sustainability due to its near-zero CO_2 emission levels, primarily due to the country's dependence on nuclear power. Any effective crisis and emergency management plan must include sustainability but in partnership with safety, security, and health. In the case of the Tokyo Electric Power Company (TEPCO) nuclear plant in Fukushima, the associated impacts to health, safety, and security were not adequately addressed. A Nuclear Accident Independent Investigation Commission (NAIIC) report concluded that the Fukushima Daiichi Nuclear Plant accident was clearly a manmade disaster that "could and should have been foreseen and prevented" (National Diet of Japan, 2012). The report stated that it was an

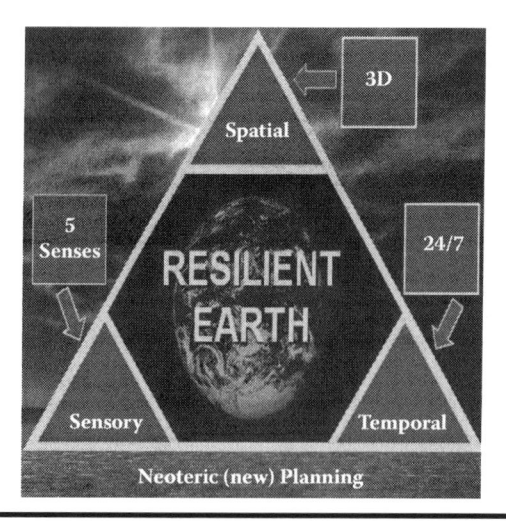

Figure 12.2 Neoteric planning elements.

act of collusion among Japan's government, the regulators, and TEPCO and a lack of governance by all parties that resulted in this catastrophic event). All 48 operable commercial nuclear reactors in the country were shut down in March, 2011. In late 2014, Japan's government approved the reopening of two reactors at the Sendai nuclear power plant, the first since the Fukushima disaster (Fackler, 2014). The Sendai reactors came back online in 2015. The issue of crisis and emergency management remains to be addressed at all of Japan's nuclear reactors sites, as do effective containment solutions and time frames.

Effective neoteric, or new, planning of our biosphere is essential and should involve the spatial (three-dimensional), temporal (time), and sensory (five human senses) parameters of Earth's habitats and infrastructure (Bragdon, 2008) (Figure 12.2). Two-dimensional planning is a myopic approach that addresses only the surface of the planet (x- and y-axes), thereby omitting aerial and subsurface features (z-axis). Consequently, a three-dimensional (3D) approach is needed, one that involves a combination of the x-, y-, and z-axes in order to be spatially comprehensive and include the air, land, sea, and space. The process of creating a resilient infrastructure becomes an economic development generator, bringing together such diverse aspects as public–private sector financing, law enforcement, cybersecurity, public health, and environmental and social justice. Resilience capacity building is essential for the future economic, social, and physical well-being of our global community. Neoteric planning can be a major stimulus to establishing global-based resiliency.

Global Trends

Several global issues must be identified, analyzed, and adequately addressed for our society to create and effectively implement a resilience-based plan. Solutions to these problems are needed to ensure that we establish a comprehensive crisis management plan with resilient attributes, thereby protecting the physical, social, and economic well-being of our global ecosystem. There are at least five areas, described below, that require global attention.

Population Growth, Distribution, and Urbanization

The Earth's human population exceeded 7.25 billion in 2015, with further rapid growth projected, perhaps reaching 11.15 billion in 2100 (Heilig, 2012). A population increase of 54% would have a profound impact on the carrying capacity of our ecosystem (Figure 12.3). Along with population growth, further urbanization is also expected. Today, nearly 55% of the world's population is urbanized, and by 2100 that number is projected to grow to 80% (IPCC, 2014). Changes in land coverage will also generate associated problems, including habitat conversion, pollutant loads, invasive species, further depletion of natural resources, challenges in adequate food production and distribution, and elevated energy demand, collectively resulting in a greater population at risk.

Our growing world population is also encroaching into the planet's coastal zone (i.e., oceans, seas, rivers, and lakes); 40% of the Earth's population resides within 62 miles of the coastline of all water bodies (NOAA, 2013). Not only is there a steady increase in people inhabiting the planet's coastlines, but the elevation above this waterline is also diminishing (below 30 feet), which is contributing to the increase in population and their associated infrastructure (e.g., housing, sewers, water supplies, utilities, transportation systems), which are subject to flooding and extreme storm events. Further urbanization is degrading coastal ecosystems that can protect against storm surge, saline intrusion, and erosion. In 2010, 39% of the U.S. population lived in coastline counties, and that figure is expected to grow to 47% by 2020 (NOAA, 2013). Coastlines and associated urban areas in the United States are going to become more vulnerable (Strauss, 2012). Five million people living in 2.6 million homes in 19 states are expected to be impacted by indefensible storm surges from Maine to Texas and from Washington to California, including 106 southern Florida cities (Strauss, 2014). A significant population in these states lives less than 4 feet above high tide level, but the sea level is expected to rise 2 to 7 feet by 2100 due to climate change and global warming. Clearly, we must "rebuild by design." The U.S. Department of Housing and Urban Development has sponsored a Rebuild by Design competition for grants to promote resilience among Hurricane Sandy-affected communities (HUD, 2013). Hoboken, New Jersey, is developing a master plan that incorporates both hard and soft infrastructure features with the goal of being able to withstand a once-in-500-years storm and significantly reducing the frequency and impact of flooding (Jaffe, 2014).

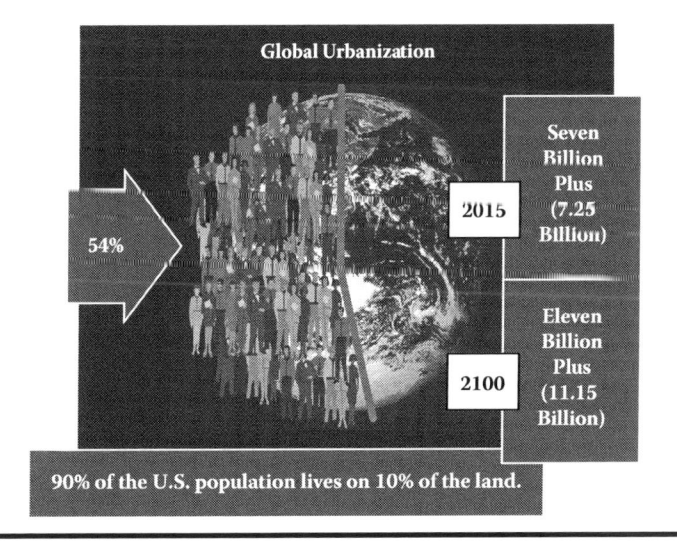

Figure 12.3 Global urbanization.

Transcommunication and Intermodalism

Transcommunication is a term used by a U.N. task force to describe the complex physical and electronic movement of people, goods, and information in urban settlements (Figure 12.4). We are a mobile society that historically has relied on physical transportation, such as ships and trains, for the effective movement of people and goods. In the United States, the growing roadway network for automobiles, trucks, buses, and motorcycles today includes over 4.1 million miles of roads, and recent Department of Transportation (https://www.transportation.gov/) statistics suggest that there are over 254 million registered vehicles. Aviation, with its associated network of 836 international airports, has further expanded the physical transportation footprint. It is predicted that 6.4 billion passengers will be carried on 59 million departing aircraft by 2030, representing an annual increase of 4.4% in passenger demand and a 3.6% annual growth rate in size of the commercial aircraft fleet (ICAO, 2013).

Mobile technology is becoming an integral partner with physical movement systems, supporting airline passengers and their baggage, as well as goods and freight. This electronic mobility augments physical mobility. Modern physical transportation is impacted by electronic mobility, as it relies on a comprehensive network of electronic systems not only to transport people and goods but also to transmit information: mobile check-in, paperless boarding passes, electronic machine-readable travel documents (eMRTDs), smartphone apps, mobility-friendly websites, and real-time monitoring of baggage and freight (Stuart, 2015).

Computer-based telecommunications systems are now integral to physical modes of movement; however, there remain fractionated and non-integrative systems of transportation and an absence of integrated transport or intermodalism (Figure 12.5). Many transport modes still are working independently, resulting in gridlock and congestion. In the United States, only 24 of the 500 commercial airports are connected to the cities they serve by a direct light rail network; consequently,

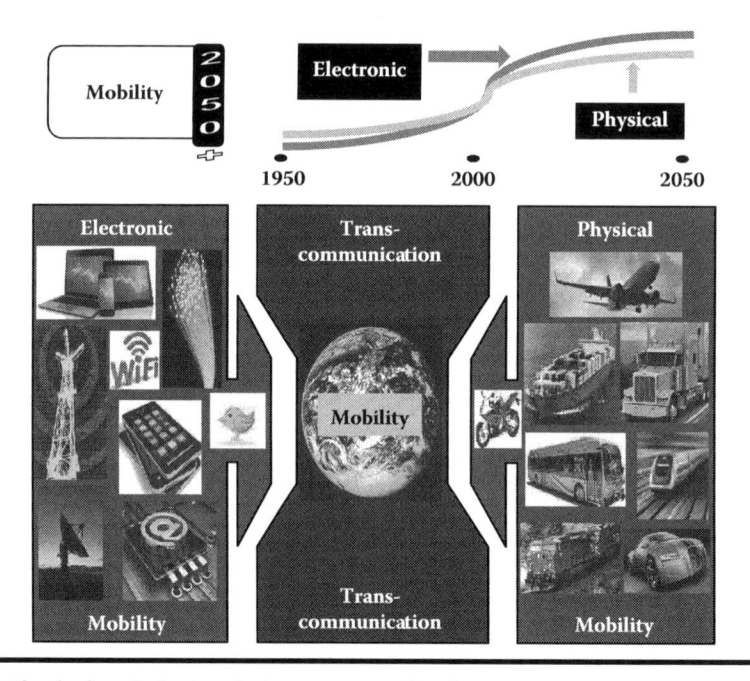

Figure 12.4   Physical and electronic transcommunication.

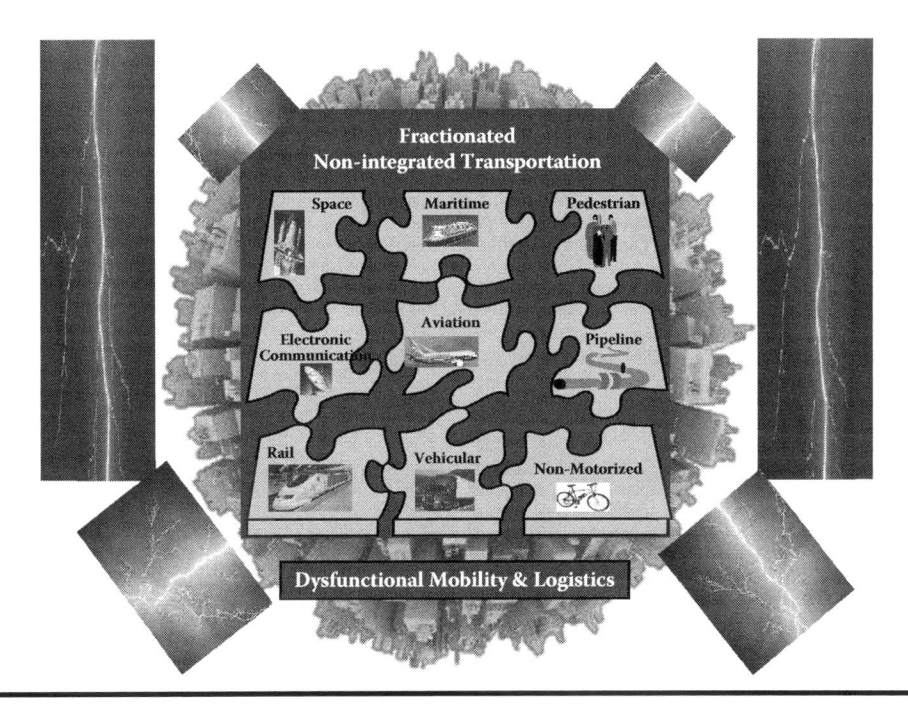

Figure 12.5 Fractionated non-integrated transportation.

airport roadway corridors remain heavily traveled by automobiles (Goetz and Vowles, 2011). In contrast to the United States, many Asian and European cities have direct rail and transit systems connected to their airports to reduce traffic and improve transportation efficiency. A large number of airports have national or inter-metropolitan rail system linkages, including those operating in France, Spain, Germany, Italy, Japan, China, and Singapore. Such a rail system does not exist in the United States (Goetz, 2011).

Congestion and Gridlock

Congestion and gridlock due to an expanding population are impairing the mobility necessary in an increasingly dense urban land mass (e.g., in the United States, 90% of the country's population lives on 10% of the land). Despite the federal government setting aside a portion (10%) of the Department of Transportation's annual budget for intermodal initiatives, over 90% of the budget supports individual modes (e.g., highways, airports, railways, seaports) as independent transportation sources (Bragdon, 2014). The passenger car is becoming an inseparable part of our lifestyle to the point that it is now influencing the shape of our cities, to the exclusion of alternative forms of mobility. Unlike Europe, the United States has adopted a drive-thru lifestyle, which in turn influences our global resilience, as the automobile is the most popular choice of conveyance (Figure 12.6). Personal vehicles are available throughout all phases of our lives, from birth to death (car burials are permitted in many American states).

The ability to be married in one's car is become increasingly popular and more convenient, with Las Vegas, Nevada, being the nuptial epicenter. The Little White Chapel annually performs over 100,000 weddings, with Valentine's Day being the most popular day, and wedding ceremonies can be performed in as little as 10 minutes (Bragdon, 2008). In close proximity to this

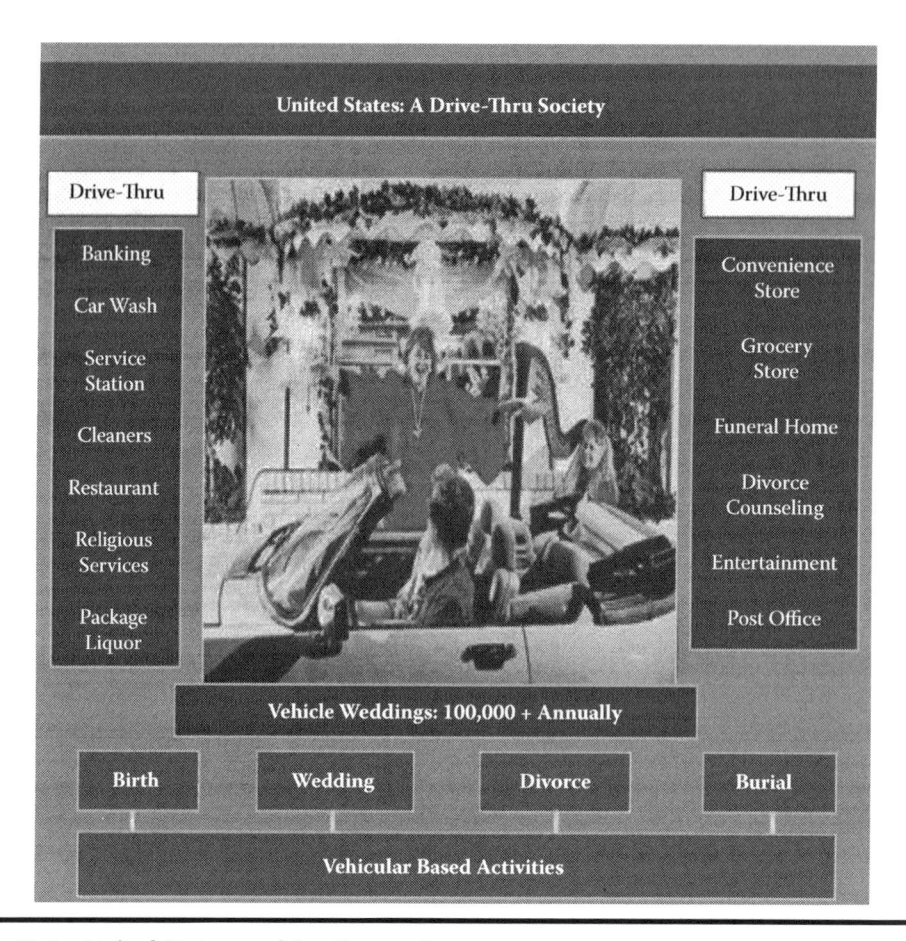

204 ■ *Global Cases in Best and Worst Practice in Crisis and Emergency Management*

Figure 12.6 United States—a drive-thru society.

wedding chapel are lawyers that the newlyweds can seek to annul the ceremony if need be. Even counseling and divorce services are available as drive-thru services. Funeral establishments are now offering a convenient drive-thru option for those desiring to view loved ones while remaining in their cars (e.g., Adams Mortuary, Compton, CA; Paradise Funeral Home, Saginaw, MI). Mortuaries with this type of drive-thru feature can currently be found in five states. The automobile has truly become an integral part of the entire human lifecycle.

The United States ranks first in motor vehicles per capita, with 809 vehicles per 1000 population and averaging 1.10 vehicles per driver; Germany is second, averaging 0.50 vehicles per 1000 population (Bragdon, 2008). China now ranks first in motor vehicle production, with 20 million vehicles produced per year, which is double the U.S. vehicle production rate. The growth in private vehicle ownership is having an adverse impact on global warming, air quality emissions, noise generation, and pavement expansion for roads and parking facilities. It has also created a general disinterest in alternative intermodal transportation scenarios.

We also need to curb both human obesity and urban obesity, by putting our cities on diets along with our citizens. Houses are becoming supersized, like most automobiles and trucks. The median size of new homes built in the United States grew from 2266 ft^2 in 2008 to 2598 ft^2 in 2013 (U.S Census Bureau, 2013). Many wealthy communities (e.g., Beverly Hills, CA; Southampton,

Figure 12.7 Carhenge c. 3000.

NY) are permitting single-family gigamansions to be built. The Ira Rennert compound for their family of five in the Hamptons is 110,000 ft^2 and has 29 bedrooms, 39 bathrooms, and an 18-car garage (Berfield, 2012). In Los Angeles, 60,000- to 90,000-ft^2 single-family homes are being approved for construction; one residence includes an underground garage capable of storing 40 cars (Haldeman, 2014). One in five new houses built in the United States have three-car garages (U.S Census Bureau, 2013). Supersizing is contrary to the resiliency benefits of good health and the conservation of resources associated with sustainability. To avoid a "Carhenge" (c. 3000), the number of hydrogen–electric hybrid vehicles needs to grow dramatically by 2020 (Figure 12.7). Congestion and gridlock will become more pervasive and severe as vehicle numbers and miles driven continue to rise, along with the use of nonrenewable energy resources and the construction of gigamansions that reflect spatial excess, or urban fat.

Natural and Manmade Threats

The threats to our biosphere are a combination of natural disasters, such as hurricanes, tornados, cyclones, earthquakes, fires, and tsunamis and their associated flooding, and manmade disasters consisting of accidents and terrorist activities. Both natural and manmade threats are a significant challenge to resiliency, especially in terms of transport modes. Air transportation has received the greatest attention from the federal government with regard to mitigating security threats to passengers. Fewer financial resources (less than 20%) are directed toward ensuring security for vehicular, mass transit, rail, maritime, or intermodal security and safety; thus, they collectively represent the greatest risk.

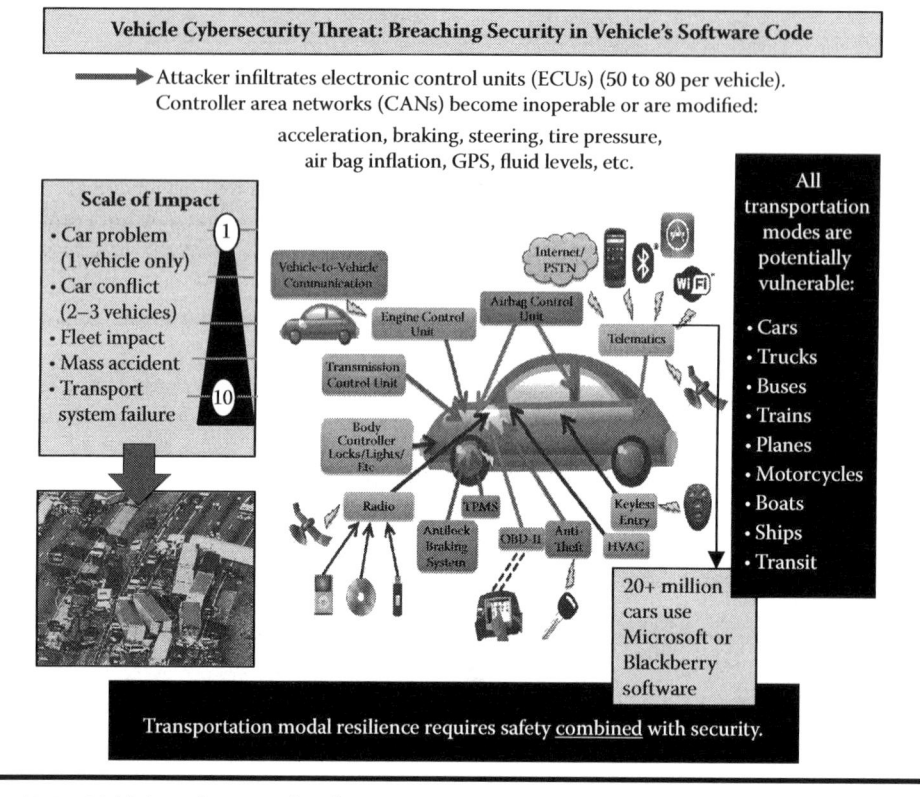

Figure 12.8 Vehicle cybersecurity threats.

Vehicle cybersecurity threats are a new frontier of concern. The newest motor vehicles contain 50 to 100 electronic control units (ECUs) that can be disabled through hacking and the use of malware (Figure 12.8). The type of vehicle functions that can be hacked include braking, engine controls, navigation systems, steering, tire pressure, air bag activation, and fluid levels, among many others (Boatman, 2014). These malware attacks can potentially impact all transportation modes. A single car mode problem could aggressively spread to an entire transport system, bringing about pandemic failure. Researchers have been able to connect remotely to onboard computers in vehicles and have impaired or disabled their safe operation (Miller and Valasek, 2014). The impact of this capability could be significant, as cybersecurity countermeasures are not currently in place for most transport modes.

Cybersecurity threats to the United States come from all over world; however, the four countries that relentlessly attack our information technology (IT) network are Russia, China, North Korea, and Iran (Figure 12.9). Also vulnerable to attacks is our infrastructure, including nuclear power plants, traffic control systems, air traffic control systems, oil and gas refineries, financial institutions, and various governmental operations (e.g., NASA, Department of Defense), which can be infiltrated through advanced supervisory control and data acquisition (SCADA) systems. Our utilities and electrical grid system could be impaired by severe weather or by cyber and physical attacks, as well as by such high-tech approaches as directed-energy weapons, electromagnetic pulses, or geomagnetically induced currents. On a small scale, utility grids in the United States have already been impacted by terrorists inflicting damage on substations and powerlines (McLarty and Ridge, 2014).

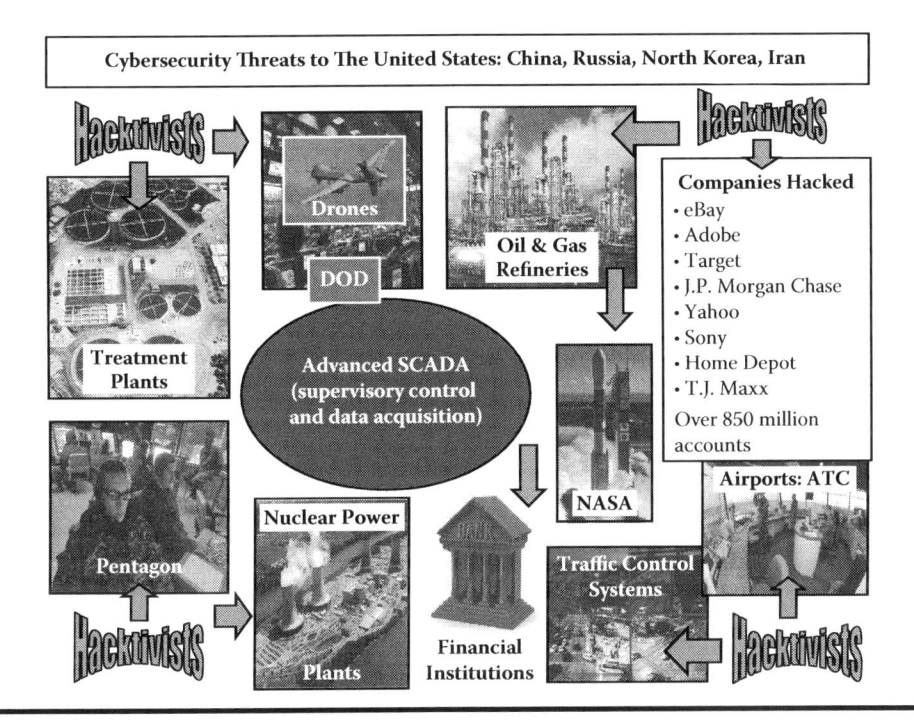

Figure 12.9 Hacktivists threatening SCAD and infrastructure.

Recent examples of computer hacking have been aimed at some of our nation's largest businesses; over 850 million accounts have been compromised in the past several years. The companies involved include eBay, Adobe, Target, J.P. Morgan, Yahoo, Sony, Home Depot, and T.J. Maxx. Cybercrime is an escalating problem globally. David DeWalt, CEO of the network security firm FireEye, suggested that 97% of all American businesses are vulnerable to hacking (Whitaker, 2014). At least 43% of companies worldwide reported being breached in 2014, with the cost to a breached company averaging $3.5 million (Poneman Institute, 2014). A breach is defined as an event in which an individual's name plus Social Security number, medical record, or a financial record or debit card is potentially put at risk. These cybercrimes have been described as a cyber-Pearl Harbor. The public sector, including governments and nonprofits, is also susceptible. Latest estimates suggest that there are over 46,000 cyber attacks a year (Figure 12.10). These breaches have affected White House computer networks, NASA, the U.S. Postal Service, the State Department, the Department of Veterans Affairs, and Goodwill Industries. Personnel records, including their Social Security numbers, financial profiles, detailed demographic information, and e-mails, have been compromised in most instances.

Economic Costs

The total economic costs (direct and indirect) of the threats to our resiliency (e.g., natural and man-made disasters, climate change, transportation congestion and gridlock, global climate change) have not been comprehensively examined; however, some studies and estimates are beginning to appear in selected categories. Globally, the cost of congestion and gridlock is estimated to be over $4.4 trillion by 2030, with the figure in the United States ranging from $350 to $700 billion (CEBR, 2014). Between 2013 and 2030, congestion costs are expected to increase between 37 and 63% in the United Kingdom, United States, Germany, and France (CEBR, 2014) (Figure 12.11).

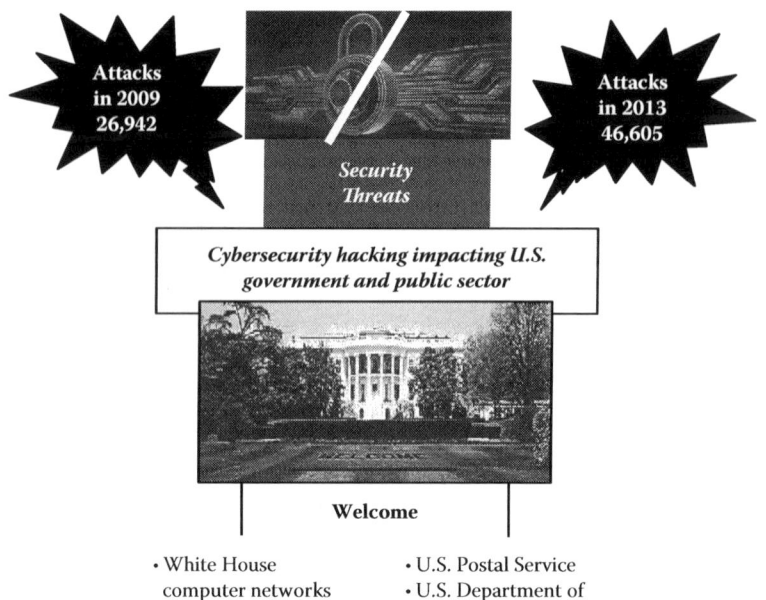

208 ■ *Global Cases in Best and Worst Practice in Crisis and Emergency Management*

Figure 12.10 Cybersecurity impact on government and nonprofits.

Figure 12.11 Cumulative costs of congestion and gridlock.

Resilience Capacity Building for Global Crisis and Emergency Management ■ 209

The problem of efficient and effective mobility impacts all modes of transportation, including roadways, airports, maritime ports, rail networks, and bicycle systems, all of which are involved in the logistical movement of people and goods. This financial burden shared by countries all over the world is significant when compared to the budgets of these same countries. The total revenue of all of the countries in the world is $22.41 trillion (CIA, 2013). The cost of congestion and gridlock around the world is equivalent to 20% of the current annual revenue of all of the countries combined. An astronomical sum of money would have to be dedicated to addressing the problem. Doing so would require the equivalent of the total revenue of the majority of the world's countries, not counting the 25 wealthiest nations. If just the 25 wealthiest countries (from the United States down to Venezuela) shouldered this problem, at least 25% of their total annual revenue would be required. The financial resources that would have to be applied to developing the transportation solutions necessary to solve the problem of gridlock and congestion would more than likely exceed the impact cost of $4.4 trillion.

Achieving global resiliency to adequately protect the world's resources is a desirable objective; however, in the process it would be necessary to minimize natural and human disasters, climate change, and transportation gridlock. Such a monumental challenge would require global changes in policies, programs, and governance, a problem that is only beginning to be recognized. This author estimates that all natural and manmade disasters, combined with the impact of climate change and transportation gridlock, on a global basis annually cost 7 to 15% of the world's gross domestic production (GDP) (Figure 12.12).

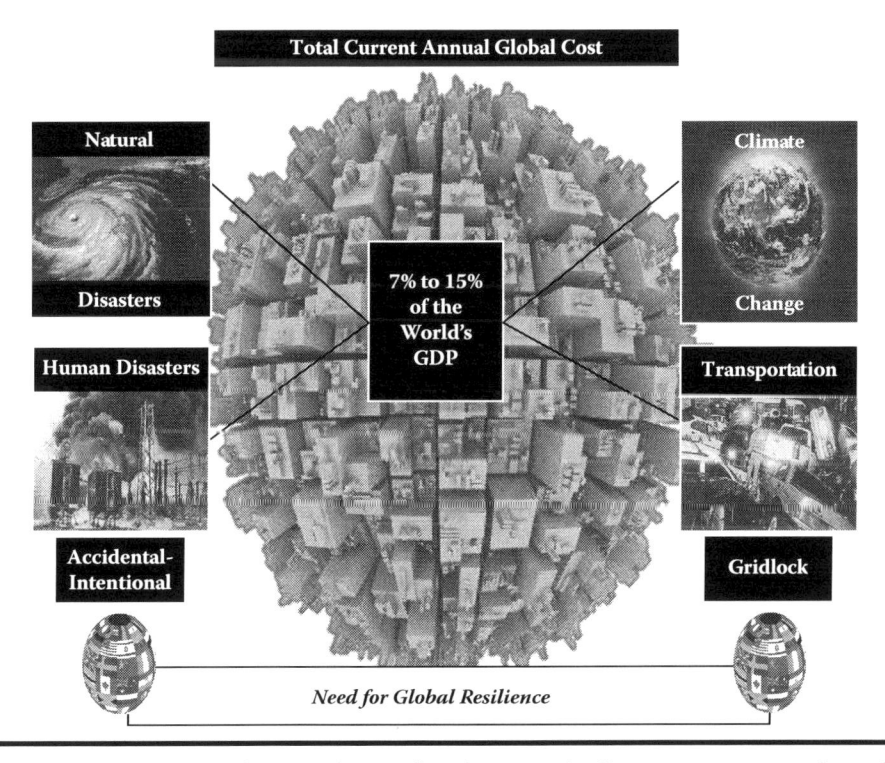

Figure 12.12 Current annual costs of natural and manmade disasters, transportation gridlock, and climate change.

Resilience Capacity Building

Our focus should not solely be on economics and costs but rather should also include the utilization of innovative technology and envisioning solutions that incorporate neoteric planning and strategic resilience principles and applications to enhance resilience capacity building for global crisis and emergency management. This will require identifying and understanding future threats and developing effective countermeasures that reinforce resilient-based solutions.

Combined Physical and Electronic Terrorism

Terrorism initiatives have evolved over time. The first attack on the World Trade Center occurred on February 26, 1993. Aimed at the physical infrastructure, the attack was an attempt to bring the towers down by detonating a bomb in the underground parking garage. Eight years later, on September 11, 2001, the World Trade Center was again the target of an attack (9/11 Commission, 2004). This time, however, the towers were destroyed by two commandeered Boeing 767 airliners, causing the loss of 2753 lives. Historically, causing physical damage to buildings and related infrastructure to cause human fatalities and injuries has been the primary tactic of terrorists; however, today, they are also using electronic means to hack sensitive databases associated with businesses, government agencies, and nonprofits. Secure files, databases, and demographic information are increasingly being accessed remotely, without any physical damage done to the buildings containing them. Fixed buildings have been the primary targets of terrorist attacks, but terrorists are growing increasingly interested in impairing transportation systems such as trains, buses, subways, and other public conveyances. Attacking the operational software and electronic control units associated with cars, trucks, and buses can result in infrastructure damage, fatalities, and injuries, leading to large-scale gridlock conditions and seriously impeding logistical movement.

Neoteric Planning

To optimize the potential of a resilient Earth and to protect our global society, neoteric planning principles must integrate spatial, temporal, and sensory elements. Currently, neoteric principles are not being effectively practiced. An effective cubic spatial approach would take a three-dimensional perspective that incorporates aerial, surface, and subsurface features, rather than just viewing the surface or land (Figure 12.13). Metes and bound property descriptions typically refer to only the two dimensions pertaining to the area or surface; however, the concept of property requires a three-dimensional examination of three spatial planes: aerial (e.g., air rights), surface (e.g., land and water), and subsurface (e.g., belowground and under water). Such a three-dimensional perspective allows us to explore, plan, and develop new spatial arrangements encompassing eco-rooftops, subterranean developments, utilidoors, air rights, vertiports, water-based communities, aquatic highways, and multipurpose subsurface logistical corridors (Bragdon, 2014). Three-dimensional thinking opens new venues but may also raise new potential threats, as the terrorist community continually seeks to determine new avenues for penetrating a nation's infrastructure.

Developing three-dimensional master plans for resiliency must become standard procedure, and it is becoming more common in military planning and installations for the tri-services to aid in their offensive and defensive missions. Fort Lewis, a U.S. Army base in Washington state, initiated the first 3D planning process in the Army, and the process has benefited the

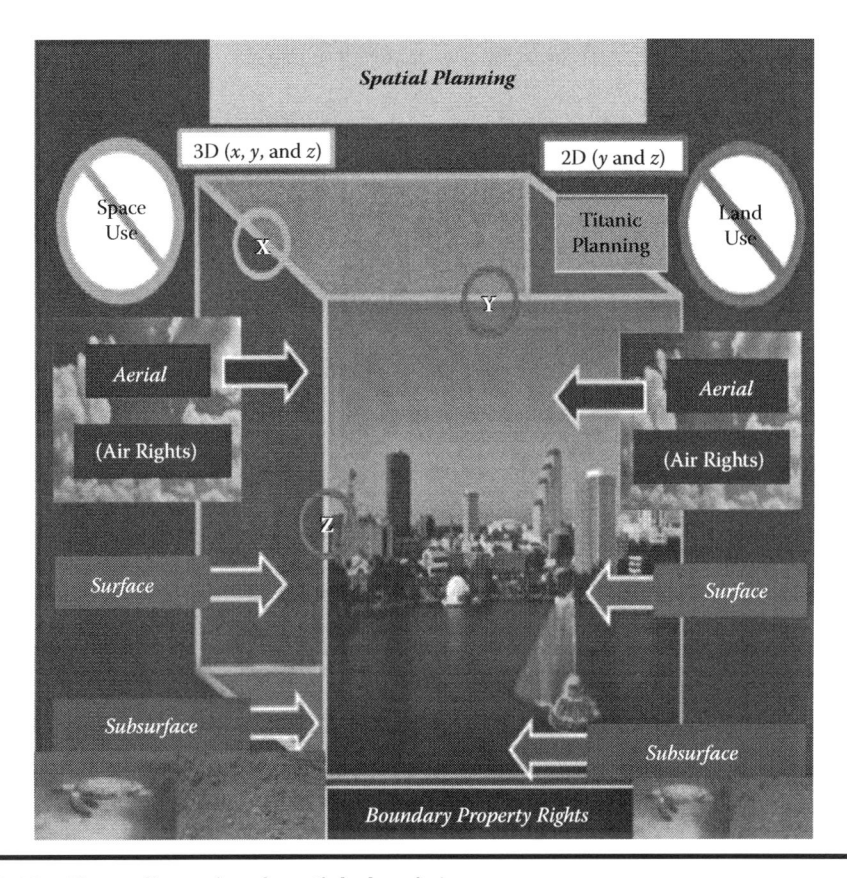

Resilience Capacity Building for Global Crisis and Emergency Management ■ 211

Figure 12.13 Three-dimensional spatial planning.

development of municipal, regional, and state space use plans (Bragdon, 2008). Spatial planning must also be combined with multisensory planning that considers all five senses (sight, hearing, touch, smell, and taste), even though sight is the dominant sense (Figure 12.14). Visual solutions have biased the disciplines of architecture, landscape architecture, urban planning, and civil engineering. Consideration of the other senses is frequently omitted, despite the fact that the sense of hearing is the only one that operates 24 hours a day and offers a 360° perspective. In the overall scheme of things, unwanted noise should be replaced by sound, aroma should replace smell and odor, and tranquility should replace shock and vibration. The result will be a more sensory-based palette that allows urbanized society to become more resilient. Temporal planning is another important neoteric planning element, as cities have become 24-hour centers of activity. Many businesses and government services are operating on a 24-hour basis, shifting traditional daytime activities to off-peak evening and nighttime hours. Good examples of businesses with considerable nocturnal activity are air cargo operations such as Federal Express and United Parcel Service (Cosmas and Martini, 2007). A sizeable portion of their employees (approximately one third) work between 10:00 p.m. and 4:00 a.m. to ensure that guaranteed deliveries are properly executed. Spatial, sensory, and temporal activities must be hardened as both businesses and governments expand operations.

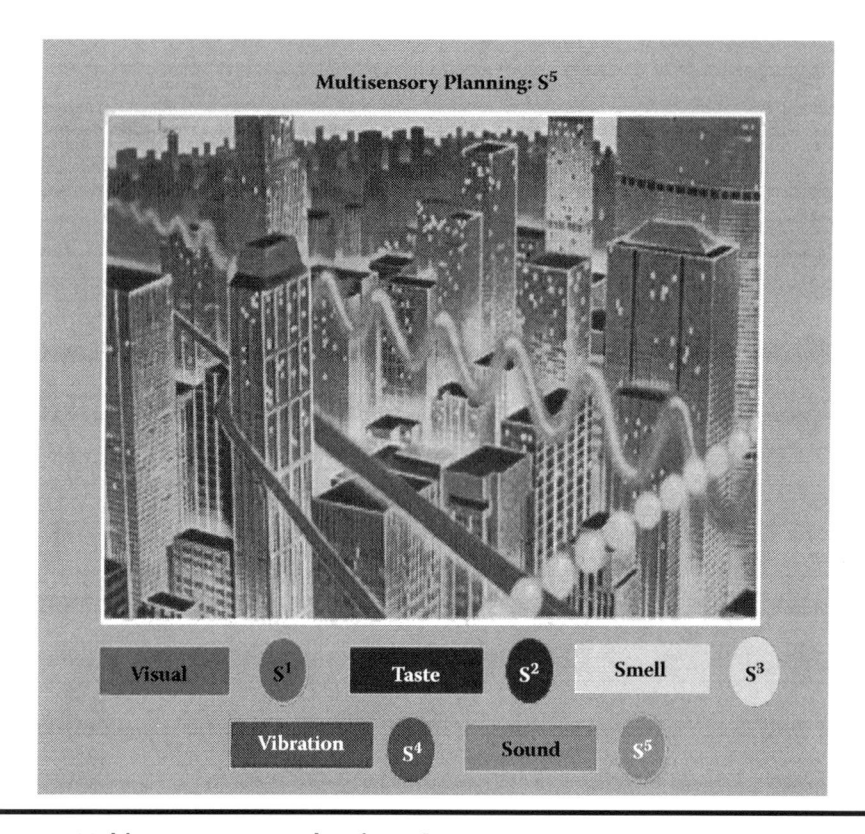

Figure 12.14 Multisensory master planning: S^5.

Resiliency: A Comprehensive and Balanced Approach

Several organizations have the methodologies and procedures in place to develop solutions to the problem of protecting the global habitat and built environment. One such entity is the U.S. Green Building Council (http://www.usgbc.org), which was established in 1993 as a private 501(c)(3) membership-based nonprofit organization that promotes sustainability in building design, construction, and operation. This organization has established a Leadership in Energy and Environmental Design (LEED) certification for both professionals and building projects. The following is a comparison of the global protection aspects of LEED and the Global Center for Preparedness and Resilience (GCPR) (Figure 12.15).

The LEED approach focuses primarily on the sustainability of commercial buildings, homes, neighborhoods, healthcare facilities, and schools, including all phases of a building's lifecycle. Its certification hierarchy (silver, gold, or platinum) for structures is based on earning a given number of credits within their rating system, with platinum being the highest level achievable. The GCPR incorporates four attributes with the intent to incorporate and balance sustainability, security, safety, and health. The scale extends well beyond a single structure by encompassing neighborhoods, communities, and government entities as part of the biosphere. LEED focuses on individual buildings, not neighborhoods, and the three attributes of safety, security, and health are not directly addressed. The LEED standards have come under criticism for not consistently creating energy-efficient buildings; the data for New York City indicate that LEED-certified buildings have performed below non-LEED buildings with regard to their energy efficiency (Scofield, 2013).

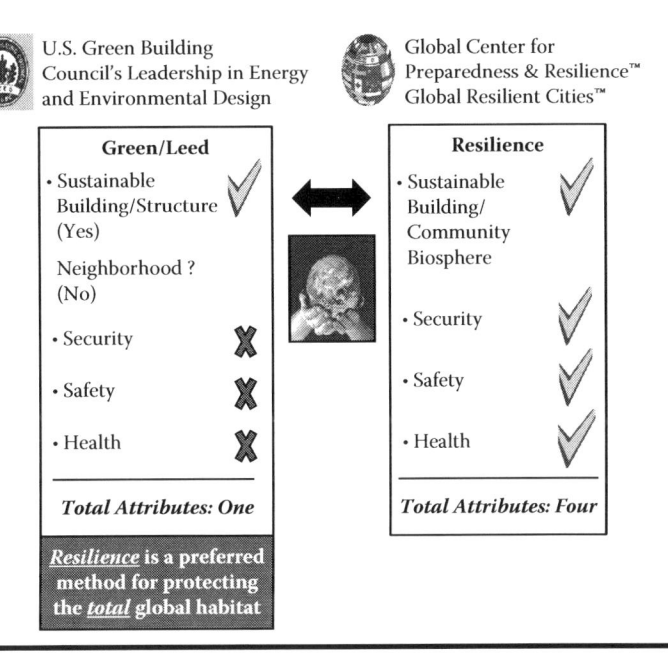

Resilience Capacity Building for Global Crisis and Emergency Management ■ 213

Figure 12.15 Global protection comparisons between LEED and GCPR.

In contrast, the GCRP believes that all four attributes must be addressed to achieve resiliency, because an emphasis on only one attribute (e.g., sustainability) does not provide adequate protection. A case in point is the Fukushima Daiichi nuclear power plant. Japan's 48 nuclear reactors gave the country a high sustainability rating, with nearly zero carbon emissions, but the attributes of safety, security, and health were inadequately addressed (Figure 12.16). As a consequence, safety

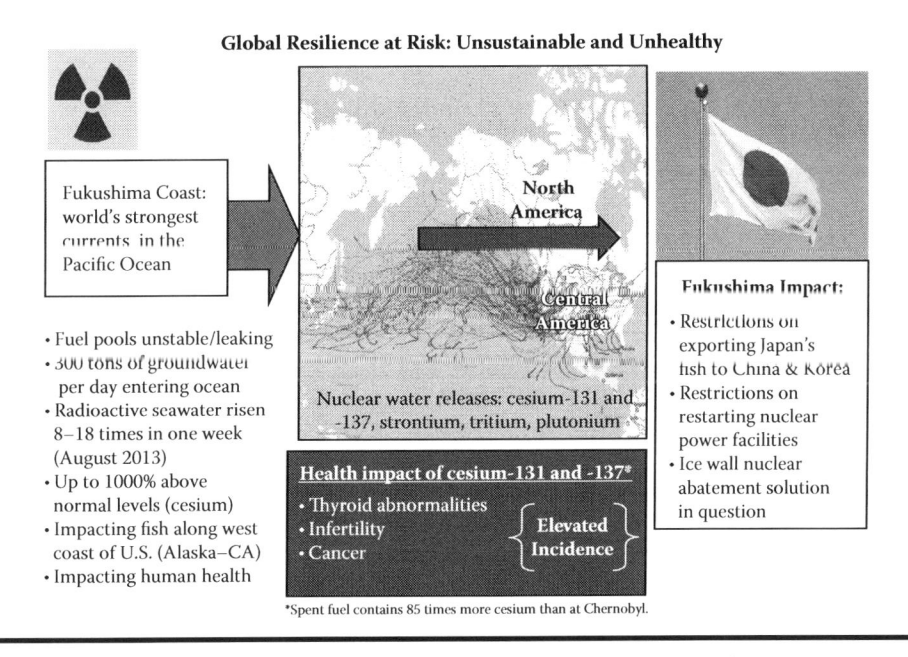

Figure 12.16 Fukushima tsunami and hurricane—global resilience at risk.

and health issues arising from the nuclear plant disaster have extended beyond the boundaries of Japan. The release into the water of cesium-131 and -137, strontium, tritium, and plutonium poses potential health risks extending as far as the west coast of North and Central America, because the Fukushima coastline possesses the strongest currents in the Pacific Ocean. Fish imports from Japan remain restricted in both China and Korea (Jun, 2013); the United States has not instituted any food restrictions. Neither the containment plans nor engineering solutions proposed by TEPCO for the Fukushima nuclear power plant have been endorsed more than 3 years after the incident. Because of the potential for future hurricanes and tsunamis and the lack of proper safety-, security-, and health-based controls at Fukushima, the site remains both a domestic and international resiliency problem (National Diet of Japan, 2012).

Resilience-Based Attributes and Applications

Each of the four resilient attributes has a specific focus, characteristics, and responsibilities with regard to protecting our global biosphere (Figure 12.17). *Safety* addresses accident reduction, enhanced worker productivity, interactive community preparedness, and social institutional awareness. *Health* includes ensuring survival and injury prevention, along with reducing stress and enhancing enjoyment among the global population. *Security* is concerned with terrorism prevention, risk reduction, protecting information technologies, and providing secure and controlled accessibility. Finally, *sustainability* is concerned with environmental protection, integrated natural and social resources, balanced economic growth, and balanced environmental sources. All four

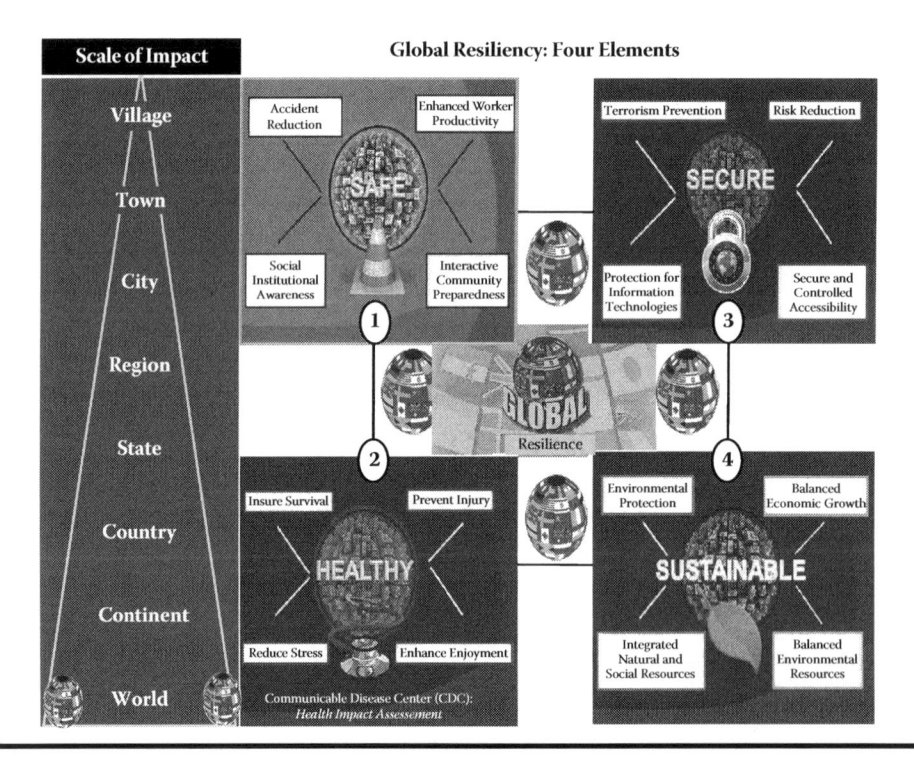

Figure 12.17 Four attributes and potential scale of impact of global resiliency.

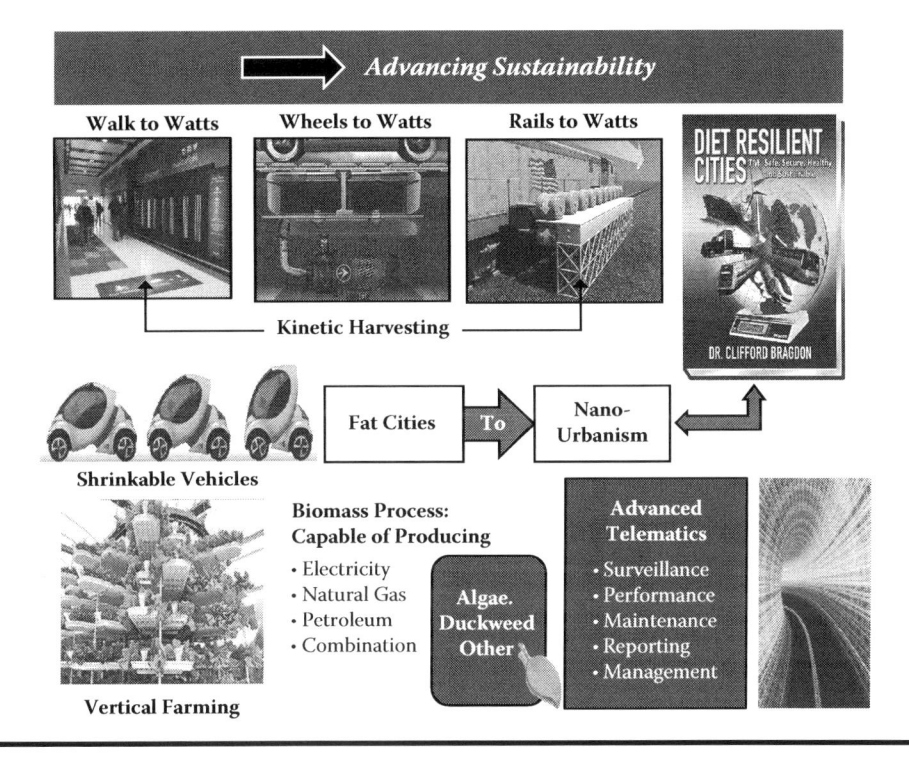

Figure 12.18 Advanced sustainability.

of these attributes must work together to provide a resilient balanced approach. Emphasizing one attribute over the others creates a dysfunctional situation and a loss of resilience, as exemplified by the nuclear power plant disaster in Fukushima. Resiliency-based approaches that address all four attributes should be applied at all governmental levels, beginning with villages, towns, and cities; extending to regions, states, and countries; and ultimately encompassing continents and the world as a whole. The sustainability attribute, like the other three, is rapidly advancing new ways to protect our biosphere through a collage of solutions, described briefly below.

Kinetic Energy Harvesting

Capturing kinetic energy related to the dynamics of movement is referred to as *kinetic energy harvesting*, which can provide electricity-based renewable energy generation through a storage-based system (e.g., lithium polymer batteries) and a wireless grid. The idea of utilizing renewable energy by harnessing the kinetic energy produced by walking or vehicular or rail passage is being actively pursued (Figure 12.18). Kinetic paver slabs developed by Pavegen Systems (Harris, 2011) have been installed at Heathrow Airport, a train station in France, and a soccer field in Brazil. The concepts of "wheels to watts" and "rails to watts," developed by SeaAway (Kroecker, 2010), are in the final development, patenting, and prototyping stages. The renewable kinetic energy associated with movement throughout the transportation-based infrastructure (e.g., sidewalks, roadways, railways, transit corridors) has the potential to be converted into electricity, a profound advance in sustainability and resilience that would reduce the reliance on nonrenewable and imported energy sources.

Advanced Telematics

Telematics involves any integrated use of telecommunication and informatics, commonly referred to as information and communications technology (ICT). Advanced methods to improve efficiency and energy management can be applied to transportation systems, including surveillance, performance, maintenance, reporting, and management (Figure 12.18). For example, truck fleet behavior can be monitored and modified in real time using ICT to enhance a fleet's operational performance and bottom line. Regulations limiting truck idling have been passed in most states and more are being considered by the U.S Environmental Protection Agency, but technology available today (e.g., Malone Specialty; Mentor, OH) can monitor trucks while they are in the field to evaluate their idling time signatures, emissions, and mileage; adjustments can be made remotely. Such technology can improve both driver behavior and mechanical operation, so cost savings and profits can be achieved.

Shrinkable Cars

It is one thing to make a small car, but even more desirable is one that folds up when parked. This was a dream of William Mitchell with the MIT Smart Cities research group over 20 years ago (Ashley, 2012). Hiriko Driving Mobility, located in the Basque region of Spain, has a folding car in the early production stages (Figure 12.18). It will be possible to park three folded Hirikos (Basque word for "urban") in one standard parking space (Ashley, 2012). The lithium-ion-powered electric car should achieve a driving range of 75 miles, with a top speed of 31 miles per hour. The four-wheel steering system is designed to make tight turns, providing maximum maneuverability in very small spaces. Prototypes have satisfied all current safety and crash tests, and it is estimated that the two-passenger Hiriko Fold model will sell for around $16,400. Many believe this vehicle would be a perfect candidate for the car-sharing business (e.g., Car2Go, Zipcar, Autolib). Hiriko appears to have a promising future if proper financing can be achieved.

Vertical Farming

The concept of growing agriculture vertically (above or below the ground) in urban environments was explored at Columbia University well over a decade ago (Despommier, 2010). The many benefits including conservation of space, farm products being produced closer to the market, simplified logistics, diversity of produce, convenient processing, greater control over the growing technology, and healthier produce (Despommier, 2010). The initial teaching and academic exercise has grown rapidly, and today vertical farms are being planned, constructed, and operated throughout the world (Figure 12.18). Our global population, now over 7 billion, requires the space nearly the size of South America to grow and harvest the necessary food; horizontal farming cannot be the sole solution. Asian countries have become ardent believers in vertical farming, as their crowded cities and scarce land make this form of agriculture very attractive. Japan is examining such farming in the Fukushima region that was ravaged by the tsunami and nuclear disaster and where land will be cleaned up robotically. VFT Global evaluated the potential for vertical farming and built an educational training center in the Florida Tech Research Park at the Melbourne International Airport to annually grow over a million heads of lettuce. Strong interest is being shown all over the United States, although attracting financing has been a problem. Nevertheless, there are enough success stories in many countries to validate and stimulate the growth of vertical farming for enhancing global resilience (Hsu, 2012).

Biomass Production for Energy

Biomass from living organisms can be utilized to create fuel or power in several ways. Bioenergy conversion to electricity, gas, and petroleum is a common practice found throughout this country with varying degrees of success (Figure 12.18). The rate of yield depends on the type of biologic material employed, the level of supply, and the production process. Capital investment varies considerably, depending on the end product desired and the associated governmental regulations. Techniques for creating petroleum byproducts, chemicals, and even pharmaceuticals are being pursued today. Algae and even duckweed are being explored as means to ultimately produce electricity through anaerobic digestion and gas conversion using a generator as part of a closed-loop biologic system. This is a promising technology that could theoretically produce a reduced kilowatt per hour energy cost (estimated to be 4 to 7¢/kWh) as part of an approved utility grid; however, these facilities are still in the development stages. Full, large-scale production would be essential to create the necessary power generation commensurate with the capital investment.

Diet-Resilient Cities

All of the sustainable examples described here demonstrate that resiliency can be enhanced by a variety of technologies, with the ultimate goal of making our cities more resilient (Figure 12.18). Kinetic energy harvesting shows promise, but it must be aggressively applied to the entire transportation-based system and supporting infrastructure, along with telematics. Nano-urbanism (the conservation of space in cities) should be practiced, as well as vertical farming, along with four-dimensional spatial, sensory, and temporal planning. Urban obesity must become a thing of the past, as remediation represents a high and undesirable cost to society. Diet-resilient cities utilizing the integrated principles of health, safety, security, and sustainability will further the development of planning and management tools and training and certification processes applicable to municipalities on a global basis.

Advancing Sustainability in the Area of Energy Technology

Numerous sustainable technologies are being developed to improve energy technology and the energy reliance of both fixed and mobile sources. For fixed operations, New York's Metropolitan Transportation Authority (MTA) has installed three CellCube vanadium flow batteries produced by American Vanadium Corp. at its headquarters building (Bowen, 2014). This is a resilient energy tool that can be utilized when the MTA experiences power disruptions (Figure 12.19). It provides resiliency in times of need, as it is capable of multiple hour and multiple-megawatt energy storage. The CellCube system provides power for extended periods of time based on an emissions-free energy supply. Vanadium provides the longest energy storage capacity currently available for grid-scale projects, and vanadium redox batteries are considered the next-generation energy storage system (Bowen, 2014). In the automotive arena, Volvo and Flybrid Automotive have jointly developed a kinetic energy recovery system (KERS) that utilizes a light carbon fiber flywheel that improves gasoline consumption (25 to 30%), improves vehicle acceleration from 0 to 60 mph by 1.5 seconds, increases power output by 80 horsepower, and saves considerable weight over existing hybrid technology (Crowe, 2014). They are currently conducting tests with a Flybrid KERS installed on the rear axle of the Volvo S60, and Volvo is considering a timetable for introducing this sustainable flywheel technology (Figure 12.19).

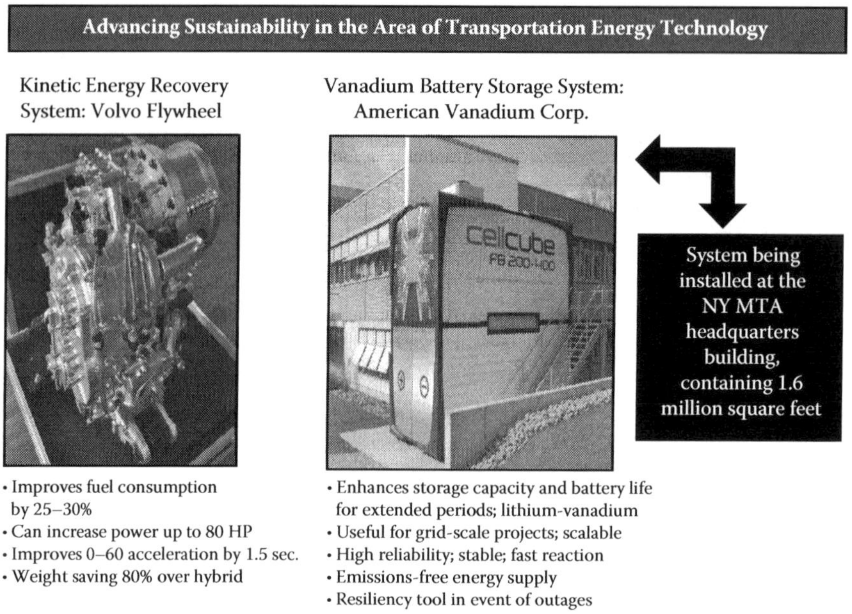

Advancing Sustainability in the Area of Transportation Energy Technology

Kinetic Energy Recovery System: Volvo Flywheel

Vanadium Battery Storage System: American Vanadium Corp.

System being installed at the NY MTA headquarters building, containing 1.6 million square feet

- Improves fuel consumption by 25–30%
- Can increase power up to 80 HP
- Improves 0–60 acceleration by 1.5 sec.
- Weight saving 80% over hybrid

- Enhances storage capacity and battery life for extended periods; lithium-vanadium
- Useful for grid-scale projects; scalable
- High reliability; stable; fast reaction
- Emissions-free energy supply
- Resiliency tool in event of outages

Figure 12.19 Advanced sustainability in transportation energy technology.

Global Applications of Resilience: U.K. Department for International Development

The U.K. Department for International Development (DFID) has developed the most comprehensive global resiliency management initiative in existence today (Figure 12.20). With work beginning in 1997, the British government has developed a global resilience manifesto for crisis management (Ashdown, 2011; DFID, 2011). This has been followed up by establishing the cabinet position of Secretary of State for International Development, responsible for all resilient activity as described in the Global Resilient Action Plan (GRAP) (Ashdown, 2012). Both public and private sectors have collaborated to develop a national resilient capabilities program through a series of 23 integrated work teams, with an emphasis on disaster resilience for vulnerable communities and disaster risk reduction and climate adaptation The programs cover a broad range of subject areas, including mass fatalities and casualty management, evacuation and shelter, humanitarian assistance, infectious and animal disease control, resilient communications, infrastructure resilience, interoperability, and chemical, biological, radiological, and nuclear (CBRN) management. Teams focused on each subject area develop response, recovery, reconstruction, and prevention plans. Each team participates in resilience-building activities that address technological–physical features, social–human issues, political frameworks, environmental–natural subject areas, and financial and economic strategies. Tangible projects are initiated in geographical areas of the United Kingdom, as well as internationally.

The U.K. Department for International Development and their GRAP provide a model that other countries should emulate. The United Kingdom is the first country to have established an office of resilience. They have put programs on the ground to address a multitude of concerns affecting vulnerable communities, in addition to writing approach papers outlining ways to deal with disaster resilience. The DFID uses this working definition of resilience: "the ability of countries, communities and households to manage change by maintaining or transforming living standards in the face of

Resilience Capacity Building for Global Crisis and Emergency Management ■ 219

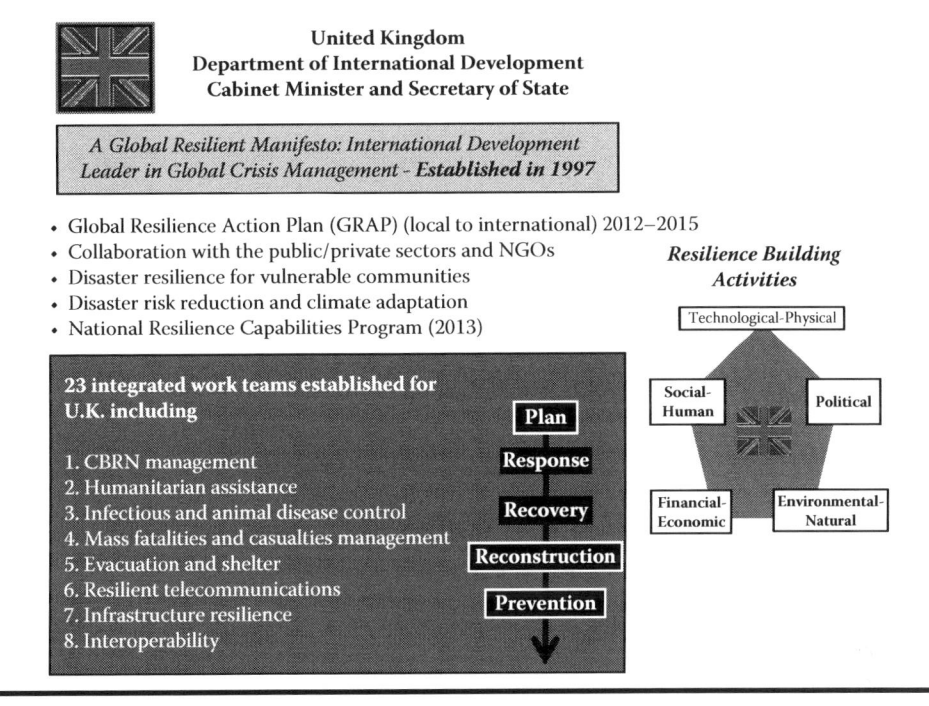

Figure 12.20 United Kingdom's approach to global resilience

shocks or stresses—such as earthquakes, drought or violent conflict—without compromising their long-term prospects" (DFID, 2011). For every disaster resilience project undertaken, the DFID is providing full case study documentation and ensuring that each plan is successfully implemented.

Lessons Learned

Resilience capacity building for global crisis and emergency management is necessary to protect our planet. The four attributes of resilience—safety, security, sustainability, and health—must be collectively addressed in a balanced manner to optimize protection of the planet's biosphere. An imbalanced approach that emphasizes fewer than all four attributes will result in a dysfunctional situation that challenges the planet's resilience capacity. Neoteric planning principles and applied technology must be utilized throughout the resiliency process, with goals, objectives, plans, and programs established and effectively implemented in a consensus-based manner. Establishing a certification in resiliency for the purposes of setting standards of excellence globally is necessary, and the Global Center for Preparedness and Resilience can help facilitate this important process (Bragdon, 2014).

Questions for Discussion

Resilience is a critical feature for both the current and future well-being of the physical, social, and economic aspects of society. The biosphere is our life-support system. It encapsulates humans, plants, and animals and the infrastructure that civilizations have created through the centuries. The following questions, based on the content of this chapter, are designed to stimulate discussion on resilience capacity building—past, present, and future.

1. With regard to the Fukushima Daiichi nuclear power plant accident, what resilient attributes were improperly addressed, thereby exacerbating the situation? Has that situation been rectified today? In retrospect, how could the attributes have been addressed in a more proactive way, in advance of either the hurricane or tsunami?
2. What are the most serious global trends that may have an adverse impact on our planet's resiliency before the next century arrives? What control strategies based on the four resilient attributes could be used to avoid future crises?
3. The United Kingdom has been identified as the country with the most comprehensive resilient approach. From an administrative and program management standpoint, how could the United States learn from their experience to improve its current approach?
4. What are some examples of potential threats to the U.S. infrastructure, and what measures could be employed to address the problem?
5. You won the presidential election, and on January 20, after taking the oath of office, you will address Congress and the citizens of the United States. Outline why we need a new approach to resiliency to protect our population, and outline measures you are going to recommend to Congress that need to be instituted on a bipartisan basis during the first year of your presidency.
6. Because of your educational qualifications (bachelor's and master's degrees in information technology and automotive engineering), along with 10 years of working at General Motors (applied research and reverse engineering), GM's new CEO has asked you to prepare a strategic plan addressing cybersecurity threats before they introduce their new line of vehicles in September, 2016. What would your plan include?

Additional Reading

Farazmand, A., Ed. (2014). *Crisis and Emergency Management: Theory and Practice*, 2nd ed. Boca Raton, FL: CRC Press.

IPCC. (2014). *Climate Change 2014: Impacts, Adaptation, and Vulnerability*. Geneva: U.N. Intergovernmental Panel on Climate Change.

Marsan, C.D. (2012). Biggest threat to corporate nets in 2011? Hactivists, not cybercriminals. *Network World*, March 22 (http://www.networkworld.com/article/2187040/malware-cybercrime/biggest-threat-to-corporate-nets-in-2011--hactivists--not-cybercriminals.html).

WEF. (2012). *Partnering for Cyber Resilience: Risk and Responsibility in a Hyperconnected World—Principles and Guidelines*. Geneva: World Economic Forum.

World Bank Group. (2012). *Toward a Green, Clean, and Resilient World for All: A World Bank Group Environmental Strategy 2012–2020*. Washington DC: The World Bank Group.

References

9/11 Commission. (2004). *The 9/11 Commission Report: Final Report of the National Commission on Terrorist Attacks Upon the United States*. New York: St. Martin's Press.

Ashdown, L. (2011). *Humanitarian Emergency Response Review*. London: Department for International Development.

Ashdown, L. (2012). *Global Resilience Action Program*. London: Department for International Development.

Ashley, S. (2012). Shrink-to-fit car for city parking. *The New York Times*, July 15, p. AU4.

Berfield, S. (2012). Versailles, the would-be biggest house in America. *Blumberg Businessweek*, March 15 (http://www.bloomberg.com/bw/articles/2012-03-14/versailles-the-would-be-biggest-house-in-america#p1).

Boatman, K. (2014). *Can Your Car Be Hacked?* Norton Security, http://us.norton.com/yoursecurityresource/detail.jsp?aid=car_computer.
Bowen, J. (2014). MTA HQ tests energy storage system. *Railway Age*, April 30, http://www.railwayage.com/index.php/management/mta-hq-tests-energy-storage-system.html.
Bragdon, C. (2008). *Transportation Security*. Burlington, MA: Butterworth-Heinemann.
Bragdon, C. (2014). Global resilience to enhance crisis and emergency management. In Farazmand, A., Ed., *Crisis and Emergency Management: Theory and Practice*, 2nd ed., Chap. 37. Boca Raton, FL: CRC Press.
CEBR. (2014). *The Future Economic and Environmental Costs of Gridlock in 2030*. London: Centre for Economics and Business Research.
CIA. (2013). *The World Fact Book 2013–14*. Washington, DC: Central Intelligence Agency.
Cosmas, A. and Martini, B. (2007). *UPS and FedEx Air Hubs: Comparing Louisville and Memphis Cargo Hub Operations*, 16.781 Term Project.
Crowe, P. (2014). Volvo testing KERS technology for your next car. *HybridCars*, March 27, http://www.hybridcars.com/volvo-testing-kers-technology-for-your-next-car/.
DFID. (2011). *Defining Disaster Resilience: A DFID Approach Paper*. London: Department for International Development.
Despommier, D. (2010). *The Vertical Farm: Feeding the World in the 21st Century*. New York: St. Martin's Press.
Fackler, M. (2012). Three years after Fukushima, Japan approves a nuclear plant. *The New York Times*, September 11, p. A6.
Gerland, P. (2014). World population stabilization unlikely this century. *Science*, 346(6206): 234–237.
Goetz, A. and Vowles, T. (2011). *A Hierarchical Typology of International Air–Rail Connections at Large Airports in the United States, Final Report*. Denver, CO: National Center for Intermodal Transportation, University of Denver.
Haldeman, P. (2014). Battle of the megamansions. *The New York Times*, December 7, p. ST1.
Harris, S. (2011). Pavegen founder Laurence Kemball-Cook. *Engineer*, November 14 (http://www.theengineer.co.uk/in-depth/interviews/pavegen-founder-laurence-kemball-cook/1010877.article).
Heilig, G. (2012). *World Urbanization Prospects: The 2011 Revision*. Geneva: United Nations Population Division.
Hsu, J. (2012). Vertical farms sprout into reality. *Innovation News Daily*, June 4 (http://www.livescience.com/20720-vertical-farms-grow-global.html).
HUD. (2013). *Rebuild by Design: An Initiative of the President's Hurricane Sandy Rebuilding Task Force*. Washington, DC: U.S. Department of Housing and Urban Development.
ICAO. (2013). *Aircraft Departures and Passengers Carried: Existing and Projected*. Montreal: International Civil and Aeronautics Organization.
IPCC. (2014). *Climate Change 2014: Impacts, Adaptation, and Vulnerability*. Geneva: U.N. Intergovernmental Panel on Climate Change.
Jaffe, E. (2014). The water next time. *Atlantic*, December (http://www.theatlantic.com/magazine/archive/2014/12/the-water-next-time/382242/).
Jun, K. (2013). Fish is off the menu in South Korea over radiation fears. *The Wall Street Journal*, November 14 (http://www.wsj.com/articles/SB10001424052702303289904579196893701088208).
Kroecker, S. (2010). *Sea Away Transportation Based Technology to Enhance Logistics and Intermodalism*, paper presented at the Third Annual Conference on Global Preparedness and Resilience, Melbourne, FL, December 8–10.
McLarty, T. and Ridge, T. (2014). *Securing the U.S. Electrical Grid*. Washington, DC: Center for the Study of the Presidency and Congress.
Miller, C. and Valasek, C. (2014). A Survey of Remote Automotive Attack Surfaces, paper presented at Black Hat USA 2014, Las Vegas, NV, August 2–7.
National Diet of Japan. (2012). *The Official Report of the Fukushima Nuclear Accident Independent Investigation Commission*. Tokyo: National Diet of Japan.
NOAA. (2013). *National Coastal Population Report: Population Trends from 1970 to 2020*. Washington, DC: National Oceanic and Atmospheric Administration.
Poneman Institute. (2014). *Cost of Data Breach Study: Global Analysis*. Traverse City, MI: Poneman Institute.

Scofield, J. (2013). Efficacy of LEED certification in reducing energy consumption and greenhouse gas emission for large New York City office buildings. *Energy Buildings*, 67: 517–524.
Strauss, B. (2012). *Surging Seas: Climate Central Report for 2030*. Princeton, NJ: Climate Central.
Strauss, B. (2014). *Florida and the Surging Sea*. Princeton, NJ: Climate Central.
Stuart, D. (2015). Mobile Engagement, paper presented at Passenger Terminal World Showcase 2015, January.
U.S. Census Bureau. (2013). *Highlights of Annual 2013 Characteristics of New Housing*. Washington, DC: U.S. Census Bureau.
Whitaker, B. (2014). *What Happens When You Swipe Your Card?* [video]. New York: CBS News (http://www.cbsnews.com/news/swiping-your-credit-card-and-hacking-and-cybercrime/).

Chapter 13

Building Disaster Resilience: The Communities Advancing Resilience Toolkit (CART)

Rose L. Pfefferbaum

Contents

Chapter Goals	224
Introduction	224
Importance and Meaning of Resilience	224
Differences between Personal and Community Resilience	224
Chapter Overview	225
Description of the Communities Advancing Resilience Toolkit	225
Synopsis	225
CART Process	225
CART Instruments	227
CART Domains	228
Analysis of a CART Application	228
Overview of Application	228
CART Assessment Survey Results	229
Best, Worst, or Ugly Case?	229
Implications of Lessons Learned	233
Summary and Conclusions	233
Questions for Discussion	234
Acknowledgments	234
Additional Reading	234
References	235

Chapter Goals

After studying this chapter, readers should be able to

1. Distinguish between community resilience and personal resilience.
2. Describe the Communities Advancing Resilience Toolkit (CART), including the CART process, CART instruments, and CART domains.
3. Describe how CART has been used to enhance community resilience.
4. Explain the importance of community assessment, public engagement, and community resilience building for disaster management.

Introduction

Importance and Meaning of Resilience

Community resilience has emerged as both a vision for and a mechanism to support disaster readiness, response, and recovery. Resilience is defined differently in various disciplines (e.g., ecology, economics, engineering, geography, health, physical science, psychology, sociology) that use the concept in assorted contexts and for diverse purposes. Resilience can be defined as an attribute (e.g., ability or capacity), a process, and/or an outcome associated with successful adaptation to, and recovery from, adversity. For a discussion of differences in these definitions of resilience, see CARRI (2013) and R.L. Pfefferbaum (2014).

Differences between Personal and Community Resilience

Although both personal resilience and community resilience refer to successful adaptation to and recovery from adversity, community resilience is not simply a collection of personally resilient individuals responding individually to adversity. Community resilience requires deliberate, purposeful, collective activity; hence, a community of personally resilient individuals would not necessarily be resilient. For the community to be resilient, individuals must be able to work together in ways that support readiness, response, and recovery for the whole. According to Brown and Kulig (1996, p. 43), a community should be viewed as a dynamic interactive set of relations between individuals so that community resilience occurs when individuals "in communities are resilient together, not merely in similar ways." In addition, a community's social and physical conditions and structures must support individual and collective action so that resilience can emerge in the face of disaster (Brown and Kulig, 1996; B. Pfefferbaum et al., 2007; R.L. Pfefferbaum et al., 2008).

For many adversities in which the general public contributes to response and recovery efforts, the existence of personally resilient individuals will likely benefit others in the community. Such benefits are less likely to occur during a disaster that affects many members of the community if individuals focus primarily on themselves and their own families. Disasters overwhelm communities, requiring collective action as well as internal and external systems and services for response and recovery.

Just as the collection of personally resilient individuals does not ensure resilience of the community, a resilient community does not ensure the resilience of individual members. Although factors that contribute to community resilience may strengthen the personal resilience of some members (B. Pfefferbaum et al., 2007) (e.g., social and material support systems that address the needs of vulnerable members such as the poor and those with emotional and physical disabilities), the resilience of a community does not guarantee the resilience (or survival) of individual members. Communities may demonstrate resilience to disasters even when individual members do not.

Chapter Overview

This chapter describes the Communities Advancing Resilience Toolkit (CART) (R.L. Pfefferbaum et al., 2011, 2013b), a community intervention designed to enhance community resilience to disasters and other adversities through assessment, group processes, planning, and action. Developed by the Terrorism and Disaster Center (TDC), a member of the National Child Traumatic Stress Network, CART has been implemented in many communities. To illustrate the use of CART, one of these applications is described and analyzed. Lessons learned from CART applications and implications for emergency management are presented.

Description of the Communities Advancing Resilience Toolkit

Synopsis

The Communities Advancing Resilience Toolkit (CART) is one of few available interventions designed specifically to assess and build community resilience (Chandra et al., 2011). CART is publicly available, community driven, theory based, and evidence informed. The intervention has potential application in any community to foster community development and disaster preparedness. CART recognizes that resilience is a dynamic process that must be sustained over time to support healthy adaptation to new and ongoing stressors. Fortunately, resilience-enhancing skills can be learned and practiced, and resilience-supporting resources can be acquired and developed at individual (Butler et al., 2003) and community levels (McGee et al., 2009). The CART process and CART instruments provide the structure and avenues to information to guide analysis of community concerns from the perspective of resilience.

CART Process

The CART process, illustrated in Figure 13.1, engages community stakeholders in collecting and using assessment data to develop and implement strategies for building community resilience. CART may be implemented by stakeholders (referred to as CART users) who represent a homogeneous or heterogeneous mix of community leaders, neighborhood members, selected professionals, and representatives of community organizations convened by the local organizational sponsor of a CART application. Groups of participants (underlined in Figure 13.1) use various instruments to address and analyze the community at each stage of the process (shown in the boxes). Solid arrows in the figure represent data and information flows. At each stage, data and information flow from the community following the use of CART instruments. Data and information also flow from stage to stage as each stage builds on and augments work in earlier stages. Dotted arrows show the potential effects of CART activities on community members and relationships and on community resilience.

```
                                    ┌─────────────────────────────────┐
                                    │ 1. Generate a Community Profile │
                                    │    CART Sponsors and Partners    │
                                    │    CART assessment survey        │
                                    │    Key informant interviews      │
         ╭─────────────╮            │    Data collection framework     │
         │  Community  │            │    Other assessments             │
         │  Resilience │←─ ─ ─ ─ ─ ─└─────────────────────────────────┘
         ╰─────────────╯                         │
                                                 ↓
         Community              ┌─────────────────────────────────┐
         Members and  ←─ ─ ─ ─ ─│ 2. Refine the Profile            │
         Relationships          │    Community Work Groups         │
                                │    Community conversations       │
                                │    Neighborhood infrastructure maps │
                                │    Community ecological maps     │
                                │    Stakeholder analysis          │
                                │    SWOT analysis                 │
                                │    Capacity and vulnerability assessment │
                                │    Additional assessment         │
                                └─────────────────────────────────┘
                                                 │
   ┌────────────────────────┐    ┌─────────────────────────────────┐
   │ 4. Implement the Plan  │←───│ 3. Develop a Strategic Plan     │
   │    Community Leaders and Groups │ Community Planning Groups  │
   │    Dissemination and adoption   │ Goals and objectives       │
   │    Evaluation and refinement    │ Strategies and action plan │
   └────────────────────────┘    └─────────────────────────────────┘
```

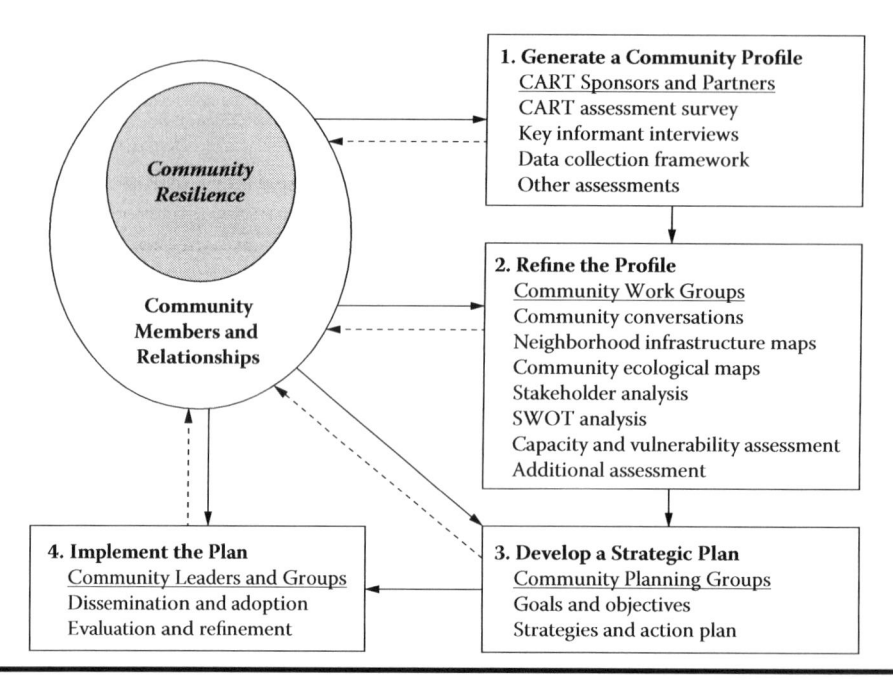

Figure 13.1 The CART process. The solid arrows show data and information flows. The dotted arrows show potential changes in or effects of the CART intervention on community members and relationships and on community resilience. (From Pfefferbaum, R.L. et al., *Communities Advancing Resilience Toolkit (CART): The CART Integrated System®*, Terrorism and Disaster Center, University of Oklahoma Health Sciences Center, Oklahoma City, OK, 2011.)

In the first stage of the process, CART users generate a preliminary community profile based on local demographics, CART assessment survey data, and information gathered through CART key informant interviews. Information from other assessments, which may be available from previous local, county, or state studies, can contribute to the profile. Such studies may have been conducted by a variety of community organizations, foundations, newspapers, public and private agencies, universities, or other entities. The collection of assessment data at this stage can be guided by the CART data collection framework (one of the CART instruments described below).

In the second stage, as they refine the profile, CART users may identify gaps in information that suggest the need for additional assessment. CART instruments for conducting community conversations, infrastructure mapping, ecological mapping of local relationships, stakeholder analysis, SWOT (strengths, weaknesses, opportunities, and threats) analysis, and capacity and vulnerability assessment, along with other group processes, can be used to identify and more completely analyze a community's needs and assets, threats and opportunities, and other internal and external considerations in community development and disaster management.

The third stage involves the development of a strategic plan, including the endorsement of goals and objectives, selection of activities to accomplish them, and creation of an action plan. Ideally, formal as well as informal community leaders participate in this stage. CART users may begin to identify goals, objectives, and strategies while refining the community profile, and they may recognize the need for additional assessments while developing strategies. Thus, stages two and three may overlap.

The fourth stage involves the adoption and implementation of the strategic plan. Typically, the first activity is to disseminate the plan among community members, organizations, and leaders which introduces additional people, with new ideas and suggestions, into the process. A strategy oversight group may be needed to decide if and how to incorporate the new ideas and suggestions, especially if these ideas and suggestions introduce conflict. Although dissemination may prolong the process, the introduction of new ideas and suggestions may improve the plan and garner the support of important community allies. Activities associated with gathering and incorporating new input can contribute to community resilience by bringing people together in discussions that reveal values, promote understanding, and foster collaboration. Action items should assign responsible parties, establish a timeline, and determine measures of success. Not every action will succeed. Some may prove to be undesirable, impractical, or ineffective; many may take years to complete; others may fail from neglect. The process should include an evaluation of each action item and outcomes of the plan.

Though ideally they would elect to do so, CART users need not complete all stages in the process. Flexibility is one of the strengths of the CART design. Even partial implementation of the process may generate information that enhances a community's resilience by helping to identify community issues, creating new relationships, and establishing cooperative ventures.

CART Instruments

The online version of CART (R.L. Pfefferbaum et al., 2011) includes the rationale, instructions, templates, and a discussion of special considerations for using the following instruments:

- *CART assessment survey*, which is a field-tested questionnaire for assessing a community's resilience
- *Key informant interviews*, which are designed to yield qualitative information from people who are knowledgeable about a community and/or an issue
- *Data collection framework*, which identifies the types and some sources of available data that may be used in strategic planning to build community resilience
- *Community conversations*, which involve the exchange of ideas, information, and opinions among individuals assumed to have useful knowledge about a specific issue
- *Neighborhood infrastructure maps*, which detail the physical infrastructure of a neighborhood with a focus on features and structures relevant for disaster management
- *Community ecological maps (eco-maps)*, which are visual tools for describing the nature and strength of relationships within a community
- *Stakeholder analysis*, which involves identifying individuals and entities with relevant influence, describing their influence, and creating strategies to gain their support and limit their opposition
- *SWOT analysis*, which assesses the internal strengths and weaknesses and the external opportunities and threats associated with an initiative or organization that can be used to develop strategies for maximizing and utilizing an organization's strengths, limiting and overcoming its weaknesses, identifying and exploiting its opportunities, and identifying and protecting against its threats
- *Capacity and vulnerability assessment*, which provides a framework for analyzing the long-term strengths and weaknesses of individuals and groups within a community which helps to determine the differential impact of a disaster on them

In addition, the online version of CART includes an appendix with questions addressing various aspects of community resilience, the CART domains (described below), terrorism preparedness, and public engagement. These questions can be used as part of key informant interviews, community conversations, or other assessment activities. They can be adapted to suit the community and type of disaster of concern to the user.

CART Domains

Early versions of the CART assessment survey were based on eight community resilience factors identified by R.L. Pfefferbaum et al. (2008) in their review of the community competence and capacity literature (Cottrell, 1976; Goeppinger and Baglioni, 1985; Goodman et al., 1998; Labonte and Laverack, 2001a,b; Gibbon et al., 2002). The eight factors are (1) connectedness, commitment, and shared values; (2) participation; (3) support and nurturance; (4) structure, roles, and responsibilities; (5) resources; (6) critical reflection and skill building; (7) communication; and (8) disaster management. Because these attributes overlapped and contained substantial interactions, they were refined through exploratory factor analysis conducted after each of four early CART survey field tests. These factor analyses identified four interrelated domains representing the foundation for the current version of the CART assessment survey (R.L. Pfefferbaum et al., 2013a):

- *Connection and caring*, which includes participation, relatedness, shared values, support and nurturance, equity, justice, hope, and diversity
- *Resources*, which includes natural, physical, information, human, social, and financial resources
- *Transformative potential*, which derives from the ability of a community to frame collective experiences, collect and analyze relevant data, assess performance, and build skills
- *Disaster management*, which addresses prevention and mitigation, preparedness, response, and recovery.

Communication is an attribute associated with all four domains.

Analysis of a CART Application

Overview of Application

In this application, the CART assessment survey was conducted as a partnership between TDC and a faith-based nonprofit organization that seeks to restore the foundation of safe and caring communities by rebuilding a system of caring relationships. Survey and follow-up activities were implemented in five high-poverty neighborhoods of a southern United States metropolitan area that serves as a regional commercial and cultural center. Based on U.S. 2000 census data (U.S. Census Bureau, 2000), poverty rates for the five neighborhoods were estimated by the local CART partner to range from 16 to 65%, and unemployment rates were estimated to range from 28 to 68%. In accordance with instructions for administering the CART assessment survey, TDC worked with staff from the local partner to define the neighborhoods to be surveyed and to develop additional survey items of particular importance to them. Trained staff and volunteers interviewed community residents ($N = 352$) at their homes in late 2008. Missing data for 12% of the total sample resulted in a sample of 309 participants with complete data. Most of the sample was female (66%), African American (83%), 30 to 59 years of age (55%), and unmarried (76%) (R.L. Pfefferbaum et al., 2013a).

CART Assessment Survey Results

Table 13.1 displays results associated with individual community resilience survey items and domains for the five neighborhoods. Relative strengths for the community are associated with survey items with the greatest percentage agreement, defined for this sample as greater than 80% agreement. Relative strengths for the five poverty neighborhoods suggest that people feel like they belong (84.47% agreement), help each other (81.88% agreement), and have hope about the future (80.26% agreement). All three strengths are within the connection and caring domain. Relative challenges for the community are associated with survey items with the least percentage agreement, defined for this sample as less than 70% agreement. Relative challenges for the five poverty neighborhoods are associated with survey items indicating that the community has the resources it needs to take care of its problems (59.22% agreement), actively prepares for future disasters (66.67% agreement), has effective leaders (67.64% agreement), and develops skills and finds resources to solve its problems and reach its goals (69.58% agreement) along with survey items indicating that people are able to get the services they need (66.99% agreement) and know where to go to get things done (67.64% agreement).

It is understandable that the greatest percentage agreement is associated with the connection and caring domain and the lowest with the resources domain. At the time of the survey, the local TDC partner involved in this CART application had been active within the metropolitan area for more than a decade, building personal relationships, operating neighborhood centers, and providing various programs and services that connected residents to their neighborhoods, demonstrated commitment and fair treatment, engendered hope, and fostered helping behavior among residents, all of which contribute to connection and caring. Chronically high poverty rates within the five neighborhoods suggest that resources for local problem solving, leadership, and knowledge of and access to services would be limited, thereby resulting in relatively low endorsement of survey items associated with the resources domain.

Best, Worst, or Ugly Case?

As a best case, CART is designed to utilize and advance the resilience of a participating community. CART users learn about their community and generate sources of information while engaging in meaningful communication, clarifying issues, and addressing problems. Critical analysis based on a commitment to shared values and community development is required for strategic planning. The implementation of action plans, which typically engages additional individuals and organizations, increases participation and encourages connection. CART promotes social and human capital development by engaging community members in a process through which they learn about their community, gain an appreciation of roles and responsibilities, and examine local issues.

The CART process helps communities to examine their strengths and challenges and to identify ways to use their assets to address problems. Clearly, communities that lack individual and communal resources, engaged members, and able leadership will face greater problems in undertaking community development and disaster management than will communities that are better endowed. Nonetheless, focusing on assets recognizes that community development is enhanced when community members invest themselves and their resources in local development efforts (Kretzmann and McKnight, 1993). The CART process creates a consciousness of community resilience, reinforces the notion that resilience can be cultivated, and emphasizes the importance of intentional collective action in promoting community well-being over time. The CART process also calls attention to the importance of disaster management in the long-term viability of a community.

Table 13.1 CART Findings for Five Poverty Neighborhoods of a U.S. Metropolitan Area

CART Domains	Survey Items[a]	% Agree[b]
Connection and caring		
	People in my neighborhood feel like they belong to the neighborhood.	80.26
	People in my neighborhood are committed to the well-being of the neighborhood.	84.47
	People in my neighborhood have hope about the future.	77.35
	People in my neighborhood help each other.	80.26
	My neighborhood treats people fairly no matter what their background is.	81.88
Resources		77.35
	My neighborhood has the resources it needs to take care of neighborhood problems (resources include money, information, technology, tools, raw materials, and services).	65.37
	My neighborhood has effective leaders.	59.22
	People in my neighborhood are able to get the services they need.	67.64
	People in my neighborhood know where to go to get things done.	66.99
Transformative potential		67.64
	My neighborhood works with organizations and agencies outside the neighborhood to get things done.	72.57
		75.40

(Continued)

Table 13.1 (Continued) CART Findings for Five Poverty Neighborhoods of a U.S. Metropolitan Area

CART Domains	Survey Items[a]	% Agree[b]
	People in my neighborhood communicate with leaders who can help improve the neighborhood.	72.17
	People in my neighborhood are aware of neighborhood issues that they might address together.	75.08
	People in my neighborhood discuss issues so they can improve the neighborhood.	70.55
	People in my neighborhood work together on solutions so that the neighborhood can improve.	70.55
	My neighborhood looks at its successes and failures so it can learn from the past.	75.08
	My neighborhood develops skills and finds resources to solve its problems and reach its goals.	69.58
	My neighborhood has priorities and sets goals for the future.	72.17
Disaster management		71.52
	My neighborhood tries to prevent disasters.	75.40
	My neighborhood actively prepares for future disasters.	66.67
	My neighborhood can provide emergency services during a disaster.	72.49
	My neighborhood has services and programs to help people after a disaster.	71.52

[a] Response options: 0, no opinion; 1, very strongly disagree; 2, strongly disagree; 3, disagree; 4, agree; 5, strongly agree; 6, very strongly agree.

[b] Calculations for % agree: Agreement required responses of 4, 5, or 6; responses of 0, 1, 2, and 3 were considered not to agree. The sample for these calculations excluded respondents who failed to answer one or more items. Calculations do not include "no opinion" responses. N = 309.

Although the CART application described above did not involve a random sample (ideal for research studies), it could reasonably be considered a best case in terms of its contributions to community resilience. As described below, these contributions included increased connections; skill development; improved awareness of local concerns, disaster preparedness, and community resilience; and the introduction of readiness, response, and coping interventions into the community.

Consistent with its focus on relationships and skill development, the local CART sponsor chose to train its staff and volunteers from each of the five neighborhoods to conduct survey interviews. Curricula and initial training, provided by TDC as part of the TDC Disaster Research Training Program (B. Pfefferbaum et al., 2010), included instruction in principles of disaster research, survey interviewing, focus group facilitation, community resilience, and CART. The local CART sponsor has contributed to the sustainability of its efforts by continuing to train locally as needed for ongoing and new projects. The sponsor subsequently also has used interview surveys for other efforts, providing opportunities for trainees to use their new skills and generating additional assessment data.

The CART community conversations held in each of the five neighborhoods to discuss survey results revealed an interest on the part of the sponsor's staff and community residents to know more about their neighborhoods. This interest was evidenced by participants' earnest review of survey findings, their input into the interpretation of these findings, and their requests for more detailed information about their neighborhoods. Residents demonstrated knowledge of their neighborhoods, interest in local concerns, and disappointment in the lack of involvement of some of their neighbors. Residents also participated in preliminary problem solving, sharing information about existing efforts to address local concerns and discussing how neighborhoods could assist each other.

The CART process revealed a need for interventions in neighborhood preparedness, response, and child coping and resilience. These needs led to the development and implementation of TDC's Neighborhood Preparedness Screen (R.L. Pfefferbaum, 2010), which was implemented in conjunction with a Department of Justice grant to the CART sponsor to develop and field test a model for emergency, terrorism, and disaster preparedness. The Neighborhood Preparedness Screen addresses personal, family, and community preparedness; willingness and ability to assist neighbors and to be trained; and personal exposure to disasters. Psychological first aid (PFA) training (e.g., Brymer et al., 2006; Schreiber and Gurwitch, 2006; ARC, 2012) was provided for the CART sponsor's staff and neighborhood residents who were previously unfamiliar with PFA, basic PFA principles, and the delivery of core PFA actions. Working with neighborhood residents and the sponsor's staff, TDC also implemented a Resilience and Coping Intervention (RCI) (Allen, 2011) for children. RCI couples a strengths-based child assessment with a skill-enhancing group coping exercise (Allen et al., 1999; Allen and Dlugokinski, 2002) which can be administered in a single session and repeated as indicated. RCI helps children to identify thoughts and feelings related to psychological, behavioral, and relationship issues following a traumatic or other problematic experience and to identify appropriate and successful coping strategies. Neighborhood preparedness surveying, PFA training, and RCI sessions could have occurred independent of the CART application, but it was the leadership of a committed organizational sponsor and the engagement of local residents in the CART process that clarified the need for and interest in these additional interventions, in addition to facilitating their implementation. Thus, CART demonstrated its ability to serve as a vehicle for delivering programs, services, and interventions to communities.

Implications of Lessons Learned

Community resilience has emerged over the last decade as a construct in disaster management that is viewed alternatively as a goal or as a mechanism for achieving readiness, response, and recovery. It requires professionals and policymakers to generate strategies for building disaster-resilient communities as part of disaster management efforts. R.L. Pfefferbaum (2014) described seven general strategies for building community resilience to disasters: (1) know the community and share that knowledge, (2) bolster connections, (3) stimulate asset-based community development, (4) foster economic development, (5) adopt a holistic wellness focus, (6) undertake effective disaster management, and (7) create a consciousness of community resilience. She also identified guiding methodological principles for the implementation of these strategies: to involve a breadth of community stakeholders as appropriate, to build awareness and consensus when possible, and to empower community members to take action when feasible.

The CART process is guided by these methodological principles, and, depending on decisions made by CART users, the community-driven intervention potentially addresses the recommended strategies. The CART application described above demonstrates that the CART process can (1) use community assessment to prompt and facilitate asset-based community development, (2) initiate and reinforce community connections, (3) contribute to disaster management, and (4) create a consciousness of community resilience.

Lessons learned from CART implementation in a variety of communities (R.L. Pfefferbaum et al., 2013c) attest to the following implications for disaster management:

- Public engagement can generate direct and indirect benefits for disaster management. Participation of community members can stimulate an interest in community concerns and heighten awareness of local threats and vulnerabilities and disaster preparedness.
- Community assessment is essential for effectively managing disasters and building community resilience. Information acquired through assessment can help emergency managers and community leaders to detail community assets, challenges, opportunities, and threats.
- Communities can be remarkably resourceful when fortified with appropriate information, tools, and training. Awareness of community assets, as well as needs, can help to guide community member involvement in problem solving and may encourage greater personal investment in community progress with concomitant gains for community resilience.
- Efforts to build community resilience in the context of a variety of adversities can benefit disaster management if such efforts involve meaningful collective action on the part of community members to transform their environment or if they create local conditions and structures that support readiness, response, and recovery. That is, efforts to build community resilience need not focus on disasters *per se* in order to benefit disaster management.

Summary and Conclusions

Community resilience is a construct that both supports and necessitates disaster management. CART is a publicly available, community-driven, theory-based, and evidence-informed intervention designed to assess and build community resilience to disasters. The CART process involves assessment, feedback, planning, and action. Available instruments include a field-tested community resilience assessment survey and other assessment and analytic tools. The implementation of

CART can increase awareness of and contribute to the resilience of participating communities by establishing and positively reinforcing relationships built on mutual respect and benefit and by improving the capacity for meaningful collective action in support of readiness, response, and recovery. Although time and labor intensive, community participation in the CART process contributes to the development of human and social capital, both of which are essential to community resilience. The collaboration, skill building, resource sharing, and meaningful action that are part of a successful CART experience should increase the transformative potential of a community.

Questions for Discussion

1. The CART process involves community users in assessment, feedback, planning, and action, which typically are time and labor intensive. What are the advantages for community resilience? Could these advantages accrue through other processes? Explain.
2. Discuss how implementing the CART process can contribute to the four CART domains: connection and caring, resources, transformative potential, and disaster management.
3. Note that communication is an attribute associated with each of the four CART domains. Discuss its role in each of the domains. Why is communication important in community resilience and disaster management?
4. The CART assessment survey can be administered by interview (over the telephone or in person), online, or in written formant (delivered in person or via postal or electronic mail). What are the pros and cons of each of these approaches to administering the survey? What issues should be considered in determining which method is most likely to engage local community members? Why are these issues relevant?

Acknowledgments

The Communities Advancing Resilience Toolkit (CART) was developed by the Terrorism and Disaster Center (TDC), located at the University of Oklahoma Health Sciences Center, Oklahoma City, Oklahoma. TDC is a partner in the National Child Traumatic Stress Network (NCTSN), which is funded by the Substance Abuse and Mental Health Services Administration (SAMHSA), U.S. Department of Health and Human Services (USDHHS). Support for the development of CART also was provided by the National Consortium for the Study of Terrorism and Responses to Terrorism (START), located at the University of Maryland, College Park, Maryland, which is funded by the U.S. Department of Homeland Security (USDHS), and by the Centers for Disease Control and Prevention (CDC). The findings, conclusions, opinions, and contents of this chapter are those of the author and do not represent the official position of the CDC, NCTSN, SAMHSA, START, TDC, USDHHS, or USDHS.

Additional Reading

Aldrich, D.P. (2012). *Building Resilience: Social Capital in Post-Disaster Recovery*. Chicago, IL: University of Chicago Press.
Bruneau, M., Chang, S.E., Eguchi, R.T., Lee, G.C., O'Rourke, T.D. et al. (2003). A framework to quantitatively assess and enhance the seismic resilience of communities. *Earthquake Spectra*, 19(4): 733–752.

Cutter, S.L., Barnes, L., Berry, M., Burton, C., Evans, E., Tate, E., and Webb, J. (2008). *Community and Regional Resilience: Perspectives from Hazards, Disasters, and Emergency Management*, CARRI Research Report 1. Oak Ridge, TN: Community and Regional Resilience Institute (http://www.resilientus.org/publications/research-reports/).

Longstaff, P.H. (2005). *Security, Resilience, and Communication in Unpredictable Environments Such as Terrorism, Natural Disasters, and Complex Technology*. Cambridge, MA: Program on Information Resources Policy, Harvard University (http://www.pirp.harvard.edu/pubs_pdf/longsta/longsta-p05-3.pdf).

Norris, F.H., Stevens, S.P., Pfefferbaum, B., Wyche, K.F., and Pfefferbaum, R.L. (2008). Community resilience as a metaphor, theory, set of capacities, and strategy for disaster readiness. *Am. J. Commun. Psychol.*, 41: 127–150.

UNISDR. (2012). *How to Make Cities More Resilient: A Handbook for Local Government Leaders*. Geneva: U.N. International Strategy for Disaster Reduction (http://www.unisdr.org/campaign/resilientcities/toolkit/handbook).

UNDP, UNEP, World Bank, and World Resources Institute. (2008). *World Resources 2008: Roots of Resilience—Growing the Wealth of the Poor*. Washington, DC: WRI (http://www.wri.org/publication/world-resources-2008).

References

Allen, S.F. (2011). *Resilience and Coping Intervention Guide: Listen to the Children (RCI-Child)*. Oklahoma City, OK: Terrorism and Disaster Center, University of Oklahoma Health Sciences Center (http://www.oumedicine.com/TDC).

Allen, S.F. and Dlugokinski, E.L. (2002). Assisting children in recovering from a traumatic community event. *Dir. Clin. Couns. Psychol.*, 12(1): 1–11.

Allen, S.F., Dlugokinski, E.L., Cohen, L.A., and Walker, J.L. (1999). Assessing the impact of a traumatic community event on children and assisting with their healing. *Psychiat. Ann.*, 29(2): 93–98.

ARC. (2012). *Psychological First Aid: Helping Others in Times of Stress (Instructor's Manual)*, revised ed. Washington, DC: American Red Cross.

Brown, D.D. and Kulig, J.C. (1996). The concept of resiliency: theoretical lessons from community research. *Health Can. Soc.*, 4(1): 29–50.

Brymer, M., Jacobs, A., Layne, C., Pynoos, R., Ruzek, J., Steinberg, A., Vernberg, E., and Watson, P. (2006). *Psychological First Aid: Field Operations Guide*, 2nd ed. Los Angeles, CA: National Child Traumatic Stress Network and National Center for PTSD (http://www.nctsn.org/content/psychological-first-aid).

Butler, L.D., Hobfoll, S.E., and Keane, T.M. (2003). *Fostering Resilience in Response to Terrorism: A Fact Sheet for Psychologists Working With Adults*. Washington, DC: American Psychological Association Task Force on Resilience in Response to Terrorism (http://deep.med.miami.edu/x427.xml).

CARRI. (2013). *Definitions of Community Resilience: An Analysis*. Oak Ridge, TN: Community and Regional Resilience Institute (http://www.resilientus.org/publications/resilience-publications/).

Chandra, A., Acosta, J., Stern, S., Uscher-Pines, L., Williams, M.V., Yeung, D., Garnett, J., and Meredith, L.S. (2011). *Building Community Resilience to Disasters: A Way Forward to Enhance National Health Security*, Report TR-915-DHHS. Santa Monica, CA: Rand Corporation (http://www.rand.org/content/dam/rand/pubs/technical_reports/2011/RAND_TR915.pdf).

Cottrell, Jr., L.S. (1976). The competent community. In Kaplan, B.H., Wilson, R.N., and Leighton, A.H., Eds., *Further Explorations in Social Psychiatry*, pp. 195–209. New York: Basic Books.

Gibbon, M., Labonte, R., and Laverack, G. (2002). Evaluating community capacity. *Health Soc. Care Comm.*, 10(6): 485–491.

Goeppinger, J. and Baglioni, Jr., A.J. (1985). Community competence: a positive approach to needs assessment. *Am. J. Comm. Psychol.*, 13(5): 507–523.

Goodman, R.M., Speers, M.A., McLeroy, K., Fawcett, S., Kegler, M. et al. (1998). Identifying and defining the dimensions of community capacity to provide a basis for measurement. *Health Educ. Behav.*, 25(3): 258–278.

Kretzmann, J.P. and McKnight, J.L. (1993). *Building Communities from the Inside Out: A Path Toward Finding and Mobilizing a Community's Assets.* Chicago, IL: ACTA Publications.

Labonte, R. and Laverack, G. (2001a). Capacity building in health promotion. Part 1. For whom? And for what purpose? *Crit. Public Health*, 11(2): 111–127.

Labonte, R. and Laverack, G. (2001b). Capacity building in health promotion. Part 2. Whose use? And with what measurement? *Crit. Public Health*, 11(2): 129–138.

McGee, S., Bott, C., Gupta, V., Jones, K., and Karr, A. (2009). *Public Role and Engagement in Counterterrorism Efforts: Implications of Israeli Practices for the U.S.: Final Report.* Arlington, VA: Homeland Security Institute (http://www.hstoday.us/images/public_role_in_ct_israeli_practices_task_08-22.pdf).

Pfefferbaum, B., Reissman, D.B., Pfefferbaum, R.L., Klomp, R.W., and Gurwitch, R.H. (2007). Building resilience to mass trauma events. In Doll, L.S., Bonzo, S.E., Sleet, D.A., Mercy, J.A., and Haas, E.N., Eds., *Handbook of Injury and Violence Prevention*, pp. 347–358. New York: Springer.

Pfefferbaum, B., Houston, J.B., Reyes, G., Steinberg, A.M., Pynoos, R.S., Fairbank, J.A., Brymer, M.J., and Maida, C.A. (2010). Building national capacity for child and family disaster mental health research. *Prof. Psychol. Res. Pract.*, 41(1): 26–33.

Pfefferbaum, R.L. (2010). *Neighborhood Preparedness Screen.* Oklahoma City, OK: Terrorism and Disaster Center, University of Oklahoma Health Sciences Center (http://www.oumedicine.com/psychiatry/research/terrorism-and-disaster-center/products).

Pfefferbaum, R.L. (2014). Advancing community resilience to disasters: considerations for theory, policy, and practice. In Farazmand, A., Ed., *Crisis and Emergency Management: Theory and Practice*, 2nd ed., pp. 691–710. New York: CRC Press.

Pfefferbaum, R.L., Reissman, D.B., Pfefferbaum, B., Wyche, K.F., Norris, F.H., and Klomp, R.W. (2008). Factors in the development of community resilience to disasters. In Blumenfield, M. and Ursano, R.J., Eds., *Intervention and Resilience after Mass Trauma*, pp. 49–68. Cambridge, UK: Cambridge University Press.

Pfefferbaum, R.L., Pfefferbaum, B., and Van Horn, R.L. (2011). *Communities Advancing Resilience Toolkit (CART): The CART Integrated System®.* Oklahoma City, OK: Terrorism and Disaster Center, University of Oklahoma Health Sciences Center (http://www.oumedicine.com/TDC).

Pfefferbaum, R.L., Neas, B.R., Pfefferbaum, B., Norris, F.H., and Van Horn, R.L. (2013a). The Communities Advancing Resilience Toolkit (CART): development of a survey instrument to assess community resilience. *Int. J. Emerg. Ment. Health*, 15(1): 15–30.

Pfefferbaum, R.L., Pfefferbaum, B., Van Horn, R.L., Klomp, R.W., Norris, F.H., and Reissman, D.B. (2013b). The Communities Advancing Resilience Toolkit (CART): an intervention to build community resilience to disasters. *J. Public Health Manage. Pract.*, 19(3): 250–258.

Pfefferbaum, R.L., Pfefferbaum, B., Van Horn, R.L., Neas, B.R., and Houston, J.B. (2013c). Building community resilience to disasters: CART® applications. *J. Emerg. Manage.*, 11(2): 151–159.

Schreiber, M. and Gurwitch, R.H. (2006). *Listen, Protect, and Connect: Psychological First Aid for Children and Parents.* Los Angeles: School of Public Health, University of California (http://www.ready.gov/sites/default/files/documents/files/PFA_Parents.pdf).

U.S. Census Bureau. (2000). *United States Census 2000.* Washington, DC: U.S. Census Bureau (http://www.census.gov/main/www/cen2000.html).

Chapter 14

Learning from Transboundary Crises and Disasters: The 2010 Haiti Earthquake

Alka Sapat and Ann-Margaret Esnard

Contents

Chapter Goals	238
Chapter Purpose	238
Introduction	238
Defining Crises and Disasters	239
Theoretical Foundations: Transboundary Crises and Disasters	240
Transboundary Crises: Macro-, Meso-, and Microlevel Effects	241
Diasporas as Transnational Policy Actors	242
Haitian Diaspora in the United States	243
Case Study and Methodology	244
2010 Haiti Earthquake	244
Research Design	244
Transboundary Effects of the 2010 Haiti Earthquake on Diaspora Organizations and Networks	245
Macro- and Mesolevel Changes in Institutions and Policy	245
Changes in U.S. Immigration Policy	245
Mobilization of Diaspora Organizations and the Rise of Emergent Umbrella Organizations	246
Provision of New Venues for Policy Change and Participation	247
Microlevel Effects	247
Change in Attitude by the Haitian Government Toward the Diaspora	247
Diaspora Sentiments and Attitudes	248
Management of the Haiti Disaster from Within and Outside	249
Sheltering and Housing	250
Recovery and Rebuilding	250

Learning from the 2010 Haiti Earthquake 252
Conclusion...253
Questions for Discussion..253
Acknowledgments 253
Additional Reading 254
References 254

Chapter Goals

After studying this chapter, readers should be able to

1. Understand what is meant by a "transboundary crisis" and describe its component attributes.
2. Explain what is meant by a diaspora organization and describe activities undertaken by some diaspora organizations.
3. Describe formal and informal transnational networks and the ways in which these networks play a role in transboundary events.
4. Understand the impact of the 2010 Haiti earthquake.
5. Understand that the management of catastrophic disasters is sometimes led from outside the impacted country and understand the implications of externally driven disaster management.
6. Understand how local, national, and international institutions can leverage the power of diaspora organizations.

Chapter Purpose

In an increasingly globalized world, crises and disasters have repercussions not just within the nation-states in which they occur; their impacts may also be felt beyond national and other boundaries. However, there is a lacuna in research on understanding the linkages between disasters and crises, their transboundary effects, and transnational advocacy groups. The purpose of this chapter is to fill this gap by focusing on the 2010 earthquake in Haiti as a transboundary crisis and using this as a case study to look at the lessons that can be learned from this event to improve the management of such events from both outside and within. Haiti "had displacement levels equivalent to 19 per cent of its total population (1.9 million people) during the years 2008 to 2012—the highest relative level of displacement experienced by any country" (IDMC, 2013, p. 7). Our findings show that diaspora coalitions in South Florida, Boston, New York, and Atlanta played a vital role in the post-disaster recovery period. These coalitions maintain formal and informal transnational networks that are social, economic, and political in nature. Additionally, coalition resources, behavior, and attitudes showed signs of change after the earthquake.

Introduction

Crises or disasters have been analyzed as focusing events that open windows of opportunity for policy entrepreneurs, interest groups, and coalitions to push for policy change (Birkland, 2006). Disaster research primarily focuses on the effects of crises and disasters on these groups and policy actors at a local, state, or national level. However, in a rapidly globalizing world, crises or disasters

Learning from Transboundary Crises and Disasters: The 2010 Haiti Earthquake ■ 239

have repercussions not just within the nation-states in which they occur; their impacts may also be felt beyond nation-state boundaries. For example, the 2004 Indian Ocean tsunami affected thousands of people in coastal communities and tourists, businesses, and other groups around the world. The 2010 earthquake in Haiti resulted in the displacement of survivors across Haiti and into the United States and other countries. The 2011 Tohuku earthquake and its effects within Japan disrupted supply chains around the world and spread fears of nuclear radiation far beyond its borders. More recently, the Ebola outbreak originated in one part of the world but within a short span of a few months had global repercussions due to fears of a potential epidemic. Overall, although scholarly research on disasters and disaster recovery has steadily grown in the last few decades (e.g., Dynes, 1970; Quarantelli, 1983; Mileti, 1999; Birkland, 2006; Smith and Wenger, 2006; Oliver-Smith, 2009; Nohrstedt, 2010; Nohrstedt and Weible, 2010; Smith, 2011), there is still a gap in the research on understanding the linkages between disasters and crises and between disasters and their transnational and transboundary effects, including their effects on transnational actors and advocacy groups such as diasporas.

The purpose of this chapter is to fill this gap by focusing on the 2010 earthquake in Haiti as a transboundary crisis and using this as a case study to look at the role played by diaspora groups and networks in transboundary events. Our findings show that more attention needs to be paid to transboundary crises and disasters and the role played by transnational groups such as diaspora coalitions. Diaspora groups have and maintain formal and informal transnational networks that are social, economic, and political in nature and can be leveraged by local, national, and international institutions. The case study also reveals insights about the management of the Haiti earthquake and the lessons that can be learned from this disaster.

We begin by first briefly defining the terms *crises* and *disasters*, followed by a discussion of the theoretical understandings and definitions of transboundary crises and disasters. We then focus on the 2010 Haiti earthquake as an example of a transboundary disaster. We also provide some background and context on diaspora groups and the Haitian–American diaspora, along with a brief history of Haitian–American relations and on the 2010 Haiti earthquake. Next, we discuss the effects of this transboundary disaster on formal and informal groups and networks, including institutional and attitudinal changes. We then discuss how the management of the response and recovery process is being handled from within and outside Haiti. Finally, we discuss some of the lessons learned from this Haiti case and the implications of this study.

Defining Crises and Disasters

The terms *crises*, *disasters*, and *catastrophes* are defined in myriad ways in the disaster literature (Perry and Quarantelli, 2005; Birkland, 2006; Quarantelli, 2006; Boin and Rhinard, 2008) but remain contested terms generating much debate on the ways in which they are similar and yet different. In the transboundary crisis literature, the term *crisis* is defined as "a threat to core values or life-sustaining systems, which requires an urgent response under conditions of deep uncertainty" (Boin and Rhinard, 2008, p. 3). In this research, a "transboundary crisis is when the functioning of multiple, life-sustaining systems is acutely threatened" (Boin and Rhinard, 2008, p. 4). A *disaster* is in turn defined as a "crisis with a bad ending" and "thus involves a normative judgment concerning the crisis outcome" (Boin and Rhinard, 2008, p. 3). Within the discussion of focusing events, Birkland (2006, pp. 2–3) relies on Faulkner's (2001) distinctions between crisis and catastrophe, where a crisis is defined as being "induced by the actions or inactions of an organization" and disasters are a result of "induced natural phenomena or external human action." The U.S. Federal Emergency

Management Agency (FEMA) defines a catastrophic incident as "… any natural or manmade incident, including terrorism, that results in extraordinary levels of mass casualties, damage, or disruption severely affecting the population, infrastructure, environment, economy, national morale, and/or government functions" (DHS, 2008, p. 42). Quarantelli (2006) noted that catastrophes require some different kinds of planning and management than major disasters, and that the differences between disasters and catastrophes can be especially seen at the organizational, community, and societal levels. Some specific ways in which these differences are highlighted include the severity and extent of the impact; local officials being overwhelmed; nearby communities being unable to assist; everyday community functions severely interrupted; the amount and extent of coverage by national mass media; and the involvement of the national government and top-level officials. Given the conceptual contestation in the literature and because our focus in this research is on immediate organizational responses and on long-term actions taken to respond to a natural phenomenon, we use both terms, crisis and disaster, for the Haiti earthquake.

Theoretical Foundations: Transboundary Crises and Disasters

Transboundary crises and disasters affect populations and groups beyond their borders. The disruptive nature of such crises and the ways in which they are perceived, framed, and managed by policymakers, leaders, and citizenry of affected nation-states requires deeper understanding by disaster and policy researchers (Clifford, 1956; Rosenthal, 1990; Scanlon, 1994; Rosenthal and 't Hart, 1998; Wachtendorf, 2000; Boin and Sundelius, 2007). More recently, there has been greater attention paid to this phenomenon and its implications, particularly in the context of crises and disasters that extend beyond politically and socially constructed borders (Wachtendorf, 2000, 2009; Boin and Rhinard, 2008; Boin, 2009a,b; Ansell et al., 2010).

Some of this work has focused on defining the concept of crises that cross boundaries; for example, Quarantelli et al. (2006) coined the term *trans-system social ruptures* (TSSRs) to refer to events that reach beyond societal boundaries and disrupt multiple social systems. Characteristics of TSSRs by this definition are that they spread quickly, initially have no known central or clear point of origin, have impacts that extend across national political boundaries, potentially impact a large number of people, lead to emergent behavior, and do not lend themselves to local-level solutions (Quarantelli et al., 2006).

Wachtendorf (2009) extended research on TSSRs to look at the effects of them not only on national systems as envisaged by Quarantelli et al. (2006) but also on the transnational systems. She discussed transnational systems as mutually dependent cross-border systems such as healthcare, trade, and transportation, using the example of such systems between Canada and the United States, and also argued that the extent of the linkages between national and transnational systems and TSSRs impact the vulnerability and resilience of the systems themselves. In discussing areas for future theoretical development, Wachtendorf (2009, p. 390) observed that, "TSSRs are about significant cross-system disruption and about the people who occupy distinct national or transnational systems." This point is directly relevant to our research as we seek to understand the groups that occupy transnational systems and how they understand and frame crises and disasters to advocate for policy change.

Boin (2009b) has also furthered our understanding in this area by defining transboundary crises as those that cross both geographical and functional boundaries, overwhelming organizations that are designed with traditional crises and disasters in mind. To explore this concept further, Boin and Ekengren (2009) studied the capacity of institutions to deal with transboundary crises, focusing in particular on the European Union (EU). They noted that, although capacities to deal with transboundary crises have grown within the EU, this development has also been marked by fragmentation and many obstacles. Similarly, Herman and Dayton (2009) analyzed the decision-making challenges that transboundary crises pose to crisis leaders and argued that the manner in which decision-makers perceive unfolding events informs the crisis decision-making process. Boin and Rhinard (2008) and Boin (2009b) also noted that, with tighter economic, political, and societal linkages increasingly driven by technology, the potential for transboundary crises increases.

Other related policy research also helps in fostering the idea of policies extending beyond neat boundaries. For example, discussions of boundary-spanning policies and "messy policies" (May et al., 2009; Jochim and May, 2010) and trans-subsystems (Jones and Jenkins-Smith, 2009) support the notion of transboundary effects that extend beyond a single policy subsystem. Similarly, some past research has also sought to understand the transnational aspirations of groups. Litfin (2000) applied the advocacy coalition framework (ACF) to understand the transnational aspirations of advocacy coalitions, and Hirschi and Widmer (2010) sought to understand the influence of coalitions in foreign policy. Litfin (2000) concluded that advocacy coalitions should be understood as operating increasingly along a domestic–foreign frontier as globalization and the internationalization of environmental affairs blur the distinction between some policy subsystems and the international arena, a concept that is useful to understandings in this chapter.

Past research on transboundary and trans-system ruptures has also examined the impacts of these on national and transnational systems (Quarantelli et al., 2006; Wachtendorf, 2009), on leaders and institutions (Boin, 2009b; Boin and Ekengren, 2009), and on capacities and tools (Santella et al., 2009) to respond to these crises. However, it is still an area that is, as described by Boin (2009b), *terra incognita*. To explore this area further, we examine the case of the Haiti earthquake as a *transboundary crisis and disaster*, which we view or define in this chapter as affecting both national and transnational communities of interest. We also seek to fill some of the gaps in knowledge by focusing on the impact of transnational crises and disasters on an area that has not hitherto been the subject of much research either in disaster studies or public policy—that is, the impact of such transboundary crises and disasters on *transnational actors and groups*, in particular on diasporas groups and actors.

Transboundary Crises: Macro-, Meso-, and Microlevel Effects

Transboundary crises and disasters may be varied in size, scope, intensity, and saliency; consequently, we suggest that their effects could potentially range from those at the macro-level to more microlevel effects. Macrolevel transboundary effects of disasters/crises could be those that affect broader policies or phenomena—for example, disruptions of global supply chains or effects that engender changes in national foreign policies to an event. Mesolevel transboundary effects may also ensue; we envisage these as those affecting institutions and possibly mesolevel economic, legal, and social policies within nation-states and across them. Examples of mesolevel effects are when the U.S. Centers for Disease Control (CDC) has responded to the threat of Ebola in Africa and its potential spread to the United States or when the U.S. Department of Agriculture (USDA) responded to the mad cow crisis in Europe. Other instances are when a country may change its internal laws and policies to deal with displaced survivors immigrating to their country following a disaster. Mesolevel transboundary effects can also be found at the group level, such as the actions taken by transnational advocacy groups in response to a transboundary crisis event, such as the reactions of Greenpeace International to the Fukushima nuclear crisis. Microlevel effects are those that affect individual behavior. Effects on and responses by individuals to transboundary crises such as fears of eating contaminated beef during the mad cow crisis or voicing their protest against nuclear power stations after the fallout that occurred after Fukushima are some examples of microlevel effects.

Although we categorize transboundary crises and disasters into these three levels, a caveat is also needed here. These levels presented here are by no means an exhaustive set of possibilities; these are primarily a categorization to allow us to structure our thinking, distinguish between the potential effects of transboundary crises and disasters, and to situate the focus of this chapter, which will be on meso- and microlevel effects of such events. These effects are explored within the context of the 2010 Haiti earthquake in terms of their impact on transnational groups and actors—in this case, the Haitian–American diaspora.

Diasporas as Transnational Policy Actors

The term *diaspora* for the purposes of this chapter simply refers to Haitian emigrants who have settled in the United in the last decades.* Diaspora groups are sometimes viewed as being synonymous with ethnic groups or are seen as a subsection of ethnic immigrants (Ambrosio, 2002); however, their deep connections to their homelands and their transnational activities make the term *diaspora* more indicative of their identities. As noted by Hall (1990) and Anthias (1998), diaspora involves a conception of identity that avoids the essentialism associated with much of the discussion on ethnic and cultural identities and refocuses attention on their role in transnational processes and commonalities. Sheffer (2003, pp. 9–10) aptly defined a diaspora as "a social–political formation created as a result of voluntary or forced migration" whose members "maintain regular or occasional contacts with what they regard as their homelands and with individuals and groups of the same background residing in other host countries."

In order to determine the impact of crises and disasters in homeland countries on diaspora groups it is important to first understand the nature and structure of these groups. Diaspora groups retain economic, political, and social connections and networks within these multiple subsystems that distinguish them from traditional interest groups and their networks. Past research on diaspora groups has noted that members of diasporas "establish trans-state networks that reflect complex relationships among the diasporas, their host countries, their homelands, and international actors" (Sheffer, 2003, pp. 9–10). These networks enable diaspora actors to be active across the boundaries of different policy systems and policy regimes. Although this phenomenon might seem self-evident in discussions of diasporas, the extent and structure of networks vary widely from one diaspora group to the next; for example, some diaspora groups are perceived to have closer networks and ties to their homeland then others. What comes through very clearly from our research, however, is the notion that diasporas operate as transnational actors and that diaspora groups and coalitions maintain formal and informal transnational networks that are social, economic, and political in nature.

---

* Diasporas are not defined by the status or length of time their members have spent in a host country as much as by their commitment and action (Fagen et al., 2009). Scholars also consider people who have not lived in their countries of origin but recognize their linkages to it and to co-nationals in other countries as part of diasporas. Although diasporas often maintain cultural legacies and other forms of identity with their country of origin, these national identities tend to weaken over time and across generations (Fagen et al. 2009).

Haitian Diaspora in the United States

According to Nwosu and Batalova (2014), the number of immigrants from Haiti in the United States tripled in number between 1990 and 2012. The majority of all Haitian immigrants reside in three states: New York, Florida, and Massachusetts (Fagen et al., 2009; Terrazas, 2010), with Florida and New York serving as home to more than 70% of these immigrants, and the metro areas of Miami, New York City, Boston, Orlando, and Atlanta serving as home to 75% of these immigrants (Nwosu and Batalova, 2014). These are also places where most Haitian diaspora organizations and groups are based, most of which have been in existence for a number of years. As noted earlier, diasporas, their groups, and their networks operate as transnational policy actors. This is primarily through their social, economic, and political activism in multiple policy systems.[*] The Haitian–American diaspora is no exception and their activism in these arenas is as follows:

1. *Social activism*—Diaspora groups provide a vast array of community services in their countries of settlement, such as medical services (e.g., clinics, outreach, education), immigration services (e.g., free legal advice clinics), religious services, media channels, and social services (e.g., adult education, vocational guidance, childcare). They engage in numerous development activities (Merz et al., 2007; Brinkerhoff, 2008). They also provide similar services to their countries of origin by sending contingents of experts, as well as building schools, hospitals, churches, and other community services for their hometowns (Fagen et al., 2009; Newland, 2010; Esnard and Sapat, 2011). To provide services to their hometowns, diaspora members often come together to benefit particular communities and create hometown associations (HTAs) with which the HTA members identify. These groups typically work to benefit the areas to which they have familial and community roots (Orozco and Welle, 2006). Their activities normally include the construction of a school, hospital, or clinic in their hometowns, usually smaller scale projects restricted to select activities. By some estimates, there were about 200 HTAs in Miami, Boston, New York, Montreal, Ottawa, and the French Caribbean (Felix, 2008) before the earthquake. It is not clear how much growth in HTAs has been experienced since the earthquake.
2. *Economic and social activism through remittances*—On an individual or collective level, this is the primary manner in which diaspora members maintain ties and networks with their homeland. Haitians have an especially deep commitment to giving back to their country of origin, and the issue of remittances[†] is especially important for the Haitian diaspora (Ratha, 2010). Citing a World Bank report, Fagen et al. (2009) noted that Haiti is estimated to be the world's most remittance-dependent country as measured by remittances' share of household income and of GDP; remittances from diaspora members represent around 30% of Haiti's GDP. Annual remittances from the United States to Haiti are estimated at over $2 billion, nearly double the $1.15 billion pledge made by the United States at the 2010 Haiti Donor Conference (USDOS, 2011). Along with economic remittances, scholars have also researched the role of *social remittances* that diaspora members convey. As noted in Sapat and Esnard (2012), social remittances are the norms, practices, identities, and social capital that flow from receiving- to sending-country communities (Levitt, 1998). Social remittances

---

[*] National identities tend to weaken over time and across generations (Fagen et al., 2009).
[†] Remittances are defined as the transfer of money or goods sent by migrants and received by individuals who, generally, are family members of these migrants. The senders are motivated by various objectives, including the wish to meet basic family needs, such as health and education, and by the hope that the funds can be invested productively to generate continuing income (Fagen et al., 2009).

can change ideas, beliefs, and practices about gender, politics, and religion and can be transferred in different ways with differential impacts (Levitt, 1998, 2001; Jiménez, 2009). With increasingly rapid forms of communication by cell phones, Internet, and other forms of social media, the diffusion of ideas through social remittances is also gaining in speed and scale, and we view these ideas as a form of transnational social capital that is vitally important in disaster response, recovery, and resilience.

Overall, diaspora links and networks with their homeland are so closely coupled that one newspaper in Haiti opined that, "When the diaspora coughs, Haiti gets a fever" (Fagen et al., 2009). The Haitian diaspora also plays a critical role during times of disaster, such as the numerous floods, hurricanes, and other political disasters that have beset Haiti. They did the same after the 2010 earthquake discussed below.

Case Study and Methodology

2010 Haiti Earthquake

The catastrophic magnitude 7 earthquake that struck Haiti on January 12, 2010, impacted over 1.5 million people directly and devastated the island (Bilham, 2010; EERI, 2010; Fierro and Perry, 2010). Affected communities included Leogane and the cities of Jacmel and Port-au-Prince, Haiti's capital. Estimates of the actual death toll vary widely based on source. According to the U.S. Geological Survey, 222,570 people died in the quake (USGS, 2011); however, according to the Haiti government about 316,000 people were killed by the earthquake (Gaestel and Brown, 2011). What is unquestionable is the deadly catastrophic nature of the earthquake for the island of Haiti. Bilham (2010) described the earthquake as more than twice as lethal as any previous magnitude 7 event, especially for those living in Port-au-Prince and its surrounding environs. Population displacement levels reached 2.3 million, and hundreds of thousands of residents have been affected by the earthquake's aftermath and the cholera epidemic that followed (Esnard and Sapat, 2014). According to EERI (2010), approximately 150,000 Haitians left the country. The latter group of Haitians were mostly those with the means or the necessary immigration status to return to countries of residence. According to Florida's Department of Children and Families (DCF, 2014), 26,671 total individuals arrived in Florida through the emergency repatriation program in a one-month period from January 15 to February 20, 2010; about 77% were U.S. citizens.

Research Design

The research design for our study is based on a qualitative approach blending in-depth semi-structured interviews with secondary data. The secondary data (coalition documents, reports, newspaper articles, website information, and prior research) were used to understand the history and missions of the groups and agencies being interviewed, to help map coalition policy beliefs, to understand the type of policy subsystems in which diaspora coalitions operate, to generate a purposive sample of experts, and to start a snowball sample of respondents for in-person interviews (Singleton and Straits, 1993; Kempter et al., 2003; Sapat and Esnard, 2012). Because qualitative research and snowball sampling have their limitations, including problems of generalizability and external validity, in order to minimize the limitations of this method the interview sampling method and strategy (Miles and Huberman, 1994) were designed to (1) allow a valid means by which to answer the research questions under study; (2) provide rich and textured data given the descriptive nature of the study; (3) be ethical and follow all the required approvals and consents; and (4) allow the results generated to be transferable and generalizable to other Haitian enclaves beyond our study area.

The findings presented herein are based on 63 semi-structured interviews conducted with representatives of agencies, organizations, and institutions in South Florida (16), Boston (21), New York City (15), Atlanta (9), and Washington, DC (2). The interviews lasted an average of 45 minutes and were conducted from June 2010 to September 2014. The majority of interviewees represented nonprofit Haitian diaspora organizations and professional coalitions. Other interviewees represented other local and international nonprofits and government agencies, including schools and multiagency task forces, faith-based organizations, media, immigration advocates, and federal agencies. All interviewees were provided with a short description of the project and a consent form, and all of the recorded interviews were fully transcribed and returned to the interviewees for clarifications and edits.

Transboundary Effects of the 2010 Haiti Earthquake on Diaspora Organizations and Networks

From our analysis of the 2010 Haiti earthquake as a transboundary crisis, we find that as a transboundary crisis the 2010 Haiti earthquake had macro-, meso- and microlevel effects. At the macro- and mesolevels, it led to (1) a major shift in U.S. immigration policy, (2) the mobilization of diaspora organizations and the rise of new emergent umbrella organizations, and (3) and the provision of new venues for policy change and participation. At the microlevel, it led to changes in the attitudes of the Haitian government toward the diaspora and within the diaspora itself.

Macro- and Mesolevel Changes in Institutions and Policy

Changes in U.S. Immigration Policy

A transboundary macrolevel effect of the 2010 Haiti earthquake was a change in U.S. immigration policy, more specifically with respect to Temporary Protected Status (TPS). TPS is a temporary immigration status granted to eligible nationals of a certain country designated by the Secretary of Homeland Security because that country has experienced temporary negative conditions, such as armed conflict or an environmental disaster. TPS allows qualified individuals from designated countries (or parts of those countries) who are in the United States to continue to legally reside here for a limited time period (DHS, 2010). Such conditions prevent nationals of the country from returning safely or the country to handle their return adequately. As noted in Sapat and Esnard (2012), Haitians who had experienced negative conditions and who were political refugees prior to the earthquake had requested TPS but were always denied the status, despite concentrated lobbying efforts, letter campaigns, marches, and protests, which did not change the administration's position on granting TPS to Haitians. Efforts by various groups to put TPS into effect after the 2008 hurricanes and flooding in Haiti were also unsuccessful; however, after the 2010 Haiti earthquake, TPS was finally granted to allow immigrants already in the United States to continue living and working in the country for an initial period of 18 months following the disaster. On May 17, 2011, DHS Secretary Janet Napolitano announced another 18-month extension of TPS for Haitians through January 22, 2013 (DHS, 2011). TPS was extended again and most recently has been extended through July 22, 2017 (DHS, 2014; Nwosu and Batalova, 2014).

Mobilization of Diaspora Organizations and the Rise of Emergent Umbrella Organizations

At the mesolevel, the 2010 earthquake led to the mobilization of Haitian–American diaspora organizations and groups, as evidenced by the rise of umbrella organizations and the mobilization of coordinated efforts between coalitions. Although the rise of emergent group processes (Stallings and Quarantelli, 1985), networks (Drabek, 1987; Drabek and McEntire, 2002), and umbrella organizations (McEntire, 1998) following disasters has been extensively studied, there has not been much understanding of transnational diaspora groups and networks and their role in response to disasters occurring in other geographical areas. The rise of umbrella organizations and informal networks within the Haitian diaspora as an emergent process was similar to other emergent group processes in that it was based on a new normative imperative that "something had to be done" (Drabek and McEntire, 2002, p. 198). However, the level and extent of coordination that emerged within the Haitian diaspora to respond to the Haiti earthquake were unprecedented for the diaspora. For much of its history, the Haitian diaspora has been characterized by a lack of coalition cooperation; at times, it has been akin to an adversarial subsystem (as termed by Nohrstedt and Weible, 2010). The links, coordination, and unity between different diaspora groups are, for the most part, fragmented and sometimes tenuous, and they are often divided and isolated along political, religious, and regional lines. Further, Haitian diaspora groups are often distinguished and distinguish themselves by class, educational level, and political loyalties (Fagen et al., 2009); the latter are typically legacies from their home countries (Newland, 2010). In a newspaper report by East and Fleshler (2010), Alex Stepick, director of the Immigration and Ethnicity Institute of Florida International University, made reference to the lack of interaction between Haitians of different classes and was quoted as saying, "Haitians of different social classes live separate lives in the United States."

After the earthquake, however, because sentiments about the homeland were affected, there was a new unity forged in emergent umbrella organizations that sprang up to coordinate relief and advocacy efforts among existing diaspora coalitions. One notable emergent organization that formed since the earthquake was the Haiti Advocacy Working Group (HAWG), consisting of 30 Haitian and non-Haitian member organizations. It was formed shortly after the earthquake to coordinate advocacy efforts for disaster relief, reconstruction, and long-term U.S. development policy toward Haiti. Interestingly, this umbrella organization combines the efforts not only of Haitian diaspora coalitions but also of other diaspora coalitions such as the American Jewish World Service and other nonprofit organizations such as Partners in Health and Grassroots International. The advocacy efforts of HAWG target U.S. foreign policies, the policies of the Haitian government, and the policies of international aid agencies. These efforts encompass a variety of issues, ranging from promoting Haitian civil society, inclusion and leadership in relief and reconstruction, and encouraging local procurement and decentralization of aid to supporting fair immigration policies for Haitians and pushing for the Haitian diaspora to be allowed greater involvement in disaster recovery and reconstruction.

In light of these factors, the effects of the earthquake led to the mobilization of diaspora coalitions and engendered a "rally around the flag effect" that has been noted after crises within the United States (Mueller, 1970, 1973). The earthquake drove some of these groups to unite to achieve common goals by forming umbrella organizations and coordinating and cooperating with each other. The unity and activism that emerged after the crisis are not without precedence among other diaspora groups. For example, after Turkey invaded Cyprus in 1974, the Greek–American diaspora (whose members had been divided in their attitudes toward the then-ruling military junta in Greece) was roused into unprecedented unity and activism and formed more than 20 new lobbying organizations, mainly to advocate for a ban on U.S. military assistance to Turkey (Newland, 2010).

Like most rally effects, this one was also short lived for some emergent organizations; prior disasters, such as the 2008 hurricanes in Haiti, had also led to similar unifying efforts, albeit not as extensive, which dissipated after a few months. Future research and time can shed more light on the duration, maintenance, and effectiveness of these unified coalitions.

Provision of New Venues for Policy Change and Participation

At the mesolevel, this high-profile catastrophe also had an effect by leading to resources for transnational organizations and networks in the form of new venues and forums for participation. Venues for political participation are considered a resource (Sabatier and Weible, 2007) with regard to influencing public policy. The earthquake provided the political wherewithal for a much emboldened diaspora to lobby and push for issues and goals that they considered important; for example, March of 2010 marked an important month for Haitian diaspora coalitions with two key events that provided opportunities for their input (Sapat and Esnard, 2012). These two events were the Haitian Diaspora Forum held at the Organization of American States (OAS) Headquarters from March 21 to 23 and the Haiti Donors Conference held at the United Nations Headquarters in New York on March 31. The OAS forum focused on a strategic plan for reconstruction and development in Haiti and specifically on how the Haitian diaspora could engage in capacity and nation building (OAS, 2010). The forum was co-organized by the OAS and Haitian diaspora organizations (several based in South Florida), and the outcome and results were presented to the Haitian government at the March 31 donors conference in New York. According to one member of the diaspora, "This was the first time in the annals of the diaspora that the diaspora had been considered as an institution versus a separate entity of one to one" (interviewee code 007). Other venues that were opened up to Haitian–American diaspora groups were due to increased attention by key policymakers and congressional committees; over 17 congressional hearings were held in the 4 months following the earthquake. At those hearings, Haitian–American academics, experts, and coalition members provided testimony at hearings on the rebuilding of Haiti and on issues related to foreign assistance and international development (Farmer et al., 2011). Tangible outcomes of these meetings remain to be seen.

Microlevel Effects

Change in Attitude by the Haitian Government Toward the Diaspora

When people emigrate from their homelands, their relationship with the latter can be characterized by bipolar or schizophrenic notions of both love and hate for their homelands: attachment because it signifies their roots and disengagement, or hate, because their emigration is often due to factors that push them away, such as oppressive, dictatorial, and often brutal regimes; poor economic conditions; negative social situations; or other similarly negative factors (Laguerre, 1998). Attitudes by homeland governments toward diaspora members are also tempered by similar contradictory negative and positive sentiments. Those who "have gone away" are both reviled for abandoning their homelands for greener political or economic pastures and envied or even sought after for their potential economic prowess or wealth. Some even note that the word *diaspora* remains a contested term that has often been used pejoratively in the Haitian context (interviewee code 026).

The 2010 earthquake did lead to some change in sentiment toward Haitian diaspora groups, who were being sought out not just for their monetary contributions but also for other contributions, such as being called on to provide more information and input. Our interview data show that Haitian–Americans began to feel for the first time in decades that their contributions were being valued more by the Haitian government after the earthquake and that their input and information would be welcome. This marked a change in relationships that existed previously; despite the presence of a Haitian Ministry for Haitians Living Abroad (MHAVE) for a number of years, an uneasy and at times even hostile relationship existed between the diaspora and the Haitian government. Thus, the vast devastation wrought by the earthquake did lead to some changes in Haitian government policies and sentiments toward the diaspora: Once shunned, Haitian emigrants began to feel that their services and contributions were needed (Dewan, 2010). According to one member of the diaspora, "At the OAS conference, the consensus was reached that it should not be two Haitis—one inside and one outside" (interviewee code 003).

Diaspora Sentiments and Attitudes

The data indicate attitudinal changes by Haitian–Americans, likely propelled by a surge of patriotism and a feeling of the reinforcement of their links and identity to their homeland. The earthquake also seems to have galvanized the feelings and perceptions of the diaspora that they needed to unify and coordinate with each other through existing and new networks to achieve more in terms of their policy goals, including a sense that more cooperation was feasible with the Haitian government itself. There were several mentions by interviewees of a sense of unity and of coming together to make policy changes. As noted by one interviewee (interviewee code 010),

> As a member of the diaspora I feel really strongly that if Haiti is going to be what we imagine it to be we have to be involved. There is so much skill in the diaspora here—there really is. And you know like me … a lot of people in the diaspora had become discouraged about the future of Haiti and the politics and the division and I think Jan. 12th changed that for a lot of us.

Similarly, another interviewee noted the need for cooperation between different Haitian diaspora advocacy groups (interviewee code 003):

> Basically, our group deals mainly with policy issues as an advocacy group. What we have done is, on January 16th after the earthquake … what we saw was the need to be proactive … take a more long-term approach, by convening the Haitian diaspora, for the first time because the Haitian diaspora is very complicated.

In the South Florida and Boston regions, for example, diaspora groups networked with school districts, social service agencies, and nonprofit organizations to coordinate relief efforts, and the success of the coordination among the networks was noted by one interviewee (interviewee code 009):

> The beauty of the success is that people came together. All the mainstream organizations recognized this and let it happen. In [name redacted] this is not a Haitian crisis, it is OUR crisis. So we are going to work together. You need to understand the historical significance of KONBIT in Haiti. When you have KONBIT and you have a piece of land everyone comes to help and we all make it happen together.

Others noted how coordination among diaspora coalitions and the effectiveness of existing networks improved after the earthquake (interviewee code 015):

> The mission of [our coalition] is networking, strengthening each organization's mission and vision and getting the different associations to work together. Because of the earthquake, we got closer and started working together even more closely on our vision and collaboration. The coalition meets once a month—but after the earthquake, our interactions have become more frequent. We got more organized than before. Because of the earthquake we got closer and we have better relationships and we are more organized than before.

However, the short-lived nature of the rally effect of the earthquake in increasing unity and mobilizing sentiments was already in evidence in terms of perceptions and attitudes as noted by some of the interviewees. As the months turned into yearly anniversaries of the earthquake, the tone, for those who chose to respond to our questions about unity and coordination among the diaspora groups, became less optimistic. This was based in part on their frustration with the slow pace of disaster recovery and with those who they deemed responsible for it, including the Haitian government and the lack of strong civic institutions in Haiti. The declining levels of optimism and rising frustration are evident in the following interview excerpt (interviewee code 011):

> We are included in every conversation but when action is being taken we are not called upon and this is very frustrating.

This rising sense of frustration, coupled with the difficulties that diaspora coalitions face due to a lack of financial and other resources, may render it difficult for these groups to maintain and continue their coordination and unifying efforts. Further, a number of diaspora coalitions are run primarily by volunteers and have few active members, often with meager resources, which exacerbate problems of sustained coordination; this may lead to coalition competition and conflict over a period of time.

Management of the Haiti Disaster from Within and Outside

The catastrophic nature of the 2010 Haiti earthquake and the scale of the destruction and damage to the existing infrastructure in the country cannot be overstated. The Presidential Palace, National Assembly buildings, and more than half of the government and administrative buildings were destroyed, as was the nation's largest port (Haddow et al., 2014). Existing administrative apparatus was critically affected; the toppling of 28 out of 29 Haitian Ministry buildings and the United Nations (UN) compound killed nearly 18% of the Haitian civil service and 101 senior UN employees (USDOS, 2011). Given that the Haitian government was operating in a state of emergency, it was inevitable that international aid and assistance were paramount in the initial response to the quake. Based on prior engagement with Haiti and the history of U.S.–Haitian relations, it was also inevitable that the United States played the largest and most predominant role in the response, although there were also a number of other countries, government and international institutions, and non-governmental organizations (NGOs) that responded in large measures. The country continues to face significant humanitarian challenges, including a cholera outbreak that dealt a serious blow to recovery efforts, as well as looming questions and concerns about accountability. The source of the cholera outbreak remains a point of contention as human rights lawyers have filed class-action lawsuits in U.S. federal courts accusing the United Nations of gross negligence and misconduct on behalf of victims of the cholera outbreak (Watson and Vaccarello, 2013). Given the scale of the disaster, recovery efforts are still ongoing and will take a number of years; only time will reveal the overall effectiveness of the management of this disaster. Overall, while progress has been made along several fronts, many challenges remain, as discussed below.

Sheltering and Housing

During the initial phase of response, the number of Haitians who lived in camps reached 1.5 million at its peak in July 2010 (Maloney, 2014). Among the various agencies, the U.S. Agency for International Development (USAID) and the Office of Foreign Disaster Assistance (OFDA) were two of the main organizations that aided the response effort. Among other things, USAID and its partners coordinated search and rescue activities, constructed over 29,100 transitional shelters, repaired more than 5800 structures to shelter over 8100 households, and provided hosting support to over 27,200 households and rental vouchers to roughly 1200 households; overall, more than 328,000 individuals were housed through these various programs (USAID, 2014). The Cash for Work program that was initiated employed more than 350,000 people (about half of whom were women) in the first year after the earthquake through short-term, cash-for-work jobs, injecting more than $19 million into the local economy (USAID, 2014).

Other organizations such as the International Organization for Migration, which serves as the global cluster lead on Camp Coordination and Camp Management (CCCM), played a key role in helping internally displaced populations (IDPs) move from camps to housing (IOM, 2013). Several initiatives were also adopted, such as the International Federation of Red Cross and Red Crescent Societies' Safe Spaces assessment methodology, which was piloted for the first time in Haiti as a community-led protection approach to help residents prevent, mitigate, and respond to violence (IFRC, 2012). This was a community-led approach that combined "a mapping of safe and unsafe spaces, a community safety audit, and participant-led discussions implemented through community focus groups" (IFRC, 2012, p. 53). One of the major initiatives launched by the Haitian government in conjunction with humanitarian partners was the Strategic Recovery Framework for Haiti, which was adopted in February 2011 (IFRC, 2012), with a focus on camp decongestion and neighborhood recovery programs to help families move out to safer, more resilient communities. Other programs adopted in Haiti included a self-sheltering solutions program which provided a US$500 resettlement grant for displacees to rent a property or live with a host family, supported by an unconditional grant of US$150 to enable families to meet their most pressing needs (IFRC, 2012).

Five years after the earthquake, however, problems remained. Large-scale reconstruction efforts had been hampered by the lack of plans and land tenure issues. Maloney (2014) noted the concerns of Amnesty International with regard to the lack of permanent housing solutions for most people who were relocated from the camps, as well as forcible evictions from camps built on public land and by landowners who want to reclaim their land.

Recovery and Rebuilding

The slow pace of recovery in Haiti is unquestionable. Rebuilding efforts are ongoing based on projects and programs initiated within and outside Haiti. Two of the main entities in the immediate aftermath of the earthquake were (1) the Interim Haiti Reconstruction Commission (IHRC), and (2) the Haiti Reconstruction Fund (HRF). The IHRC was co-chaired by then-Prime Minister

Jean-Max Bellerive and by President Bill Clinton. They envisioned a structure similar to the Reconstruction and Rehabilitation Agency, which was set up in Indonesia after the 2004 South Asia tsunami (Bellerive and Clinton, 2010). The IHRC approved projects for consideration that aligned with the Government of Haiti's action plan for recovery (Rouzier, 2014). The HRF, on the other hand, was chaired by Haiti's Minister of Finance and administered by the World Bank. HRF made the decisions on how to fund projects, along with partner entities such as the World Bank, United Nations, and Inter-American Development Bank (Rouzier, 2014). One diaspora interviewee applauded the formation of the IHRC but cautioned the need to remain an "interim" vs. "permanent" commission (interviewee code 009):

> It is a good thing on a short term basis because that gives the umbrella for the international community to feel safe to invest … more or less. In the long term I am not sure if this is the way to go forward. I do not think that you can formulate any kind of good policies when the outside world is paying the bills for you.

There have been also been questions raised about the IHRC's work in facilitating recovery and reconstruction in Haiti (O'Grady, 2014), particularly by the Haitian–American diaspora. Some of the early frustration by some members of the diaspora stemmed from having their hopes dashed by the make up of the commission (i.e., one member instead of the two requested by the diaspora at the March 2010 meetings previously discussed) and the lack of voting power of the diaspora representative on the IHRC. According to one of our interviewees during the first year of our research (interviewee code 010):

> I think we were discouraged when the interim reconstruction commission decided they would have a representative from the diaspora but that person would not have a vote … personally I think it's a slap in the face. Their explanation is that everyone that has a vote has contributed financially but the diaspora contributed 1/3 the GDP of Haiti through remittances. So, I think that's very telling of how they feel about the diaspora.

As previously mentioned the diaspora remains a continuous lifeline for their families in Haiti through economic remittances, critical to the rebuilding and reconstruction of individual houses. Other philanthropic initiatives by Haitian-led NGOs and hometown associations (previously mentioned) are also worth noting, as rebuilding of schools and other community amenities are vital to the recovery process.

Other international players who were and continue to be critical to the response and recovery process in Haiti are international NGOs. These organizations have been essential partners in providing shelter, emergency food supplies, medical services, educational services, counseling services, final support, etc. Their presence and activities, however, remain bitterly contested and are seen as a double-edged sword; these organizations play a humanitarian role but are also seen as exacerbating aid dependence (Sapat and Esnard, 2014). Within Haiti, NGOs are seen by some as serving as instruments of global neoliberal regimes and furthering their interests (Schuller, 2009, 2012). Even more concerns have been raised about the billions of dollars that were raised and dispersed and who benefited in the recovery process. By 2012, almost $6 billion had been disbursed in official aid to Haiti and an estimated $3 billion had been donated to NGOs in private contributions in addition to official aid; of this aid, the Government of Haiti had received just 1% of the humanitarian aid and somewhere between 15 and 21% of longer term relief aid (Ramachandran and Walz, 2012). As one of our diaspora interviewees succinctly noted (interviewee code 2001):

A lot of the money spent in the Beltway of Washington. So it comes back to Washington.

There was also a sense among our interview respondents that, if recovery was to be successful, then it was necessary to include Haitians in the process. In talking about how recovery should proceed, one of interviewees stated (interviewee code 1004):

> … we were convinced that if the Haitians were to own the reconstruction in any way, they needed to be at the table, they needed to be offering critique, input, they needed to be active participants. And I think our idea—and USAID supported it—that if it's just the World Bank comes in, USAID comes in, DFID comes in, French aid comes in, you know, honestly, where are the Haitians in the whole recovery process?

Many challenges thus remain in Haiti and this research shows that several lessons can be learned from the Haiti case as discussed below.

Learning from the 2010 Haiti Earthquake

Overall, several lessons can be learned from the Haiti case as a transboundary crisis, in light of the close ties that diasporas have to their homelands. These lessons relate to the role of diaspora groups as well as overall disaster recovery processes. For diaspora groups, one takeaway from this research is that, although they are often invisible actors, the research here shows that diaspora groups can play a major role. Institutions at local, national, and international levels could more effectively leverage and harness the power of diaspora groups in transboundary disasters by (1) incorporating diaspora perspectives in tandem with local perspectives and goals within decision-making processes to develop more culturally appropriate responses in disaster response and recovery policies; (2) using their expertise and resources (human and financial) where appropriate, as well as providing opportunities and funding for capacity building in areas such as grant-writing; (3) using diaspora media outlets to communicate with groups both within the United States and within the affected country; (4) tapping diaspora knowledge of local areas to target disaster aid more usefully and effectively; and (5) helping diaspora groups maintain unity by providing a coordinating mechanism, which would allow them to continue their focus on long-term disaster recovery.

With respect to disaster management processes more generally, the case of Haiti shows that

1. Long-term recovery can span more than a decade.
2. Catastrophic disasters increasingly require involvement of multiple entities, including international organizations, agencies, and institutions, and that coordination and collaboration between these institutions and local civil society organizations are important.
3. More transparency is needed in disaster management and recovery processes.
4. Aid mechanisms that are *ad hoc* and temporary create a volatility that does not help engender sustainable recovery processes.
5. Inclusion of the local society—in this case, the Haitian state and Haitian civil society—in the recovery processes is critical for sustainable disaster recovery. Greater integration with local goals and needs can help target aid more usefully and effectively.

Conclusion

Transboundary crises and disasters can garner attention from a number of actors and groups, yet not enough attention has been paid to them or the actors that they affect. The 2010 Haiti earthquake served as an important transnational crisis whose effects extended well beyond Haiti. This case shows that more attention needs to be paid to "invisible" transnational actors, such as diasporas, and the role they play in disasters. We argue and find that transboundary crises and disasters can have macro effects and lead to changes in policy; meso- and microlevel effects can lead to the mobilization of groups and coalitions, including the creation of emergent umbrella organizations, and engender transnational rally-around-the-flag sentiments. Findings from this research also support the notion that, with increasing globalization and linkages between diaspora groups and their homelands, the expression of policy preferences and activities by coalitions may not always be confined to the boundaries of a nation-state; rather, the transnational and border-crossing practices of coalitions and actors are also worthy of study.

We must note that the findings here are based on research on one diaspora group, which is subjective and subject to various other limitations of qualitative and case study research. Surveys or other types of quantitative data and a broader discussion of diaspora groups may present a different picture. It is also important to note that diaspora group and NGO activities can *supplement* but not *supplant* the role of the state. This is particularly so in an age of globalization that requires new state administrative capacities and sound governance (Farazmand, 1999, 2009). These issues are likely to become even more critical, given the potential effects of climate change combined with increasing interconnectedness that will lead to a growth in the transboundary effects of disasters.

Questions for Discussion

1. What is a transboundary crisis and why is the Haiti earthquake a good example?
2. Why are some of the transboundary effects of crises and disasters?
3. What role can diaspora organizations and networks play in disasters?
4. When did the Haiti earthquake take place and what effect did it have on groups within the United States?
5. What are some examples of macro, meso, and micro changes in institutions and policy after the 2010 earthquake?
6. What can local, national, and international institutions do to leverage the power of formal and informal diaspora networks and organizations?
7. Are there findings from the research on the role of the Haitian diaspora in the United States that can be generalized to other diaspora groups? Why? Why not?
8. What are some of the challenges inherent in managing such catastrophic disasters in low-income countries?

Acknowledgments

The material in this chapter is based on research supported by the U.S. National Science Foundation Grants (NSF Grant Nos. CMMI-0726808, CMMI-1034667, and CMMI-1162438). Any opinions, findings, and conclusions or recommendations expressed in this material are those of the authors and do not necessarily reflect the views of the National Science Foundation. Due to institutional guidelines and guarantees of interviewee confidentiality, we cannot include the names of the various Haitian-American diaspora and other non-governmental organizations who participated in this research, but we are extremely grateful to their representatives for their time and insight. This work would not have been possible without data collection and overall research assistance provided by dedicated graduate research assistants Lorena Schwartz and Jean Pierre, doctoral students, School of Public Administration, Florida Atlantic University; Anne-Christine Carrie, School of Urban and Regional Planning, Florida Atlantic University; and Emefa Sewordor, doctoral student, Department of Public Management and Policy, Georgia State University. We thank Lorena Schwartz for her invaluable assistance in helping to complete the cumbersome tasks related to reference lists and citations.

Additional Reading

Boin, A. (2005). *The Politics of Crisis Management: Public Leadership Under Pressure*. Cambridge: Cambridge University Press.
Crisp, J., Morris, T., and Refstie, H. (2012). Displacement in urban areas: new challenges, new partnerships. *Disasters*, 36(S1): S23–S42.
Farmer, P. (2011). *Haiti After the Earthquake*. Philadelphia, PA: Public Affairs.
FEMA. (2011). *A Whole Community Approach to Emergency Management: Principles, Themes, and Pathways for Action*. Washington, DC: Federal Emergency Management Agency (http://www.fema.gov/media-library/assets/documents/23781).
Gutmann, A., Kunreuther, H., Kettl, D.F., and Daniels, R.J. (2006). *On Risk and Disaster: Lessons from Hurricane Katrina*. Philadelphia: University of Pennsylvania Press.
IDMC. (2014). *Global Estimates 2014: People Displaced by Disasters*. Geneva: Internal Displacement Monitoring Centre (http://reliefweb.int/sites/reliefweb.int/files/resources/201409-global-estimates.pdf).
Katz, J. (2013). *The Big Truck That Went By: How the World Came to Save Haiti and Left Behind a Disaster*. New York: Palgrave Macmillan.
Klarreich, K. and Polman, L. (2012). The NGO republic of Haiti. *Nation*, 295(21): 11–17.
Laguerre, M. (2006). *Diaspora, Politics, and Globalization*. New York: Palgrave Macmillan.
Quigley, F. (2014). *How Human Rights Can Build Haiti: Activists, Lawyers, and the Grassroots Campaign*. Nashville, TN: Vanderbilt University Press.
Rahill, G.J., Ganapati, N.E., Clérismé, J.C., and Mukherji, A. (2014). Shelter recovery in urban Haiti after the earthquake: the dual role of social capital. *Disasters*, 38(S1): S73–S93.

References

Ambrosio, T., Ed. (2002). *Ethnic Identity Groups and U.S. Foreign Policy*. Westport, CT: Greenwood Publishing Group.
Anthias, F. (1998). Evaluating 'diaspora': beyond ethnicity. *Sociology*, 32(3): 557–576.
Ansell, C., Boin, A., and Keller, A. (2010). Managing transboundary crises: identifying the building blocks of an effective response system. *J. Contingencies Crisis Manage.*, 18(4): 195–207.
Bellerive, J.-M. and Clinton, B. (2010). Finishing Haiti's unfinished work. *The New York Times*, July 11, p. A19.
Bilham, R. (2010). Lessons from the Haiti earthquake. *Nature*, 463(18): 878–879.
Birkland, T. (2006). *Lessons of Disaster: Policy Change After Catastrophic Events*. Washington, DC: Georgetown University Press.
Boin, A. (2009a). The new world of crises and crisis management: implications for policymaking and research. *Rev. Policy Res.*, 26(4): 367–377.

Boin, A. (2009b). Meeting the challenges of transboundary crises: building blocks for institutional design. *J. Contingencies Crisis Manage.*, 17(4): 203–205.

Boin, A. and Rhinard, M. (2008). Managing transboundary crises: what role for the European Union? *Int. Stud. Rev.*, 10: 1–26.

Boin, A. and Sundelius, B. (2007). Managing European Emergencies: Considering the Pros and Cons of a European Union Agency, paper presented at the 4th ECPR General Conference, Pisa, Italy, September 6–8 (http://www.epc.eu/documents/uploads/103667278_EPC%20Working%20Paper%2027%20 Managing%20Emergencies.pdf).

Boin, A. and Ekengren, M. (2009). Preparing for the world risk society: towards a new security paradigm for the European Union. *J. Contingencies Crisis Manage.*, 17: 285–294.

Brinkerhoff, J. (2008). *Diasporas and Development: Exploring the Potential.* Boulder, CO: Lynne Rienne.

Clifford, R.A. (1956). *The Rio Grande Flood: A Comparative Study of Border Communities in Disaster*, Publ. No. 458. Washington, DC: National Academy of Sciences, National Research Council.

DCF. (2014). *Haiti: Efforts and Resources: Time Line of Events.* Tallahassee: Florida Department of Children and Families (www.dcf.state.fl.us/initiatives/haiti/timeline.shtml).

Dewan, S. (2010). Scattered émigrés Haiti once shunned are now a lifeline. *The New York Times*, February 3, p. A16 (http://www.nytimes.com/2010/02/04/us/04diaspora.html?scp=1&sq=haitian expatriates&st=cse#).

DHS. (2008). *National Response Framework.* Washington, DC: U.S. Department of Homeland Security, Chap. 2 (http://www.fema.gov/pdf/emergency/nrf/nrf-core.pdf).

DHS. (2010). Statement from Homeland Security Secretary Janet Napolitano on Temporary Protected Status (TPS) for Haitian Nationals [press release]. Washington, DC: U.S. Department of Homeland Security (http://www.dhs.gov/ynews/releases/pr_1263595952516.shtm).

DHS. (2011). Secretary Napolitano Announces the Extension of Temporary Protected Status for Haiti Beneficiaries [press release]. Washington, DC: U.S. Department of Homeland Security (http://www.dhs.gov/ynews/releases/pr_1305643820292.shtm).

DHS. (2014). Temporary Protected Status Extended for Haitians [press release]. Washington, DC: U.S. Department of Homeland Security (http://www.uscis.gov/news/temporary-protected-status-extended-haitians-0).

Drabek, T.E. (1987). *The Professional Emergency Manager: Structures and Strategies for Success.* Boulder: Institute of Behavioral Science, University of Colorado.

Drabek, T.E. and McEntire, D.A. (2002). Emergent phenomena and multi-organizational coordination in disasters: lessons from the research literature. *Int. J. Mass Emerg. Disasters*, 20(2): 197–224.

Dynes, R.R. (1970). *Organized Behavior in Disaster.* Lexington, MA: Heath Lexington.

East, G. and Fleshler, D. (2010). Earthquake could mean major changes for South Florida Haitians. *Sun Sentinel*, February 19 (http://articles.sun-sentinel.com/2010-02-19/news/fl-haitian-communities-20100219_1_haitian-american-south-florida-haitians-haitian-communities).

EERI (2010). The 12 January 2010 Haiti Earthquake: Emerging Research Needs and Opportunities, paper presented at Earthquake Engineering Research Institute Haiti RAPIDs and Research Needs Workshop, Arlington, VA, September 30–October 1.

Esnard, A.-M. and Sapat, A. (2011). Disasters, diasporas and host communities: insights in the aftermath of the Haiti earthquake. *J. Disaster Res.*, 6(3): 331–342.

Esnard, A.-M. and Sapat, A. (2014). *Displaced by Disasters: Recovery and Resilience in a Globalizing World.* New York: Routledge.

Fagen, P.W., Dade, C., Maguire, R., Felix, K., Nicolas, D., Dathis, N., and Maher, K. (2009). Haitian Diaspora Associations and their Investments in Basic Social Services, paper prepared for the Inter-American Development Bank.

Farazmand, A. (1999). Globalization and public administration. *Public Admin. Rev.*, 59(6): 509–522.

Farazmand, A. (2009). Building administrative capacity for the age of rapid globalization: a modest prescription for the twenty-first century. *Public Admin. Rev.*, 69(6): 1007–1020.

Farmer, P., Concannon, B., Rohr, B., and Maguire, R. (2011). *How to Rebuild Haiti After the Quake.* New York: Council on Foreign Relations (http://www.cfr.org/haiti/rebuild-haiti-after-quake/p23781).

Faulkner, B. (2001). Towards a framework for tourism disaster management. *Tourism Manage.*, 22(2): 135–147.

Felix, K. (2008). Presentation at United Nations Institute for Training and Research (UNITAR) Seminar on Labor Migration: Protection, Gender, and Development, October 2.

Fierro, E. and Perry, C. (2010). *Preliminary Reconnaissance Report—Haiti Earthquake 2010*. Berkeley: Pacific Earthquake Engineering Research Center, University of California (http://peer.berkeley.edu/publications/haiti_2010/documents/haiti_reconnaissance.pdf).

Gaestel, A. and Brown, T. (2011). Haitians recall 2010 quake "hell" as death toll upped. *Reuters*, January 13 (http://www.reuters.com/article/2011/01/13/us-haiti-quake-anniversary-idUSTRE7094L420110113#0EHM6KVtX5Kl6YZu.97).

Hall, S. (1990). Cultural identity and diaspora. In Rutherford, J., Ed., *Identity: Community, Culture, Difference*, pp. 223–237. London: Lawrence & Wishart.

Haddow, G.D., Bullock, J.A., and Coppola, D.P., Eds. (2014). *Introduction to Emergency Management*, 5th ed. New York: Butterworth-Heinemann.

Hirschi, C. and Widmer, T. (2010). Policy change and policy stasis: comparing Swiss foreign policy toward South Africa (1968–94) and Iraq (1990–91). *Policy Stud. J.*, 38(3): 537–563.

Herman, M.G. and Dayton, B.W. (2009). Transboundary crises through the eyes of policymakers: sense making and crisis management. *J. Contingencies Crisis Manage.*, 17(4): 233–241.

IDMC. (2013). *Global Estimates 2012: People Displaced by Disasters*. Geneva: Internal Displacement Monitoring Centre (http://www.internal-displacement.org/publications/2013/global-estimates-2012-people-displaced-by-disasters/).

IFRC. (2012). *World Disasters Report 2012: Focus on Forced Migration and Displacement*. Geneva: International Federation of Red Cross and Red Crescent Societies (http://www.ifrcmedia.org/assets/pages/wdr2012/).

IOM. (2013). *Compendium of IOM Activities in Disaster Risk Reduction and Resilience*. Geneva: International Organization for Migration (http://www.iom.int/compendium-iom-activities-disaster-risk-reduction-and-resilience).

Jimenez, L.F. (2009). De Paisano a Paisano: Mexican Migrants and the Transference of Political Attitudes to Their Countries of Origin, doctoral dissertation, University of Pittsburgh.

Jochim, A.E. and May, P.J. (2010). Beyond subsystems: policy regimes and governance. *Policy Stud. J.*, 38(2): 303–327.

Jones, M.D. and Jenkins-Smith, H. (2009). Trans-subsystem dynamics: policy typography, mass opinion, and policy change. *Policy Stud. J.*, 37(1): 37–58.

Kempter, E.A., Stringfield, S., and Teddlie, C. (2003). Mixed methods sampling strategies in social science research. In Tashakkori, A. and Teddlie, C., Eds., *Handbook of Mixed Methods in Social and Behavioral Research*, pp. 273–296. London: Sage.

Laguerre, M. (1998). *Diasporic Citizenship: Haitian Americans in Transnational America*. New York: Palgrave Macmillan.

Levitt, P. (1998). Social remittances: migration driven local-level forms of cultural diffusion. *Int. Migr. Rev.*, 32(4): 926–948.

Levitt, P. (2001). *The Transnational Villagers*. Berkeley: University of California Press.

Litfin, K. (2000). Advocacy coalitions along the domestic-foreign frontier: globalization and Canadian climate change policy. *Policy Stud. J.*, 28(1): 236–253.

Maloney, A. (2014). *Haitians Still Homeless, 'Suffering in Despair' 4 Years After Quake—Amnesty*. London: Thomson Reuters Foundation (http://www.trust.org/item/20140113063728-6lwyr/).

May, P., Sapotichne, J., and Workman, S. (2009). Widespread policy disruption and interest mobilization. *Policy Stud. J.*, 37(4): 793–815.

McEntire, D.A. (1998). *Towards a Theory of Coordination, Umbrella Organizations and Disaster Relief in the 1997–1998 Peruvian El Nino Disaster*, Quick Response Report No. 105. Boulder, CO: Natural Hazards Research and Information Applications Center, University of Colorado.

Merz, B.J., Chen, L.C., and Geithner, P.F., Eds. (2007). *Diasporas and Development*. Cambridge, MA: Harvard University Press.

Miles, M.B. and Huberman, M.A. (1994). *Qualitative Data Analysis: An Expanded Sourcebook*. Thousand Oaks, CA: Sage.

Mileti, D.S. (1999). *Disasters by Design: A Reassessment of Natural Hazards in the United States*. Washington, DC: National Academy Press.
Mueller, J.E. (1970). Presidential popularity from Truman to Johnson. *Am. Polit. Sci. Rev.*, 64(1): 18–34.
Mueller, J.E. (1973). *War, Presidents, and Public Opinion*. New York: Wiley.
Newland, K. (2010). *Voice After Exit: Diaspora Advocacy*. Washington, DC: Migration Policy Institute.
Nohrstedt, D. (2010). Do advocacy coalitions matter? Crisis and change in Swedish nuclear energy policy. *J. Public Admin. Res. Theory*, 20(2): 309–333.
Nohrstedt, D. and Weible, C.M. (2010). The logic of policy change after crisis: proximity and subsystem interaction. *Risk Hazards Crisis Public Policy*, 1(2): 1–32.
Nwosu, C. and Batalova, J. (2014). Haitian immigrants in the United States. *Migr. Info. Source*, May 29 (http://www.migrationpolicy.org/article/haitian-immigrants-united-states/).
OAS. (2010). *Haitian Diaspora Forum: Contributing to a Strategic Plan for Reconstruction and Development in Haiti*. Washington, DC: Organization of American States (http://www.oas.org/en/ser/dia/docs/recommendations - haitian diaspora forum - consolidated.pdf).
O'Grady, M.A. (2014). Bill, Hillary and the Haiti debacle: Haitians are upset by the reconstruction effort managed by the Clintons. *The Wall Street Journal*, May 18 (http://www.wsj.com/articles/SB10001424052702304547704579564651201202122).
Oliver-Smith, A. (2009). Introduction: development-forced displacement and resettlement: a global human rights crisis. In Oliver-Smith, A., Ed., *Development & Dispossession: The Crisis of Forced Displacement and Resettlement*, pp. 3–23. Santa Fe, NM: SAR Press.
Orozco, M. and Welle, K. (2006). Hometown associations and development: ownership, correspondence, sustainability and replicability. In Merz, B., Ed., *New Patterns for Mexico: Observations on Remittances, Philanthropic Giving, and Equitable Development*, pp. 157–179. Cambridge, MA: Harvard University Press.
Perry, R.W. and Quarantelli, E.L., Eds. (2005). *What Is a Disaster? New Answers to Old Questions*. Philadelphia, PA: Xlibris.
Quarantelli, E.L. (1983). *Emergent Behavior at the Emergency Time Periods of Disasters*. Columbus, OH: Disaster Research Center.
Quarantelli, E.L. (2006). *Catastrophes Are Different from Disasters: Some Implications for Crisis Planning and Managing Drawn from Katrina*. New York: Social Science Research Council (http://understanding-katrina.ssrc.org/quarantelli/).
Quarantelli, E.L., Lagadec, P., and Boin, A. (2006). A heuristic approach to future disasters and crisis. In Rodriguez, H., Quarantelli, E.L., and Dynes, R.R, Eds., *Handbook of Disaster Research*, pp. 16–41. New York: Springer.
Ramachandran, V. and Walz, J. (2012). *Haiti: Where Has All the Money Gone?*, Paper 004. Washington, DC: Center for Global Development (http://www.cgdev.org/content/publications/detail/1426185).
Ratha, D. (2010). *Helping Haiti Through Migration and Remittances*. Washington, DC: The World Bank (http://blogs.worldbank.org/peoplemove/helping-haiti-through-migration-and-remittances).
Rosenthal, U. (1990). Cross-National Approaches to Disasters and Disaster Research, paper presented at the World Congress of Sociology, Research Committee on Disasters, Madrid, July 9–13.
Rosenthal, U. and 't Hart, P. (1998). *Flood Response and Crisis Management in Western Europe: A Comparative Analysis*. Berlin: Springer-Verlag.
Rouzier, P. (2014). Setting the record straight on Haiti's recovery. *The Huffington Post*, May 21 (http://www.huffingtonpost.com/patrick-rouzier/setting-the-record-straig_19_b_5367438.html).
Sabatier, P.A. and Weible, C.M. (2007). The advocacy coalition framework: innovations and clarifications. In Sabatier, P.A., Ed., *Theories of the Policy Process*, 2nd ed., pp. 189–220. Boulder, CO: Westview.
Santella, N., Steinberg, L., and Parks, K. (2009). Decision making for extreme events: modeling critical infrastructure interdependencies to aid mitigation and response planning. *Rev. Policy Res.*, 26(4): 409–422.
Sapat, A. and Esnard, A.-M. (2012). Displacement and disaster recovery: transnational governance and socio-legal issues following the 2010 Haiti earthquake. *Risk Hazards Crisis Public Policy*, 3(1): 1–24.
Sapat, A. and Esnard, A.-M. (2014). Collaborative Networks and NGOs in Disaster Recovery, paper presented at the 72nd Annual Midwest Political Science Association Conference, Chicago, IL, April 3–6.

Scanlon, J. (1994). The role of EOCs in emergency management: a comparison of American and Canadian experience. *Int. J. Mass Emerg. Disasters*, 12(1): 51–75.

Schuller, M. (2009). Gluing globalization: NGOs as intermediaries in Haiti. *PoLAR*, 32(1): 84–104.

Schuller, M. (2012). *Killing with Kindness: Haiti, International Aid, and NGOs*. New Brunswick, NJ: Rutgers University Press.

Sheffer, G. (2003). *Diaspora Politics: At-Home Abroad*. Cambridge, UK: Cambridge University Press.

Singleton, Jr., R.A. and Straits, B.C. (1999). *Approaches to Social Research*, 3rd ed. New York: Oxford University Press.

Smith, G. (2011). *Planning for Post-Disaster Recovery: A Review of the United States Disaster Assistance Framework*. Fairfax, VA: Public Entity Risk Institute.

Smith, G. and Wenger, D. (2006). Sustainable disaster recovery: operationalizing an existing agenda. In Rodriguez, H., Quarantelli, E.L., and Dynes, R.R., Eds., *Handbook of Disaster Research*, pp. 234–257. New York: Springer.

Stallings, R.A. and Quarantelli, E.L. (1985). Emergent citizen groups and emergency management. *Public Admin. Rev.*, 45: 93–100.

Terrazas, A. (2010). *Haitian Immigrants in the United States*. Immigration Research Information, http://www.immigrationresearch-info.org/report/migration-policy-institute/haitian-immigrants-united-states.

USAID. (2014). *Earthquake Overview*. Washington, DC: U.S. Agency for International Development (http://www.usaid.gov/haiti/earthquake-overview).

USDOS. (2011). *Post-Earthquake USG Strategy for Haiti: Toward Renewal and Economic Prosperity*. Washington, DC: U.S. Department of State (www.state.gov/documents/organization/156448.pdf).

USGS. (2011). *Haiti Dominates Earthquake Fatalities in 2010*. Washington, DC: U.S. Geological Survey (http://www.usgs.gov/newsroom/article.asp?ID=2679#.VkoTxsoZ0lYp).

Wachtendorf, T. (2000). When disasters defy borders: what we can learn from the Red River Flood about transnational disasters. *Aust. J. Emerg. Manage.*, 15(3): 36–41.

Wachtendorf, T. (2009). Trans-system social ruptures: exploring issues of vulnerability and resiliency. *Rev. Policy Res.*, 26(4): 379–393.

Watson, I. and Vaccarello, J. (2013). UN Sued for 'bringing cholera to Haiti,' causing outbreak that killed thousands. *CNN*, October 10, http://www.cnn.com/2013/10/09/world/americas/haiti-un-cholera-lawsuit/.

Chapter 15

Planning for Response to Weapon of Mass Destruction and CBRNE Events: A Local and Federal Partnership

Frances L. Edwards

Contents

Chapter Goals	260
Impetus for Weapons of Mass Destruction Planning	260
Federal Response: Legislation and Directives	261
Domestic Preparedness Program	264
Financial Support for Counterterrorism	265
Domestic Preparedness Partner Agencies	268
Future of Sustained Response	268
Training Needs	268
Pharmaceuticals	269
Dual-Use Equipment	269
Medical Community	270
Biological Response	270
Nunn–Lugar–Domenici: Development or Devolution	270
Local Capability for WMD and CBRNE Events	271
Financial Considerations	272
Staffing Challenges	272
MMST Mutual Aid	273
Lessons Still Unlearned	274
Future of MMST/MMRS	276

Conclusion 277
Questions for Discussion 277
Additional Reading 278
References 279

Chapter Goals

After reading this chapter, readers should be able to

1. Understand the risk of weapons of mass destruction/disruption CBRNE events.
2. Understand the history of the legislative response to planning for such events.
3. Understand the local and federal agencies' partnerships.
4. Understand the evolution of the role of the National Guard Civil Support Teams.

Impetus for Weapons of Mass Destruction Planning

For many years, Americans considered terrorism an activity that took place abroad, typified by events such as the IRA bombings in London; however, since 1993 it has become clear that large-scale terrorist attacks can occur within the United States. Terrorism is defined in the *Code of Federal Regulations* as "the unlawful use of force and violence against persons or property to intimidate or coerce a government, the civilian population, or any segment thereof, in furtherance of political or social objectives" (28 CFR 0.85). Events such as the attacks against the World Trade Center in New York on February 26, 1993 (Jehl, 1993) and on September 11, 2001 (Kleinfield, 2001) and the attack against the Pentagon that same day (Van Natta and Alvarez, 2001) show that foreign terrorists can attack within the United States. The attempted bombing of the New York City subway, the failed car bomb in Times Square (Karmon, 2013), and even the Boston Marathon bombing of 2013 show that foreign nationals inside the United States have been able to use improvised explosive devices (IEDs) for ideological purposes against civilian targets (Eligon and Cooper, 2013; Karmon, 2013; Seelye et al., 2013). The bombing of the Murrah Federal Building in Oklahoma City in 1995 (Kifner, 1995) and the attacks by environmental terrorists against selected corporate and university sites (FBI, 2002) and animal control employees (FBI, 2006) demonstrate that domestic terrorism remains a real threat.

Although their leader, Osama bin Laden, was killed in 2011 (Cooper, 2011), al-Qaeda remains a threat. On January 31, 2013, they issued a new map of areas they plan to attack, including the United States and its allies Great Britain, France, and Denmark (Herridge, 2013). Their heightened activity has been stimulated by France's support of the government of Mali against al-Qaeda-backed rebels. Their communications have stated that they are planning "earth-shattering, shocking and terrifying attacks" threatening "the heart of the land of unbelief," the United States (Tomlinson, 2013).

Terrorists have employed a variety of weapons, but explosives have been the most common; for example, the 1993 World Trade Center and 1995 Murrah Federal Building attacks used vehicle-borne improvised explosive devices (VBIEDs). The 9/11 attacks used airplanes as guided missiles (Steinhausler and Edwards, 2005), a very sophisticated application of VBIEDs. In 2004, terrorists bombed the subways in Moscow (Myers, 2004) and Madrid (Golden and Van Natta, 2004), and bombed them twice in London in 2005 (Van Natta and Sciolino, 2005). These attacks caused significant damage and loss of life, but the effects were limited to the immediate area of the attack. This has led experts to characterize most terrorist weapons making use of explosives as "weapons of mass victimization" (WMVs); these are weapons that cause loss of life and economic harm without doing catastrophic damage to the larger community (Edwards and Steinhausler, 2007). Catastrophic terrorism, on the other hand, has been defined as attacks causing more than 1000 deaths at a single site (Wilkening, 1999), such as the World Trade Center attack in 2001 where about 2800 people died (Cauchon, 2001).

Although explosive devices have been the typical weapons used by terrorists, terrorist organizations have also attempted to create military biological and chemical weapons. The Aum Shinrikyo cult in Japan experimented with a variety of biological agents in the mid-1990s (Broad, 1998) and then attacked the Tokyo subway with Sarin, a military weapon (Kristof, 1995). As terrorists branch out from the use of WMVs to the use of militarized material with a greater potential for catastrophic effect, civilian authorities must be trained to respond to these weapons of mass destruction (WMDs), such as chemical, biological, radiological, nuclear, or high-yield explosive (CBRNE) devices, with the power of catastrophic impact. These WMD and CBRNE agents have the potential to create chaos within the civilian community; disable large numbers of police, fire, and emergency medical personnel (first responders); and engender a major media event, thus highlighting the terrorist's "cause."

Federal Response: Legislation and Directives

Recognizing that the former Soviet Union had control of numerous WMD and CBRNE agents and weapons, the U.S. Congress passed the Nunn–Lugar Threat Reduction Initiative in 1991 which was designed to "support the destruction and deactivation of much of the former Soviet Union's (FSU) nuclear arsenal. [At a cost of $400 million per year] … missiles … have been dismantled and stored … thousands of weapon scientists are now employed on civilian projects, and key nuclear facilities … have been made more secure" (Selden, 1997). This legislation was named for the bill's co-sponsors: Senator Sam Nunn (D-Georgia) and Senator Richard Lugar (R-Indiana). The resulting Cooperative Threat Reduction Program hired former Soviet military scientists for peaceful scientific work and incrementally purchased portions of the Soviet WMD stockpile for destruction. By the end of 1996, nuclear weapons in the hands of the Ukraine, Kazakhstan, and Belarus had all been removed through this program. These weapons were deactivated and returned to Russia, where the nuclear material was reprocessed into fuel rods for civilian power reactors (Allison, 2005). As a result of the success of this program, the threat of terrorists acquiring nuclear material from the former Soviet Union states was greatly reduced.

The presence of fissile material in the global supply chain provides another possible source of radiological material that could be used in dirty bombs, conventional improvised explosive devices that include radiological material as shrapnel (NRC, 2012). Beginning in 1987, the United States signed treaties with the nations of the former Soviet Union to reduce the nuclear arsenals. The Megatons to Megawatts program, with the United States Enrichment Corporation (USEC) at the lead, has obtained fissile material from bombs and "downblended" the highly enriched uranium (HEU) used in bombs to low-enriched uranium (LEU) used to fuel power plants. "By mid-2009, the USA had received 10,500 tonnes of LEU from Russia that had been downblended from 367 tonnes of HEU (equivalent to over 14,500 nuclear warheads, according to USEC). By September 2010 the total had risen to 400 tonnes HEU downblended" (WNA, 2015).

Other nations were also identified by international intelligence sources as having chemical weapons (CWs) and biological weapons (BWs). Iran, Iraq, Libya, North Korea, and Syria are on the U.S. State Department's list of states that sponsor terrorism, and all of these states had CW and/or BW programs (Wilkening, 1999). Terrorist groups could be given these weapons by state sponsors or can acquire them on the black market, making urban areas vulnerable to WMD attack. However, little effort had been made to protect civilian targets or prepare civilian first responders for a WMD attack.

As a result of the government's analysis of the potential for terrorist events within the United States, then-President Bill Clinton issued Presidential Decision Directive 39 (PDD-39; U.S. Policy on Counterterrorism), on June 21, 1995 (White House, 1995). It detailed the responsibilities of a variety of federal departments and agencies in the domestic counterterrorism effort. The Federal Bureau of Investigation (FBI) was mandated to be the lead agency for crisis management, which was defined as primarily a federal obligation and law enforcement oriented. The Federal Emergency Management Agency (FEMA) was the lead agency for consequence management, which was defined as "measures to protect public health and safety, restore essential government services, and provide emergency relief to governments, businesses, and individuals affected by the consequences of terrorism" (PDD-39, Terrorism Incident Annex). Consequence management is defined as primarily a state obligation, and federal agencies were directed to work with states to ensure that their plans were adequate.

Section 4 of PDD-39 focuses on nuclear, biological, or chemical (NBC) consequence management: "The United States shall give the highest priority to developing effective capabilities to detect, prevent, defeat and manage the consequences of nuclear, biological or chemical (NBC) materials or weapons use by terrorists. The acquisition of weapons of mass destruction by a terrorist group, through theft or manufacture, is unacceptable. There is no higher priority than preventing the acquisition of this capability or removing this capability from terrorist groups potentially opposed to the U.S." (White House, 1995).

Funding for these activities was to come from agency budgets. Congressional budgetary processes apportioned the new support among 40 federal agencies "eager for part of the billions of dollars that Congress began appropriating for anti-terrorism programs" (Miller and Broad, 1998b). At this point, the counterterrorism effort was a congressionally sponsored and managed program.

Under the National Defense Authorization Act for Fiscal Year 1997 (Public Law 104-201), funding was provided for the Department of Defense "to enhance the capability of federal, state and local emergency responders in incidents involving nuclear, biological and chemical terrorism" (CBDCOM, 1999). This legislation is generally referred to as the Nunn–Lugar–Domenici Domestic Preparedness Program, after its principal sponsors: Senators Nunn, Lugar, and Pete Domenici (R-New Mexico). This legislation charged the U.S. Army's Chemical Biological Defense Command (CBDCOM) with "enhancing existing metropolitan response capabilities to include nuclear, chemical and biological incidents." This legislation, whose formal title is "Defense Against Weapons of Mass Destruction Act of 1996," contains five subtitles: (A) Domestic Preparedness; (B) Interdiction of Weapons of Mass Destruction and Related Materials; (C) Control and Disposition of Weapons of Mass Destruction and Related Materials Threatening the United States; (D) Coordination of Policy and Countermeasures Against Proliferation of Weapons of Mass Destruction; and (E) Miscellaneous. This chapter focuses on Subtitle A, Domestic Preparedness.

On April 10, 1998, President Clinton participated in discussions with seven scientists and Cabinet members about the threats of bioterrorism. His interest in the subject was piqued by the book *The Cobra Event* (Preston, 1998), a fictional account of a biological attack against the United States. Informed sources stated that the panel urged the President to develop better response capacity for antidotes, vaccines, and antibiotics, as well as a stronger medical surveillance system (Miller and Broad, 1998a). At this point the initiative in counterterrorism returned to the Executive Branch.

On May 22, 1998, President Clinton issued two additional Presidential Decision Directives on counterterrorism topics: PDD-62 (White House, 1998a,b) and PDD-63 (White House, 1998c,d). On the same day, he articulated a new role for the National Guard, and he highlighted defense against biological weapons in his commencement speech at the Naval Academy (Clinton, 1998). The two new PDDs provided for two new approaches to counterterrorism. PDD-62 (Combating Terrorism), according to a White House press release, created "a new and more systematic approach to fighting the terrorist threat" (White House, 1998b). It addressed many agencies in the Executive Branch of government, bringing them into the program to apprehend and prosecute terrorists, increase transportation security, enhance response capabilities, and protect the computers "that lie at the heart of America's economy" (White House, 1998b). Specifically, PDD-62 established the Office of the National Coordinator for Security, Infrastructure Protection and Counterterrorism, to oversee "counterterrorism, protection of critical infrastructure, preparedness and consequence management" for WMD events. The Office led in the development of guidelines necessary for crisis management.

The other Presidential Decision Directive, PDD-63 (Critical Infrastructure Protection), followed recommendations made by the Commission on Critical Infrastructure Protection, which was convened in 1997. It set "a goal of reliable, interconnected, and secure information system infrastructure by the year 2003, and significantly increased security to government systems by the year 2000" (White House, 1998d). New initiatives included a National Infrastructure Protection Center in the FBI, and public–private partnerships for infrastructure security. Essential government services were included for development of heightened security.

As the Cold War waned, National Guard units were seeking peacetime missions. On May 22, 1998, President Clinton's commencement address at the Naval Academy announced that ten states would get specially trained National Guard units "to help local and state officials respond to potential terrorist attacks with chemical, biological or even nuclear weapons" (Schafer, 1998). Each unit would have ten full-time and ten reserve members, with a $49.2 million budget for their salaries, training, and equipment. According to Defense Secretary William Cohen, "The teams ... will be able to deploy rapidly, assist local first responders in determining the nature of an attack, provide medical and technical advice, and pave the way" for other federal resources (Lee, 1998). Other reserve units were trained to assist these ten teams in reconnaissance and decontamination. Because of legal restrictions on the domestic role of military units, the National Guard plays a support role with local resources (Lee, 1998; Schafer, 1998).

The length of time required for deployment and employment of National Guard units, however, precludes them from assuming a first-responder role, as chemical agents and nuclear or radiological weapons wreak irreversible havoc within the first hour after an attack, a period when local officials may not yet have analyzed the evidence leading to a conclusion that the event is a WMD or CBRNE event. By the time a WMD or CBRNE event is confirmed and a request for state resources is placed, assembly and travel time would place the National Guard's arrival too late for its stated mission of providing analysis and advice.

In the same Naval Academy commencement speech, President Clinton announced that "we will undertake a concerted effort to prevent the spread and use of biological weapons," and that we will "pursue the fight against biological weapons on many fronts," including improvement of national medical surveillance, a widening of the initiative to prepare local first responders, and the creation of "stockpiles of medicines and vaccines to protect our civilian population against the kind of biological agents our adversaries are most likely to obtain or develop" (Clinton, 1998).

The two new PDDs, along with the new mission for the National Guard, provided additional support for the local first-responder partnership known as the Metropolitan Medical Strike Team (MMST)/Metropolitan Medical Task Force (MMTF) developed under the Nunn–Lugar–Domenici Domestic Preparedness Program.*

Domestic Preparedness Program

In order to create the capability to respond to WMD or CBRNE events at the local level, six federal agencies were designated to participate in the Nunn–Lugar–Domenici Domestic Preparedness Program. The Department of Defense (DoD), in conjunction with FEMA and the Department of Energy (DOE), is required by Subtitle A of the Defense Against Weapons of Mass Destruction Act of 1996 to establish a program to provide training and advice to federal, state and local officials responsible for crisis and consequence management in a nuclear, radiological, chemical or biological emergency. Of the funds authorized for this purpose, a portion is to be made available for the establishment of medical response teams (Subtitle A, Section 1411). Thus, a new program was begun that created a partnership among six federal departments/agencies and local emergency responders and emergency managers. The federal partners were the Department of Defense (DoD), Department of Energy (DOE), Federal Bureau of Investigation (FBI), Public Health Service (PHS), Environmental Protection Agency (EPA), and the Federal Emergency Management Agency (FEMA).

Washington, DC, was the site of the first prototype MMST, followed by Atlanta, Georgia, in preparation for the 1996 Olympics (Knouss, 1998). Twenty-five additional cities were selected for the 1997 nationwide program: the next 23 largest cities plus Honolulu and Anchorage because of their isolation. Unlike most federal programs, which require grant applications or some request to participate, the cities were selected at the federal level and contacted in the spring of 1997 with the information that they were on the list. In April 1997, a meeting was held at Dulles International Airport in the suburbs of Washington, DC, to announce this program to the participating cities. The notices were sent out less than a week in advance of the meeting date, resulting in a low level of participation by cities outside of the Eastern seaboard.

Faxes were sent to the mayors of the 27 cities asking them to designate the principal point of contact for the program immediately. This procedure ignored the reality that many of the cities function under a council/manager form of government, with a mayor whose powers are mostly ceremonial (ICMA, 2007). There was also no provision made for regional- or state-level coordination, even though several states had multiple cities among the first 27, such as California with Los Angeles, San Diego, San Jose, and San Francisco. Others cities were added in subsequent years, with a final participation of 122 cities and two regions: New England and Texas Border. These cities are listed below:

Akron, OH	Anchorage, AK	Aurora, CO
Albuquerque, NM	Arlington, TX	Austin, TX
Amarillo, TX	Arlington, VA	Bakersfield, CA
Anaheim, CA	Atlanta, GA	Baltimore, MD

---

* Note that in states that were using the Incident Command System (ICS) for command and control, such as California, the name was changed to the Metropolitan Medical Task Force, because in ICS terminology a strike team is a group of the same resource, such as an ambulance strike team, while a task force is made up of various types of equipment and personnel.

Baton Rouge, LA
Birmingham, AL
Boston, MA
Buffalo, NY
Charlotte, NC
Chattanooga, TN
Chesapeake, VA
Chicago, IL
Cincinnati, OH
Cleveland, OH
Colorado Springs, CO
Columbus, GA
Columbus, OH
Corpus Christie, TX
Dallas, TX
Dayton, OH
Denver. CO
Des Moines, IA
Detroit, MI
El Paso, TX
Fort Lauderdale, FL
Fort Wayne, IN
Fort Worth, TX
Fremont, CA
Fresno, CA
Garland, TX
Glendale, AZ
Glendale, CA
Grand Rapids, MI
Greensboro, NC
Hialeah, FL
Honolulu, HI
Houston, TX
Huntington Beach, CA
Huntsville, AL
Indianapolis, IN
Irving, TX
Jackson, MS
Jacksonville, FL
Jersey City, NJ
Kansas City, KS
Kansas City, MO
Knoxville, TN
Las Vegas, NV
Lexington-Fayette, KY
Lincoln, NB
Little Rock, AR
Long Beach, CA
Los Angeles, CA
Louisville, KY
Lubbock, TX
Madison, WI
Memphis, TN
Mesa, AZ
Metairie, LA
Miami, FL
Milwaukee, WI
Minneapolis, MN
Mobile, AL
Modesto, CA
Montgomery, AL
Nashville, TN
New Orleans, LA
New York, NY
Newark, NJ
Newport News, VA
Norfolk, VA
Oakland, CA
Oklahoma City, OK
Omaha, NB
Orlando, FL
Philadelphia, PA
Phoenix, AZ
Pittsburgh, PA
Portland, OR
Providence, RI
Raleigh, NC
Richmond, VA
Riverside, CA
Rochester, NY
Sacramento, CA
Salt Lake City, UT
San Antonio, TX
San Bernardino, CA
San Diego, CA
San Francisco, CA
San Jose, CA
Santa Ana, CA
Seattle, WA
Shreveport, LA
Spokane, WA
Springfield, MA
St. Louis, MO
St. Paul, MN
St. Petersburg, FL
Stockton, CA
Syracuse, NY
Tacoma, WA
Tampa, FL
Toledo, OH
Tucson, AZ
Tulsa, OK
Virginia Beach, VA
Warren, MI
Washington, DC
Wichita, KS
Worcester, MA
Yonkers, NY

Financial Support for Counterterrorism

Federal funds to support this domestic preparedness effort initially came from three sources—DoD, Department of Health and Human Services (HHS), and FBI—each with a slightly different set of goals and rules. Although the 122 cities were the same for the DoD and HHS efforts, the FBI's program varied by region. The FBI provided training and tabletop exercises to communities based on its intelligence about potential threats in a given region. Furthermore, the Office of Justice Programs grant program used 120 entities, including counties as population entities, significantly changing the list of eligible communities.

The DoD had funding to create and deliver a set of "train the trainer" courses, written by consultants, to bring DoD training materials to the civilian level. These courses were designed to equip local government first responders with the tools to respond safely and to save the maximum number of victims of a WMD or CBRNE event. Course titles included First Responder Awareness, Operations, Incident Command, Hazardous Materials Technician, Emergency Medical Technician, and Hospital Provider. These six courses were intended to be delivered to police, fire, and emergency medical services personnel and to Emergency Operations Center staff. In addition, a course was developed for the executive management of a community.

Before a city received training, there was a two-day meeting with representatives of the six federal partner agencies. Each agency outlined its responsibilities and its counterterrorism assets available to local government. The local government then outlined its current strengths and training needs. This meeting theoretically formed the basis for the week of train-the-trainer courses. There were four days of repeated delivery of the six courses. On the last day there was a tabletop exercise/facilitated discussion that included all levels of WMD and CBRNE response. Work groups for the breakout sessions included the incident site team, emergency operations center team, operational area team, regional/state team, and federal team. A scenario formed the basis for this last class, providing an interactive learning environment for all the participants.

The DoD recruited, trained, and paid for all the instructors and instructional materials for the train-the-trainer courses. In addition, $300,000 worth of instructional support material was provided to the selected cities. The standard training equipment set of training aids included audiovisual and written materials to support the six courses, simulators to train personnel to use various detection devices, a set of personal protective equipment, decontamination equipment, and detection equipment. The DoD also created new resources to support the local counterterrorism response: a website, a specialized team, and a helpline. A military website outlined the resources, training, and future plans for local assistance in counterterrorism.

Also supporting a local government's response was a Chemical/Biological Rapid Response Team (C/B-RRT) located on the East Coast. The C/B-RRT was deployed to support the FBI and assist state and local responders "in the detection, neutralization, containment, dismantlement, and disposal of weapons of mass destruction containing chemical, biological, or related materials" (Public Law 104-201, Section 1414(a)). The basis of the team was the U.S. Army's Technical Escort Unit's Chemical Biological Rapid Response Teams. The Tech Escort was to be deployed within four hours. Additional resources included U.S. Army Chemical Biological Defense Command, Aberdeen Proving Ground, Maryland; U.S. Army 52nd Ordnance Group; U.S. Army Medical Research Institute for Infectious Diseases (USAMRIID), Fort Detrick, Maryland; U.S. Army Medical Research Institute for Chemical Defense, Aberdeen Proving Ground, Maryland; U.S. Army Material Command Treaty Lab, CBDCOM, Aberdeen Proving Ground, Maryland; U.S. Navy Medical Research Institute, Bethesda, Maryland; U.S. Navy Environmental and Preventive Medicine Units; and the U.S. Naval Research Laboratory in Washington, DC.

Another resource was a toll-free chemical/biological help line run by CBDCOM at Aberdeen Proving Ground. The number was available for first responders such as police, fire, hazardous materials technicians, emergency medical technicians, and emergency management officials. In addition, bomb squad members, dispatchers, and other support personnel had access to the information line. Security of the information was ensured through a call screening process. Information on preparedness was available during non-emergency periods. It was also available to support emergency personnel during a response. Toll-free phone lines, fax, e-mail, and Internet sites all supported this effort.

The second source of funding for local government WMD and CBRNE device preparedness was the Department of Health and Human Services (HHS), managed by U.S. Public Health Service (PHS) officers. Recognizing that a major impact on medical facilities from victims of WMD or CBRNE events would require assets with specialized training and equipment, HHS was given funds to contract with 27 cities to create Metropolitan Medical Strike Teams (MMSTs) and the wider Metropolitan Medical Strike Team System (MMSTS), later called Metropolitan Medical Response System (MMRS). The contracts were made for an average of $350,000, with a planning standard of up to 1000 victims. The funds were designated for specific activities that resulted in the creation of a local WMD or CBRNE emergency response capability. The MMST included police personnel tasked with the search for secondary devices, security, crowd and traffic control, and evidence collection. It included fire department personnel who are emergency medical technicians (EMTs), paramedics, hazardous materials technicians, and incident commanders. It also included medical specialists who could research the signs and symptoms to determine the particular agent and the best antidotes or countermeasures. The wider system included emergency medical transportation personnel, emergency medical care providers in hospitals, police and fire dispatchers, emergency public information officers, and emergency operations center leaders. The DoD courses provided the backbone of the training for this team.

In addition to the materials provided as part of the DoD training cache, the PHS funds permitted the purchase of specific types of support equipment, such as personnel protective equipment for first responders, detection equipment, decontamination equipment, specialized communication equipment, medical equipment, and pharmaceuticals. A PHS project officer was assigned to each of the 27 cities to oversee the development of the MMST, its supporting plans, and the lists of goods to be purchased with HHS funds. The allocation was roughly $100,000 for pharmaceuticals and $250,000 for equipment. No vehicles were included.

In support of this system, a series of plan documents was developed by the MMST. First was a planning process, followed by a training plan that included the DoD training but also covered ongoing training and refresher training. Third was a MMST system plan that outlined the relationships among the various jurisdictions and occupational specialties within the community. Finally, specific lists of pharmaceuticals and equipment were approved by the PHS project officer, along with custody plans for each group of equipment.

The third partner offering financial support to the counterterrorism effort was the FBI. They offered competitive grants for an average of $250,000 per eligible jurisdiction (cities and counties), depending on the population size, for assets to support the multijurisdictional/multitask activities of the community in counterterrorism. Competitive grant applications for these funds included equipment not covered by the HHS funds, such as law enforcement resources. For example, one major city was awarded funding to purchase personal protective equipment for the bomb squad that provided splash protection, inhalation protection, and protection against explosives.

The FBI's primary role within the Nunn–Lugar–Domenici program's local preparedness element was as the principal trainer for the terrorism awareness portions of the courses. In addition to participating in the DoD training modules, the FBI provided its own briefings and conducted tabletop exercises to develop integrated terrorism response plans. The issue of turnover of responsibility for the investigation and evidence collection at a terrorist event had been subject to some controversy in the past; however, the FBI's counterterrorism plan included a complementary role for local law enforcement and the development of a Joint Operations Center that included local participation (FBI, 1998).

Domestic Preparedness Partner Agencies

The Department of Energy is a training partner. As the experts on nuclear materials, they offer specialized courses on managing both the victims and the community consequences of radiological or nuclear events. They presented a free conference in Washington, DC, in 1998 that covered a variety of planning, preparedness, and response skills. The principal consequence management agency is FEMA. Originally it was envisioned that FEMA would manage a WMD event as it manages natural disasters; however, early in the planning stages it became clear that there was a need to enhance FEMA's legal authority to spend funds for WMD and CBRNE consequence management because the Stafford Act, which was passed in 1988 and provides the basis for most disaster assistance to affected communities, covered only natural hazards, and it did not cover law enforcement activities. Ultimately, the Terrorism Incident Annex to the Federal Response Plan resolved the roles of local, state, and federal entities in responding to and paying for terrorism's consequences (Larson and Peters, 2000).

Future of Sustained Response

The philosophy behind the Nunn–Lugar–Domenici program was the development of a permanent counterterrorism capability at the local level. In order to create this at the least cost, a "delta" concept was created for the delivery of training and equipment. The concept was that the federal partners would use their expertise and federal funds to enhance existing hazardous materials response capabilities, emphasizing only the delta information where the standard hazardous materials response branches off into the specialized fields of chemical and biological weapons. Many of the techniques and considerations are the same for the management of a hazardous materials event and the management of a WMD or CBRNE event. The delta falls within two major areas: (1) equipment—more sophisticated detectors and more stringent personal protective equipment requirements of a WMD or CBRNE event; and (2) victims—many more severely injured people needing decontamination and unusual definitive medical care. These victims may also require extensive applications of medical technology and large quantities of pharmaceuticals.

Training Needs

Although a large cadre of trainers was trained by the DoD in each selected community, over time these people had to be replaced by additional local trainers. The addition of counterterrorism coursework in fire and police academies and the delivery of this training to other public employees, such as airport and stadium workers, drained local training budgets. For example, San Jose, California, spent $1 million in overtime costs for the police alone in the first year of the MMST program. No money was provided through any MMST-related federal funding process to pay for the overtime costs of delivering the DoD classes to public employees.

Also, no money was provided for the ongoing costs of training supplies once the DoD "loaned training equipment" was used up or became outdated. At a cost of $4000 each and with a maximum shelf-life of five years, Level A hazardous materials suits were unlikely to be stockpiled in sufficient quantities at city expense to protect the public safety staff needed to respond to 1000 victims. City budgets, already strained by current community needs and demands, could not absorb the new federally mandated activities required to remain prepared for potential WMD or CBRNE events. Homelessness, affordable housing, and other immediate social problems competed for scarce public resources with overall disaster preparedness, of which terrorism was just one component. Expensive terrorism countermeasures were ultimately unsustainable over the long term without additional federal support.

Pharmaceuticals

The initial federal funds were not sufficient to completely prepare a community for a WMD or CBRNE response, even as an enhancement of existing hazardous materials and emergency medical response capabilities. Exotic pharmaceuticals for up to 1000 victims would have overwhelmed the funding, without any other purchases. Local staffs were forced to set priorities for the use of the $350,000 HHS MMST funds that promised the greatest benefit to the community in the event of a terrorist attack. Rather than purchasing a cache of expensive drugs that would become outdated in a few years, communities allocated their funds for commonly used but necessary drugs, such as atropine and antibiotics, that might be able to be cycled through the normal medical system in an attempt to create a sustainable cache. However, to ensure the timely delivery of treatment, some pharmaceuticals with no routine use had to be replaced within MMST resources. For example, a WMD or chemical event would require such a large quantity of atropine that all of the cached supplies, as well as local supplies with Food and Drug Administration (FDA) approval, would be exhausted. Access to non-traditional sources within the community was needed to boost local capabilities. Some communities planned on assistance from veterinarians, and others extended the shelf-life of caches through careful storage and regular testing of samples. Some cities stockpiled their pharmaceutical caches within the county hospital system as an oversupply. FDA guidelines on supply limits created some challenges. Even when it was possible, fully rotating a 1000-patient, single-event cache of antidotes and antibiotics might not occur within the shelf-life of the products, except in the largest metropolitan areas. Another challenge was that for-profit institutions did not want to allocate the storage space for portions of the MMST drug cache, even if the drugs were originally purchased through federal funds. Another strategy was having Veterans Affairs hospitals serve as the cache location, but they were not strategically located to serve all of the 27 original cities, and even less so to care for the 122 cities on the final list. Finally, some cities proposed having military medical facilities stockpile the expensive, exotic drugs and pharmaceuticals, notably vaccines and antitoxins. The drawback for most areas is the time required to deliver them from the nearest military facility. In many cases, these items must be administered to patients within one to two hours to be effective, and it is unlikely that a stockpiled cache from a military base could be mobilized that quickly. Considering that it will take about an hour before the first contaminated victim can receive definitive care (following extrication and decontamination), it may not be realistic to plan to use this type of storage.

Dual-Use Equipment

Funds allocated for equipment that has multiple uses proved to be a better investment; for example, equipment such as decontamination tents can be used for hazardous materials responses. Such use is more frequent than counterterrorism use, guaranteeing that staff members continue to be familiar with the procedures for locating and setting up the equipment. Multiple-purpose items are more likely to be inspected periodically. An unmet challenge remains how to stockpile expensive and fragile medical equipment, such as ventilators. Although vendor-managed stockpiles have been adopted as the answer by most jurisdictions, there has been a concern that many cities are relying on the same vendors, who are unlikely to be able to meet all the contractual agreements within a region at the time of a WMD or CBRNE crisis (Prior, 2004).

Medical Community

Maintaining the training of the medical community was also challenging. Although emergency medical technicians and paramedics in fire departments were included in department-wide refresher training, it is difficult to keep other medical personnel up to date after they have been initially trained. Emergency medical transportation and hospital services are typically provided by for-profit organizations, which see no financial benefit in investing staff time in counterterrorism training. Alternatives such as web-based independent studies can fill the knowledge gap but do not provide for practical applications. Other federal programs such as the Urban Area Security Initiative (UASI), State Homeland Security Grant Program (SHSGP), and Health Resources and Services Administration (HRSA) grants have provided some financial support for ongoing training. The need for awareness and decontamination training classes is especially important in medical facilities, but the Occupational Safety and Health Administration (OSHA) requirements for refresher training for people assigned personal protective equipment have impacted the number of people that a hospital can afford to train and equip for WMD and CBRNE responses. HRSA grants and the Joint Commission's Environment of Care standards have provided incentives for hospitals to maintain a minimal level of WMD and CBRNE preparedness (Joint Commission, 2008). Reaching physicians is especially difficult, given their status as independent professionals and the value of their time.

Biological Response

Although the medical community plays an important part in a chemical weapon response, it is even more critical to saving lives in a biological event. It is the medical community whose epidemiology and disease reporting systems will most likely give the first hint of a biological attack. PDD-62 highlighted the need to improve medical surveillance, and the Centers for Disease Control and Prevention (CDC) began work on a national disease surveillance system, the National Electronic Disease Surveillance System (NEDSS), in 1998. By 2006, the CDC had begun hosting a national web-based version of NEDSS that allows for electronic exchange of information on emergency room visits and laboratory test results. By 2007, the system covered 25% of the U.S. population, with over 900 users. By 2012, 46 states, New York City, and Washington, DC, were using NEDSS to report disease surveillance information to the CDC (CDC, 2012), and the reporting time for communicable diseases had shrunk from 24 days to 3 days (CSC, 2007). Reports of multiple cases of unusual diseases in one area, such as smallpox or anthrax, can be the first warning that an attack has occurred. Mass vaccination of the public and definitive care for the victims are now possible as NEDSS provides near-real-time disease surveillance. Although the MMST/MMTF system contract required the cities to make a long-term training plan, each city has had little or no control over many of its MMST system partners, especially those in private practice and for-profit institutions. Incentives such as earning continuing education units (CEUs) toward licensure for CBRNE training encouraged participation in training by some practitioners, but grant funding for overtime and exercise expenses proved to be the most important factor in maintaining competence.

Nunn–Lugar–Domenici: Development or Devolution

The federal programs designed to create a level of domestic counterterrorism capability at the local government level represent an interesting exercise of federal power. Although the federal government has been distributing federal funds to support specific local government programs since the New Deal, in the past most of these programs were managed as grants. Although the ability to apply might have been offered, the elected officials of a community usually had to make a decision to apply for the grant or program. This decision process allowed the local government's professional staff to analyze the costs to the community of participation in the federal program. They could advise the elected officials on the overall cost–benefit to the community and of the budgetary impact in each year of participation in the grant. It is true that few federal grants cover all of the costs for a community to participate, but the community generally can make a conscious decision about accepting a federal program and its package of costs and revenues.

Local Capability for WMD and CBRNE Events

Prior to the Nunn–Lugar–Domenici legislation, acts of terrorism were handled either as local crimes and managed as a law enforcement response or as a national problem that was managed by the FBI. This new program created a new responsibility for local governments that ultimately required ongoing federal funding. Cities that were selected for participation in the program generally reacted toward the notification as if it were a mandate. Most cities simply added the creation of the MMST to the existing work load of a senior city administrator, who had to engender support for the program from the most impacted departments: police, fire, and emergency medical services resources. In general, department heads felt compelled to cooperate while decrying the impact on budgets that were already minimal. Federal funding was strictly limited to the acquisition of a specific list of supplies and equipment, in most cases items that the local government did not previously intend to purchase. These goods became the responsibility of the local governments, and eventually the replacements were acquired with funding from other grants that were created after 9/11, such as the Homeland Security Grant Program and the Urban Area Security Initiative (FEMA, 2012). In the beginning, the development of WMD or CBRNE capability was a leap of faith, but the reality of domestic and international terrorism in the United States proved the investments to be worthwhile.

The program created a new duty at the local government level: the duty to be prepared to respond to a WMD or CBRNE attack on the community. In the past, such attacks had been considered acts of war, and it was anticipated that military resources would be deployed to manage the response and recovery. Now local governments have been "empowered," without prior consultation, to take over this technical and dangerous role. Police and fire employee unions in some cities initially questioned whether this was a meet-and-confer issue because they considered it a change of working conditions, as they had never before been expected to deal with CBRNE devices. Exposure to Sarin during an emergency response is quite different from exposure to a methamphetamine lab or an industrial chemical release, both of which have been part of urban policing's environment.

Federal leaders viewed the development of the local response capabilities as empowering local government to provide effective service to their communities; however, local governments often viewed the program as a transfer of responsibility from the federal government to the local government. Local governments now face a limitless future of maintaining a new capacity that is unlikely to be used but has proven to be necessary in the post-9/11 world. Former FBI Director Louis J. Freeh suggested in his Senate hearing testimony on April 23, 1998, that WMD and CBRNE events were "a phenomenon which is of low probability, based on the cases that we know about, but extremely catastrophic consequence" (Weiner, 1998). Given the demands on local government to develop emergency response capabilities to high-probability events, the development of MMST capability may not appear to be a good application of scarce resources; however, the realization that such capability also improves response to all mass casualty events, even a train accident or a bus accident, has also improved the value of the teams in the eyes of the community.

Many communities made the MMST a multiple-use group, whose equipment and skills may be applied in industrial chemical accidents, multiple casualty accidents, and similar more frequent events. This approach has benefited all parties, as skills are maintained and familiarity with equipment is maintained when the team and its supplies are multipurpose and have actual response experiences.

Financial Considerations

The financial issue was a second problem created by the federal selection of communities for Nunn–Lugar–Domenici funding. The program became an unfunded mandate for training. Federal contractors provided information to the selected cities about the "free" training. In fact, the cost to a city to receive the training is very high. The federal program developers did not factor into the development process the cost of the time for local government employees to sit in classrooms to receive the training. Some employees might be able to be trained during on-duty time; however, the DoD-developed courses can last up to 12 hours, and only rarely can so much time be provided during normal working hours for most public safety personnel, who typically spend their working hours in the field. Therefore, most police, fire, and emergency medical services personnel have taken the DoD training courses either on overtime themselves or while being covered in the field by someone else on overtime.

The cost to the San Jose Fire Department to receive the train-the-trainer courses in 1998 exceeded $65,000, not including the personnel time cost for the trainers from the Office of Emergency Services, public information officers, police department, or the partner county public health department and private sector hospital and ambulance personnel. These trainers had to train the rest of their departments, at additional cost in personnel time. With overtime budgets stretched thin by natural hazards responses, economic downturns, and decreasing revenue overall, this additional expense has had a significant budgetary impact. Because MMST capability requires the use of unique equipment (notably, military warfare chemical detectors), ongoing training to maintain proficiency means that the training costs can continue indefinitely.

Furthermore, the MMST process requires the development of a series of plans: plans to write the plans, plans for emergency response, training plans. All of these have to be coordinated with local MMST development oversight committees. The cost of staff time to undertake this planning and plan writing process was not included in any budget, nor in any presentation on the process. The $350,000 in equipment was seen as a *quid pro quo* that should have been an acceptable trade for the staff time. Considering that most of that equipment is single use and nothing that local governments have been anxious to possess, local governments have been forced to make an investment in personnel effort for which they often see little overall value added to the city's response capabilities. The same amount of planning time invested in a higher consequence natural disaster event, such as an earthquake or hurricane, could have had more immediate benefit to the community.

Staffing Challenges

In most local governments, the extra work of MMST development has been absorbed by senior and executive staff in the affected departments—people on salary. Staff members at this level typically have little time that is not programmed for specific projects. The initial rollout of this federal project was not announced until April, too late in the local governments' annual budget cycle to be included in personnel resource planning. Therefore, initially much of the MMST development work was actually paid for with "volunteer" time "donated" by these salaried people after normal working hours or through lost opportunity costs, as other work was deferred. After 9/11, the demands from the Department of Homeland Security (DHS) accelerated. Target capabilities and universal tasks were overlaid on the original MMST planning and training requirements (Edwards, 2007). Many emergency managers complained that they became full-time grants managers, to the detriment of community outreach and natural hazards programs' planning and training efforts.

Finally, the federal program developers appear not to have considered the political ramifications at the local level of participation in the program. After reviewing the requirements for participation in the MMST program, the City of San Diego initially chose not to participate. Citing the lack of financial and staff capacity to support a new program, the city deferred the effort to the county's health department. For the purposes of developing a MMST within San Diego County, the law enforcement and fire roles initially were filled by federal employees in the Department of the Navy's fire and security services.

Other communities have found that smaller surrounding jurisdictions assume that, because they received funding for the development of a MMST program, the receiving community is now a regional resource and has some obligation for training and response in other communities. The federal contracts for the original MMSTs specifically stated that local teams were not deployable; however, because the state was left out of the planning and development process, issues related to mutual aid and regional responsibilities remained murky. Smaller communities tend to think that larger communities receive the train-the-trainer capability to train them. When the MMST was modified and renamed the Metropolitan Medical Response System (MMRS), a regional approach was built into the program that created problems for the older teams that were based on a single community approach.

MMST Mutual Aid

The relationship among MMSTs was also unclear. Mutual aid among MMSTs was anticipated in Arizona and California as part of their existing and robust mutual aid systems, but the multidisciplinary nature of the MMST created some managerial problems for mutual aid deployment, such as which profession is authorized to deploy the entire team on a mutual aid mission. Clearly, a 49-person team would be overwhelmed by the 1000 victims postulated by the planning parameters, so cross-border mutual aid seems inevitable during an event. Yet, operational considerations have to temper mutual aid decisions. Could team members be spared from their own community if a MMST city in the region had been the subject of attack? National, deployable National Medical Response Teams exist in Los Angeles, Denver, and North Carolina (Knouss, 1998), but their response times for most of the first 27 cities would not be rapid enough to make a difference to the victims.

Further, the involvement of the National Guard Civil Support Teams (CSTs) poses yet another intergovernmental dilemma. The National Guard is a state asset, deployed by the governor. Except when federalized they are not part of the U.S. military; yet, the WMD and CBRNE mission was announced by federal authorities without consultation with state organizations responsible for the National Guard. When questioned about the statement that the National Guard would become first responders, one law enforcement executive who was also a National Guard officer said, "Well, they would be the first *military* responders." By 2012, there were 57 teams staffed by full-time personnel throughout the nation. "Each team consists of 18 Army Guardsmen and four Air Guardsmen—six officers and 12 non-commissioned officers (NCOs) from the Army, and one officer and three NCOs from the Air Guard" (Viana, 2012).

A 2007 National Guard fact sheet stated that the role of the 55 existing National Guard Civil Support Teams was "to assess a suspected weapons of mass destruction (WMD) attack, advise civilian responders on appropriate action through on-site testing and expert consultation, and facilitate the arrival of additional state and federal military forces" (National Guard, 2007). The fact sheet postulated a 90-minute window for deployment of the first team and a 3-hour deployment for the rest of the team. Each state and territory has one team except for California, New York, and Florida, which each have two teams. Travel time would have to be added to this deployment schedule, including traffic obstructions from the disaster.

The role assigned in former President Clinton's announcement was reconnaissance and decontamination (Anon., 1998). Is this reconnaissance of the crime scene? The local FBI and local government law enforcement personnel will have long since completed scene reconnaissance and probably have begun evidence collection. What are they going to decontaminate? The scene of the event? All of the victims will have been decontaminated, triaged, and treated within the first few hours. The untreated will no longer be salvageable victims but will be deceased. What use are these reconnaissance and decontamination activities 24 to 48 hours after the event? By then the role is recovery and consequence management, a role more suited to psychologists and environmental specialists than to a military unit.

By 2011 a broader mission had been developed for the CSTs (Viana, 2012):

> In fiscal year 2011, CSTs were deployed throughout the United States in support of civil authorities 128 times. These missions included white powder incidents, suspicious substances, chemical hazards, clandestine labs, the BP *Deepwater Horizon* oil spill and Hurricane Irene recovery operations. They were also called upon for 504 standby missions in support of large-scale events, including national and state special security events, stadium and arena sporting events and political gatherings where the WMD-CSTs, in cooperation with local first responders, provided air sampling and chemical detection or similar activities.

These pre-event deployments, not foreseen in the original design, provide a better opportunity for CST capabilities to assist local first responders than trying to deploy distant units after an event. Their analytical laboratory can communicate with the CDC for specimen analysis and communication vans enhance interoperability among federal, state, and local responders to an event—once they arrive (Viana, 2012).

Lessons Still Unlearned

The Nunn–Lugar–Domenici Domestic Preparedness Program is a good example of an idea being released before it has been fully developed. A variety of issues in federalism remain unexamined. First, what does the original "direct to the cities" approach say about federalism in 1998? The federal government, in the guise of two senators and their staffs and committees, arbitrarily selected 27 communities, based principally on population, to participate in a new counterterrorism initiative. There was no consultation with the states about the communities within their jurisdiction that were selected nor about the relationship between the federally formed MMSTs and each state's own internal resource management system. There was no needs assessment by the states or local governments.

The one-size-fits-all approach to boilerplate training resulted in sophisticated fire departments with hazardous materials response teams receiving the same training as departments with limited or single-industry-focused hazardous materials response capabilities. Departments with public ambulances and those with private contractors received the same guidelines for team development. Communities that tried to use the MMST funds to bolster existing capabilities often found that contractors hired for the nationwide list review balked at their equipment selection, insisting that they lacked some critical capability simply because they had not bought it from federal funds. Some items, such as cyanide kits and biological "smart tickets," became required items, even when communities questioned their usefulness in an actual event.

Also, the implications of deploying a MMST within a community, county, region, or state were not considered before the program was announced and the contractual deadlines set. Cities were notified in April 1997, with contractual deadlines established to meet the needs of federal budget cycles, rather than local planning cycles. DoD contractors presented a schedule of training classes followed by a full-scale field exercise within six months; yet, the training equipment had not been delivered to most cities as long as eight months after the training was received. Rather than ordering the training equipment on which there was no disagreement, DoD reviewers held up the entire list while a community justified its need for a particular item. Even delaying the full-scale exercise until nine months after the training resulted in training equipment coming barely in time to be used in the exercises.

When significant new programs requiring large commitments of unfunded resources by local governments are proposed, they should be offered on a grant basis, and time should be built into the schedule for a thorough analysis of the investment required by the recipient community. According to Senator Nunn, the imperative for this program was the three-pronged wake-up call embodied in the 1993 World Trade Center bombing, 1995 Tokyo subway Sarin attack, and 1995 Murrah Federal Building explosion. Impelled by these events, Congress used the budget to propel the MMST and DoD training programs into the local communities. Staff members assigned to manage the programs have struggled to rationalize the process and create a manageable program. Los Angeles County already had a counterterrorism task force working on countywide planning issues, so they were more prepared than most to develop the new initiatives. Their existing committee formed a nucleus to develop the MMST and receive the DoD training across the 88 cities that make up Los Angeles County's 9.9-million population base. Most communities started from nothing to create a MMST system that met federal mandates and local needs. Although the experience generated beneficial relationships across professional lines that will be useful in other responses, the costs in time and lost opportunities to complete other pressing work have yet to be calculated.

Although the federal government took the position that local government would guide the MMST development process in each community (local control), this control was actually very carefully circumscribed by both the DoD and DHHS headquarters units. Local requests for multi-use equipment and multipurpose teams initially met with resistance at the national level. There was a clear message that the Nunn–Lugar–Domenici funds were not to be applied to handling everyday events that were seen as the local government's responsibility. However, multi-use training and equipment represented a more efficient use of time and money, guaranteeing ongoing proficiency and frequent capability exercising. Repeated iteration of this message has had only a moderate effect on national-level responses to local requests for MMST-funded equipment.

Post-9/11 programs went to the other extreme, cutting the nation's largest cities out of the State Homeland Security Grant Program funds. The Urban Area Security Initiative (UASI) grants were intended to provide ongoing support for urban counterterrorism efforts, but regionalization of the UASI grants and the blending of law enforcement state and urban grants, along with MMRS, Emergency Management Performance Grants, and Citizen Corps money, ended up confusing and diluting the system (FEMA, 2012).

In 2000, the MMSTs were converted to Metropolitan Medical Response Systems (MMRSs), and the focus shifted to medical planning, to the detriment of field team capabilities. Some of the last MMRS cities to be appointed had no field response capability, leading to confusion in Congress regarding their purpose, which had been intended as a coordinating role among hospital-based resources, public health, and first-responder teams. This loss of clearly explained focus led to federal budget battles for funding almost every budget cycle, especially after 9/11 when everything was suddenly about prevention and interest in preparedness was lost. Executive branch staffers asked how much money could be usefully spent on medical planning for WMDs, while the leadership of the Department of Homeland Security (DHS)-based MMRS program struggled to interpret the crucial field response embodied in this large, ten-year investment.

Future of MMST/MMRS

Financial continuity and independence have been a struggle for the MMRS program after the attacks of 9/11 demonstrated just how prescient urban area preparedness for terrorist attacks was. Rather than supporting the existing multidisciplinary capability, the federal government lost the MMST/MMRS program in a sea of reorganization and bureaucratic infighting. The multiple funding streams supporting the MMRS were disrupted as the Department of Homeland Security was formed by the merger of existing federal entities. Grants moved from FEMA to a new DHS office that was moved out of the Department of Justice's criminal justice area. Oversight of the MMRS program moved from HHS to FEMA, dominated by fire department influence and where the multidisciplinary, multigovernment mission of MMRSs was poorly understood.

In the post 9/11 period, preparedness grants proliferated for cities and states and transit (e.g., 16 separate grants created by 2012). MMRS funding ultimately was delivered through the Urban Area Security Initiative process. In the combined regional UASIs, as in the San Francisco Bay Area, multiple teams at differing levels of development and capability were vying for the small amount of available funds. As the cost of maintaining the pharmaceutical cache rose, the cost of disposal of expired drugs rose, and the available funds were no more than the 2000 level of $350,000 per city at best. MMRS began to lose capability and participation, often defaulting back to the fire department, which is home to the hazardous materials response and emergency medical services components, resulting in the loss of robust participation from other entities that decided it was no longer their job.

In 2012, the National Emergency Management Association (NEMA) proposed merging all 16 separate grant funds into a new National Preparedness Grant Program. The Department of Homeland Security appears to have adopted this approach in its 2013 grant "vision document" (DHS, 2012) in support of President Barak Obama's reframing of HSPD-8 into Presidential Policy Directive 8 (PPD-8; National Preparedness), issued in 2011 (White House, 2011). The new directive covers "the threats that pose the greatest risk to the security of the nation, including acts of terrorism, cyber attacks, pandemics, and catastrophic natural disasters." It covers not just federal departments but "is also aimed at facilitating an integrated, all-of-nation, capabilities-based approach to preparedness."

The DHS's proposed merger of the grant programs, excluding Emergency Management Performance Grants (EMPGs) and Fire Grants, reflects an interest in enhancing local initiative by allocating some funding to a baseline level for states with a population-driven formula and then placing most of the funding in a block grant approach that requires a competitive process among the states, based on meeting a specific capability gap identified in the threat analysis (UASI, 2012). However, this cuts the cities and major metropolitan areas out of the process, as only states and tribes may apply (DHS, 2012). This may mark the end of most MMST/MMRS programs, as states have no stake in the MMST/MMRS program because it was designed as a nondeployable local asset.

Even those teams, such as California's, that struggled to create a statewide mutual aid system found no support from the state, and their plans remain a gentlemen's agreement with no legal standing. All newly funded grant supported projects and programs will have a two-year implementation cycle to avoid congressional criticism that the allocated funds were unspent at the end of the fiscal year (DHS, 2012). Previous grant cycles have not taken into account the time the state spends analyzing the federal grant documents and then creating their own guidance for their local jurisdictions. The result was that the application process and grant approval took most of the first year, with equipment ordering and delivery consuming another year before training could begin and the capability could be realized. Nothing in the new guidance suggests that this lesson in timing has been learned.

Another aspect of the National Preparedness Grant Program vision document is the inclusion of the development of deployable capability in the funding process, focusing on "capabilities that are cross-jurisdictional, readily deployable, and multipurpose" (DHS, 2012). This was a gap in the original MMST design. New initiatives will include a plan for cross-border use of the newly developed assets, equipment, and capabilities funded in the future. States will have to work out the multidisciplinary mutual aid issues in advance of receiving funding for capability development. Given the power of the sheriffs over law enforcement mutual aid in most states, it will be a challenge to get an equitable arrangement for management of a team such as the MMST/MMRS that is dominated by fire and medical response planning, yet cannot operate without the bomb squad and force protection work of the law enforcement members.

Conclusion

The effort represented by the MMST/MMRS programs to provide counterterrorism capabilities at the local government level is a worthwhile part of an important mission. Without a permanent stream of federal funding to support the training of the participants and the maintenance of supplies and equipment, however, the MMST/MMRS program will disappear, just as the civil defense efforts of earlier times did. If the country truly considers domestic terrorism an ongoing threat that deserves countermeasures, a financial commitment to maintain local preparedness is essential. Without an ongoing commitment to the MMST, communities will be left with an outmoded cache of response materials and no trained first responders. The domestic counterterrorism effort, including field responders in the MMSTs, deserves the serious consideration of Congress and a federal financial commitment into the future, based on realistic funding at the local level, a realistic analysis of costs and benefits to local governments, and the intelligent application of federal stockpiling capabilities nationally. DHS may determine that independent teams that can collaborate in time of need may be easier to manage than the well-integrated system embodied in MMST/MMRS programs.

Questions for Discussion

1. What are the WMD or CBRNE event risks in your community? What groups or organizations would be likely to use them?
2. What programs are in place to create a community response to such an event?
3. What local/federal partnerships were created? What local/state partnerships were created? What challenges to the federal system are demonstrated by the need to coordinate across local, state, and federal organizations for a public safety response that includes fire and emergency medical assets?

Additional Reading

Adams, J.A. and Marquette, S. (2002). *First Responders Guide to Weapons of Mass Destruction*. Alexandria, VA: American Society for Industrial Security.

Anon. (1997). Domestic prep program on target despite military oversight: experts. *Emergency Preparedness News*, December 10, p. 3.

Anon. (1998b). Anniversary stirs painful thoughts. *San Jose Mercury News*, April 19, p. 16A.

Anon. (1998c). Marines to be trained in warfare amid skyscrapers. *The New York Times*, May 2, p. 8A.

Barnes, C. (1998). Big bang theory. *Metro*, August 20 (http://www.metroactive.com/papers/metro/08.20.98/terrorism-9833.html).

Brandeau, M.L., Zaric, G.S., Freiesleben, J., Edwards, F.L., and Bravata, D.M. (2008). An ounce of prevention is worth a pound of cure: improving communication to reduce mortality during bioterrorism responses. *Am. J. Disaster Med.*, 3(2): 65–78.

Broad, W.J., Dunn, S., and Miller, J. (1998). Scope of cult attacks revealed. *San Jose Mercury News*, May 26.

CSIS. (1995). *Postscript: Chemical Terrorism in Japan*. Ottawa: Canadian Security Intelligence Service (http://www.csis-scrs.gc.ca).

Edwards, F.L. (2006). Law enforcement response to biological terrorism: lessons learned from New Orleans after Hurricane Katrina. *Law Enforc. Exec. Forum*, 6(1): 139–148.

Edwards, F.L. and Goodrich, D.C. (2007). Organizing for emergency management. In Waugh, W. and Tierney, K., Eds., *Emergency Management: Principles and Practice for Local Government*. Washington, DC: ICMA Press, pp. 30–54.

FEMA. (1996). *Emergency Response to a Criminal/Terrorist Incident: Participant Handbook*. Washington, DC: Federal Emergency Management Agency.

FEMA. (2000). *Emergency Response to Terrorism: Job Aid*. Washington, DC: Federal Emergency Management Agency.

FEMA. (2003). *Terrorism Incident Annex*. Washington, DC: Federal Emergency Management Agency.

Gillert, D.J. (1997). Combating terrorism at home. *J. Civil Defense*, 31(1): 4–7.

Graham, B. (1997). Standing guard for toxic attacks. *San Jose Mercury News*, December 14.

Hicks, V.L. (1998). One faithful man's descent into cult terrorism. *San Jose Mercury News*, June 6.

Howitt, A.M. and Pangi, R.P. (2003). *Countering Terrorism: Dimensions of Preparedness*. Cambridge, MA: MIT Press.

Institute of Medicine and National Research Council. (1999). *Chemical and Biological Terrorism: Research and Development to Improve Civilian Medical Response*. Washington, DC: National Academy Press.

Johnston, D. and Sack, K. (1998). Blasts connected. *San Jose Mercury News*, February 27.

JPEO-CBD. (2015). Joint Program Executive Office for Chemical and Biological Defense website, http://www.jpeocbd.osd.mil/packs/Default2.aspx?pg=0

Kayyem, J.N. and Pangi, R.L. (2003). *First to Arrive: State and Local Responses to Terrorism*. Cambridge, MA: MIT Press.

Kuntz, T. (1998). Word for word/Jane's fighting germs: the grim do's and deadly don'ts of handling chemical attacks. *The New York Times*, March 8 (http://www.nytimes.com/1998/03/08/weekinreview/word-for-word-jane-s-fighting-germs-grim-s-deadly-don-ts-handling-chemical.html?pagewanted=all).

Lederberg, J., Ed. (1999). *Biological Weapons: Limiting the Threat*. Cambridge, MA: MIT Press.

Manning, F.J. and Goldfrank, L., Eds. (2002). *Preparing for Terrorism: Tools for Evaluating the Metropolitan Medical Response System Program*. Washington, DC: National Academies Press.

Marine Terrorism Response Team. (2006). *Marine Terrorism Response Plan*. Vol. III. *Emergency Response to Terrorism Response: Field Operations Guide, Maritime Edition*. Washington, DC: Maritime Terrorism Response (marineresponse.org/mtr-seattle/pdf/MTR_Plan_Vol_III.pdf).

Miller, J. and Broad, W.J. (1998). U.S. fails secret exercise simulating a germ-weapon attack. *The New York Times*, April 26.

Morris, R. (1998). Bioterrorism threat is real. *San Jose Mercury News*, August 11.

Safire, W. (1998). On language: weapons of mass destruction. *The New York Times*, April 19 (http://www.nytimes.com/1998/04/19/magazine/on-language-weapons-of-mass-destruction.html).

Salmon, J.L. (1998). Preparing for the worst: Pentagon drill tests local, federal response to a terrorist attack. *Washington Post*, May 31.

Sidell, F.R., Patrick III, W.C., and Dashiell, T.R. (1998). *Jane's Chem-Bio Handbook*. London: Jane's Information Group.

Simon, S. (1998). A growing fear of toxic terrorism. *Los Angeles Times*, February 24 (http://articles.latimes.com/1998/feb/24/news/mn-22390).

Stern, J. (1998). Taking the terror out of bioterrorism. *The New York Times*, April 8, p. A25.

Sylves, R.T. (2008). *Disaster Policy and Politics*. Washington, DC: CQ Press.

Tucker, J. (2000). *Toxic Terror: Assessing Terrorist Use of Chemical and Biological Weapons*. Cambridge, MA: MIT Press.

U.S. Army. (1995). *Medical Management of Chemical Casualties Handbook*, 2nd ed. Aberdeen Proving Ground, MD: U.S. Army Medical Research Institute of Chemical Defense.

U.S. Department of Health and Human Services. (1995). *Proceedings of the Seminar on Responding to the Consequences of Chemical and Biological Terrorism*, July 11–14, 1995. Washington, DC: U.S. Department of Health and Human Services.

Waugh, W. and Tierney, K. (2007). *Emergency Management: Principles and Practice for Local Government*. Washington, DC: ICMA.

Winik, L.W. (1998). We live in a dangerous world. *Parade*, April 5.

Winslow, F.E. (1999). The first-responder's perspective. In Drell, S., Sofaer, A.D., and Wilson, G., Eds., *The New Terror: Facing the Threat of Biological and Chemical Weapons*, pp. 375–389. Stanford, CA: The Hoover Institution Press.

Zuckerman, M.J. (1998). Anti-terror 'czar' to coordinate $7B effort. *USA Today*, May 4, p. 1A.

References

Allison, G. (2005). *Nuclear Terrorism: The Ultimate Preventable Catastrophe*. New York: Holt.

Anon. (1998). A bottom line in war on terrorism: how to best spend the money. *USA Today*, May 4.

Broad, W.J. (1998). Sowing death: a special report; how Japan germ terror alerted world. *The New York Times*, May 26, p. A10 (http://www.nytimes.com/1998/05/26/world/sowing-death-a-special-report-how-japan-germ-terror-alerted-world.html?pagewanted=all).

Cauchon, D. (2001). For many on Sept. 11, survival was no accident. *USA Today*, December 20 (http://usatoday30.usatoday.com/news/sept11/2001/12/19/usatcov-wtcsurvival.htm).

CBDCOM. (1999). *Domestic Preparedness Fact Sheets*. Aberdeen, MD: Chemical and Biological Defense.

CDC. (2015). *National Notifiable Diseases Surveillance System (NNDSS): NEDSS/NBS*. Atlanta, GA: Centers for Disease Control and Prevention (http://wwwn.cdc.gov/nndss/script/nedss.aspx).

Clinton, B. (1998). Remarks by the President at the United States Naval Academy Commencement, Annapolis, MD, May 22.

Cooper, H. (2011). Obama announces killing of Osama bin Laden. *The New York Times*, May 1 (http://thelede.blogs.nytimes.com/2011/05/01/bin-laden-dead-u-s-official-says/).

CSC. (2015). *CSC Creates National Electronic Disease Surveillance System*. Falls Church, VA: CSC (http://www.csc.com/ca_en/ds/11414/17218-csc_creates_national_electronic_disease_surveillance_system).

DHS. (2012). *FY 2013 National Preparedness Grant Program Vision Document*. Washington, DC: U.S. Department of Homeland Security (http://www.fema.gov/pdf/government/grant/fy2013_npgp_grant_program_overview.pdf).

Edwards, F.L. (2007). Federal intervention in local emergency planning: nightmare on Main Street. *State Local Gov. Rev.* 39(1): 31–43.

Edwards, F.L. and Steinhausler, F. (2007). *NATO and Terrorism—On Scene: New Challenges for First Responders and Civil Protection*. Dordrecht: Springer.

Eligon, J. and Cooper, M. (2013). Blasts at Boston Marathon kill 3 and injure 100. *The New York Times*, April 16, p. A1 (http://www.nytimes.com/2013/04/16/us/explosions-reported-at-site-of-boston-marathon.html?nl=todaysheadlines&emc=edit_th_20130416).

FBI. (1998). *Unified Command*. Washington, DC: Federal Bureau of Investigation.
FBI. (2002). *Terrorism 2000/2001*. Washington, DC: Federal Bureau of Investigation (https://www.fbi.gov/stats-services/publications/terror/terrorism-2000-2001).
FBI. (2006). *Terrorism 2002–2005*. Washington, DC: Federal Bureau of Investigation (http://www.fbi.gov/stats-services/publications/terrorism-2002-2005/terror02_05.pdf
FEMA. (2012). *FY 2012 Homeland Security Grant Program*. Washington, DC: Federal Emergency Management Agency (http://www.fema.gov/fy-2012-homeland-security-grant-program).
Golden, T. and Van Natta, D. (2004). Carnage yields conflicting clues as officials search for culprits. *The New York Times*, March 12, p. A1.
Herridge, C. (2013). Al Qaeda affiliate in Africa looking to strike more Western targets, intelligence officials say. *Fox News*, January 31 (http://www.foxnews.com/politics/2013/01/31/al-qaeda-affiliate-in-africa-aspiring-to-strike-more-western-targets/).
ICMA. (2007). *Council–Manager Form of Government: Frequently Asked Questions*. Washington, DC: International City/County Management Association (http://icma.org/en/icma/knowledge_network/documents/kn/Document/2705/CouncilManager_Form_of_Government_Frequently_Asked_Questions_brochure).
Jehl, D. (1993). Explosion at the Twin Towers: the background; a long list of possible suspects, as inquiry into the bombings begins. *The New York Times*, February 28 (http://www.nytimes.com/1993/02/28/nyregion/explosion-twin-towers-background-long-list-possible-suspects-inquiry-into.html).
Joint Commission. (2008). *Emergency Management*. Oakbrook Terrace, IL: The Joint Commission (http://www.jointcommission.org/emergency_management.aspx).
Karmon, E. (2013). The Boston marathon bombing, Israel and the Jews. *Haaretz*, April 21 (http://www.haaretz.com/misc/article-print-page/the-boston-marathon-bombing-israel-and-the-jews-1.516745?trailingPath=2.169%2C2.216%2C2.217%2C).
Kifner, J. (1995). Terror in Oklahoma City: the overview—at least 31 are dead, scores are missing after car bomb attack in Oklahoma City wrecks 9-story federal office building. *The New York Times*, April 20, p. A1 (http://www.nytimes.com/1995/04/20/us/terror-oklahoma-city-overview-least-31-are-dead-scores-are-missing-after-car.html?pagewanted=all).
Kleinfield, N.R. (2001). A creeping horror: buildings burn and fall as onlookers search for elusive safety. *The New York Times*, September 12, p. A1 (http://www.nytimes.com/2001/09/12/nyregion/12SCEN.html?pagewanted=all).
Knouss, R.F. (1998). *Testimony on Anti-Terrorism Measures by Robert F. Knouss, M.D.* Washington, DC: U.S. Department of Health and Human Services (http://www.hhs.gov/asl/testify/t981002c.html).
Kristof, N.D. (1995). Japanese police raid the offices of a sect linked to poison gas. *The New York Times*, March 22, p. A1.
Larson, E.V. and Peters, J.E. (2000). *Preparing the U.S. Army for Homeland Security: Concepts, Issues, and Options*, Santa Monica, CA: Rand Corporation.
Lee, D.R. (1998). *Protecting Americans at Home*. Washington, DC: Office of the Assistant Secretary of Defense for Manpower and Reserve Affairs (http://fas.org/spp/starwars/program/wmdresponse/deblee.html).
Miller, J. and Broad, W.J. (1998a). Clinton set to OK anti-terror plan. *San Jose Mercury News*, April 26.
Miller, J. and Broad, W.J. (1998b). Exercise finds U.S. unable to handle germ war threat. *The New York Times*, April 26, p. A1 (http://www.nytimes.com/1998/04/26/world/exercise-finds-us-unable-to-handle-germ-war-threat.html).
Myers, S.L. (2004). 19 die in Moscow as bomb goes off—on subway train. *The New York Times*, February 7, p. A1.
National Guard. (2007). *The National Guard's Role in Homeland Defense: National Guard Civil Support Teams Fact Sheet*. Washington, DC: National Guard.
NRC. (2012). *Fact Sheet on Dirty Bombs*. Washington, DC: U.S. Nuclear Regulatory Commission (http://www.nrc.gov/reading-rm/doc-collections/fact-sheets/fs-dirty-bombs.html).
Preston, R. (1998). *The Cobra Event*. New York: Ballantine.
Prior, S.D. (2004). *Who You Gonna Call? Responding to a Medical Emergency with the Strategic National Stockpile*. Washington, DC: Center for Technology and National Security Policy, National Defense University (www.dtic.mil/cgi-bin/GetTRDoc?AD=ADA476356).

Schafer, S.M. (1998). Washington among 10 states chosen for anti-terrorism teams. *Associated Press*, May 22.

Seelye, K.Q., Rashbaum, W.K., and Cooper, M. (2013). 2nd bombing suspect caught after frenzied hunt paralyzes Boston. *The New York Times*, April 20, p. A1 (http://www.nytimes.com/2013/04/20/us/boston-marathon-bombings.html?pagewanted=all&_r=0).

Selden, Z. (1997). *Nunn–Lugar: New Solutions for Today's Nuclear Threats*. Washington, DC: Business Executives for National Security.

Steinhausler, F. and Edwards, F.L. (2005). *NATO and Terrorism: Catastrophic Terrorism and First Responders*. Dordrecht: Springer.

Tomlinson, S. (2013). U.S. faces new Al Qaeda threat as terror group's 'strike map' is revealed. *Daily Mail*, January 31 (http://www.dailymail.co.uk/news/article-2271146/Al-Qaeda-issues-new-threat-carry-earth-shattering-terrifying-attacks-U-S-Europe.html).

UASI. (2012). The fiscal year (FY) 2013 National Preparedness Grant Program (NPGP). *Urban Area Security Initiative Blog* (http://urbanareas.org/blog/the-fiscal-year-fy-2013-national-preparedness-grant-program-npgp/).

Viana, L.P. (2012). Guard's WMD civil support teams can respond faster than other federal assets. *Homeland Security Today*, May 14 (http://www.hstoday.us/briefings/correspondents-watch/single-article/guards-wmd-civil-support-teams-can-respond-faster-than-other-federal-assets/af2160975c8dc3d-4ab7f17f0942bdcdc.html).

Van Natta, Jr., D. and Alvarez, L. (2001). Attack on military; a hijacked Boeing 757 slams into the Pentagon, halting the government. *The New York Times*, September 12, p. A5.

Van Natta, Jr., D. and Sciolino, E. (2005). Timers used in blasts, police say; parallels to Madrid are found. *The New York Times*, July 8, p. A1 (http://www.nytimes.com/2005/07/08/world/europe/timers-used-in-blasts-police-say-parallels-to-madrid-are-found.html).

Weiner, T. (1998). Reno says U.S. may stockpile medicine for terrorist attacks. *The New York Times*, April 23 (http://www.nytimes.com/1998/04/23/us/reno-says-us-may-stockpile-medicine-for-terrorist-attacks.html).

White House. (1995). *Presidential Decision Directive 39*. Washington, DC: U.S. Government Printing Office (http://fas.org/irp/offdocs/pdd39.htm).

White House. (1998a). *Presidential Decision Directive 62*. Washington, DC: U.S. Government Printing Office (https://fas.org/irp/offdocs/pdd-62.htm).

White House. (1998b). *Fact Sheet: Combating Terrorism: Presidential Decision Directive 62*. Washington, DC: U.S. Government Printing Office (https://fas.org/irp/offdocs/pdd-62.htm).

White House. (1998c). *Presidential Decision Directive 63*. Washington, DC: U.S. Government Printing Office (http://fas.org/irp/offdocs/pdd/pdd-63.htm).

White House. (1998d). *Fact Sheet: Protecting America's Critical Infrastructure: PDD 63*. Washington, DC: U.S. Government Printing Office (http://fas.org/irp/offdocs/pdd-63.htm).

White House. (2011). *Presidential Policy Directive/PPD-8: National Preparedness*. Washington, DC: U.S. Government Printing Office (http://www.dhs.gov/presidential-policy-directive-8-national-preparedness).

Wilkening, D. (1999). BCW attack scenarios. In Drell, S., Sofaer, A.D., and Wilson, G., Eds., *The New Terror: Facing the Threat of Biological and Chemical Weapons*, pp. 76–114. Stanford, CA: Hoover Institution Press.

WNA. (2015). *U.S. Nuclear Power Policy*. London: World Nuclear Association (http://www.world-nuclear.org/info/inf41_US_nuclear_power_policy.html).

Index

A

accountability, in Japan, 36, 42, 49
acts of God, 22, 24
adaptive management, 29
advocacy coalition framework (ACF), 241
A Failure of Initiative, 127
air piracy, 151
al-Farabi, Abu Nasr, 180
Algeria, 192
alienation, 4
Allbaugh, Joseph, 130, 152
al-Qaeda, 2, 150, 260
al-Sisi, Abdel Fattah, 188
anthrax, 164, 270
anticipatory surprise management, 20, 23, 27–28
antiterrorism, 10, 152
Arab Spring, 7, 180, 182, 183, 184, 187, 189, 190, 191
Arab states, governance in, 179–193
    deficiencies, 182, 191
    lessons learned, 190–192
    popular uprisings, 180, 181, 182, 183, 186, 187, 188, 190, 191
    resurgance of political Islam in, 186–189
Aristotle, 180
Aum Shinrikyo cult, 261
Aviation and Transportation Security Act, 153
aviation, yearly number of passengers carried, 202

B

Bahrain, 181, 191
Bam Citadel, 137, 142
Bam earthquake, 28, 135–146
    crisis management and emergency governance, 138–142
    lessons learned, 143–146
        chaos management, 143–144
        leadership, 143
        mistakes to avoid, 145–146
        organization and coordination, 144
        policy and administration, 144
        post-disaster recovery, 145
        public health challenges, 144–145
        volunteers, 145, 146
        thefts during, 146
behavior, ethical/unethical, 111
bin Laden, Osama, 150, 151, 260
bioenergy, 217
biological weapons, 261–262, 263, 268, 270
bioterrorism, 262–263
Blackwater, 111
Boston Marathon bombing, 260
Brazil, accidental radiation exposure in, 92, 95
breach, computer, 207
Broward County Sheriff's Office, 163–166, 173, 175, 176
Brown, Michael, 25, 112, 127, 128, 129–130, 132, 152
butterfly effect, 24

C

Cajun humor, 114–115
campaign contributions, 185
Camp Coordination and Camp Management (CCCM), 250
capacity and vulnerability assessment, 226, 227
capacity building, 4, 9, 20, 22, 26, 27–28, 29, 50, 51
    resilience, 197–219
capitalism, 2, 3, 4
carbon dioxide emissions, 199
catastrophes, defined, 239–240
catastrophic terrorism, 261
Category 5 hurricane, 25, 126, 127, 165
CellCube vanadium flow batteries, 217
central command, 5–6, 21, 23, 25, 26, 139–141, 144, 192
Central Intelligence Agency (CIA), 151
chaos, 2, 5, 8, 9, 18, 19, 21, 25, 27, 28, 135–146, 261
    and order, relationship between, 136
    destabilizing forces of, 5, 20
    -driven crises, 2, 5, 20, 136
    management, 18, 26, 29, 140–141
        Bam earthquake and, 143–144
    opportunists, and, 8
    political, 191
    theory, 5, 9, 11, 20, 22, 24, 28, 136

284 ■ *Index*

Chemical Biological Defense Command (CBDCOM), 262, 266
chemical, biological, radiological, nuclear, or explosive (CBRNE) devices, 91, 218, 259–277
Chemical/Biological Rapid Response Team (C/B-RRT), 266
chemical weapons, 141, 261–262, 270
Chernobyl nuclear reactor accident, 38, 41, 89–103
    communication failure, 97
    decontamination of affected area, 99
    evacuation, 101
    lessons learned, 95–102
    media role, 97–98
    medical data, 96
    site remediation, 100
Chertoff, Michael, 112, 131
China, *see* Qinglong County, Tangshan earthquake
China Earthquake Agency (CEA), 55, 56, 57, 62
cholera outbreak in Haiti, 244, 249–250
Civil Support Teams (CSTs), National Guard, 273–274
climate-positive community, 199
cloud shine, 99
coastal ecosystems, 201
code red system, 170
Cold War, 2, 97, 263
collaboration, 6, 21, 25, 29, 158, 176, 227, 234, 249, 252
collaborative emergency management, 173–174
command-and-control systems, 8, 157, 159
communication, 3, 4, 10, 29, 152, 153, 164, 165, 166, 173, 228, 229; *see also* transcommunication
    failure, 25
        Chernobyl, 97
        Three Mile Island, 96, 101
    Fukushima nuclear disaster, and, 33–51, 98
    Great Tangshan Earthquake, and, 57–59
    plan, 95, 96
    systems, 110
communications, redundant, 164, 173
communism, 186
Communities Advancing Resilience Toolkit (CART), 223–234
    application, 228–232
    domains, 228
    instruments, 227–228
    lessons learned, 233
    process, 225–227
community resilience, 224–225, 227, 229, 232, 233
    factors, 228
    strategies for building, 233
complexity-driven management system, 19
complexity theory, 22, 28, 146
congestion, 203–205, 207–209
consequence management, 156, 262, 263, 264, 268, 274
consequential crises, 18
Continuity of Operations (COOP) planning, 174
Cooperative Threat Reduction Program, 261
coordination, Hurricane Katrina, and, 26

counterterrorism, 91, 150, 151–152, 153, 155, 156, 259–277
    financial support for, 265–267
creative breakdowns, 5, 20
crises
    capitalism, and, 3
    chaos-driven, 2, 5, 20, 136
    consequential, 18
    defined, 239–240
    governability, 4
    governance, in Arab states, 179–192
    modern, characteristics of, 6
    nature of, 6–7
    preeminent concerns, 110
    transboundary, 238–253
    two types of, 7
crisis communication, Fukushima nuclear disaster, and, 33–51
crisis management, 7–9, 26, 136
    anticipatory, 28
    Bam earthquake, 138–142
        chaos management, 140–141, 143–144
        command structure, 139–140
        response system, 138–139
    case study approach to, 9–10
    ethics, and, 110
    false assumptions, 6, 22
    Fukushima nuclear disaster, 33–51
    Hurricane Katrina, 19–29
    Presidential Decision Directive 39, and, 262
    public administration implications, 175–176
    theoretical knowledge, 4–6
    theories, 20–23
    U.K. Department for International Development, and, 218
Cuban Missile Crisis, 6, 7, 21
culture, defined, 114
curfews, 166
cybersecurity, 199, 206–207

D

damage assessment, 8, 110, 173
decontamination, 91, 263, 266, 267, 268, 269, 270, 274
    at Chernobyl, 99
Defense Against Weapons of Mass Destruction Act, 264
Democratic Republic of the Congo, 180
democratization, 183–184, 188–189, 190–191
Department for International Development (DFID), 218–219
Department of Defense (DoD), 264, 265–266, 267, 268, 272, 275
Department of Health and Human Services, 265, 267
Department of Homeland Security, 131, 153, 154–157, 158, 273, 276
    Hurricane Katrina, and, 127
    problems encountered, 155–156

diaspora, 238, 239, 241, 242, 244, 252
    as transnational actors, 242, 253
    defined, 242
    Haitian, 243–249, 251; *see also* Haitian–American diaspora
dictatorial regime, 5, 21
diet-resilient cities, 217
dirty bomb, 91, 261
disaster awareness, 59
disaster management, 10, 11, 24, 26
    2010 Haiti earthquake, 252
    Bam earthquake, 144, 146
    community resilience, and, 226, 227, 228, 229, 233
    Fukushima nuclear disaster, 36, 48, 49
    Hurricane Katrina, 19, 24
    Tangshan earthquake, 57
disaster mitigation, 9, 36, 50, 51, 56, 57, 59
disasters, defined, 239–240
displacement, 238, 239, 244
Document No. 69, 55–56, 57, 58, 61–62, 83–84
dogs, search-and-rescue, 140, 145
drills, disaster emergency preparedness, 49, 50, 51
drive-thru lifestyle, 203–204

E

early warning, earthquake, 53–86
earthquakes, 4, 18, 20, 27, 151, 205, 219
    2010 Haiti, 11, 238–254
    Bam, 28, 135–146
    Fukushima nuclear disaster, and, 94, 102, 199
    Great East Japan, 33–51
    in Iran, 26, 137
    predictions of, 55, 57, 62
    recovery from, 61
    Tangshan, 10, 53–86
East Rockaway, New York, 169–172
Ebola outbreak, 239, 241
economic costs of threats to resiliency, 207–209
edge of chaos, 24, 29, 135–146
Egypt, 181, 182, 183, 186, 187–188, 189, 190, 191, 192
elected officials, visibility of, 174
electronic control units (ECUs), 206
electronic machine readable travel documents (eMRTDs), 202
emancipatory politics, 182
emergency governance
    Bam earthquake, 138–144
    case study approach to, 9–10
    policies and actions, 8–9
    surprise management theory, and, 29
    Tangshan earthquake, 54, 59
    theoretical knowledge, 4–6
    theories, 20–23
emergency management, 1–11, 63, 136, 138
    Bam earthquake, 138–143, 144
    collaborative, 173–174
    Fukushima nuclear disaster, 45, 48, 49–50, 51
    government communication issues, 36
    Hurricane Katrina, 17–29, 109–119, 125, 126–131, 132
    public administration implications, 175–176
    radiological events, 90–103
    resilience capacity building, and, 197–219
    September 11, 2001, terrorist attacks, 149–158
Emergency Management Performance Grants (EMPGs), 276
emergency operations center (EOC), New York City, 152
emergency regimes, 5, 21
emergency vs. routine disturbance, 6, 21
ethical culture, 113–114
ethical leadership, 110–111
ethicality, Foucalt's assessment of, 116–117
evacuation
    Fukushima nuclear disaster, and, 38, 42, 49, 50, 51, 101
    Hurricane Katrina, 25, 112, 127
    prior to Great Tangshan Earthquake, 56–57, 58, 60, 61, 62, 63
    radiological event, 90, 93, 95, 100–101, 102
    September 11, 2001, and, 153, 166
executive-centered management, 156, 157, 158

F

fallout, 92
favoritism, 112, 181, 191
Federal Bureau of Investigation (FBI), 151–152, 262, 264, 265, 266, 267
Federal Emergency Management Agency (FEMA), 6, 22, 25, 93, 111, 127, 128, 129–130, 138, 139, 150, 151, 152, 154–157, 170, 171, 240, 262, 264, 268, 276
first-responder protection, 98
Flood Control Acts, 125, 132
foci, 29
folding car, 216
Foucault's assessment of ethicality, 116–117
Freedom and Justice political party, 187
Freedom to Manage Act, 157
fuel supply, importance of, 173
Fukushima nuclear disaster, 33–51, 199–200, 213–214, 216, 242
    communication during, 98
    decommissioning and radioactive water issues, 45
    evacuation, and, 38, 42, 49, 50, 51, 101
    government organizations established as a result of, 44
    institutional reforms, 43
    lessons learned, 49–50, 89–103
    management of, analysis, 38–49
    ongoing effects of, 45
    organizations involved in, 37
    sequence of events, 38–40, 46–48

G

Gaddafi, Muammar, 181
gigamansions, 205
Global Center for Preparedness and Resilience (GCPR), 212–213, 219
Global Resilient Action Plan (GRAP), 218
global trends, 200–209
globalization, 2, 3–4, 5, 19, 21, 27, 184, 238–239, 253
    adverse consequences, 3
governability crises, 4
governance crises, in Arab states, 179–192
government transparency, Fukushima nuclear disaster, and, 42–43, 49–50
Great East Japan earthquake, 33–51
    communication failure, 41–43
    initial damage, 35
    lessons learned, 49–50
Great Hanshin-Awaji Earthquake, 48
Great Tangshan Earthquake, 53–86
    Activism Matrix, 60
    declaration of a state of emergency, 61–62
    emotional effect on people, 62
    lessons learned, 57–62
    loss of life, 54, 55, 61
    prediction of, 55–56, 58
    property damage, 61
Greek–American diaspora, 246–247
gridlock, 203–205, 207–209, 210
Guggino, Principal Laura, 172–173

H

hacking, 206–207
Haiti Advocacy Working Group (HAWG), 246
Haiti earthquake (2010), 237–253
    case study and methodology, 244–245
    death toll, 244
    lessons learned, 252
    management of disaster, 249–252
        recovery and rebuilding, 250–252
        shelter and housing, 250
    official aid provided, 251–252
    transboundary effects of, 245–249
Haiti Reconstruction Fund (HRF), 250–251
Haitian–American diaspora, 239, 242, 243–244, 246–247, 251
    sentiments and attitudes, 248–249
Haitian Ministry for Haitians Living Abroad (MHAVE), 248
hazardous materials, 90
head of the fish, 110, 111
Health Resources and Services Administration (HRSA), 270
healthcare response, Bam earthquake, 144–145
Hebei Province, 55–56
Hempstead, Town of, 168–169, 170
highly enriched uranium (HEU), 261
hijacking, 7, 151
Hiriko Driving Mobility, 216
Hiroshima, 95
Homeland Security Act, 154
Homeland Security Grant Program, 271
hometown associations (HTAs), 243
Hurricane Andrew, 8, 152
Hurricane Guno, 27
Hurricane Hugo, 130, 152
Hurricane Irene, 169, 172, 175, 274
Hurricane Katrina, 6, 17–29, 109–119, 123–132, 150, 156, 157, 165
    coordination, 26
    cost of, 125
    Department of Homeland Security, and, 127
    disaster management, 19, 24
    emergency management response, 126–131
    evacuation, 25, 112, 127
    impact of, 124–125
    lessons learned, 26–27, 131–132
    patronage, and, 127–131, 132
    psychological impact, 124
    unethical behavior, and, 110–111
Hurricane Pam Exercise, 126
hurricane preparedness, 125–126
Hurricane Sandy, 162, 167–173
    lessons learned, 173–174
    public administration implications, 175
Hurricane Wilma, 162, 163–167, 169
    lessons learned, 173–174
    public administration implications, 175
    unusual aspects of, 163

I

Immigration and Customs Enforcement (ICE), 156
improvised explosive devices (IEDs), 260, 261
information and communications technology (ICT), 216
information disclosure/sharing, 36
    Fukushima nuclear disaster and, 41–43, 49
    Qinglong County, and, 54, 57
    radiological events, and, 95–98
    September 11, 2001, 156
    transparent, 36, 42–43, 49–50
infrastructure
    Bam, 138, 143, 145
    damage, 54, 61, 173, 210
    global, 199
    maps, 226, 227
    New Orleans, 26, 126, 132
    resilient, 200, 218
    security, 206, 210, 263
    urban, 3
institutional authority, 111

Interim Haiti Reconstruction Commission (IHRC), 250–251
intermodalism, 202–203
internally displaced populations (IDPs), 250
International Nuclear Events Scale (INES), 35, 38, 45
Iran, 7, 18, 20, 21, 26–27, 261; see also Bam earthquake
    as cybersecurity threat, 206
    as state that sponsors terrorism, 261
Iraq, 7, 18, 22, 137, 140, 146, 182, 183, 184, 192, 261
    as state that sponsors terrorism, 261
ISIL, 2
Islam, 180, 186–189, 190, 191
Israel, 18, 189
Israeli–Palestinian conflicts, 22, 184–185

J

Jefferson, Represenative William, 111
Joint Commission's Environment of Care standards, 270
Jordan, 183, 189, 191

K

kinetic energy harvesting, 215, 217
kinetic energy recovery system (KERS), 217
Kohlberg's hierarchy of moral development, 117, 118

L

leadership failure, 25
Leadership in Energy and Environmental Design (LEED), 212
Lebanon, 18, 181, 183
legal–rational authority, 128
legitimacy crisis, 18
levees, New Orleans, 10, 19, 25, 124, 125, 126, 127, 132
Libya, 181, 182, 188, 189, 190, 191, 192
    as state that sponsors terrorism, 261
loci, 29
Louisiana's ethical culture, 113–116
low-enriched uranium (LEU), 261

M

macrolevel transboundary effects, 241–242, 245–247, 253
Mahlab, Prime Minister Ibrahim, 188
Management Agenda, President Bush's, 156–157
managerial incompetence, 7
mass monitoring, 62
media relations, 164, 174
media role, radiological events, and, 97–98
medical information/misinformation, 95–98
medical isotopes, 90
medical response teams, 264
Megatons to Megawatts program, 261

Melucci, School Superintendent Roseanne, 170–172
memorials, 158
merit, politics and, 128, 132
mesolevel transboundary effects, 241–242, 245–247, 253
Metropolitan Medical Response System (MMRS), 273, 276–277
Metropolitan Medical Strike Team (MMST)/Metropolitan Medical Task Force (MMTF), 264, 267, 268, 269, 270, 271, 272–273, 274–277
    mutual aid, 273–274
Metropolitan Transportation Authority (MTA), 217
microlevel transboundary effects, 241–242, 247–249, 253
military bureaucracy, 5, 21
military rule, Arab states, 187–188, 192
mitigation, disaster, 9, 36, 54, 58, 63, 156
Morocco, 189, 191
Morsi, Mohamed, 187, 188
motor vehicles per capita, 204
Mubarak, Hosni, 181, 188, 192
multisensory planning, 200, 211, 217
Murrah Federal Building bombing, 150, 260, 275
Muslim Brotherhood, 187, 188
Muslims, 184, 185, 189

N

Nagasaki, 95
Nagin, Mayor Ray, 110, 111, 112–113, 116
nano-urbanism, 217
Nassau County, 168–173
    Board of Cooperative Educational Services (BOCES), 171
Nasser, Abdel, 188, 192
National Counterterrorism Center, 151
National Defense Authorization Act, 262
National Electronic Disease Surveillance System (NEDSS), 270
National Emergency Management Association (NEMA), 276
National Flood Insurance Program, 125
National Guard, 263, 273–274
National Infrastructure Protection Center, 263
National Preparedness Grant Program, 276, 277
National Response Plan, 23, 136
National Salvation Front, 187
National Weather Service, 156
natural disasters, 4, 6, 7, 10, 18, 22, 27, 38, 54, 60, 61, 102, 110, 137, 150, 152, 153, 156, 158, 205–207, 268, 272, 276
neoteric planning, 200, 210–211, 219
nepotism, 192
New Orleans, 19, 24, 111, 116; see also Hurricane Katrina
    levees, 10, 19, 25, 124, 125, 126, 127, 132

Mayor Ray Nagin, 110, 111, 112–113, 116
    readiness of for Hurricane Katrina, 124–126
NFPA 1600: Standard on Disaster/Emergency Management and Business Continuity Programs, 153
non-governmental organizations (NGOs), 249, 251, 253
North Korea
    as cybersecurity threat, 206
    as state that sponsors terrorism, 261
nuclear, biological, or chemical (NBC) consequence management, 262
nuclear power plants, 35, 37, 91–93, 95; *see also* Fukushima nuclear disaster
nuclear weapons, 90–91, 261
Nunn–Lugar–Domenici Domestic Preparedness Program, 262, 264–265, 267, 268–277
    biological response, 270
    dual-use equipment funds, 269
    financial considerations, 272
    lessons unlearned, 274–276
    local capability, 271–272
    medical community training, 270
    pharmaceuticals for victims, 269
    staffing challenges, 272–273
    training needs, 268–269
Nunn–Lugar Threat Reduction Initiative, 261
nursing home drownings, 111, 125

O

obesity, 204–205
Occupy Wall Street, 4
Office of Foreign Disaster Assistance (OFDA), 250
Office of the National Coordinator for Security, Infrastructure Protection and Counterterrorism, 263
Oklahoma City bombing, 150, 260, 275
opportunists, 8, 141

P

Palestinian–Israeli conflicts, 22, 184–185
passenger cars, 203–204
patronage, Hurricane Katrina and, 127–131, 132
performance review, post-crisis, 117–119
personal resilience, 224–225
pharmaceuticals, for victims of WMD events, 269
Plato, 180
plume shine, 95
political Islam, 186–189, 191
political order, perception of, 186
politics–administration dichotomy, 128
Ponyo, Augustin Matata, 180
popular uprisings, Arab states, 180, 181, 182, 183, 186, 187, 188, 190, 191
population growth, distribution, and urbanization, 201
population of world, 198–199, 201
Port Everglades, 166–167
positions, strategic, 29
post-crisis performance review, 117–119
potassium iodide, 98
Powell, Donald, 112
preparedness, emergency management and, 9
Presidential Decision Directive 39 (PDD-39), 151, 262
Presidential Decision Directive 62 (PDD-62), 263, 270
Presidential Decision Directive 63 (PDD-63), 263
Presidential Policy Directive 8 (PPD-8), 276
process-oriented crises, 7
psychological first aid (PFA), 232
psychological impact
    Bam earthquake, 142
    Chernobyl nuclear reactor accident, 101
    Hurricane Katrina, 124
    radiological events, 101–102
    September 11, 2001, 151
public administration, crisis and emergency management and, 175–176
public servants as victims, 174

Q

Qinglong County, 53–86
    Activism Matrix, 60, 86–88
    events analysis, 64–82
    lessons learned, 57–60
    reasons for lack of casualties, 57

R

radiation monitoring, 37
radiation sickness, 92
radioisotopes, 91–92
radiological events
    emergency planning for, 95–102
        lessons learned about community protection and evacuation, 100
        lessons learned about first-responder protection, 98
        lessons learned about psychological impacts, 101–102
        lessons learned about public information, 95–98
        lessons learned about victim care, 99
    psychological impacts of, 101–102
radiological hazards, 90–92
radiological materials, 90
    sources of, 261
radon, 90
Rebuild by Design competition, 201
recovery, emergency management and, 9
reform preconditions, 183–184
refugee crises, 2
remittances, 243–244

renewable energy, 215
resilience, 223–234
    attributes, 199, 214–217, 219
    capacity building, 50, 51, 197–219
        lessons learned, 219
    defined, 224
Resilience and Coping Intervention (RCI), 232
resource deployment, 8
response, emergency management and, 9
Rhame Avenue Elementary School, 170–173
Romano, Vice Mayor Bruno, 169–170
Rome, 4, 20
Rubel character map, 116, 117, 119

S

Sadat, Anwar, 188, 192
Salafis, 189
Santino, Anthony J., 168–169
Sarin, 261, 271, 275
search-and-rescue dogs, 140, 145
September 11, 2001, 7, 149–158, 210, 260, 273
    counterterrorism policy before, 151–152
    emergency management, 152
        impact on, 153
    memorials, 158
Shelter Object, 100, 101
smoke detectors, 90
social activism, Haitian diaspora, 243
social remittances, 243–244
sound governance, 4
sovereign power, 5, 21
spatial planning, 200, 210–211, 217
Stafford Act, 268
Standard on Disaster/Emergency Management and
    Business Continuity Programs, 153
State Homeland Security Grant Program (SHSGP), 270
storm surge, 201
    Hurricane Katrina, 124
    Superstorm Sandy, 162, 163, 167, 170, 171, 172, 176
strategic management, key components of, 29
Strategic Recovery Framework for Haiti, 250
Sudan, 192
sudden ruptures, 7
suitcase nukes, 91
Superdome, 25
Superstorm Sandy, 162, 167–173
    lessons learned, 173–174
    public administration implications, 175
surprise management, 19, 27–29
    theory of, 9, 28–29, 146
surprises, 7
    anticipation of, 174
sustainability, 199, 205, 214, 217
SWOT (strengths, weaknesses, opportunities, and
    threats) analysis, 226, 227

synthetic groups, 8
Syria, 181, 188, 189, 192
    as state that sponsors terrorism, 261

T

Tangshan earthquake, 53–86
    Activism Matrix, 60
    declaration of a state of emergency, 61–62
    emotional effect on people, 62
    lessons learned, 57–62
    loss of life, 54, 55, 61
    prediction of, 55–56, 58
    property damage, 61
Tech Escort, 266
telecommunications, 202
telematics, 216, 217
temporal planning, 200, 211, 217
Temporary Protected Status (TPS), 245
terrorism, 2, 5, 7, 18, 20, 21, 95, 102, 141, 146, 149–158,
    164, 205–207, 210, 214, 228, 232, 240,
    260–262, 267, 268, 269, 271, 276; *see also*
    antiterrorism, counterterrorism, September
    11, 2001
    catastrophic, 261
    defined, 260
    federal response to, 261–264
    war on, 26, 150, 153
    weapons of mass destruction, 259–277
Terrorism and Disaster Center (TDC), 225, 228, 232
threat advisory, color-coded, 156
three-dimensional planning, 200, 210
Three Mile Island, 41
    communication failure, 96
    evacuation, 100–101
    lessons learned, 89–103
    psychological counseling, and, 102
thyroid cancer, 96, 98, 99
Tohuku earthquake, 239
Tokyo Electric Power Company (TEPCO), 35, 36, 37,
    42, 45, 199–200, 214
Top Officials (TOPOFF) counterterrorism program, 156
Town of Hempstead, 168–169, 170
transboundary crises, 237–253
    defined, 240–241
    macro-, meso-, microlevel effects, 241–242
transcommunication, 202–203
transformational breakdowns, 5, 20
transnational actors, 239, 241, 242, 243, 253
transparent information disclosure, 36, 42–43, 49–50
Transportation Security Administration (TSA), 153
trans-system social ruptures (TSSRs), 240–241
tsunamis, 10, 18, 22, 34, 35, 102, 205, 214, 239, 251; *see
    also* Fukushima nuclear disaster
Tunisia, 181, 182, 183, 187, 188–189, 190, 191
two-dimensional planning, 200

U

U.K. Department for International Development, 218–219
umbrella organizations, 246, 253
unethical behavior, 110–113
   consequences of, 116–117
Unified Command Post (UCP), Broward County Sheriff's Office, 165, 166
United Nations International Strategy for Disaster Reduction (UNISDR), 48
United States, 3, 6, 8, 19, 21, 23, 24, 25, 146, 149–158, 161–176, 183, 184, 186; *see also* Hurricane Wilma, September 11, 2001, Superstorm Sandy
   airports, 202–203
   congestion in, 203–204, 207
   cybersecurity threats to, 206
   elections, 185
   governance, 183, 184
   Haitian diaspora in, 243–244, 252
   immigration policy, 245
   miles of roads, 202
   motor vehicles per capita, 204
   new homes built in, 204–205
   nuclear power generated in, 92
   storm surges in, 201
   weapons of mass destruction, and, 260, 261, 262, 271
United States Enrichment Corporation (USEC), 261
Urban Area Security Initiative (UASI), 270, 271, 275, 276
urban obesity, 204–205, 217
urbanization, 201
urgency, 5, 7, 8, 18, 21
U.S. Agency for International Development, 250
USA PATRIOT Act, 153
U.S. Army's Chemical Biological Defense Command (CBDCOM), 262, 266
U.S. Army's Technical Escort Unit's Chemical Biological Rapid Response Teams, 266
U.S. Department of Energy, 268
U.S. Green Building Council, 212
U.S. immigration policy, 245
U.S. Policy on Counterterrorism, 262
U.S. Public Health Service (PHS), 267
utilities, loss of, 174

V

vanadium flow batteries, 217
vehicle-borne improvised explosive devices (VBIEDs), 260
vehicle cybersecurity, 206
vertical farming, 216, 217
Village of East Rockaway, 169–172
visibility of elected officials, 174
volunteers
   Bam earthquake, and 138–139, 140, 141, 145–146
   Hurricane Katrina, and, 25, 126, 127
   Hurricane Wilma, and, 167
   September 11, 2001, and, 152, 156
   Superstorm Sandy, and, 169, 170, 174
   Tangshan earthquake, and, 56, 57, 59, 62, 63, 84

W

war on terrorism, 26, 150, 153
Washington Consensus, 184
weapons of mass destruction, 259–277
weapons of mass victimization (WMVs), 260–261
weasel activity, earthquakes and, 60
whos, strategic management, 29
Witt, James Lee, 152, 156
World Trade Center, 150, 151, 210, 260, 275; *see also* September 11, 2001

Y

Yemen, 2, 181, 182, 188, 189, 190, 191, 192